A Traveler's Guide

AMERICA'S LIVING HISTORY

THE EARLY YEARS

A Traveler's Guide

AMERICA'S LIVING HISTORY

THE EARLY YEARS

Suzanne & Craig Sheumaker

www.AmericasLivingHistory.com

RED CORRAL
PUBLISHING

Jackson, California

A Traveler's Guide
America's Living History – The Early Years

Red Corral Publishing
505-1 South Highway 49, #240, Jackson, CA 95642
www.AmericasLivingHistory.com

Publisher's Cataloging-in-Publication

Sheumaker, Suzanne.
    America's living history : the early years / Suzanne
& Craig Sheumaker.
    p. cm.
    Includes index.
    ISBN-13: 978-0-9792598-0-7
    ISBN-10: 0-9792598-0-0

    1. United States--History--Guidebooks. 2. Historical
museums--United States--Guidebooks. 3. Open-air museums
--United States--Guidebooks. 4. Historical reenactments
--United States--Guidebooks. I. Sheumaker, Craig.
II. Title. III. Title: At head of title: Traveler's guide.

E158.S54 2007   917.304'931
                           QBI07-600024

Printed in the United States of America.
First Printing 2007.

The purpose of this book is to both educate and entertain. The text should be used only as a general guide and not as the ultimate source for history and travel information. Although every effort has been made to ensure the accuracy and completeness of information up to the printing date, the authors and publisher assume no responsibility for errors, inaccuracies, omissions or inconsistencies herein. Any slights of people, places or organizations are unintentional.

Photos on Contents page:

On-A-Slant Mandan Village council lodge, Mandan, ND

Jamestown Settlement, two of its three ships, Williamsburg vicinity, VA

Mission San Fernando, Rey de España reredos, San Fernando, CA

Fort Ticonderoga re-enactment, Ticonderoga, NY

Chesapeake & Ohio Canal National Historical Park mule-drawn canal boat, Washington, DC

Colonial Michilimackinac church and other buildings, Mackinaw City, MI

CONTENTS

INTRODUCTION

Our goal with this guidebook is to provide accurate, timely information as well as insight into a past that is sometimes mysterious, often surprising and always intriguing. The term "Living History," as we use it, refers to places and experiences which immerse us in history, making real through direct exposure what otherwise can only be imagined through books, lectures, museums and films. A substantial portion of our recommended travel destinations are National Parks, National Monuments or State Historic Sites. Six have been designated as World Heritage Sites by UNESCO. Many others are privately operated attractions, made exceptional because of the hard work and commitment of proud, dedicated Americans.

Our Selection Criteria

America's Living History - The Early Years covers a long span of time – from the development of widely varied Indian cultures, to the discovery and domination of our land by European powers, and finally to the emergence of an independent nation. It ends for the most part in the early 1840s, before the concept of Manifest Destiny extended America's reach from the Atlantic to the Pacific. To help you experience whatever part of that heritage interests you most, we have compiled a set of recommendations based on the following criteria:

making real through direct exposure what otherwise can only be imagined

1. The destinations are as historically accurate and complete as possible, based on archaeological findings and historic records. Attention has been given to not only the buildings, furnishings and personal items but also the gardens, farm fields and livestock.
2. Where possible, the sites have history-based activities, re-enactments and other special events. Staff members typically include individuals in period clothing who share information through third-person discussions or first-person portrayals.
3. They show many aspects of early life – community, household, agriculture, arts and crafts, business, public affairs and military actions. Every effort is made to replicate historical reality in fun and interesting ways.
4. The historical atmosphere is superior. Excluded are amusement parks and sites that have not properly restored or maintained their properties. Conventional museums also have been excluded because they display their collections out of context with real-life use. However, we could not resist "museum plus" destinations, whose exceptional exhibits include creative re-creations and historic buildings.
5. Our focus is on pre-1840 destinations. For the sake of completeness, though, a few exceptions have been made. Most notable is 'Iolani Palace in Hawai'i, which was occupied during the late 1800s at the turning point in Native Hawaiian history. To exclude it would be to leave untold an important part of the Hawaiian story.
6. The majority of recommended sites are substantial enough to be the primary destination in a particular locale. However, most are within close proximity to other popular tourist attractions.
7. In a few instances, such as listings of the California missions and the Shaker villages, we have included all of the visitable sites for the benefit of readers who are interested in completeness. Those that we believe to be the best of the group are featured attractions.

Historical Perspective

Each chapter of this book opens with a summary overview of relevant historical information. In addition, we have sidebars on special-interest subjects throughout the book. Because of their brevity, these sections are necessarily incomplete. Our intent is not to teach history but to enhance your travel experience. You can learn much more at the destinations themselves, simply by asking questions. Living History interpreters at the featured sites tend to be well trained. They welcome the opportunity to share their extensive knowledge and talk about their hands-on understanding of America's past.

Choosing Your Travel Itinerary

Our list of historical sites is sizable. Even with our strict selection criteria, *America's Living History - The Early Years* recommends 300 destinations that provide exciting contact with America's early heritage. To help you make travel choices, we have organized them by region following this introduction and by field of interest within each chapter.

Please keep in mind that things change. Hours of operation may vary; visitor attractions may be under renovation or expansion; their offerings may change;

and places may even have closed since the publication of this book. We provide phone numbers and website addresses to help ensure that you have access to the most up-to-date tourist information. However, sometimes even these change; so we recommend doing an Internet search rather than assume that a particular destination is no longer in operation.

Ideal Times to Visit

Most attractions are open from Memorial Day through Labor Day; many are open longer; national parks are usually open year-round. (See site descriptions for specifics.) Interpretive events typically are scheduled for mornings and early afternoons during the summer and less frequently during other seasons. Furthermore, weekends tend to include more interpretive programs than weekdays. So if you want to experience the widest range of Living History or are traveling with children, you probably will prefer summer weekends.

Because of our own penchant for talking with interpreters, we tend to prefer weekday visits when these people may have more time to chat. A potential distraction is the presence of school classes during morning hours, especially in springtime. In some cases, afternoon visits are more satisfying. You might want to call ahead before making this choice for yourself.

Some sites have food and beverage concessions. A few (such as Plimoth Plantation and Colonial Williamsburg) have restaurants that are history-inspired. We recommend that you check in advance if this is important to you, and plan accordingly.

Begin Your Discovery

Before exploring individual chapters, take a moment to review the summary timeline on pages 24-25. It will help you place key sites and events in context with their times. It may also surprise you. What is happening in America today is a striking reflection of all that has come before. Ours is a country built by people caught up in the quest for a better world, no matter what the cost. Whether out of choice or by force, our ancestors uprooted their lives, leaving behind friends, family and everything familiar to start over in a strange new land. In contrast to the pattern of history in most other nations, America's development is a story of discovery, exploration and migration; of escape from old civilizations and old ways of thinking; of the search for economic advancement, religious independence and personal fulfillment. It is also the story of lessons learned "the hard way" and great progress made in spite of serious challenges.

Whether history is a life-long passion for you or a new-found pleasure, we hope this book will excite your imagination and stimulate new travel adventures.

> **timeline on pages 24-25 will help you place key sites and events in context**

ACKNOWLEDGEMENTS

We have not attempted to cite the many authorities and historical resources drawn upon during the creation of this guidebook. The list is voluminous. Suffice it to say that our research was extensive and included our own observations while visiting each of the featured destinations during recent years.

We do, however, wish to say "thanks" again to the historians, managers and communications professionals at the sites themselves. Featured travel destinations were asked to review our content for accuracy and completeness. There was no obligation or cost to them – we simply wanted to ensure that everything was fairly stated and up-to-date. They were very helpful. A few even provided photographs when needed. (We have credited them beside the pictures.)

We were delighted to learn through these contacts that several sites had grown even more enjoyable since our visit. Key among them were Historic Jamestowne, Jamestown Settlement and George Washington's Mount Vernon home, which added major new offerings that coincided with the 400th anniversary of the founding of Jamestown, Virginia – mid-May 1607, the sentimental "birth" of America. This fact provides an important reminder: Never fall into the trap of saying "I've already been there." Change is inevitable, and the best sites typically get better and better.

CONTACT US

We welcome comments and suggestions. Please feel free to email us at redcorralpub@aol.com or send us a letter c/o Red Corral Publishing, 505-1 South Highway 49, #240, Jackson, CA 95642. Thanks for your interest!

300 PREMIER DESTINATIONS

DESTINATIONS:
NORTHEAST

More than anywhere else in America, the Northeast presents a vivid and unforgettable story of our nation's multi-cultural, multi-religious heritage and unrelenting pursuit of freedom. You will find many opportunities to explore Living History here while also enjoying exceptional natural beauty, charming rural communities and numerous big-city pleasures.

The Northeast was not the first area to be settled by our European ancestors, but it soon became the most developed. The English began establishing northern

▲ Mayflower II, Plymouth, MA

▶ Fort Stanwix drummer, Rome, NY

▶ Jonathan Corwin House, Salem, MA, captain's cabinet with portrait of Reverend George Corwin.

colonies in 1620 Massachusetts, the Dutch in 1614 New York and the Germans in 1683 Pennsylvania. They came not to a wilderness but to a land that had been cleared and settled earlier by Native Peoples. In many cases, the Indians initially allowed them to coexist in their territories. In other cases, whole tribes already had vacated the area in advance of the "white man" or died due to smallpox, the plague and other fatal diseases brought earlier by foreign fishermen and explorers.

In the Northeast, Puritans from England comprised the largest group of early Euro-Americans. Close behind them came other devout Protestants as well as the Quakers, Shakers, Amish, Huguenots, Jews and various secular groups. These were people who built their own communities and lived by group rules and values. Over time, they learned to expect the freedoms of life, liberty and the pursuit of happiness. So when tensions grew between the colonies and "Mother England," the Northeast became the hotbed of rebellion.

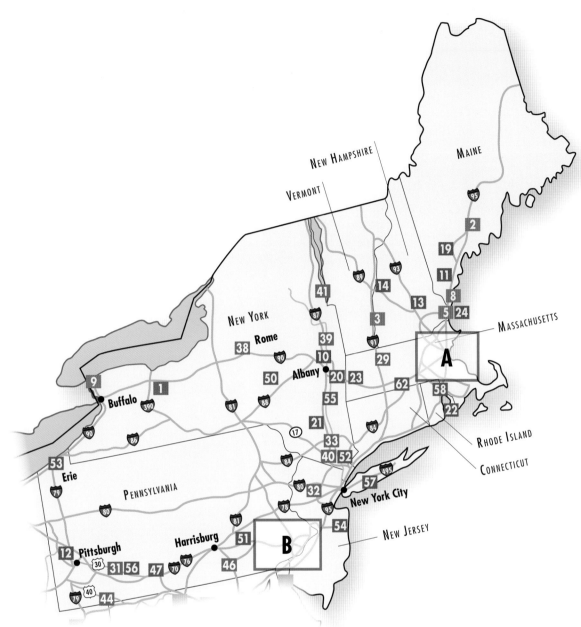

NEW HAMPSHIRE

VERMONT

MAINE

95

19

11

8

41

14

13

5 24

89

93

NEW YORK

Rome

38

39

3

29

MASSACHUSETTS

87

10

91

90

50

Albany

20 23

62

58

9

1

55

22

Buffalo

81

88

390

21

84

RHODE ISLAND

17

CONNECTICUT

33

90

86

40 52

53

84

495

Erie

80

32

57

PENNSYLVANIA

78

95

New York City

79

81

54

12

Pittsburgh

Harrisburg

51

B

NEW JERSEY

30

31 56

47 70 76

46

79 40

44

A

2

49 28

6 61

30 93

7

Salem

90

27

Boston

60

495

3

95

24

Plymouth

4

B

Reading

476

43

222

26

45

42

48 422

35

16

15

276

17 Lancaster

36

95

18

76

30

3

37 59

295

25

202

Philadelphia

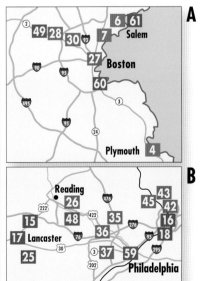

▲ Saugus Iron Works undershot paddle wheel, Saugus, MA

▶ Hancock Shaker Village grape press, Pittsfield, MA

▶ Old Bethpage Village Restoration gander, Old Bethpage, NY

▶ Colonial Pennsylvania Plantation wagon barn, Philadelphia vicinity, PA

■ ROAD TO INDEPENDENCE

■ OUR NEW NATION

DESTINATIONS:
MID-ATLANTIC & SOUTHEAST

This highly diverse and colorful region offers a little bit of everything for the Living History traveler, along with gracious hospitality, lush scenery and a temperate-to-tropical climate.

The Spanish, French and English each attempted to establish their first American colonies here; but initially they all failed. Spanish St. Augustine, founded in 1565 Florida, was the first permanent European settlement. Soldiers from this fortified community forced out the French, who did not attempt to establish a major new

▲ Colonial Williamsburg windmill for grinding cornmeal and wheat flour, Williamsburg, VA

settlement in America until 1699 in Biloxi, Mississippi. Jamestown, founded in 1607 Virginia, was the first successful English settlement. Of course, Native Peoples preceded the "white man" into this region by many thousands of years. You can see authentic re-creations of the early Indian villages and European colonies at numerous Living History sites.

Many major advances also had their beginnings in the Mid-Atlantic and Southeast. Particularly interesting are sites devoted to our fight for independence; the establishment of Washington, DC, as our nation's political power-base; and the emergence of the Industrial Revolution. You can tour one of America's most powerful early businesses (du Pont's gunpowder works) at the Hagley Museum; float down portions of the Chesapeake & Ohio Canal, which opened up a vast area to efficient travel and transportation; visit historical settings where influential people came together; and see where our early Presidents enjoyed their private lives. Even remnants of our nation's first Gold Rush (in North Carolina) await you.

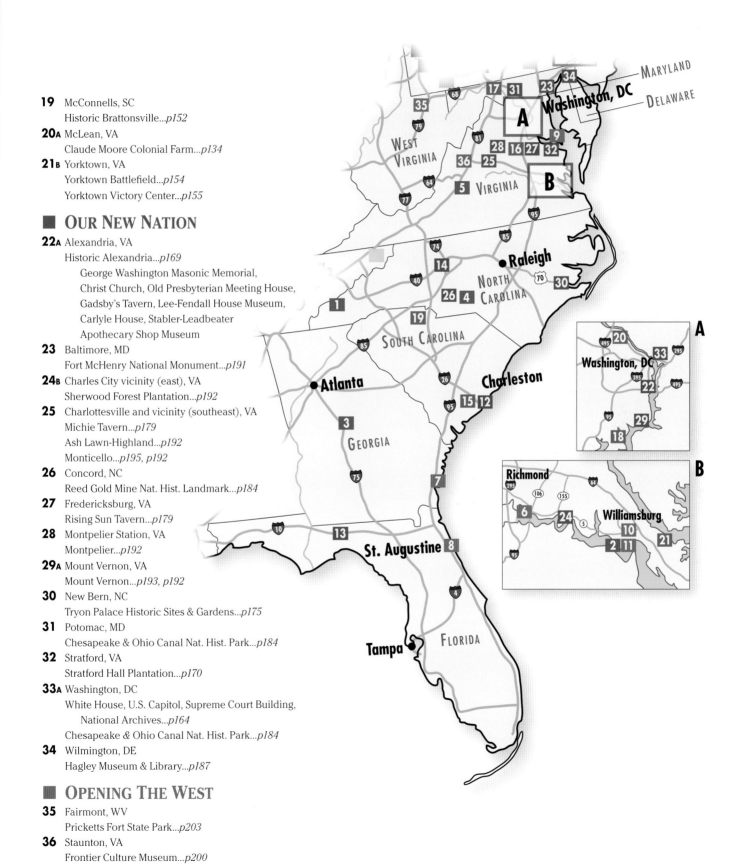

DESTINATIONS:
CENTRAL & SOUTH

As different as they seem, the northern Great Lakes region, the Ohio River Valley and the Deep South all have a very important thing in common: these were the areas populated by our Euro-American ancestors as they began to make their way west. By the early 1800s, vast numbers of people were developing the land. As a result, these were among the earliest territories to gain statehood after the Original Thirteen Colonies.

▲ The French Quarter, New Orleans, LA

▶ French settlement of Colonial Michilimackinac, Mackinaw City, MI

Here is your opportunity to explore a wide range of fascinating historic subjects – from ancient Native American cultures to early French communities; from the Shakers, Amish and Moravians to the Mormons and other religious groups; from frontier forts to the first signs of industry and prosperity; from log cabin communities to President Andrew Jackson's Federal-style estate. The variety is startling.

Translating all this into a Living History trip is more fun than challenging. You also might want to add a few more-modern delights. Consider, for example, including the Henry Ford Museum & Greenfield Village in Dearborn, Michigan; Circus World Museum in Baraboo, Wisconsin; cultural, art and history museums in Cincinnati, Ohio, and Indianapolis, Indiana; the big-city attractions of Chicago, Illinois; horse racing at Churchill Downs in Louisville, Kentucky; the Grand Ole Opry and country music clubs in Nashville, Tennessee; U.S. Space and Rocket Center in Huntsville, Alabama; Vicksburg National Military Park west of Jackson, Mississippi; Cajun food and Creole music in Louisiana.

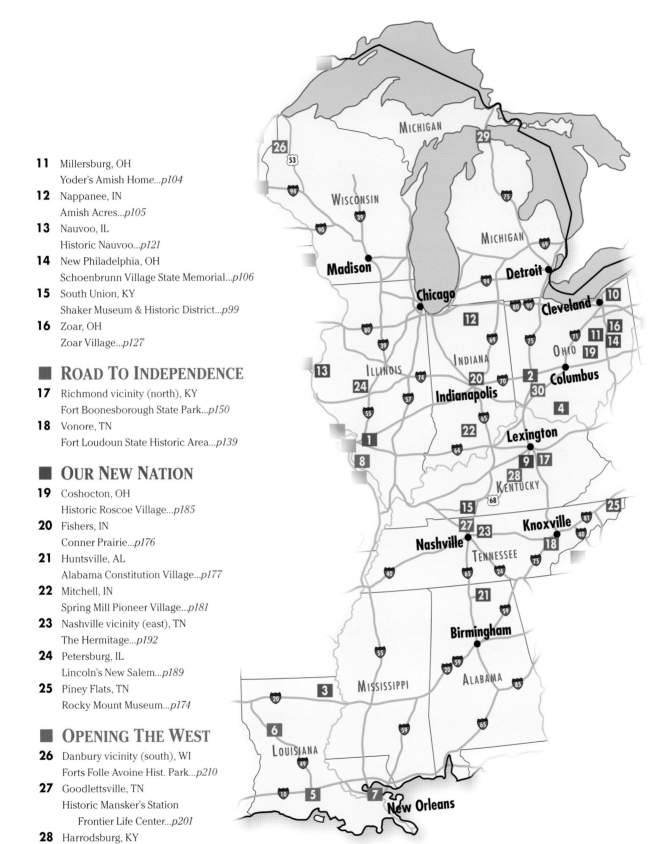

DESTINATIONS:
MOUNTAINS & PRAIRIES

Here is good, solid land – the Bread Basket of America, the heart of the fur trade and the spark igniting America's fascination with the "Wild West." Well into the 1800s, it was mostly Indian territory and the prime hunting ground for the American "buffalo" (actually bison) and other fur-bearing animals.

Despite the region's remoteness, courageous Europeans took the long trip inland to make their mark on the land here. The Spanish padres established a

▲ Bent's Old Fort,
La Junta vicinity, CO

series of missions in Texas, determined to convert the Native Peoples to Catholicism. The French built settlements in Missouri. The Amana developed their exceptional communal society in Iowa. Fur traders built forts throughout much of the region and came together at various sites for a summer rendezvous of trading, story-telling and partying. The men of the Lewis & Clark Expedition took the northern route from Missouri westward, exploring the rivers and mountains, establishing friendly relations with dozens of Indian tribes, and spending the winter of 1804-1805 in North Dakota. Other explorers mapped out central areas, seeking a more accessible route west. Later, their findings would guide pioneering settlers across the country – typically through what is now northern Kansas and the southern parts of Nebraska, Wyoming and Idaho to Oregon and California.

For the Living History traveler of today, this early frontier period comes back to life at a variety of fascinating historic sites, villages and forts.

■ AMERICA'S NATIVE PEOPLES

■ EUROPEAN COLONIZATION

■ RELIGIOUS & SECULAR GROUPS

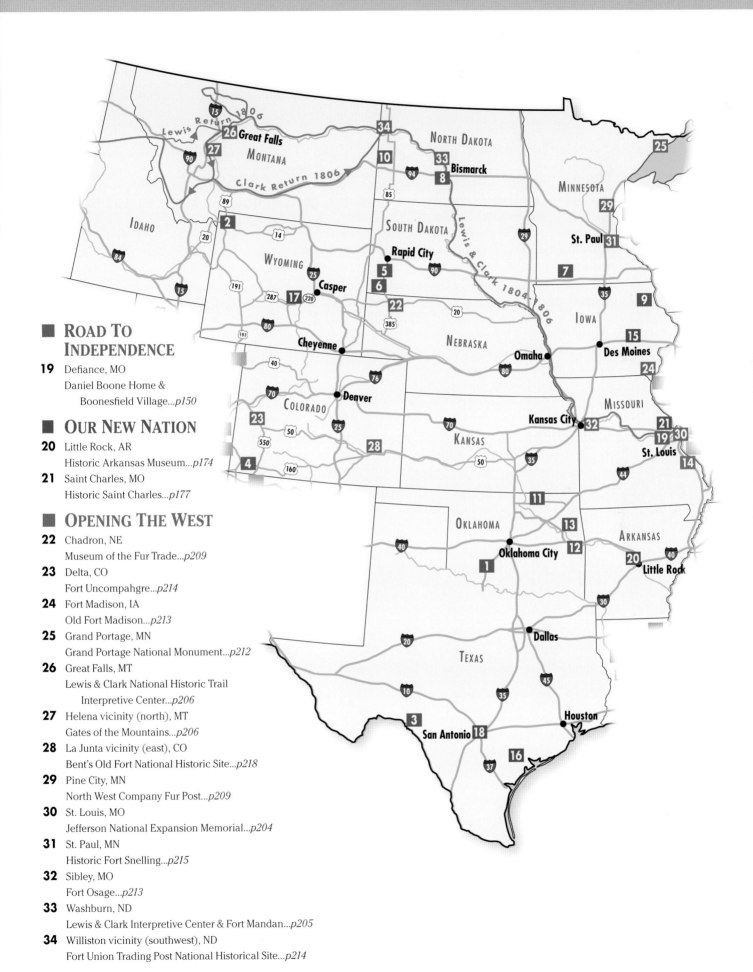

■ ROAD TO INDEPENDENCE

■ OUR NEW NATION

■ OPENING THE WEST

DESTINATIONS:
DESERT SOUTHWEST

Sunshine, a defensible terrain and nature's bounty lured many Native Peoples to the Southwest long before Europeans arrived. Estimates are as high as 100,000 or more in New Mexico alone by the time the Spanish began to settle here in the 1600s, and their local ancestry extended back 10,000 years or more.

The history they created speaks of diverse and often sophisticated cultures. These Native Peoples built complex adobe villages and stone cities. They clocked the path of stars and tied astrological signs to major events in their lives. They carved tens of thousands of petroglyphs to communicate with one another and the spirit world. They shared goods through a vast trading network that extended into what is now central Mexico.

▲ Chaco Culture National Historical Park, Nageezi vicinity, NM

▶ Heritage Village, This is the Place Heritage Park, Salt Lake City, UT

They not only hunted for meat and collected plant foods from the land; they also farmed crops, often using expert systems for watering and pest control.

But this is just the beginning of the great Southwest story. The Spanish heritage in Arizona and New Mexico is beautiful; so too is the Mormon world in Utah. For a change of pace, there are the modern adult playlands of Reno and Las Vegas, Nevada, plus an array of breathtaking scenic parks: Arches, Bryce, Canyonlands, Capitol Reef, Dinosaur, Escalante and Zion in Utah; Canyon de Chelly, Chiricahua, Grand Canyon, Monument Valley, Oregon Pipe, Painted Desert and Petrified Forest in Arizona; Carlsbad Caverns and White Sands in New Mexico; Red Rock and Great Basin in Nevada. Mix and match. This is a wonderful region!

■ AMERICA'S NATIVE PEOPLES

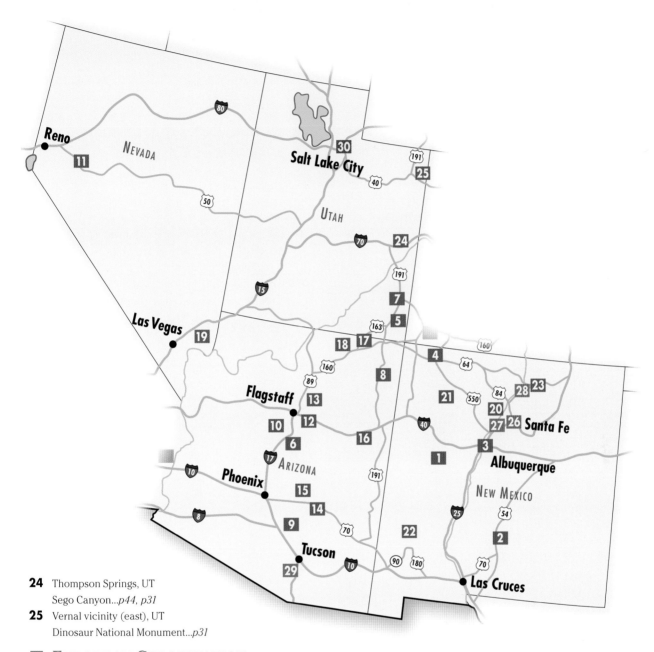

■ EUROPEAN COLONIZATION

■ RELIGIOUS & SECULAR GROUPS

DESTINATIONS:
FAR WEST

Europeans did not arrive in influential numbers in the Far West until the latter part of the 1700s. Alaska received the Russian missionaries as well as the Russian, French and American fur traders. Oregon and Washington saw the trappers, fishermen and explorers. California took a decidedly Spanish direction with the arrival of Catholic padres and their mission system. Hawai'i faced the impact of English Protestant missionaries as well as American and European businessmen.

▲ Fort Clatsop, Lewis & Clark National Historical Park, Astoria, OR

▶ Mission San Luis, Rey de Francia, San Luis Rey, CA

What remains from those early days is unique to the region and often a blend of cultures. In Hawai'i, for example, America's only royal palace is distinctively Native Hawaiian, but it also incorporates design features typical of the grand homes of Europe. In Alaska, Colonial Russian buildings are protected in a park that also includes many towering Alaska Native totem poles. In Washington and Oregon, reconstructed forts show the influence of both Native American and Euro-American lifestyles. In California, the Spanish missions reflect the unique personality of each commanding padre and his band of Indian converts. And while little evidence remains of the first inhabitants, you will find restored missions and fur posts, re-created Native villages, marvelous petroglyphs and even a set of intaglios (carvings in the land) that somehow have survived the passage of time.

■ AMERICA'S NATIVE PEOPLES

■ RELIGIOUS & SECULAR GROUPS

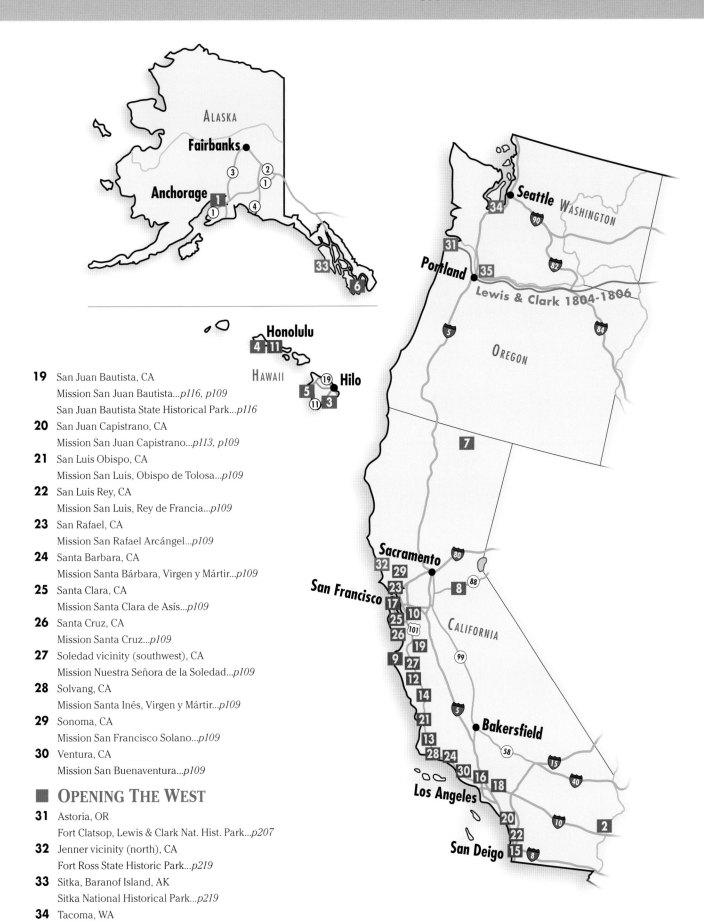

▓ Opening the West

HISTORICAL TIMELINE:
THE EARLY YEARS

Before exploring our Living History recommendations, take a quick look at what occurred during the formative period covered by this book.

Pre-history to 1500s

When the first Europeans arrived in the "New" World, America was already a very old place. It had seen entire civilizations rise and fall through power struggles, religious differences, climate changes, etc. The Native Peoples – descendants of the ice age travelers who arrived on this continent 18,000-30,000 years ago – transformed themselves from foragers to farmers, and from clans to nations. In the process, they achieved rich cultural diversity, elaborate political structures, highly cooperative societies, imaginative art and architecture, complex religions and belief systems, and much more that rivaled what was happening elsewhere in the world. Although often misunderstood by outsiders, they could not fairly be viewed as either primitive or uncivilized.

1500s to 1630

Christopher Columbus' voyages to this continent from 1492-1504 opened the door to significant changes. But European colonization did not come easily. The first settlements – Spanish in 1526, French in 1562 and English in 1585 – all failed. African slaves left behind by the Spanish were the first permanent settlers. The Spanish fort/city of St. Augustine, FL (c. 1565) became the first surviving colony. The first successful English settlement was in 1607 at Jamestown, VA. Africans arrived there in 1619. (Listed as "servants" in historic records, they may have been either indentured servants or slaves.) The Dutch settled on Manhattan Island in 1614. The French didn't succeed until the late 1600s. All told, the impact on Native Peoples was devastating: battles, enslavement, displacement and deadly disease.

1630 to 1764

An increasing number of Europeans confiscated Indian lands and destroyed Native societies. The Indians fought back, often aggressively, but to little avail. At the same time, the African slave trade emerged as a big business. All thirteen English colonies had slaves by 1690, and Charleston, SC, was the principal slave port. Land changed hands too: the English took Manhattan Island from the Dutch (1664), and the French led the race to occupy the Louisiana Territory (late 1600s). Religious fervor and conflict were widespread. Fears of witchcraft reached the level of hysteria, culminating in the Salem witch trials and executions of 1692.

Growth continued at a rapid pace. The colonial population stood at 275,000 by 1700, increased to over one million by 1750 and more than doubled in the next 25 years. Numerous battles over territorial rights were waged between Great Britain, France and Spain as well as between Colonial Americans and Native Peoples.

First People 18,000-30,000 Years Ago	First Successful Spanish Colony: St. Augustine, FL	Central Atlantic Coast Claimed by England	First Successful English Colony: Jamestown, VA		First Indian Reservations	Salem Witch Trials
Spanish Explore Southwest and Southeast; Bring Slaves			First African "Servants" Arrive in English Colonies	Mayflower Arrives / First White Man (French) West of Great Lakes	Dutch Give Up Manhattan To English / Pueblo Indian Revolt Against Spanish	French Claim Louisiana Territory

1550 · **1600** · **1650**

AMERICA'S NATIVE PEOPLES

EUROPEAN COLONIZATION

RELIGIOUS & SECULAR GROUPS

As a result, the French lost much of their territory to the British and Spanish; whole tribes of Indians were virtually eliminated; and major Indian territories were lost to European encroachment. Attempting to protect its interests, Britain introduced a plan of imperial reorganization in 1763, which infuriated colonists.

1764 to 1783

Public opinion was further inflamed by Britain's attempts to rebuild its dwindling financial resources by levying taxes. When opposition proved futile, the Original Thirteen Colonies united against the Mother Country. At issue were political, economic, cultural and geographic matters. War erupted in 1775. The Declaration of Independence was formally approved on July 4, 1776. After American successes at the Battles of Saratoga, France stepped in to help with substantial military and financial aid. Our first constitution, called the Articles of Confederation, was informally adopted in 1777 and ratified in 1781. America became an independent nation in 1783, bounded on the north by the Great Lakes and St. Lawrence River, on the west by the Mississippi River and on the south by Spanish Florida.

1783 to 1840+

The Articles of Confederation had established a loose union of largely independent states and granted only limited power to a central government. It was a weak solution. A new Constitutional Convention was held in 1787; the Articles of Confederation was scrapped; and the Constitution of the United States of America became our supreme law. In 1789, our national government met for the first time, with George Washington as President.

Still, numerous difficulties marred the nation's early years. Among them: partisan politics, attacks by Barbary pirates, the Whiskey Rebellion against taxation, diplomatic issues with Great Britain and France, unpopular public policies, and the controversial Louisiana Purchase. Then came the War of 1812 (our second war of independence), during which the British invaded Washington, DC, and burned the White House.

A superficial "Era of Good Feelings" followed the war's end and continued until 1825. It was a time when political rivalries were minimal and a spirit of nationalism prevailed. Literature and technology flourished. Much of the country's attention was focused on transportation systems, industry and westward expansion. But then came more problems: the Spoils System (government jobs given to political supporters), Tariff of Abominations (high tariff on imports), the nullification crisis (South Carolina, angry over the tariff, threatened to secede), more tensions with Britain, and mounting discontent over Mexico's hold on California. In addition, the population nearly doubled, from 9,650,000 in 1820 to 17,060,000 in 1840. America's early years weren't easy; but they certainly were interesting.

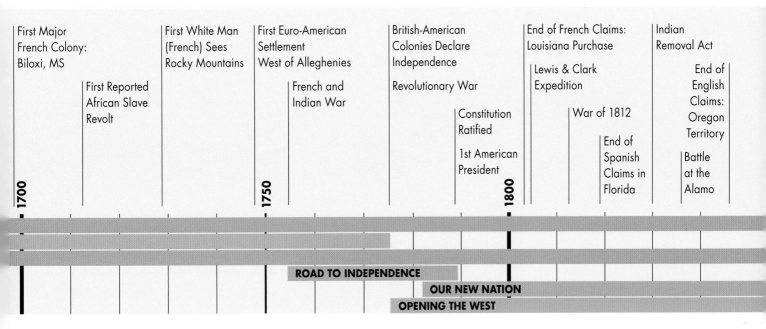

▲ Abrupt rock formations create dramatic landscapes throughout the American Southwest.

▲ Rather than live in tipis or wigwams, the Cherokees preferred more permanent dwellings. So when they saw colonial log houses, they quickly adapted this design to suit their needs, as seen at Oconaluftee Indian Village in NC.

▲ Occupied by the Salado culture, Besh-Ba-Gowah pueblo may have served as a major ceremonial and food storage complex. Today's archaeological park in Globe, AZ, provides fascinating insight.

◄ Early Southwest Indian pottery may be viewed as art, but most vessels were simply meant for everyday use.

AMERICA'S NATIVE PEOPLES

Discovering the true heritage of America's Native Peoples

requires overcoming long-held stereotypes. We grow up with tales

about primitive nomads subsisting on nature's bounty, small villages

surrounded by wilderness, and violent savages on the warpath.

But we only touch the surface. In actuality, America's Native Peoples

comprised hundreds of complex cultures with highly diverse lifeways.

Millions lived here when the Europeans arrived, and they had tamed

much of the land. While many were hunters and gatherers, most

lived in farming communities; some built large stone cities populated

by thousands of people. Major tribes participated in multi-nation

alliances, vast trade networks and semi-democratic governments.

What's more, when the time came for America to become

a nation, our Founding Fathers looked at the spirit of cooperation

that guided Native Peoples. Here they found inspiration.

HISTORICAL PERSPECTIVE:
AMERICA'S NATIVE PEOPLES

A Native American teacher noted: "The ancient ones were just like everyone else. They lived. They loved. They fought. They made mistakes. They adapted. What makes them seem so different – even today – are their religious, political and cultural backgrounds."

millions of Indians died from diseases brought by the whites

To understand America's Native Peoples, we must realize that, with few exceptions, any contact they had with outsiders ended when they came here during the ice age. Various DNA and archaeological findings suggest that waves of people traveled to our continent over the Bering Strait land bridge from Asia and possibly also along the northeastern ice sheet from Europe beginning as far back as 18,000-30,000 years ago. They headed south, gradually populating the land. (The oldest known cultural site – Meadowcroft in Avella, Pennsylvania – is 16,000 years old.) When temperatures warmed, the Bering Strait land access flooded, and the northeastern ice sheet melted. Undoubtedly some migrations continued by sea. For the most part, though, America's early inhabitants were separated from the rest of the world, as if living on a huge Galápagos Island.

▶ Among the plains Indians, the Pawnee were particularly industrious builders. By the mid-1400s, they had created palisaded communities of domed, partially buried earth lodges which provided year-round comfort and security. As shown in this round lodge at Indian City USA in Oklahoma, the Pawnee also had an elaborate belief in the sacredness of the circle.

Clash of Lifestyles

By the time Europeans arrived, Native Peoples had achieved much that was beyond the "white man's" comprehension. Their social systems were often complex. Their trading networks were extensive. Their spiritual practices were unique. And their understanding of the natural world was highly sophisticated.

Communications between the "whites" and "Indians" were tenuous at best. Most Europeans viewed the Indians as Stone Age savages. The Indians, in turn, saw the Europeans as undisciplined, smelly brutes having no manners, no respect for the rights of others and no sense of protocol. Even so, when they first came into contact, Indians treated the whites as their equals. Unfortunately, the same could not be said in reverse.

Battles were inevitable and often vicious. The Indians wanted their freedom and long-established lifeways; the whites wanted the Indians' land and rich resources. The more peace-loving tribes moved to new territories, far from European settlements. Others fought back, ultimately using the white man's rifle and horse in heavy combat. Still, by the late 1800s, the majority found themselves penned in western reservations, forced to give up nearly everything they held dear. There were only a few exceptions – including Seminoles who hid in the Florida Everglades and a group of Cherokees who purchased land in the North Carolina mountains.

Devastating Diseases

With European contact came a long series of epidemics that nearly annihilated many Indian nations. The first diseases (typhus, smallpox and measles) came with the Spanish explorers in the 1500s and eventually killed 75 to 90 percent of Indians in the Southeast. A smallpox epidemic in 1617, apparently brought by fishermen, wiped out up to 90 percent of the coastal Indians in the Northeast. Other epidemics spread throughout the continent – not only smallpox, bubonic plague, measles and typhus, but also influenza, tuberculosis, diphtheria and cholera. As a unit, they were perhaps the most important event in American history. Millions of Indians died. In their stead, Europeans settled lands already cleared by Native farmers, established critical trade relationships with weakened tribes and claimed huge territories, meeting relatively little resistance.

Benevolence Among Enemies

Ironically, early settlers needed the Native Peoples. Having come ill prepared for life on this continent, whole colonies suffered due to insufficient food, poor housing and inadequate knowledge about everyday survival here. The indigenous peoples taught them how to fish, successfully grow crops, hunt for wild foods, make clothing from animal hides, and even build suitable shelters. Such generosity was part of their culture. Before being overrun by white civilization, Indians throughout the continent believed in a world meant for all to share. While many engaged in territorial

raids, and some were very violent, they believed in the sacredness of life – even the life of an enemy. Out of respect, Indians customarily gave gifts of food, clothing and other valuable items during diplomatic missions, tribal gatherings and times of need.

Political Influences

Many historians look at Indian systems of governance and believe that these, too, had an immeasurable impact on America. Although controversial, the evidence was strong enough to support a joint Congressional resolution passed in 1988. (Go to http://www.senate.gov/reference/common/faq/Iroquois_Constitution.shtml). It says in part: "Whereas the original framers of the Constitution, including, most notably, George Washington and Benjamin Franklin, are known to have greatly admired the concepts of the Six Nations of the Iroquois Confederacy; Whereas the confederation of the original Thirteen Colonies into one republic was influenced by the political system developed by the Iroquois Confederacy as were many of the democratic principles which were incorporated into the Constitution itself...be it

resolved by the House of Representatives (the Senate concurring), that...Congress, on the occasion of the two hundredth anniversary of the signing of the United States Constitution, acknowledges the contribution made by the Iroquois Confederacy and other Indian Nations to the formation and development of the United States..."

The Iroquois Confederacy (more aptly called Six Nations of the Haudenosaunee) was a northeastern union of the Mohawk, Onondaga, Seneca, Oneida, Cayuga and, later, Tuscarora Indian Nations. It was guided by the Great Law of Peace (an oral constitution) conceived to govern a large domain democratically. Each member nation made its own laws and governed itself; but joint laws took precedence when matters affected other members. Rule was by councils of leaders chosen by the electorate to serve the people. Decisions were made by compromise and consensus. Sound familiar?

Recaptured Spirit

Today, Native Americans are in the midst of a cultural renaissance. They are correcting inaccurate representations of their history, regaining some ancestral lands or being compensated, and reasserting their rights as sovereign nations. Native American art is highly prized by collectors. Native American cookery is taking its rightful place in regional cuisine. Most valuable of all, Native American philosophy, spiritual insight and environmental practices are helping to make our country a better place in which to live. For travelers and social explorers, America has several Living History museums and historic places which offer a personal look at the "old ways" of truly great peoples.

▲ Before the arrival of Europeans, most of America's Native Peoples lived in semi-permanent encampments such as this one at Monacan Indian Village, VA. They inhabited these sites for several years, coming and going as needed to take advantage of natural resources.

◄ Out west, the Miwok lived in cedar bark houses (u'macha) and stored their food in caches made of woven cedar boughs. (Cedar deters insects and small animals.) This representative cache can be seen at Indian Grinding Rock State Historic Park near Pine Grove, CA. Nearby are an estimated 1,185 mortar holes and petroglyphs made by the Miwok while grinding acorns into a coarse flour. They comprise the largest collection of bedrock mortar holes in all of North America. The park also has an interesting museum.

ANCIENT CULTURES

Although archaeological remains are not "living" history in the strictest sense, many are well-enough preserved to provide a very interesting, in-depth understanding of what America was like before European contact.

Cliff and Canyon Dwellings

The Pueblo people of the Southwest are believed to be descendants of nomadic hunters and gatherers who arrived an estimated 10,000-12,000 years ago in what is now the Four Corners area (where New Mexico, Arizona, Utah and Colorado converge). Initially, these early inhabitants lived in small, scattered bands. Over time, they formed larger groups, spreading throughout the region and constructing distinctive multiroomed apartment complexes. Tens of thousands settled on high mesas and later moved to elaborate cliff dwellings. Others established a progressive and prosperous world in Chaco Canyon and outlying communities. These large settlements reached their height in the mid-1100s to mid-1400s but then died out or dispersed, probably due to a long period of devastating droughts and accompanying warfare.

Ancestral Puebloans (formerly known as "Anasazi") were intelligent, peaceful people whose cliff-high homes and canyon-bottom cities were so well constructed that even after a thousand years several remain remarkably complete. Oral histories tell us that numerous southwestern Native Americans, including Navajo clans who apparently intermarried with Pueblo people, claim Chaco Canyon as their ancestral center. Many Pueblo people in northwestern New Mexico and on the Hopi mesas in northern Arizona are descendants of those who left Mesa Verde. Similarly, residents of San Ildefonso Pueblo and Cochiti Pueblo in New Mexico are descendants of villagers from the Bandelier area.

Other ancestral Native Peoples also developed sophisticated cultures in the Southwest. The Hohokam in southern Arizona established a system of canals

▲ Mesa Verde National Park, CO, is a showcase of Ancestral Puebloan culture. Cliff Palace is its greatest alcove structure. Shown here is just a small section of this remarkably well-preserved site, protected by a massive cliff overhang.

to irrigate crops. The Sinagua in central Arizona interfaced with so many tribes that they developed a melting pot of building techniques and sociological enlightenment. The Salado in southern Arizona became prolific artisans, especially adept at making pottery and weavings of grass or cotton. And in the mountains of New Mexico, the Mimbres branch of the Mogollon perfected black-on-white pottery. Early dwellings have survived these indigenous cultures, preserved by the desert air and, in some cases, by the stabilization and restoration techniques of modern archaeology. Among the most interesting and accessible places to visit:

▦ ANCESTRAL PUEBLO SITES
Aztec Ruins National Monument, NM
Bandelier National Monument, NM
Canyon de Chelly National Monument, AZ
Chaco Culture National Historical Park, NM
Hovenweep National Monument, UT and CO
Mesa Verde National Park, CO
Monument Valley Navajo Tribal Park, AZ
Navajo National Monument, AZ

▦ HOHOKAM SITES
Casa Grande Ruins National Monument, AZ

▦ MOGOLLON SITES
Gila Cliff Dwellings National Monument, NM

▦ SALADO SITES
Besh-Ba-Gowah Archaeological Park, AZ
Tonto National Monument, AZ

▦ SINAGUA SITES
Montezuma Castle National Monument, AZ
Tuzigoot National Monument, AZ
Walnut Canyon National Monument, AZ
Wupatki National Monument, AZ

Large-Scale Earthworks

In the eastern half of the continent was another extraordinary group of Indian Nations known collectively today as the Mississippians, or mound builders. Developing over several hundred years before the arrival of European explorers, they had hierarchical societies in which certain tribal members and religious leaders were separated from the masses. Their gigantic, flat-topped earthworks elevated the elite and ceremonial above the everyday world. Some of their creations were burial mounds; others were multi-acre platforms for political and spiritual structures that overlooked a central plaza.

◄ Ocmulgee National Monument, GA, has eight temple and burial mounds – intriguing reminders of a powerful, ancient culture.

In contrast to these were the effigy mounds – earthen likenesses of animals. These too were huge: many bird effigies, for example, had wingspans extending several hundred feet. In addition, octagons, circles and squares stretched for hundreds of yards to define and protect sacred sites; tall conical and loaf-shaped mounds stood nearby. Hundreds of these earthworks appeared across what are now parts of America's central, southern and southeastern states. While most have long since disappeared into the landscape, the following are protected, popular attractions for modern visitors:

Cahokia Mounds State Historic Site, IL
Effigy Mounds National Monument, IA
Ocmulgee National Monument, GA
Poverty Point National Monument, LA
Serpent Mound State Memorial, OH
Spiro Mounds Archaeological Park, OK
Town Creek Indian Mound, NC

Carved or Painted Rock Images

It is staggering, the amount of Native American "picture writing" that remains from the long-distant past. Nearly everywhere that indigenous peoples lived, they communicated through what we view today as artworks. Petroglyphs (ancient carvings) were pecked or ground into the dark desert varnish or weather patina on the surface of rocks. Pictographs (ancient paintings) were created by applying a mixture of animal fat and pigment on protected rocks under overhangs, in caves or even in dwellings. The resulting human-like figures, animals and abstract symbols are as diverse as the creators themselves and reveal a way of life that we can only imagine today. Perhaps these images had spiritual significance. Perhaps they told of great hunting grounds or pointed the way to seasonal gatherings. Perhaps they memorialized major events. Perhaps they were graffiti. Regardless, they are fascinating to behold.

Our nation also has intaglios reminiscent of the giant on-the-ground images of South America. Best seen from the air, these larger-than-life human, animal and geometric designs were carved into the earth by removing layers of sand and dirt. So far, more than 200 intaglios have been discovered in the Southwest, mostly near the Colorado River. Best known are the Blythe Intaglios, 15 miles north of Blythe, California.

Most rock art is situated in remote areas, but the following sites are fairly easy to reach:

Blythe Intaglios, CA
Chaco Culture National Historical Park, NM
Dinosaur National Monument, UT
Grimes Point Archaeological Site, NV
Jeffers Petroglyphs State Park, MN
Newspaper Rock, UT
Petrified Forest National Park, AZ
Petroglyph National Monument, NM
Petroglyph Point, Lava Beds National Mon., CA
Pu'u Loa Petroglyphs, Hawai'i Volcanoes Nat. Pk.
Sego Canyon area, UT
Seminole Canyon State Historical Park, TX
Three Rivers Petroglyph Site, NM
Valley of Fire State Park, NV

▲ We may never know the meaning of geoglyphs scattered around our nation. Local Native Americans believe this man-like intaglio north of Blythe, CA, relates to the Creation Myth. It measures 105.6 feet from head to toe and 91.8 feet across its outstretched arms. The image was made by scraping away the layer of dark desert gravel and exposing the lighter sand beneath.

Chaco Culture National Historical Park

SEE MAP PAGE 21, LOCATION #21
Nageezi vicinity (southwest), New Mexico
Phone: (505) 786-7014, ext. 221
http://www.nps.gov/chcu

▲ The great kiva at Casa Rinconada was a semi-subterranean ceremonial place. It once had a flat roof supported by massive pine logs brought from 40 miles away. A stone bench built into the circular wall may have served as seating.

▶ The Chacoans were highly skilled masons. At Pueblo Bonito, they created thick rock walls that had an inner core of rubble set in mud. Faced with a stone veneer, these walls provided a strong support for multistoried structures. Originally, the fine stonework pictured here was hidden behind a coating of mud plaster.

Chaco Canyon was and is a very special place. From the mid-800s to the 1200s, nine planned towns plus monumental public buildings and numerous villages grew up along a nine-mile area. The largest and most important of these was Pueblo Bonito, its beautifully shaped stonework rising four stories high and extending in a huge sweeping arc. It had more than 600 rooms and 40 circular ceremonial chambers (kivas). And yet, few people lived here – Pueblo Bonito was a spiritual center and meeting place. A system of water gates and canals diverted runoff from summer storms into nearby farm fields. Over 400 miles of arrow-straight roads, 30 feet wide, radiated to outlying communities and resource areas. Broad stairways were cut into sheer cliffs to provide access into high terrain. Everyone united by this vast network benefited from a farming and turquoise-based economy, common religious practices and a far-reaching bureaucratic structure.

During its golden age, Chaco was the place to be. Thousands of friends and relatives traveled to pilgrimage fairs, participating in the religious rituals and engaging in active trade. In the good crop years, they may have brought food to exchange for turquoise, macaws or copper bells. In the bad crop years, they may have traded turquoise for more immediate needs, such as food for their clan. The Chacoans controlled the market for turquoise, which served an important role in rituals and ceremonies, and they became affluent enough to import an array of luxury items from distant peoples.

Even today, visiting this World Heritage Site is awe-inspiring. We suggest taking a ranger-led tour before exploring the several well-preserved sites on your own. If you're feeling adventurous, hike up the plateau to view Chaco Canyon from above.

Located in northwestern NM. From 3 miles east of Nageezi on US 550, take County Roads 7900 south and 7950 west. The last 13 miles to the park boundary are unpaved road but well maintained. Phone ahead for road conditions during inclement weather. Open daily except Thanksgiving, December 25 and January 1. Per vehicle admission charged.

SOPHISTICATED TIME-KEEPERS

Time was not taken lightly among America's Native Peoples. In fact, careful observations and precise measurements of celestial movements were often considered essential to managing daily life. The Pueblo people in Chaco Canyon constructed an ingenious seasonal "clock" with the sun's rays striking particular points on a spiral. Elsewhere, the Pawnee timed their spring Thunder Ritual to begin with the appearance of the "Swimming Ducks," a pair of stars. The Pomo scheduled their fishing expeditions based on the position of Ursa Major (which includes the Big Dipper). The Klamath Indians used the changing position of Orion to determine the passage of time during winter months. These tribes and many others also used celestial movements to mark the best times of year for planting and harvesting, to predict rainfall or major animal migrations, and to determine the best dates to hold important events.

Mesa Verde National Park

SEE MAP PAGE 19, LOCATION #4
Cortez vicinity (east), Colorado
Phone: (970) 529-4465
http://www.nps.gov/meve

A showcase of Ancestral Puebloan culture, this World Heritage Site is one of the most extensive and well preserved archaeological sites in America. It offers excellent examples of almost every stage of Ancestral Puebloan development – the single-family subterranean pithouses of A.D. 500, the mesa-top apartment-style pueblos built between 750 and 1100, and the sprawling cliff cities constructed during the late 1200s. Twenty-four contemporary Native American tribes trace their ancestral lineage to this remarkable area.

The people who lived here were farmers, taking advantage of the fertile mesa-top soil, long growing seasons and dependable rains to produce beans, corn, squash and melons. They enjoyed good hunting in the lush mesa country and had no need to raise animals for meat. Turkeys were domesticated for their feathers, which were bound by plant fibers and then decoratively woven into blankets and capes. Dogs were domesticated as sentries and pack animals.

For centuries, the people enjoyed a life of relative plenty during which the arts flourished. Weaving was perfected, and pottery reached its peak. But then, a major upheaval shook the population. Perhaps it was an enemy invasion or increasingly dry, harsh weather or internal squabbles. Whatever the reason, the people moved down from the mesa into cliff alcoves, carrying with them millions of building stones; yet they still

returned to the mesa top for food and water. When a 23-year drought began around 1276, it was time to continue the southward migration which had brought them here long ago. By 1300, Mesa Verde was deserted.

Today, an estimated 4,000 archaeological sites are protected within the national park boundaries; 600 of them are cliff dwellings. Some have been excavated and are accessible to visitors, primarily through ranger-guided tours. Hopi dances, cultural demonstrations, lectures and other special events are presented during the summer and fall. Very enlightening!

Located an hour from Cortez, CO, heading east on Highway 160. Open daily but on a limited basis in winter. Admission charged.

▲ Cliff Palace, only a portion of which is shown here, can be visited on a one-hour ranger-guided tour. It is the largest cliff dwelling in America, with 151 rooms and 23 kivas. The Ancestral Puebloans constructed this protected cliff city using local sandstone, which they shaped into blocks and mortared with a mixture of soil, water and ash.

◀ Square Tower House, like other dwellings built high in the canyon walls, is representative of the last 75 to 100 years of occupation at Mesa Verde. In the end, within one or two generations, the people had all moved away.

FARMING INGENUITY

Did you know that nearly half of the world's leading food crops can be traced to America's Native Peoples? Early farmers domesticated a wide variety of vital plants which were indigenous to their territory or traded from Mexico – including potatoes, tomatoes, beans, sweet potatoes, squash, peanuts, sunflowers and corn (now produced on every continent except Antarctica). We can be happy to have such varied foods, but the real story is their far-reaching impact. Native Peoples introduced these crops to the Europeans centuries ago. Initially, this helped to reduce serious hunger and nutritional problems both here and across the Atlantic. Ultimately, it changed the world economy. (Where would the Irish be without potatoes or the Africans without corn?) Native Peoples also introduced colonists to tobacco. Despite today's health concerns, tobacco proved vital to the financial survival of early English settlements. As such, it may even have been pivotal to the development of our nation's English-based political, cultural and economic systems.

Aztec Ruins National Monument

SEE MAP PAGE 21, LOCATION #4
Aztec, New Mexico
Phone: (505) 334-6174
http://www.nps.gov/azru

▲ Nowhere else can you find such a remarkable reconstructed Great Kiva. Based on early archaeological findings, it includes remnants of the original structure and is open to visitors at Aztec Ruins National Monument. (Kivas are underground or partly underground chambers used by Pueblo men for ceremonies, councils and other important gatherings.)

▶ For a different perspective, Bandelier National Monument allows visitors to climb inside cave rooms carved into the volcanic tuff in Frijoles Canyon, much as the original Indian inhabitants did hundreds of years ago.

▶ The West Ruin is the largest of the great houses at Aztec, once stretching 360 feet and rising three stories around a central plaza. It probably was not so much a living space as a public building, akin to modern civic centers or places of worship.

Of the more than 150 communities closely affiliated with Chaco Canyon, Aztec appears to have been a center of administrative, trade and ceremonial affairs during the 1100s and 1200s. Clearly important, it was laid out according to a grand design, with purposeful landscape modifications to elevate large buildings, to formally define the space and to provide roadways. Ultimately it included at least three monumental public buildings (great houses), the last of which consisted of about 450 contiguous rooms and several ceremonial kivas.

Like many other sites in the Four Corners region, Aztec was abandoned in the late 1200s and fell into ruin. Centuries later, white settlers carted away at least a quarter of the stones for their own use. But what remains is still staggering – a huge excavated complex and a reconstructed Great Kiva. Buy the trail guide!

Located just north of Aztec, NM, and reached via US 516 and Ruins Road. Open daily except Thanksgiving, December 25 and January 1. Admission charged.

Bandelier National Monument

SEE MAP PAGE 21, LOCATION #20
Los Alamos vicinity (south), New Mexico
Phone: (505) 672-3861, ext. 517
http://www.nps.gov/band

Centuries ago, thousands of villages and cliff dwellings were built in the area now protected by Bandelier National Monument. The most accessible are located in Frijoles Canyon near the Visitor Center and were inhabited from the 1100s to mid-1500s. Excavated and partially restored, they include cave rooms hewn out of the soft volcanic tuff, stone houses built on the talus slopes, and a multistoried village on the valley floor.

Like Ancestral Pueblo people elsewhere, the Indians of Bandelier grew beans, corn and squash. They supplemented their farming diet with native plants and hunted for meat. They made garments from animal hides and from cotton obtained in trade, wove their own cloth, made their own pottery, and crafted their own tools from bones, wood and local stone. They also participated in an active trade network that extended south into central Mexico and west to Baja California. Sometime between the years 1500 and 1550, these Ancestral Pueblo people left the Bandelier area, apparently moving to settlements along the Rio Grande River.

Today, you can take a self-guided walk around the park and into some of the rooms. Even better, you can join guided tours, offered regularly in the summer and occasionally at other times. In addition, you can enjoy a variety of interpretive programs and Native craft demonstrations during the summer months.

Located 16 miles south of Los Alamos, NM, an hour from Sante Fe. Take US 285 to SR 502 and SR 4. Open daily except December 25 and January 1. Admission charged.

Gila Cliff Dwellings National Monument

SEE MAP PAGE 21, LOCATION #22

Silver City vicinity (north), New Mexico
Phone: (505) 536-9461
http://www.nps.gov/gicl

This is an excellent opportunity to enter the former cliff homes and glimpse the lives of the Mimbres Mogollon (muh-gah-YONE) who lived in the Gila (HEE-la) Wilderness from the late 1200s to early 1300s. Seven natural caves are located high in the southeast-facing cliff of a side canyon; five contain dwellings constructed of stone harvested within the caves more than 700 years ago. Although what remains is not extensive, the dwellings are almost completely original. They are accessible on a relatively easy one-mile trail that leads not only to but through several of them. It is a unique experience.

We encourage you to follow the trail guide and take time to listen to ranger interpretations at the dwellings. Look out into the canyon. Imagine what life was like when everything was either obtained from the environment or made "from scratch," when the only available water had to be collected from the nearby stream, and when the nighttime light came from the moon and a flickering fire. Since the surrounding mountains and forest were America's first designated wilderness area, the environment probably looks much as it did when an estimated 10 to 15 Mogollon families lived here.

Guided tours are offered twice daily at the cliff dwellings, and a self-guided tour can be enjoyed at any time. Special programs may be offered at the park, depending on staff availability.

Located 2 hours north of Silver City, NM, via SR 35. (SR 15 also provides access, but it is a winding mountain road and, while shorter, is no quicker.) Cliff dwellings open daily. Visitor Center open daily except December 25 and January 1. Admission charged.

Walnut Canyon National Monument

SEE MAP PAGE 21, LOCATION #12

Flagstaff vicinity (east), Arizona
Phone: (928) 526-3367
http://www.nps.gov/waca

The Sinagua (sin-AH-wah) occupied Walnut Canyon for more than 800 years, beginning around A.D. 600. Initially they lived in one-room pithouses on the rim, using water-conserving techniques such as check dams and terraces to farm the land. They also hunted deer and small game, gathered native plants and traded with neighbors. Between the years 1100 to 1250, the people moved into the canyon, constructing rock homes within the natural recesses. Centuries after these were abandoned, pot hunters took artifacts and dynamited walls. Thankfully the Civilian Conservation Corps (CCC) and our National Park Service saved and stabilized what was left, to help us see into the past. Today these dwellings are the only such remains of the northern Sinagua culture. Rimtop sites and 25 cliff rooms are accessible. (Be prepared for a safe but strenuous 0.9 mile round-trip walk to the cliff dwellings, with 240 stairs back to the Visitor Center.)

Located 7 1/2 miles east of Flagstaff, AZ. Take I-40 exit 204 and drive south 3 miles. Open daily except December 25. Admission charged.

▲ Tucked into the recesses of Walnut Canyon are over 300 rooms that housed several hundred people and provided ample storage space.

◄ Gila Cliff Dwellings are probably the best preserved of any Mogollon buildings. They comprise about 40 rooms built into five adjacent, natural caverns, safely hidden 180 feet above the floor of a narrow, densely wooded canyon.

◄ As you walk the trail at Walnut Canyon, you see a tangible past. Here are ancient fingerprints, pressed into the clay mortar during construction; smoke-blackened stains from cooking fires that burned eight centuries ago; and T-shaped entryways that once controlled air flow into the various rooms.

Canyon de Chelly National Monument

SEE MAP PAGE 21, LOCATION #8

Chinle, Arizona
Phone: (928) 674-5500
http://www.nps.gov/cach

▲ When the Navajo first entered the labyrinth called Canyon de Chelly, they found a good location for farming and sheep herding, as well as protection from potential enemies.

▶ Among many Native Peoples, ball games served as vital links between individuals, neighbors and distant trading partners. The original ball court at Wupatki is the only known masonry court in the Southwest and has been faithfully reconstructed.

▶ The pueblos within Canyon de Chelly were deserted long before the Navajo arrived. The White House remains date from about A.D. 1050 and are some of the oldest in the park.

▶ The red-rock structures at the Wupatki National Monument sit exposed in an open valley near Sunset Crater, rather than hidden in cliffs. This one, called Wukoki, is small but impressive and easily accessible.

Canyon de Chelly (deh-SHAY) is more than a national monument. It is also part of the Navajo Reservation, a physical and spiritual home of the Diné (din-EH), or Navajo people, and one of the longest-inhabited landscapes in America. As such, this strikingly beautiful place provides unique insight into both the past and present life of southwestern Native Americans.

Ancient pueblo dwellings and rock images are visible from lookout points along the scenic North Rim and South Rim drives. Navajo crafts are presented for sale at established locations.  Fields of alfalfa and corn, small fruit orchards, sheep and traditional Navajo hogans dot the canyon floor. And a 2½ mile round-trip trail beckons visitors to walk down into the canyon for a closer view of the White House pueblo remains. Keep in mind: This is Navajo land. Any travel other than on the White House trail or to park overlooks requires a guide. Ask the Visitor Center about special tours and guides.

Located in northeastern AZ, off of I-191 about 2 miles east of Chinle. Open daily except major holidays. Admission charged. Note: The Navajo Reservation observes daylight-saving time; the rest of Arizona does not. During summer months, Canyon de Chelly clocks read one hour ahead of most other visitor attractions.

Wupatki National Monument

SEE MAP PAGE 21, LOCATION #13

Flagstaff vicinity (north), Arizona
Phone: (928) 679-2365
http://www.nps.gov/wupa

The former inhabitants at Wupatki (wuh-PAHT-kee) are believed to have been ancestors of the Hopi and Zuni Indians. After the volcanic eruption of nearby Sunset Crater in about A.D. 1064, they established relatively small but rich and influential communities reaching out to thousands of people within a day's walk. They farmed the arid land but knew the risks of drought and were prepared with stored food and water. They also

engaged in a far-reaching trade network which brought them turquoise, shell jewelry, copper bells, parrots and other exotic items. That was in the 1100s. After 1250, the pueblos were silent until others made this place their home – Basque sheepherders, Diné ranchers, park rangers. Several major sites, including one just outside the Visitor Center, are easily seen on self-guided trails.

Located north of Flagstaff, AZ. Take US 89 for 12 miles; turn right toward Sunset Crater Volcano and Wupatki; drive 21 miles to Visitor Center. Open daily except December 25. Admission charged.

On-A-Slant Mandan Village

SEE MAP PAGE 19, LOCATION #8
Mandan, North Dakota
Phone: (701) 667-6380
http://www.fortlincoln.com

Unlike many tribes on the midwestern plains centuries ago, the Nu'eta, or Mandan Indians, were not nomads. They lived for generations in stable villages and were farmers and craftspeople, at the height of their wealth and power around A.D. 1650-1750. They built solid homes – 20 to 40 feet in diameter and 15 to 20 feet high – and they developed a culture lasting over two hundred years in south-central North Dakota. Smallpox devastated the people in 1781 and again in 1837, but their descendents have survived as one of the Three Affiliated Tribes of the Fort Berthold Indian Reservation.

Fort Abraham Lincoln State Park provides extraordinary insight into a Mandan village once populated by about 1,500 people. The original was deserted by the time Lewis and Clark camped nearby during their cross-country explorations in 1804, but archaeological excavations have been able to piece together a captivating picture. The village, now called "On-A-Slant" for its location on the sloping banks of the Missouri River, contained about 86 circular earth lodges, closely grouped and facing a center courtyard. The dwellings were built and owned by the women, and each housed 12 to 15 people.

Four circular dwellings and a circular council lodge have been reconstructed as authentically as possible at the original site on a low bluff. Nearby depressions in the earth show the remains of other lodges, giving visitors a real sense of the village's size and layout. What is particularly gratifying, from a visitor's perspective, is the completeness of the reconstructions. One of the lodges is fully outfitted as it might have appeared during the Mandans' lifetime. In addition, guided tours provide a wealth of information about the site and its former inhabitants. This is

one of the few places in America where Living History explorers can truly grasp what life must have been like in an earth lodge community.

Fort Abraham Lincoln State Park has several well-preserved and reconstructed historic attractions. After touring On-A-Slant, stop by the fort and cavalry post that served as the home base for Lt. Col. Custer and the Seventh Cavalry before they rode into battle at the Little Big Horn in 1876. Interpreters tell an interesting tale.

Located within Fort Abraham Lincoln State Park, 7 miles south of Mandan, ND, on the Lewis and Clark Trail (SR 1806). Open daily Memorial Day-Labor Day. Small admission charged.

▲ The structural framework of Mandan lodges was covered with a dense mat of willows, topped by a layer of grass, and finished with a thick coating of clay and earth. During inclement weather, smoke holes were capped with bison-hide bullboats.

◄ Stand within the spacious interior of the replica council lodge (near photo), and feel the power of its dramatic architecture.

◄ Enter a replica family lodge (far left), and imagine life among the Mandans. Inside the doorway is a decorative screen that protects the fire from breezes. On the floor are cattail mats. Hanging from upright poles are personal items – clothing, cherry picker bags, medicine bags, drums, weapons, braided corn. In the back are curtained adult sleeping quarters, and on the right is a sweat lodge.

Cahokia Mounds State Historic Site

SEE MAP PAGE 17, LOCATION #1
Collinsville, Illinois
Phone: (618) 346-5160
http://www.cahokiamounds.com/cahokia.html

▲ All Mississippian mounds were made entirely by carrying basketloads of dirt from borrow pits to building sites. An estimated 15 million basketloads, weighing 55 pounds each, were required to build Monks Mound at Cahokia. On top stood a massive building measuring 105 feet long, 48 feet wide and about 50 feet high.

▷ Corn originally came from Mexico. Hybridized by America's Native Peoples, it became one of "The Three Sisters" cultivated by most farming communities along with beans and squash. For reasons unknown, the people of Cahokia did not grow beans. Corn, however, was a staple, as shown in the walk-through diorama.

Only remnants of the Mississippian culture's central city, Cahokia, remain for you to see today, but they represent such a rich tapestry of life from A.D. 700-1400 that this remarkable state attraction is recognized as a World Heritage Site. Just seven cultural sites in America have this distinction, and four of them are Native American.

At Cahokia's peak, around 1100-1200, an estimated 10,000-20,000 Mississippian people lived here. They were situated at the heart of an enormous trade network, and their world was one of the most sophisticated and most powerful of Native American cultures. Like all Mississippians, the Cahokian people established hierarchies with social distance between nobles and commoners. The nobility – perhaps five percent of the population – wore clothing and jewelry befitting their elite status. They also literally towered above everyone else, presiding over religious, social and political matters from huge, flat-topped, man-made, earthen mounds. Even in death, high-status adult males were elevated above others through elaborate mortuary rituals and burial in mounds.

While the Mississippian culture has been lost to time, many monumental earthworks remain. The people at Cahokia constructed at least 120 earthen mounds in their city plus another 100 in satellite centers. The primary mound – Monks Mound – is the largest ancient earthwork in the Americas, covering 14 acres at its base and rising 100 feet in terraces. Its footprint is larger than that of the Great Pyramid of Giza in Egypt.

Don't miss the site's 33,000-square-foot interpretive center. You will find it to be exceptional, with a fine orientation film, highly informative displays that provide a broad perspective, and a life-like walk-through village diorama. Also ask about special events, workshops and Living History demonstrations of ancient skills such as flint knapping, pottery making, bow making, firestarting, cordage making, fingerweaving, bone and shell carving, and gourd decorating.

Located near Collinsville, IL, about 8 miles east of St. Louis, MO. Take I-255 exit 24, and drive west 1 1/2 miles. Open daily except major holidays. Free.

GREEN CORN CEREMONY

Vestiges of the Mississippian culture survived long after the ultimate demise or disbursement of the people. Key among them was the Green Corn Ceremony held by Native Peoples throughout the Southeast. This was a time of high religious and social activity that coincided with the ripening of the late summer corn crop. Communal buildings were repaired; feuds and animosities were healed; women extinguished their fires, cleansed their houses and broke their used cooking pots; and in the town square, honored leaders gathered to fast and purify both body and spirit. In the most critical part of the ritual, the high priest ceremonially lit a new fire, and selected elders danced around the "sacred flames" accompanied by drumbeats and incantations. The new coals were then used to rekindle home fires; new cooking pots were brought out; and the villagers enjoyed a sumptuous feast of celebration and thanksgiving. To complete the sacrament, the people shared a communal bath in a nearby stream, purifying themselves for the new year ahead.

Ocmulgee National Monument

SEE MAP PAGE 15, LOCATION #3

Macon, Georgia

Phone: (478) 752-8257

http://www.nps.gov/ocmu

Ocmulgee (oak-MUL-gee) preserves a 12,000-year record of continuous human habitation in southeastern America, from ancient hunters-and-gatherers to modern Native Americans. The most outstanding period was between A.D. 900 and 1200, when the Mississippian culture established a large village and ceremonial center on the Macon Plateau here in Georgia. It was a

time of strict rule by powerful chiefs who held tight to complex religious practices that centered around the fire-sun deity. It was also a time of intensive floodplain horticulture by master farmers as well as long-distance trade that extended throughout the Southeast and well into central Mexico. As was true in other Mississippian centers, man-made earthen mounds served as burial places honoring elite adult males. They also provided platforms for ceremonial, political and residential structures built of timber, clay and thatch.

Within Ocmulgee National Monument, you will find intriguing reminders of this remarkable people, including eight temple and burial mounds as well as a restored ceremonial earthlodge with its original bird-shaped platform and seating area. Foot trails connect most attractions, and a drive leads to the large mounds.

Consider timing your visit to include one of the special events. Among the possibilities: a Lantern Light tour after dark in March; a ranger-led field trip during spring and autumn to the outlying Lamar Mounds and Village; and the Ocmulgee Indian Celebration in September.

Located on the eastern limits of Macon, GA, reached via US 80 exit 2. Open daily except December 25 and January 1. Free.

Serpent Mound State Memorial

SEE MAP PAGE 17, LOCATION #4

Peebles vicinity (north), Ohio

Phone: (937) 587-2796

http://www.ohiohistory.org/places/serpent

The largest and finest animal effigy mound remaining today, this earthwork undulates for a quarter of a mile. It is several feet high and up to 25 feet wide despite the passage of time. Early archaeologists credited the Adena culture with its creation; but the Hopewell or Fort Ancient people may be the actual builders. Radiocarbon dating of excavated wood charcoal suggests that it dates to about A.D. 1070.

Apparently the builders mapped out the form using stones and lumps of clay; they then added hundreds of thousands of basketfuls of earth. Why they did this is unknown. Some historians speculate that the serpent imagery might relate to the rattlesnake of Mississippian iconography. The rattlesnake is swift without feet, fins or wings; it is slow to attack but has the power to kill quickly; it sheds its skin every spring – a symbol of the annual renewal of life. At the same time, one cannot ignore the solar and lunar alignments. Apparently, the head points to the summer solstice sunset, and the coils point to the winter solstice sunrise or equinox sunrise.

Take the footpath around the entire mound. View details such as the spiral tail and the open mouth. It would be fun to see this creation from an airplane, since the image is a top-down view. The park offers you the next best option: stairs to the top of a nearby observation tower. Your mind will ponder. Did the serpent serve as an object of worship, a ritual space, an astronomical calendar? The mystery is intriguing.

Located north of Peebles, OH, and west of Locust Grove on SR 73. Closed in winter; generally open Wednesday-Sunday rest of the year. Admission charged.

▲ Even visitors afraid of heights find themselves climbing the observation tower stairs at Serpent Mound for a bird's-eye view of this remarkable earthwork. As we heard a boy say: Wow! To increase your understanding, be sure to explore the Visitor Center museum as well.

◀ This earthlodge was reconstructed in the 1930s over the original clay floor of a 1,000-year-old ceremonial building at Ocmulgee National Monument. Protected here is the low clay bench where political and religious leaders once sat in individually molded seats around a bird-shaped platform.

SunWatch Indian Village & Archaeological Park

SEE MAP PAGE 17, LOCATION #2
Dayton, Ohio
Phone: (937) 268-8199
http://www.sunwatch.org

▲ Five Fort Ancient buildings have been faithfully reconstructed on their original sites at SunWatch, along with sections of the encircling stockade, the solar calendar, work areas and an heirloom garden. Also visible are the original family burial plots, long ago positioned within the village and covered with large, flat stones.

▶ Wichita villages were landmarks on the southern plains. Part of a loose confederation of 200,000 people, they were comprised of large, permanent structures built cooperatively by women. The dwellings shown here were made of split cedar in the traditional way, covered with layers of willow branches and swamp grass.

▶ In addition to seeing seven mini villages and encampments, summer visitors at Indian City USA enjoy a show of ceremonial and competition dances.

In the 1970s, this 800-year-old site of a Fort Ancient village came dangerously close to becoming a sewage treatment plant. Rescued by concerned citizens of Dayton, it is now a unique Living History project where you can learn the underlying reasons for archaeological reconstructions and better understand the lifeways of sophisticated Indian agriculturists. Be sure to visit the museum and see the introductory film. Special events include lectures, workshops, Family Days and overnights.

Located just south of downtown Dayton, OH, off I-75. Take exit 51. Drive a mile west on Edwin C. Moses Boulevard, which becomes Nicholas Road; turn left onto West River Road; drive a mile south. Open Tuesday-Sunday except major holidays. Admission charged.

HOW DID EUROPE COMPARE?

"Pre-contact" Native Peoples had comfortable lives for the most part, although they were challenged by nature, limited resources and territorial battles between tribes. During the same period, however, the average European faced constant survival tests. Most were have-not serfs, trapped by their lives as unpaid workers on a Lord's land. Many in the middle and upper classes sought to increase their fortunes at the expense of others. Wars were widespread and ruthless. Health conditions were poor, and disease killed millions. The bloody Crusades confused religious zeal with political and commercial interests. Overall, much of what made Europeans feel superior to Indians did not occur until the widespread availability of gunpowder (1300s), invention of the printing press (mid-1400s) and Medici family patronage of the arts and science (1400s-1500s).

Indian City USA

SEE MAP PAGE 19, LOCATION #1
Anadarko, Oklahoma
Phone: (405) 247-5661
http://www.indiancityusa.com

America's Native Peoples were remarkably diverse. In fact, their languages, dwellings, clothing, utensils and crafts often had little in common, even when tribes shared a particular environment or actively traded with one another. Indian City USA offers fascinating insight into the lifestyles of seven plains and southwest cultures, as they existed before the first Europeans arrived.

Setting the stage during summer months are the songs, music and dance of modern Native Americans who strive to keep ancient traditions alive. After this energetic performance, visitors are invited to stroll along a wooded trail, stopping at mini Indian villages and encampments. This is a great opportunity to see the circular wood hogans of the Navajo; the brush-and-grass wickiups of the Chiricahua Apache; both the winter and summer homes of the Wichita; the portable tipi (or "teepee") of the Kiowa, Comanche, Arapaho and other nomadic tribes; the wattle-and-daub timber house of the Caddo; the hump-back earth lodges of the Pawnee; and the brick-and-adobe structures of Pueblo Indians. Each is interesting and distinctive.

Located within the Kiowa, Apache and Comanche Reservations, 2 ½ miles south of Anadarko, OK, on SR 8. Open daily except major holidays. Admission charged.

Native Resources

SEE MAP PAGE 19, LOCATIONS #11, #2, #10, #5
Mountain and Prairie States

The Tallgrass Prairie Preserve

Tallgrass prairies were one of the major ecosystems in early America, covering about 400,000 square miles with a rich diversity of plants and animals. Less than 10% of the native grassland remains today – mostly in the Flint Hills of Kansas and Oklahoma. The Nature Conservancy manages the largest protected area and welcomes visitors. Here you can see expansive rolling hills, tall grasses and a herd of approximately 2,500 free-roaming bison. The grasses – including big bluestem, Indiangrass and switchgrass – can reach up to 8 feet in height during August and September in moist, deep-soil areas. Bison calves are born from April-June. We saw a sizable portion of the herd during the rutting (mating) season, July-August. Thrilling!

Located 18 miles from Pawhuska, OK. From downtown, turn north on Kihekah Road; follow the signs. Visitor information at Preserve Headquarters. Open daily. http://www.nature.org/wherewework/northamerica/states/oklahoma/preserves/tallgrass.html

Yellowstone National Park

Try to time your visit to coincide with the early June bison migration into Madison River Valley (western Yellowstone) or the fall rutting season, when Hayden Valley (central Yellowstone) is a favorite hangout. Easy roadside viewing of bison herds is common. Elk and other animals are elusive but also visible, especially in the early morning and evening hours when they feed.

Located in northwestern Wyoming. Open mid-April to beginning of November, weather permitting; facilities have shorter season. http://www.nps.gov/yell

Theodore Roosevelt National Park

Here in the Little Missouri River Badlands of North Dakota are two bison herds – one in the North Unit and one in the South Unit of the park. We saw sizable herds grazing near the road in ridge-top and valley settings. Cities of prairie dogs (cute little burrowing animals) share the range.

Located in western North Dakota. Entrance to South Unit is just off I-94 in Medora, ND. North Unit is 50 miles north of I-94 on US 85. Visitor Centers open daily except Thanksgiving, December 25 and January 1. http://www.nps.gov/thro

Custer State Park

In the Black Hills of South Dakota is a beautiful 71,000-acre state park where you can see not only a large herd of free-roaming bison but also pronghorn "antelope," mountain goats, bighorn sheep, deer, elk and an array of bird species. All three scenic drives are enjoyable, but the Wildlife Loop Road offers the best potential for viewing the nomadic animals. Guided nature walks, chuckwagon suppers and other programs are offered Memorial Day to Labor Day. Consider attending the Buffalo Roundup and Arts Festival held in early October. At that time, approximately 1,450 bison are moved to corrals for their annual checkups, and cowhands separate out some for the November auction that helps support park operations. Also see numerous rebuilt or restored historic structures, including the 1874-1875 Gordon Stockade (first called Fort Defiance) and 1925 Badger Hole (home of Badger Clark).

Located 4 miles east of Custer, SD, on US 16A. Open daily. Peter Norbeck Visitor Center on US 16A; Wildlife Station Visitor Center on Wildlife Loop Road. http://www.sdgfp.info/parks/Regions/Custer

▲ For many Native Peoples, bison were the mainstay of life, providing food plus raw materials for making clothing, tools and shelter. While bowmen sometimes targeted lone animals, hunters usually stampeded herds into ravines, where the bison could be shot at close range. They also drove animals over cliffs now called "buffalo jumps."

◀ Pronghorn were vital game animals too. In the Great Basin, villages came together for communal drives. These annual events not only ensured a productive hunt but also enabled individuals to engage in trade, reaffirm cultural relationships and even arrange marriages.

Three Rivers Petroglyph Site

SEE MAP PAGE 21, LOCATION #2

Alamagordo vicinity (north), New Mexico

Phone: (505) 525-4300

http://www.nm.blm.gov/recreation/las_cruces/three_rivers.htm

▲ You can quickly lose track of time when walking among so many petroglyphs. At sunset, we found ourselves at the top of the hill, just halfway along the trail.

▶ This Big Horn Sheep petroglyph, sitting near the path, is a startling reminder of wildlife that thrived in what is now a relatively empty region. Animal hunts were an important part of life for Native Peoples.

▶ It seems as though every available space of desert-varnished rock served as a "canvas" for creative image-making.

Protected by the federal Bureau of Land Management (BLM), Three Rivers is one of the few places where visitors can walk freely among Native American petroglyphs. Everywhere you look on the rocky but relatively easy hillside trail – one mile, round trip – you can see carvings of human-like forms, masks, hands, animals, birds, fish, plants and a wide variety of geometric designs. Amazingly, there are more than 21,000 petroglyphs at Three Rivers, scattered over a 50-acre area. Be sure to pick up the trail guide, which provides good descriptions and points out the most noteworthy examples. If you want to see more, the surrounding landscape won't disappoint you.

Some of the petroglyphs were scratched into the dark patina on rock surfaces. Others were more painstakingly pecked deep into the rocks. While their meanings remain uncertain, they are fascinating. Through them,

we come face-to-face with the strong supernatural and religious connection that Native Peoples had with their environment. Please avoid stepping on the petroglyphs – they are fragile and can be easily damaged by carelessness.

Across the road from the picnic area is the site of a small Indian village, partially excavated and stabilized to illustrate different building types. Among the findings are an early pithouse, a multiroomed adobe structure and a masonry house. Each is believed to have been built between A.D. 900 and 1400 by the Jornado (desert dwelling) branch of the Mogollon – the same people who carved the rocks.

Located approximately 30 miles north of Alamogordo, NM, via US 54; then east on County Road B30. Open daily. Admission charged.

COMPLEX COMMUNICATIONS

Prior to European contact, America's Native Peoples apparently had no need for our version of "a written language." In addition to petroglyphs and pictographs, they had a rich oral tradition of stories, legends and remembrances. They adhered to long-established protocols for communicating with one another through actions as well as words. They learned practical matters through direct experience and specialized knowledge passed down from generation to generation. They paid close attention to the natural and spiritual worlds, using symbols, ceremonies and rituals to reinforce religious values and express tribal philosophies. What's more, they attached special meaning to a wide range of things that the whites simply enjoyed – such as color, music, dance, food, gifts and art.

Petroglyph National Monument

SEE MAP PAGE 21, LOCATION #3

Albuquerque, New Mexico
Phone: (505) 899-0205
http://www.nps.gov/petr

Preserving one of the largest rock carving sites in North America, Petroglyph National Monument stretches 17 miles along a basalt escarpment and includes an estimated 20,000 images that were carved not only by Native Peoples (beginning about 1000 B.C.) but also by early Spanish settlers. You'll see animals, handprints, masks, people, brands, crosses, abstract designs and other creations. In Boca Negra Canyon, three well-developed trails enable you to view approximately 200 petroglyphs. While short, these trails range from easy to moderately strenuous; so be sure to wear good walking shoes. The Rinconada Canyon dirt trail will take more time, but it has about 3,000 viewable petroglyphs. Special activities include ranger-guided hikes and talks, as well as craft demonstrations.

Located on West Mesa, which dominates the western horizon of Albuquerque, NM. Reached via I-40. Open daily except Thanksgiving, December 25 and January 1. Parking fee at Boca Negra.

Valley of Fire State Park

SEE MAP PAGE 21, LOCATION #19

Las Vegas vicinity (northeast), Nevada
Phone: (702) 397-2088
http://parks.nv.gov/vf.htm

This is an extraordinary place, both for its unique scenery and its ancient art. Multicolored rock landscapes stretch to the horizon. Swirls of purple stripes undulate on sandstone "fields" of pink and gold. Flaming red rock, eroded by the forces of wind and water, create fantastical shapes that tower overhead. All are the perfect complement to two impressive petroglyph sites that are accessible to visitors year-round.

◀ Macaws (large, long-tailed parrots) were a trade item brought from Mexico in ancient times. They were treasured by Native Peoples for their bright-colored plumage.

You'll exercise your muscles a bit to see the Native American carvings, but it's worth the effort. A good view of Atlatl (aht-LAH-tul) Rock, which is crowded with carvings, requires walking up a steel staircase. Easier-to-see panels are spaced along a sandy half-mile trail to Mouse's Tank, so-named for an accused criminal who hid here in the 1890s.

▲ These carvings on Atlatl Rock are like voices from the past, reminding us not only of the Native American cultural heritage but also of mankind's place in the natural world.

Located near Las Vegas, NV. Take I-15 east to SR 169. Open daily except December 25. Admission charged.

◀ Roughly 90% of the carvings at Petroglyph National Monument were made by ancestors of the Pueblo peoples.

HUNTING WEAPONS

The atlatl, or spear thrower, which appears in petroglyphs at Valley of Fire, was an important technological advance. Predating the bow and arrow, it seems to have been brought to America by ice age travelers. The handle, with a hook on its tip to position the spear, had the effect of lengthening the hunter's throwing arm, enabling him to launch a small spear with a single step forward and a whiplike snap of his forearm (somewhat like casting a fishing rod). This meant that a skilled hunter could throw spears with greater accuracy and force over a longer distance than ever before.

Sego Canyon

SEE MAP PAGE 21, LOCATION #24

Thompson Springs, Utah
Phone: (435) 259-2100 (Moab BLM Field Office)
http://www.ut.blm.gov/RockArt/index.html

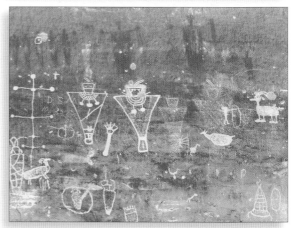

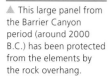 This large panel from the Barrier Canyon period (around 2000 B.C.) has been protected from the elements by the rock overhang.

▶ Many of the nearly two dozen figures seem very other-worldly to us now. It is presumed that they were used by the shamans for ritualistic purposes.

▶ Clearly people have used these surfaces for eons. The Barrier Canyon paintings (2,100 to 4,000 years old) are partly overlaid with Fremont Culture carvings (1,500 to 2,100 years old).

▶ The newest artwork, attributed to the Historic Ute, can be dated to the 1600s, when the Spanish introduced horses into the region.

The land here is rugged and feels very remote, even though the road is paved and a small community is just three miles away. A sign beckons visitors to the ghost town of Sego, an old coal mining spot just to the north. Stark sandstone cliffs tower on both sides of the roadway. Scattered trees line a winding river wash. Nothing stirs. It is the perfect prelude to the scene ahead.

If you love pictographs and petroglyphs, you won't want to miss Sego Canyon. Its large panels of ancient carved and painted images are an awesome sight. Thousands of years ago, this must have been a holy place where Native Peoples experienced religious visions. The depictions look alien and eerie. Here are larger-than-life man-like forms with bug eyes, antennae, earrings and snakes in hands. Here, too, are huge figures with triangular bodies and small heads,

wearing decorative collars and waistbands. Nearby are figures with huge torsos and skinny arms, hunting large animals with spears. Three distinct styles from three separate Native American cultures and time periods are represented: Barrier Canyon, Fremont and Historic Ute.

Excellent signage describes the cultures that created these ancient works, which were restored in the 1990s by Constance Silver, one of our nation's finest rock art restorers. Fences keep visitors a short distance away, helping to protect these fragile national treasures from curious hands. (Skin oil is damaging.) Note: The art panel near the corral across the road is on private land.

Located on BLM land about 45 minutes north of Moab, UT. Take I-70 exit 187 to Thompson Springs (2 miles west of highway rest stop and information center). Drive north through town to Sego Canyon Road and follow signs. Roadway is paved but narrow. Small parking lot at the site about 3 miles from town. The large paintings are on cliff walls, left side of the road. Open daily. Free.

Grimes Point Archaeological Site

SEE MAP PAGE 21, LOCATION #11

Fallon vicinity (east), Nevada
Phone: (775) 885-6000 (Carson City BLM Field Office)
http://www.nv.blm.gov/carson/Recreation/
Rec_grimes_pt.htm

We almost skipped this site, arriving as we did, late in the day, and thinking there was little to see. When viewing petroglyphs, the angle of light is critical to identifying their very existence. Thankfully, we returned the next morning. Grimes Point captivated us.

Approximately 150 basalt boulders on the gently sloping hillside are covered with petroglyphs. About a mile drive down the side road are a few more petroglyphs along with ancient rock shelters. They date to a time several thousands years ago when this now-arid land was a peninsula partially submerged

in water and surrounded by a marshy lake. Back then, birds, large animals and the "cattail-eater people" made Grimes Point their home.

This would have been a fine location for a hunter-gatherer society. The men could have crouched behind boulders, waiting for antelope and deer to come to the water's edge. Anthropologists believe a shaman would have performed rituals to help ensure success during the hunts. One theory is that the petroglyphs here are related to such rituals. Many of the carvings are abstract images with circles, stripes, dots and zigzags. Others represent human figures, goats, snakes and horned toads.

Located on BLM land about 11 miles east of Fallon, NV, just north of US 50. Open daily. Free.

Newspaper Rock

SEE MAP PAGE 21, LOCATION #7

Canyonlands National Park vicinity (east), Utah
Phone: (435) 587-1500 (Monticello BLM Field Office)
http://www.ut.blm.gov/RockArt/index.html

Planning to visit Canyonlands National Park? It is strikingly beautiful. Most of the northern part, however, is best seen via dirt bike or four-wheel-drive vehicle. Travelers with street cars who want to see more than long-distance views should visit the Needles District at the south end of the park. On the way, you will pass directly by a remarkable site on BLM land: Newspaper Rock.

This large panel of carvings etched in sandstone records approximately 2,000 years of history. Scholars believe that Archaic hunters and gatherers as well as the Basketmaker, Fremont and Pueblo cultures left their marks here from 700 B.C. up to A.D. 1300. More recently, Utah and Navajo tribesmen, plus a few whites, made contributions of their own.

Located an hour from Moab, UT. Take US 191 south about 40 miles; turn right onto UT-211; drive 13 1/2 miles towards the Needles District of Canyonlands in Indian Creek Canyon. Signs will direct you. Open daily. Free.

▲ Under a large arch, Newspaper Rock has a myriad of imagery laboriously carved by several cultures who occupied the area.

◀ The Grimes Point petroglyphs were carved onto rocks strewn across several acres. A marked trail allows good views of key carvings while protecting the environment from damaging feet.

◀ This lizard-like petroglyph is the iconic image from Grimes Point. It isn't located in the main rock area but, instead, a mile further down the gravel road.

◀ With space at a premium, images were carved on top of one another at Newspaper Rock as high up as people could reach. The predominant theme seems to be the hunters and their prey. Mysterious larger figures might have had religious significance.

AFTER EUROPEAN CONTACT

Much that had been Native American culture was destroyed, suppressed or assimilated into the fabric of America, lost even to the Indian Nations themselves. Still, a number of Pueblo communities and several fascinating historical parks are able to provide us with a living link between the past and the present.

▲ More than 850 years old, Acoma Pueblo was thriving long before the first Europeans arrived. It remains today – a real community, not a re-creation. Inhabitants live and work here, maintaining the heritage of their ancestors, passing on their lifeways from generation to generation, and providing visitors with an enchanting window into Native history.

Pueblo People

While the Ancestral Pueblo people were forced to relinquish substantial territories to Spanish, Mexican and American powers, many Puebloans have managed to remain on their homelands to this day, descendants of the Indians who journeyed from Chaco Canyon, Mesa Verde and other cultural centers. At least 19 Pueblos have survived in New Mexico. Most are located in the central or northern part of the state, within an hour of Albuquerque or Santa Fe. They are the oldest continuing settlements in America.

These communities have a rich cultural heritage spanning thousands of years. When the Spanish explorer Francisco Coronado arrived in the Rio Grande Valley in 1540, the region was densely settled and intensely farmed by Native Peoples. Over 100 populous towns were made up of terraced, multistoried apartments. Their concentrated mode of living allowed full exploitation of the available water and the limited fertile land along rivers and creeks. Crop growing conditions were poor, and it was a hard-won life; but the Ancestral Pueblo people were more or less comfortable and peaceful. Living in separate, close-knit communities, they developed at least eight distinct, mutually unintelligible languages as well as markedly different cultural traditions.

Even today, the Pueblos are unique, private communities. Some allow visitors to wander; others do not. Some welcome the public primarily to special events; a few are not open to casual visitors. In most cases, their buildings have been upgraded to meet today's needs. Taos and Acoma are visitor-oriented and exceptional. Since the majority of their tribal members live off-site, they have been able to maintain the integrity of ancestral buildings (with no running water and no electricity but some battery power).

On all Indian lands, tourists should be mindful of the strict rules of etiquette, including no drawings or photographs without permission and no entry into sacred areas, such as cemeteries and kivas. Whenever you visit a Pueblo, contact the tribal office or visitor center (typically on the main road) before wandering around. You need to know the visitor restrictions and to learn where tourists are welcomed.

HOW MANY INDIANS?

The most conservative viewpoint says that 1 million people occupied the territory north of Mexico pre-contact; most estimates are much higher – typically 10-20 million. While reliable early numbers are impossible to find, we do know that in 1890 the U. S. census identified 248,253 Native Peoples (including those in Indian Territory and on reservations). Any way we look at it, the population decline was staggering. Taking their toll were the white man's diseases, loss of hunting grounds, territorial wars and extensive deculturation. But there was another contributor as well: white enslavement of Native Peoples. The Spanish, English and French all exchanged trade goods for Indian slaves. In addition, the English apparently sold survivors of the Pequot War into slavery in the West Indies and Europe in the 1630s; Carolina merchants are said to have shipped 30,000 to 50,000 Indian captives to the Caribbean, Hispaniola and northern colonies from the late 1600s to early 1700s; and the French shipped much of the Natchez Nation to the West Indies in the 1730s. Some historians estimate that a quarter of all slaves were American Indians in those early years.

Great Plains and Plateau Indians

While the Pueblo people retained their heritage post-contact, nomadic Native Peoples changed dramatically. The catalyst was the Spanish horse, found running loose or taken during conflicts and then passed from tribe to tribe through raiding and trading. Horses enabled the Comanches, the Sioux, the Arapahos and many other hunters and gatherers to readily travel great distances, efficiently hunt game and swiftly overpower their enemies. Horses also improved their lives by enabling them to haul possessions on a larger travois (a type of sled). This meant that bigger, more comfortable animal-hide tipis could replace small mat tents and lean-tos, and larger quantities of meat could be carried to meet family needs. In addition, the young, sick and elderly could be moved easily during migrations.

Wanting freedom from the whites, many Indians turned to an increasingly nomadic lifestyle throughout the plains and plateaus. In the process, ownership of horses became the basis for tribal reorganization and the formation of new tribes. A chief's power – and any other person's rank – was largely determined by the number of horses one possessed. Young men marked their advancement by acquiring horses in raids, and they gave horses as gifts to a prospective bride's family to win parental consent to marry.

In addition, horse breeding became a highly respected skill, bringing wealth to the tribes. The Chickasaw Horse was considered the equal of English bloodlines; the Appaloosa, developed by the Nez Percé, also was highly prized. Indian breeds were light-weight, even-tempered and highly adaptable. What's more, their endurance was legendary. Call them what you wish – Barb, Indian Pony, Spanish Mustang, Spanish Colonial, Cayuse – they were uniquely American and vital to both whites and Indians. These horses herded cattle and drove them to market, hunted buffalo, were mounts for Pony Express riders and cavalries, and even took center stage in the art of Remington and Russell. Today, official registries keep track of their valuable pedigrees.

Sovereign Nations

From coast to coast and border to border, Indians had to change their lives in response to a white-dominated world. Few found this easy. Defining themselves as Native Americans meant walking a fine line between the allure of America's melting-pot society and the importance of maintaining their own cultural integrity. Furthermore, they did not all become American Citizens until 1924 or receive the full benefits of citizenship until the 1940s. Today, our nation has about 2.8 million Native Americans, nearly half of whom live on reservations – lands held in trust for them through the Bureau of Indian Affairs. In a complex relationship with federal organizations, over 550 tribal governments are recognized as having sovereignty and the right to govern themselves. And yet, they must still challenge old stereotypes about what it means to be "Indian." For them, Living History plays a particularly vital role, educating all Americans, including their own people.

Photo printed courtesy of California State Parks

▲ By 1900, bison were almost extinct in America. Today they are making a comeback, mostly as a commercial source of lean meat.

▼ When the Spaniards arrived in the West, the Miwok Indians were living in bug-resistant conical-shaped homes (u'macha) covered with cedar bark. Excellent examples can be seen at Indian Grinding Rock State Historic Park near Pine Grove, CA.

MATRILINEAL SOCIETIES

In many early Native cultures – among them the Six Nations in the North and the Choctaws in the South – women controlled the society. The reasons were practical. Indian men traveled extensively as hunters, warriors and traders, and they could be gone for months at a time during an ambitious military campaign. The women were left behind to defend the homes, tend to community life and plant, harvest and store seasonal crops. So everything belonged to the women except a man's weapons, clothing and personal possessions. And the line of power was through women – the important male in a family was not the husband but the wife's father, uncle or brother. Similarly, the male village chief, who presided at the center of political, religious and trade relationships, was biologically related to the most powerful female.

Taos Pueblo

SEE MAP PAGE 21, LOCATION #23
Taos, New Mexico
Phone: (505) 758-1028
http://taospueblo.com

▲ Taos Pueblo is a living community of modern Native Americans dedicated to preserving their cultural heritage by continuing the old ways, not only for themselves but for all peoples.

▶ We as visitors have been given a gift by these people. They are willing to be watched and photographed and asked a million questions by inquisitive tourists. They want us all to enjoy and learn from what they have worked so hard to maintain.

Native Peoples have lived in Taos Valley for nearly 1,000 years and most likely constructed the main parts of this village between A.D. 1000 and 1450. The Pueblo looks much as it did when the Spanish arrived in the 1500s, reflecting a culture that is determined to protect its traditions from "modernization."

Much photographed, Taos Pueblo rises nobly from the sun-baked earth with two five-story terraced communal dwellings and many flat-topped houses built side-by-side and in layers. The Pueblo is made entirely of adobe (earth, water and straw mixed together and made into sun-dried bricks). Outside surfaces are regularly replastered with thick layers of tan mud, and interior walls are coated with thin whitewashes to keep them clean and bright. True to the Taos heritage, electricity and running water are banned.

Today, approximately 1,900 Native Americans live on Taos Pueblo land – 100 full-time within the Pueblo itself. This is a living community dedicated to preserving ancient ways. Visitors are invited to have a first-hand look inside certain buildings, to meet the people and to purchase traditional and contemporary Native American products sold here. Arts and crafts, tourism and food concessions are important sources of employment. Local artists include drum makers, potters, woodworkers, jewelers, photographers, painters, musicians, pipe makers, clothing designers and various other skilled artisans.

Take your time on the easy, self-guided walking tour. Feel the ancient spirit of this World Heritage Site. Chat with some of the Native people. Ask them what life was like here centuries ago. And, with the benefit of a permit, enjoy making sketches or painting or taking outdoor photographs.

At the same time, please be mindful of these visitor guidelines: Take care to enter only doors that are clearly businesses – many of the buildings are private homes; none are museum displays. Do not photograph the people without first asking their permission. And out of respect, please do not take photographs or videos and do not make sketches while attending special ceremonies open to the public. These small sacrifices will be much appreciated and will enable you to enjoy an extraordinary glimpse into this Native American culture.

Located 2 ¹/₂ miles north of Taos Plaza in Taos, NM. Visitors welcome daily except during tribal rituals and about 10 weeks in winter and spring. Guided tours often available. Special events held year-round, especially June-December. Admission charged; extra fee for photography, sketching and painting.

BEEHIVE OVENS

Puebloan ovens look like giant clay beehives sitting in backyards or common areas. America's Native Peoples have used these ovens for hundreds of years to bake a bread that is like no other – lightly crisp on the outside; wonderfully moist and spongy on the inside. It would last longer than most store-bought breads, except that it tastes too good to keep for days. The dough is made in the evening and allowed to rise overnight. The next morning, the oven is prepared for cooking, first by building a wood fire inside and then by brushing away the ashes with a wet Juniper branch. At just the right point, when the baker judges the heat to be perfect (there is no thermometer), the loaves are placed inside the oven with a long-handled wooden paddle. They bake for about an hour. "My wife tried using the same dough in a modern oven, but it wasn't the same bread," a man at Zuni Pueblo told us. "It wasn't as moist, and it didn't taste as good."

Acoma Pueblo

SEE MAP PAGE 21, LOCATION #1
Acomita vicinity (south), New Mexico
Phone: toll-free (800) 747-0181
http://www.skycity.com/index.aspx?nav=1&level=1&pk=4&fk=

◀ While it fills the top of a high mesa, Acoma Pueblo is almost invisible, blending seamlessly with its environment.

What strikes us most about this unique Pueblo is its location on a 370-foot-high golden sandstone mesa. It is a barren but strikingly beautiful environment accessible to visitors only on a guided tour. You will ride to the top in a small bus and then walk through the village with your Acoma guide, stopping at key points along the way.

Appropriately known as "Sky City," Acoma Pueblo was built around A.D. 1150 and remains little changed despite decades of warfare with Spanish soldiers during the 1600s. The streets are narrow and winding; the homes are flat-roofed adobe, multiple stories high, with common walls and communal courtyards; and the views high above the plains are outstanding. San Esteban del Rey mission, built in 1629 as a concession to the Spanish and maintained as a final requirement for peace, remains to this day an important part of village life. Remarkably, a few dozen people still live at Acoma, even though it is remote and has no electricity or running water. The Pueblo is being safeguarded by both the Acoma people and the National Trust for Historic Preservation in Washington, DC.

Acoma artists are widely respected for their thin-walled, finely decorated pottery and other clay pieces. A major highlight of your Pueblo visit is the opportunity to meet some of these talented Native Americans, admire their work and buy from them if you feel so inclined. Typically, you will see bowls, platters, small seed pots and animal sculptures made of white clay decorated with natural pigment designs. If you just want a souvenir, consider items that are made in molds but hand-painted. If you want a piece that gains in value and is fully authentic, be sure to buy only artwork that has been both shaped and painted by hand. (All purchases must be in cash. Credit cards are not accepted.)

At the base of the mesa, Sky City Cultural Center and Haak'u Museum has exhibits, special events and scheduled lectures as well as a café, theatre and gallery shop. Artisans frequently work outside, under an adobe-style marketplace, and they welcome admirers/buyers.

Located 45 miles west of Albuquerque, NM. Take I-40 exit 102; drive 15 miles south on Road 32 (Sky City Road). Register at Sky City Cultural Center at the base of the mesa for guided tours to Acoma Pueblo. Tours offered daily except during tribal events and certain holidays. Admission charged; extra fee for photography. This is private property; so please do not explore on your own.

PUEBLO POTTERY

Traditional Native American ceramics do not come easily. Potters start from scratch, collecting their clay from the earth. They sort, grind, sift and soak the clay, sometimes repeatedly. In most cases, they add sand, broken pottery bits or some other temper to prevent shrinkage. Next, they roll and punch and twist the clay to make a consistent mixture and remove air bubbles. Finally, a "tortilla" of clay is set into a bowl-shaped support such as a basket or hollowed-out bed of sand. Coils of clay are added, around and on top of one another, dampened to make them stick, pinched into place, smoothed, shaped and sometimes textured. Then the object is set aside for several days. When it is leather hard, it can be carved if desired. When completely dry, it is sanded to finalize its shape and often finished with a thin slip of clay overall. The object is then polished with a smooth stone and painted with a yucca fiber brush. After all this, it is fired for hours – the old way, sitting on a low platform on the ground, surrounded by slow-burning fuels – to make it hard and durable.

Powhatan Indian Village

SEE MAP PAGE 15, LOCATION #2B
Jamestown Settlement, Virginia
Phone: (757) 253-4838 or toll-free (888) 593-4682
http://www.historyisfun.org/jamestown/powhatan.cfm

Monacan Indian Village

SEE MAP PAGE 15, LOCATION #5
Natural Bridge, Virginia
Phone: toll-free (800) 533-1410
http://www.naturalbridgeva.com/village.html

▶ No space was wasted in Powhatan houses. The highly functional dwellings (top and bottom photos) were covered with layers of woven reed mats which shed rain and yet allowed enough circulating air to dry freshly harvested herbs.

▶ A Monacan woman fries a fruity biscuit made with fresh berries gathered from stream banks nearby and cornmeal made from corn harvested from her garden. Her stove is a slab of river stone heated by a wood fire.

At their height of power, the Powhatan Indians held a territory that stretched from south of the Potomac River to the south side of the James River. The nearby English colonists traded goods with them. They also traded "sons," who served as interpreters and links between very different people – young Thomas Savage of Jamestown lived with the Indians, and Namontack lived with the English for short periods. While both peoples realized the mutual benefit of peaceful relations, the goodwill did not last. War erupted, and the Powhatans were crushed. Around the mid-1600s, the first Indian reservations were established; they limited the land Natives could use for hunting and fishing.

Today, the Powhatan Indian village at Jamestown Settlement is a remarkably authentic re-creation of better times. The houses, garden and ceremonial dance circle are based on eyewitness drawings and written accounts as well as archaeological findings. Interpreters in Indian attire cultivate crops, craft pottery, make bone tools, tan deerskin and weave plant fibers into rope.

Located at Jamestown Settlement, VA. (See European Colonization, page 76.) Open daily except major holidays. Admission with Jamestown Settlement.

While the Monacan (MON-ah-cuhn) people wanted little to do with English colonists, these Eastern Sioux may have been indirectly responsible for the Powhatan decision to allow Jamestown to grow. They were copper miners and traders. If war broke out with the English, the Monacans probably would have left rather than fight. This would have ended a chief source of copper that was highly prized by the Powhatan Indians.

Today, members of the Monacan Indian Nation maintain an early 1700s home for Living History visitors at Natural Bridge Park. Keeping alive their heritage, they use traditional techniques and natural resources obtained from the surrounding forest. As was true 300 years ago, their activities change with the seasons. You might see tool making, weaving, rope making, gardening, cooking, basketry, hide tanning, canoe building. Ask questions. They are proud to share their insight into a culture that dates back 10,000 years.

Located along Cedar Creek Trail at Natural Bridge Park in Natural Bridge, VA. Take SR 11 about 2 miles off I-81, exit 175 or 180. Open daily April-November; closed Thanksgiving. Admission included with park fee.

A BEAUTIFUL PEOPLE

Physically, Native Peoples fascinated early settlers. At Jamestown, John Smith observed that Powhatan men, who were tall and straight (averaging six feet), shaved the right side of their head to avoid entangling their hair in bowstrings. They allowed their remaining hair to grow long, often forming it into a knot decorated with shells, feathers, beads and even a dead enemy's hand. Robert Beverley, another official at Jamestown, noted that Powhatan women possessed an uncommon delicacy of shape and features. Colonist George Strachey was enchanted by their tattoos, commenting that they embroidered their bodies and faces with flowers and other designs drawn from nature.

Ganondagan
State Historic Site

SEE MAP PAGE 11, LOCATION #1
Victor, New York
Phone: (585) 924-5848
http://www.ganondagan.org

Ganondagan (gah·NON·dah·gan) was once a prosperous town peopled by the Seneca, one of the Six Nations of the Haudenosaunee (hoh-deh-noh-SHAW-nee), commonly referred to as the Iroquois Confederacy. But in July 1687, the Governor General of New France led an army from Canada, determined to annihilate the Seneca and thus eliminate them as competitors in the fur trade.

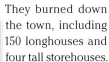

They burned down the town, including 150 longhouses and four tall storehouses.

On the site where thousands of Seneca lived 300 years ago, you can now tour a full-size replica of a traditional bark longhouse. According to oral history, such dwellings were inhabited by sizable extended families. Each was about 20 feet wide and up to 200 feet or more in length, depending on the number of residents. Two-tiered bunks lined the walls, providing sleeping quarters and storage space for individual families. Cooking and heating fires glowed in the central corridor.

Located southeast of Rochester, NY. From I-490, take Victor exit (Route 96) to downtown Victor; turn right onto Maple and right at top of hill onto Boughton Hill. Open daily mid-May through October. Admission charged.

Black Hills
Wild Horse Sanctuary

SEE MAP PAGE 19, LOCATION #6
Hot Springs vicinity (south), South Dakota
Phone: toll-free (800) 252-6652
http://www.wildmustangs.com

In the Black Hills of South Dakota, not far from Mount Rushmore, two-hour guided bus tours take visitors into a non-profit wilderness sanctuary. Here, you will see large herds of wild and semi-wild horses running freely with their foals on summer grazing lands along the Cheyenne River. How striking they are! How difficult it is for visitors to leave them behind! One can understand why horse stealing between Native tribes became the number one sport on the plains and was considered an honorable way for young warriors to gain fame.

The Sanctuary's bus tour takes visitors to lower prairie, rocky canyon and pine forest grazing areas as well as to movie locations and historic sites such as flint mines, petroglyphs and cliff dwellings. Although the ride is a bit rough, it's a fun and economical adventure.

Located in the Black Hills of SD, 14 miles south of Hot Springs via SR 71. Last 2 miles on a gravel road. Open daily April-October. Admission charged.

◀ The Bark Longhouse at Ganondagan is a very interesting replica of a 1670 Seneca multi-family home. It is complete with European and colonial trade goods as well as a wide range of Seneca-created crafts, tools, clothing, herbs and food crops.

▲ You will discover something very magical about standing in an open field surrounded by quietly grazing wild ponies (top and bottom photos). The animals are cautious but not skittish in the presence of humans.

◀ You can touch the various items inside the Bark Longhouse and ask questions of your guide. There is much to see and learn at Ganondagan.

Alaska Native Heritage Center

SEE MAP PAGE 23, LOCATION #1
Anchorage, Alaska
Phone: (907) 330-8000
http://www.alaskanative.net

▲ Most Alaska Natives lived in earthen mound shelters. They lined and supported these all-weather homes with driftwood logs that accumulated on river banks or ocean beaches during the spring ice breakup.

▶ Parkas were made of almost any material, depending on the need. From left to right: Seal intestines were used to make waterproof rain gear; bird skins were stitched together for a light, warm covering on special occasions; and furs such as wolf, caribou and wolverine could be combined to make artistic as well as functional garments.

▶ Alaska Native dances are a form of story telling, typically accompanied by drumbeats. Female dancers tend to contribute lyrical grace while male dancers express forcefulness and physical prowess. When performing in small interior spaces, the males sometimes sit so that the females can be more easily seen.

Just 12 minutes from downtown Anchorage is a premier cultural center governed primarily by Alaska Natives and guided by a 30-member Academy of Elders and Tradition Bearers. Its focus is on exploring the lifeways of Alaska's first people and keeping ancient traditions alive in the modern world.

Contemporary Alaska Natives comprise about 16 percent of the state's residents. In the large Native Heritage Welcome House, you will see exhibits of their modern art and ancient traditions, meet local artisans and enjoy Native dancing, music and other scheduled performances. Outside, on a trail that circles a two-acre lake, you will see the way their ancestors lived long ago. Here, Alaska's 11 ancient cultures have

been organized into five traditional village exhibits based on cultural similarities or geographic proximity: Athabascan; Yup'ik and Cup'ik; Inupiag and St. Lawrence Island Yupik; Aleut and Alutiiq; Eyak, Tlingit, Haida and Tsimshian. Although you can wander on your own, we recommend that you take a guided tour first. You will learn much more.

Located at 8800 Heritage Center Dr., Anchorage, AK. Take Glenn Highway; exit Muldoon Road north. Or take shuttle bus. Open daily, Mother's Day to mid-Sept.; Saturday only, Nov.-Mother's Day. Admission charged.

Anchorage Museum

SEE MAP PAGE 23, LOCATION #1
Anchorage, Alaska
Phone: (907) 343-4326
http://www.anchoragemuseum.org

Alaska has an exciting history – not only Native American but also gold fever, pioneer settlement, European power struggles, World War II battles and the oil pipeline. If you want to see an excellent overview, visit the Anchorage Museum. The Alaska Native section is particularly invaluable. In addition to traditional museum displays, it includes a number of life-size cross-sections of historical homes.

Located at 121 W. Seventh Avenue, downtown Anchorage, AK. Open daily in summer; Tuesday-Saturday from mid-September to mid-May. Admission charged. Combination ticket, with shuttle bus service, to Alaska Native Heritage Center during summer season.

A WORLD OF PLENTY

For many Alaska Natives, fishing provided the basis for an affluent way of life, with less time spent in the pursuit of food and more time focused on social, cultural and religious matters. Salmon was especially important because of its predictable life cycle. The Natives used latticework fences, wood-framed dip nets, box-like traps and fish wheels to capture huge quantities of fish during the spring and summer. In just a few weeks, several months worth of food could be caught, smoked and dried for long-term storage. By supplementing this harvest with other seafood, game animals and plant foods, Alaska Natives had a healthy diet and – except for those living in the coldest regions – time on their hands. Today, we all reap the benefits. Alaskan totem poles, baskets, masks, jewelry, weavings, clothing and elaborately carved, painted buildings are all imaginative and strikingly beautiful.

Ketchikan Totem Poles

SEE MAP PAGE 23, LOCATION #6
Ketchikan vicinity (north & south), Revillagigedo Island, Inside Passage, Alaska
Totem Bight State Historical Park - Phone: (907) 247-8574
http://www.dnr.state.ak.us/parks/units/totembgh.htm
Saxman Native Village - Phone: (907) 225-4846
http://www.capefoxtours.com/saxman.html

◀ Totem poles are not always free-standing. Sometimes they are part of the structure of a building. At Totem Bight, visitors enter the community house through the bottom section of a totem pole.

◀ All sorts of human, land and sea creatures are incorporated into totem designs. Note the bottom animal in this pole at Totem Bight – an octopus. Such artwork generally served one of four purposes: presenting the ancestry of a family, recording the history of a clan, illustrating folklore and real-life experiences, or commemorating an individual.

◀ The creation of totem poles seems to have reached its height in the late 1800s, with the availability of metal woodworking tools. This art form was very expensive and time-consuming. So the larger, more elaborate poles, such as this one at Saxman, tended to reflect the higher status of a carver or clan.

The dramatic scenery in Alaska's Inside Passage can be spellbinding. But don't let it keep you away from the local history. Two very interesting totem centers are located a short drive from the city of Ketchikan: Totem Bight State Historical Park and Saxman Native Village.

Totem Bight has 15 totem poles plus an authentic re-creation of an 1800s clan house that would accommodate 30-50 people. The totem poles are remarkable reproductions of old poles that were too deteriorated to display here. True to their heritage, modern Native carvers laid the originals beside new cedar logs and copied them using traditional techniques.

Saxman, too, has a large clan house and impressive collection of totem poles. In addition, it has a totem carving center where you can see Native craftsmen at work. Special guided tours, timed to include cruise passengers, provide a more complete experience with story telling, Native songs and dances.

Both attractions located on Revillagigedo Island, AK. Totem Bight is 8 miles from Ketchikan via the North Tongass Highway. Saxman is 2 miles from Ketchikan via the South Tongass Highway. Both are open daily mid-May through September. Free entry. Fee for tours.

TRAVELING IN ALASKA

We highly recommend driving around in Alaska. The road system is fairly good, although under constant repair because of harsh winters. Be sure to buy *The Milepost* guidebook available in most bookstores – it is very helpful. You can fly into the island ports; but ferry travel is a wonderful, carefree adventure, and you can bring your car/RV on board. Alaska Marine Highway is the name of both the state ferry system and the protected waterway from Bellingham, Washington, up the Inside Passage to Skagway, Alaska. You can catch the ferry anywhere along the way – we chose Prince Rupert, BC. You can also disembark anywhere you wish – we decided to reserve a few days each at Ketchikan, Wrangle, Petersburg, Sitka, Juneau, Haines and Skagway. It's a very flexible system, with passage fees based on your travel plans and type of vehicle. Reservations are recommended and can be made online. http://www.dot.state.ak.us/amhs/index.html

Oconaluftee Indian Village

SEE MAP PAGE 15, LOCATION #1
Cherokee, North Carolina
Phone: (828) 497-2315 or toll-free (800) 438-1601
http://www.cherokee-nc.com/oconaluftee_main.php?

▲ Each Cherokee village had its central ceremonial square where dances were performed and the tribe's stories were passed from generation to generation.

▶ One of the many arts demonstrated at Oconaluftee is that of finger weaving. With no more equipment than their ten fingers, women weave intricate designs several inches wide and many feet long, often while conversing with visitors and fellow weavers.

This re-created Native village will transport you 250 years back in time to a world where the Cherokees lived freely on 135,000 square miles of land in the East and Southeast. An estimated 200 villages existed here at the time of European contact, with 30 to 60 dwellings in each. Their structures were wood-framed, covered with woven vines and saplings, and plastered over with mud. Later, log cabins became the preference, with a smokehole or chimney in the bark-covered roof. Their Council House for meetings and religious ceremonies was a seven-sided structure representing the seven matrilineal clans of the Cherokee people – the Bird, Paint, Deer, Wolf, Blue, Long Hair and Wild Potato – and it was frequently located high on a mound built by the earlier Mississippian culture.

Cherokee tribes were loose-knit confederations with two elected chiefs: a Peace Chief and a War Chief. Sensitive to the need for consensus, their leaders did not rule absolutely. Decision-making was a substantially democratic process, with tribal members able to voice concerns and influence outcomes. Furthermore, women had an equal voice in tribal affairs.

Today, the Cherokee people comprise the second largest Indian Nation in the United States. (The Dinè, or Navajo Nation, is the largest.) Walking the trails of Oconaluftee with a Cherokee guide, you will learn much about their fascinating heritage. Discover the art of making and using blowguns, demonstrated with uncanny accuracy. See blocks of wood become elaborate ceremonial masks and logs become canoes with the aid of fire and ax. Watch craftspeople shape clay into beautiful pottery, weave river cane into intricate baskets, knap flint into specialized arrowheads, and weave strands of tiny glass beads into brightly colored belts. Learn about sweat lodges, dances, masks, rattles and feathers. Step inside the Council House to hear about various non-ceremonial facets of community life, such as the Cherokee government and language. It's all very informative!

The Oconaluftee Indians have a unique heritage, even among the Cherokee. Their ancestors purchased land in the North Carolina mountains and safely avoided a forced relocation, commonly called the "Trail

of Tears," in 1838. William H. Thomas, a white man adopted into the tribe as a child, held the property deeds for them. Today, they are part of the 13,000-member Eastern Band of Cherokee.

Located on the Cherokee Indian Reservation, 2¹/₂ miles north of Cherokee, NC, off US 441N. Guided tours given daily May to mid-October. Admission charged.

A LIFE IN BALANCE

Native Peoples knew their land well and never took it for granted. Those who farmed concentrated on the Three Sisters – corn, beans and squash. Corn stalks served as poles for the climbing beans; beans added important nutrients to the soil; and squash, growing under the corn, helped keep the soil moist. Many Indian farmers built irrigation systems and established water storage areas, rather than rely on the rains. They also hung gourd birdhouses on poles around crops to attract purple martins, which ate destructive insects and kept away crop-damaging crows and blackbirds.

Yet, successful as they were, Native Peoples rarely became dependent on farmed crops to sustain them. They believed in balance. Villages actively gathered wild plants and game, although not enough to deplete the environment. Nomadic tribes moved seasonally, from valleys to mountains and back, guided by wild harvests and game animals, with farming as a backup. Extra food was stored in caches or used as a trade item for other goods.

Cherokee Heritage Center

SEE MAP PAGE 19, LOCATION #13

Tahlequah, Oklahoma

Phone: (918) 456-6007 or toll-free (888) 999-6007

http://www.powersource.com/heritage/center.html

For another side of the Cherokee story, visit this 44-acre complex nestled in a beautiful wooded setting. Here, you will explore key time periods in Native American history at two authentically re-created villages.

Tsa-La-Gi Ancient Village

This pre-contact world, pronounced tsah-lah-gee, provides a fascinating look at the Cherokee lifestyle of the early 1500s. It features traditional homes and meeting houses comparable to those believed to have been built and inhabited before Europeans arrived in the Americas. On a guided tour, Cherokee interpreters share a variety of interesting facts and demonstrate not only daily activities but also popular games of skill.

Adams Corner Rural Village & Farm

Re-creating an 1875-1890 crossroads community, Adams Corner provides insight into the final years before the Cherokee Nation, Indian Territory lost its autonomy and, along with other Indian Nations, became part of the state of Oklahoma in 1907. You'll see several different styles of homes as well as a school, church and general store stocked with handmade items and late nineteenth-century dry goods. Take your time on a self-guided tour.

Located on original site of Cherokee Female Seminary, 3 miles south of Tahlequah, OK. Take Highway 62 to historic Park Hill; turn east on Willis Road and south on Keeler. Open daily except during the month of January; closed major holidays. Admission charged.

▲ This replica ancient village is comprised of a large, round Council House and many small, rectangular lodges. All are made in the traditional manner, primarily of wattle and daub.

◀ Adams Corner Rural Village is a compilation of typical nineteenth-century structures that reflect the Cherokee adaptation to the white man's ways.

WRITTEN LANGUAGE

When the Cherokee Nation was formally established in the early 1800s, it expanded upon the principles of democratic government long practiced by member tribes. At the heart of its rule was a constitution, a code of law and elected leaders (Chief, Vice Chief and 32 Council Members). The Cherokee Nation also had a written language, created by Sequoyah in the 1820s, with 86 characters based on individual syllables in Cherokee words. Any person who could speak Cherokee could also read and write it after learning the 86 characters. So the Cherokee Council passed a resolution establishing a newspaper to foster communication. A printing press was ordered, the type was cast, and the *Cherokee Phoenix* was born in 1828. (Side note: The giant sequoia tree and Sequoia National Park are named after the Cherokee man, Sequoyah.)

In the Cherokee language...

"Cherokee"

sounds like: tsah - lah - gee

looks like: Ꮳ Ꮃ Ᏹ

"Phoenix"

sounds like: tsoo - lay - hee - sah - nuh - hee

looks like: Ꮷ Ꮬ Ꮑ Ꮁ Ꮽ Ꮑ

Pu'uhonua o Hōnaunau National Historical Park

SEE MAP PAGE 23, LOCATION #5
Kailua-Kona and vicinity (south), island of Hawai'i, Hawai'i
Phone: (808) 328-2288
http://www.nps.gov/puho

▲ Guarded by towering ki'i statues, this reconstruction is located in the Hawaiian pu'uhonua, or place of refuge. It is representative of the ancient temple and mausoleum that housed the bones of 23 ali'i (members of the ruling class).

▲ In pre-contact days, Hawaiian men made brightly colored feather capes for their chiefs. Today this unique art is demonstrated at Pu'uhonua o Hōnaunau.

On the Hawaiian Islands were very different Native peoples. They arrived in large wa'a (canoes) from Polynesia and followed strict laws, or kapu, based on religious beliefs and social hierarchies. In their world, chiefs served as a connection between men and the gods, and priests assisted them. Inheriting their right to rule, the chiefs were trained from youth to lead, protect and inspire. Their importance was so great that to step on the shadow of a high-ranking chief was to step on his *mana* or spiritual essence and make the area unclean. This was a capital offense for a commoner, punishable by death unless he could run inside a pu'uhonua (poo-oo-OH-noo-ah).

In approximately 1550, on the southwestern shore of the "Big Island," a very important pu'uhonua was built. This "Place of Refuge of Hōnaunau" (HOH-now-now) was surrounded by a Great Wall over 1,000 feet long, 10 feet high and 17 feet wide. For the Hawaiian people, this was a safe haven, where law breakers could be absolved of crimes and where defeated warriors, elders or children could find refuge in times of war. Just outside the pu'uhonua boundaries, the chiefs lived and ruled. Their bones, which were believed to possess great spiritual power to protect the pu'uhonua, were housed in the Hale o Keawe temple at one end of the Great Wall.

Some remnants of the original pu'uhonua have survived the passage of time and the forces of nature; others have been rebuilt. Historic sites include portions of the Great Wall, temples, royal fishponds and Ki'ilae Village (including the holua slides where chiefs once rode fast-moving sleds down steep slopes). Also in the park are reconstructions of Hale o Keawe temple and several thatch-roofed structures. Cultural demonstrators can be seen at work, creating traditional Hawaiian arts and crafts. Ask at the Visitor Center for their schedules.

Nearby Attractions

For a more complete picture of Hawaiian life, we also recommend visiting the following attractions.

'Ahu'Ena Heiau

Just outside what is now King Kamehameha's Kona Beach Hotel, adjacent to the lagoon in Kailua-Kona, is the site of King Kamehameha's capitol from 1812-1819. Although much was covered by Kailua Pier and the hotel grounds, a scaled-down replica of the 'Ahu'Ena Heiau temple is interesting.

Hulihe'e Palace

This building at 75-5718 Ali'i Drive in Kailua-Kona was the vacation residence of Hawaiian royalty. Extensively remodeled in the 1880s by the last reigning king, it is an historical museum and showplace of royal furnishings.

Mokuaikaua Church

Directly across from Hulihe'e Palace is the oldest church in the Hawaiian islands. Completed in 1837, it has walls of lava rock cemented together by a mixture of sand and lime produced from burnt/crushed coral.

Kona Coffee Living History Farm

Near the town of Captain Cook, you can explore a more recent but also uniquely Hawaiian history – the coffee farm lifestyle of Japanese pioneers in the early 1900s. Guided tours weekday mornings include the planting orchards, family home (authentically furnished), coffee-processing mill, drying platforms and outbuildings.

Pu'uhonua o Hōnaunau National Historical Park is located off of Highway 11 south of Kailua-Kona, island of Hawai'i, HI. Turn onto Route 160 towards the ocean. Open daily except major holidays. Admission charged.

'Iolani Palace State Monument

SEE MAP PAGE 23, LOCATION #4
Honolulu, island of O'ahu, Hawai'i
Phone: (808) 522-0822
http://www.iolanipalace.org

The only official royal residence in the United States, this impressive structure was completed in 1882. Although beyond our designated time period, it is a necessary part of understanding Native Hawaiian heritage. 'Iolani (ee-oh-LAH-nee) Palace was used by Hawaiian royalty until the monarchy was overthrown in 1893. Now restored to its regal opulence, it is a delight to visit. Amazingly, although most of the royal possessions had been sold at public auction long ago, the historical society has managed to recover a substantial number of original furnishings and personal items.

The Palace was built by King Kalākaua (kah-lah-COH-ah), who came to the throne in 1874. Descended from a long line of kings and queens, Kalākaua believed he should live like European royalty to gain international respect and maintain his nation's independence. He also was active on the world scene, becoming the first ruling monarch (anywhere) to visit an American President and the first to take a world tour.

The main floor of 'Iolani Palace includes the Throne Room and public spaces where the King and Queen engaged in government affairs, dined and entertained. The Grand Staircase leading to private quarters on the second floor is a work of art carved of Hawaiian Koa wood. Upstairs is King Kalākaua's bedroom, decorated with some of his favorite possessions. It connects to his library of books and correspondence with important people in Europe, Asia and America. Also upstairs are the rooms of his wife, Queen Kapi'olani (kah-pee-oh-LAH-nee) and his sister, the future Queen Lili'uokalani (lee-lee-oo-oh-KAH-lah-nee). When King Kalākaua died in 1891, his sister ascended to the throne. A short but successful revolution led by non-Hawaiians removed her from office two years later. The resulting new republic ended the long reign of Hawaiian royalty.

Nearby Bishop Museum

We recommend taking a short drive from 'Iolani Palace to the Bishop Museum at 1525 Bernice Street. Here you'll see priceless artifacts, royal heirlooms and cultural objects representing Native Hawaiian, Pacific Island and Hawai'i immigrant life. Among them are the feather capes and royal standards of Hawaiian kings as well as items made of tapa "cloth" (a papery material created from the inner bark of the Mulberry tree).

'Iolani Palace is located at South King and Richard Streets in downtown Honolulu, island of O'ahu, HI. Open Tuesday-Saturday except major holidays. Admission charged for guided tours. Entry to park grounds is free.

▲ While smaller than European royal residences of its day, 'Iolani Palace had a regal elegance and contained the most up-to-date amenities, including indoor plumbing, telephone communications and electric lighting (years before electricity was installed in the White House or Buckingham Palace).

HAWAIIAN ANCESTORS

The first people to live in Hawai'i arrived by sea from Polynesia 1,400-2,000 years ago. They were overcome by a group from Tahiti 800-900 years ago. Spanish, Dutch and Japanese explorers may have stopped at various islands centuries later, but their impact appears to have been minimal. The rest of the world did not know about Hawai'i until Captain James Cook landed with his crew in early 1778. What the British saw was a world of separate chiefdoms totaling 300,000-400,000 people on eight major islands. The leaders were imposing: tall, broad-structured and decorated with elaborate tattoos, bold necklaces and colorful feather capes. The common people were generally happy, enjoying a relaxed lifestyle of farming and fishing. Appreciative of new things, these Native Peoples welcomed the changes brought by foreign visitors. The impact was devastating. In 100 years, the number of pure Hawaiians declined to an estimated 48,000 due to diseases, intermarriage with foreigners and inter-island wars using European firearms. One chief, Kamehameha the Great, took particular advantage of the new weapons and created a single nation under his control in 1810.

▲ The Northeast was ideal for early European settlement. It was thick with timber, teaming with fish and had deep, wide ports enabling ships to come and go easily.

▶ Domesticated sheep brought from the Old World provided colonists with a welcomed contrast to hunted meat and fish. Raised today at historical farms, heritage stocks differ markedly from modern species.

▶ By 1627, English settlers were thriving on the Massachusetts coast. At Plimoth Plantation, you can step back in time to witness their very different lifestyle. You can also board the Mayflower II berthed nearby.

▲ Exceptional San Xavier del Bac Mission in Tucson, AZ, reminds us that Spanish coloniz-ation was tied to the conversion of Native Peoples. Being a Spanish citizen in the New World required being a Catholic.

EUROPEAN COLONIZATION

One has to wonder: what were the early colonists thinking? The first arrivals were mostly interested in finding easy wealth and claiming vast sections of land for their governments. They cared little about basic survival needs, quarreled with one another, made enemies of the Indians and searched fruitlessly for gold. The settlers who followed were often city folks, ill-prepared to live off the land here or fish from the sea. Farmers typically arrived at the wrong time in the growing season, with seeds and plantings that frequently could not survive the trip or thrive in the New World. Worst of all, whole shiploads of people arrived with minimal supplies, assuming apparently that others would provide for them. That any of the early colonists lived to tell their story is remarkable. Their survival remains a great testimony to the power of self-determination and the sheer force of will against all odds.

HISTORICAL PERSPECTIVE:
EUROPEAN COLONIZATION

Columbus' four voyages between 1492 and 1504 dramatically changed life not only for Native Peoples but also for many Europeans. Even though Columbus himself did not set foot on North American soil, he opened the door to exploration and colonization on a grand scale. Europeans needed a New World – the old one was consumed by serious problems. And although the majority of colonists came inadequately prepared for life in a strange new land, they were determined to stay no matter how extreme the circumstances. They settled in very hostile environments; they endured

famine, plague, disastrous weather and deadly wars; they worked extraordinarily hard; and most died young. Yet, those who survived rarely returned to their native countries when the opportunity arose.

Undoubtedly, a major part of the attraction of America was its contrast to Europe. Here was a place where individuals had a chance to fulfill their dreams… where wealth and power were possible regardless of one's background…where religious and political dissenters could find peace in their own communities… and where others could achieve communal ideals in separate, utopian societies. Left behind was disease-ridden, war-torn Europe; left behind were mean-spirited neighbors, adversarial churches and harsh royal governments; ahead was hope and potential.

Hard-Fought Success

The first European settlers came in 1526 by way of the West Indies. They were Spanish and seemed well prepared for colonization; but the hardships were unbearable, their leader died, and they soon had to

▲ In the 1700s, the French built forts and houses by setting logs into the ground vertically, instead of stacking them horizontally. Examples can be seen at Fort St. Jean Baptiste in Natchitoches, LA.

▶ Spanish settlers, such as those at El Rancho de las Golondrinas near Santa Fe, NM, became experts at using native materials to survive in an inhospitable climate.

abandon their settlement at San Miguel de Guadalupe (probably in South Carolina). They left behind the first non-native permanent residents: African slaves. Undaunted, the Spanish next tried Florida, failing after two years in Pensacola (1559-1561) but finally succeeding in St. Augustine (1565). In the early 1560s, the French had hoped to gain a foothold on American soil; but they were forced out by the Spanish and didn't succeed in a major way until 1699 in Mississippi. In 1585 and again in 1587, the English attempted their first colonies at Roanoke Island (North Carolina). However, they too failed, for unknown reasons; 20 years went by before they successfully founded Jamestown, Virginia. The Dutch began their own settlements in 1614 (New York), the Swedes in 1638 (Delaware) and the Germans in 1683 (Pennsylvania). Despite the long and arduous sea voyage, the influx of colonists was huge. By 1700, the European population in America had grown to about 275,000. At that time, the only other sizable group of immigrants were Africans – mostly slaves but also sailors, soldiers, explorers and free servants.

Rich Resources

As one would expect, the commercial side of early colonization varied widely, although nearly everyone raised some crops and livestock. In the Southeast and Southwest, the Spanish built a farm economy based on Native labor and shipped a wide variety of trade goods to Spain. In Georgia and South Carolina, English farmers exported rice and, after 1750, indigo. In Virginia and Maryland, tobacco became such a valuable export crop that it shaped social development. With little need for a merchant class, the farmers built agricultural power bases and luxurious lives on large plantations. Both Native American and African slaves worked the land along with indentured servants (who had committed to several years of work in return for

The English were here to build thriving communities. This meant not only farming and harvesting natural resources, but also creating commercial operations such as the Saugus Iron Works in Saugus, MA. As was true with grist mills and sawmills, the iron works relied on readily available water to turn giant wheels, which moved a series of gears and belts, which powered tools and machinery.

their trip to America). English orphans and even some convicts also came under long-term labor contracts.

In the northern colonies, where the land was less fertile, farming was primarily a family enterprise providing a sustainable living but little for sale. Some colonists in the Connecticut Valley managed to grow tobacco for export. Others in Rhode Island developed a dairy industry. Overall though, a substantial merchant economy developed, and urban affairs were dominated by a growing mercantile minority who translated their wealth into political power. Port cities such as Philadelphia, New York and Boston thrived as centers of commercial life. Seeing this northern wealth, other nations sought to gain a foothold. Dutch-Swede rivalries turned into war, and a Dutch force seized New Sweden in 1655. Dutch control was relinquished to the English in 1664. The Dutch reclaimed the colony, but before long, control again reverted to the stronger English.

By the mid-1700s, English colonists had become the most powerful cultural group in all of America. Their overall standard of living appears to have been equal to that of their European counterparts.

Little Harmony

Land ownership and improved quality of life were driving forces behind many settlements. When personal gains infringed on others, as they invariably did, power plays and violence ensued. The Native Peoples, who were constantly being pushed aside, suffered the worst; but there were plenty of squabbles and outright wars between the colonists themselves as each sought to gain dominance. Security was a significant concern for everyone, prompting some communities to come together in loose unions for protection from outsiders.

Many settlers who came here to avoid European oppression managed to create political, religious and cultural institutions that were equally oppressive. The Puritans, for example, persecuted and even hung Quakers because of their beliefs – until they discovered a more serious threat from witches. When they became obsessed with the Salem Witchcraft Trials of 1692, the Puritans were torn apart by accusations and fear. After months of hysteria had spread throughout the colonies, 20 people were executed in Salem for supposedly practicing witchcraft. Finally, the Governor of Massachusetts Bay Colony recognized the travesty being perpetrated, forbade further witch trials and freed the dozens of remaining prisoners.

A resurgence of religious values in the 1700s, along with expanding cultural diversity, prompted Americans to turn their attention to community concerns and individual rights. Groups of English, Germans, Scots and Scotch-Irish broadened the Christian base. Jews of Spanish and Portuguese origins took the first steps toward building Jewish settlements. The sadly growing population of slaves expanded the African traditions. At the same time, a rising tide of evangelists challenged people to question what they believed and how they lived. Critical of established churches, they held emotional revival meetings, warning colonists about the dangers of falling prey to terrible sins and unholy amusements. Symptomatic of the mind-set at that time: drinking, cardplaying and dancing were major concerns in "civilized" communities.

Whatever one's background or area of interests, being an American was not easy in those early days.

standard of living equal to that of European counterparts

THE SPANISH

La Hacienda de los Martinez

SEE MAP PAGE 21, LOCATION #28
Taos, New Mexico
Phone: (505) 758-1000
http://taoshistoricmuseums.com/martinez.html

▶ Spanish buildings such as this one at La Hacienda de los Martinez had few windows. While providing security, this architectural style also helped control room temperatures. Summer heat was minimized. Corner fireplaces provided efficient winter warmth. White walls reflected fire and candlelight.

Hispanics were the earliest European colonists in what became the United States of America. Primarily Spanish explorers, soldiers and Roman Catholic missionaries, they were driven by the promise of great riches, the potential to achieve glory, and the desire to build a Spanish empire peopled primarily by Native citizens. In fact, by the time the English began active colonization on the Northeast Coast during the 1600s, the Spanish already had made a significant impact on the Southeast and Southwest, due in large part to the mission system. (See *Religious & Secular Groups*, "The Catholics," pages 108-116.) Although Spain wanted all of America, it ultimately claimed about one-third and held onto much of its territory for roughly 250-300 years – until the Mexican War of Independence in 1810-1821. The first major, long-term settlements were established in Florida and New Mexico. A series of others followed in Georgia, Texas, Arizona and California

In Florida, the Spanish sought to assimilate Native chiefdoms into their colonial realm as tributary provinces, incorporating converted Indian leaders as subordinate bureaucrats. A particularly interesting example was Mission San Luis de Apalachee (a-puh-LA-chee) in what is now Tallahassee, Florida. Built in the mid-1600s, it was a Spanish capital, home of the most powerful Apalachee chief and a center of agriculture, overseas trade and Hispanic-American culture. An estimated 1,500 Apalachee and Spanish people lived in and around the mission complex 300 years ago. Another 6,000 Apalachee lived in the surrounding region.

Despite such success in the Southeast, the Spanish employed a different strategy in the Southwest, where religious conversion of the Native Peoples seems to have been the primary focus. The initial result was not positive. The Indians resented the intrusion into their long-held lifeways. In New Mexico, for instance, approximately 70 pueblos revolted in unison during 1680, killing about 400 of the estimated 2,500 colonists (including Catholic padres) and forcing others to flee south to Mexico or east to Texas. In the end, though, the Spanish did win. The power of religious teachings plus the impact of guns and horses were certainly persuasive factors.

a significant impact on the American Southeast and Southwest

Remnants of America's Spanish Colonial heritage extend across the southern regions, from Florida to California. Our review of these visitor attractions begins with one of the most recent – a reminder that much of America still belonged to Spain well into the 1800s.

Built between 1804 and 1827, La Hacienda de los Martinez was a private home and trade center for the northern boundary of the Spanish Empire. Its 21 rooms and two inner placitas (courtyards) have been restored beautifully and furnished with period re-creations as well as more than 400 artifacts. Here is a rare glimpse into the everyday world of a powerful family when New Mexico was still a rugged frontier.

Living History demonstrations are presented periodically. During the last weekend in September, the Hacienda hosts the Old Taos Trade Fair.

Located 2 miles southwest of Taos Plaza on Lower Ranchitos Road, Taos, NM. Open daily May-October. Call for winter hours. Admission charged.

▶ With security as a primary concern, the exterior of the Hacienda was built to look more like a fortress than a home and trade center.

Historic Santa Fe

SEE MAP PAGE 21, LOCATION #26

Santa Fe, New Mexico
Phone: (505) 983-7317
http://www.santafe.org

The "Kingdom of New Mexico" was first claimed for the Spanish Crown by Francisco Vasquez de Coronado in 1540, and its first capital was established in 1598 at San Juan Pueblo, 25 miles north of present-day Santa Fe. When the original Governor-General retired, the new leader preferred the small cluster of European-style buildings at Santa Fe. So he moved the capital in 1609, and Santa Fe grew to become the seat of power for the entire Spanish Empire north of the Rio Grande River. The indigenous population in New Mexico alone numbered approximately 100,000 people at the time.

Palace of the Governors

When the Pueblo Indians revolted against the Spanish in 1680, they sacked Santa Fe but spared one building, the Palace of Governors. Constructed in 1610, this long, low adobe structure now houses history exhibits and the Palace Print Shop and Bindery, which operates nineteenth-century printing presses and other equipment. Under a covered porch facing the city's central plaza, modern Native Americans present their hand-crafted artwork and jewelry for sale. You will find quality pieces here – all of the artists must be accepted by a committee that sets high standards.

Mission of San Miguel of Santa Fe

Burned by Indians during the Pueblo Revolt, the original Spanish church was reconstructed by order of the governor, The Marquez de la Peñuela, in 1710. Repairs have been made over the years, and stone buttresses were added to strengthen the walls, tower and façade. Still, it remains a wonderful place. Priceless artworks adorn the interior. The altar screen dates from 1798. The bronze Spanish bell, which is now displayed in the gift shop, was cast in northern New Mexico in 1856.

▲ Mission of San Miguel of Santa Fe is one of our country's oldest continuously operating churches and noteworthy for its historic Spanish Colonial artwork.

◀ The staircase in Loretto Chapel is both marvelous and mysterious. The carpenter's identity is unknown, and his innovative methods of construction continue to spark curiosity.

Loretto Chapel

This former Catholic church is not as old – it dates to the late 1870s – but it does have something quite remarkable: a spiral staircase that rises 22 feet to the choir loft with two 360 degree turns and no visible means of support. The carpenter is said to have used no nails to build the staircase – only wooden pegs. Small but elegant, Loretto Chapel was built in the Gothic-Revival style with sandstone walls, apparently influenced by French clergy in Santa Fe.

Located on or near the central plaza in Santa Fe, NM. Within an easy walk, you will find other historic buildings as well as fine painting and Native American art galleries, various other shops and a variety of restaurants.

SO MANY MISSIONS!

It would be an oversimplification to say that the Spanish missions were built for religious purposes. In actuality, they were agencies of Spain, supported by the government as a means of persuading Native Peoples to become loyal subjects. Protection of the Spanish Empire was paramount at this point in history, and missions could serve as strongholds. So the conversion of Indians, as part of their training to become Spanish citizens, became an incentive for Jesuit and Franciscan support. Spanish padres and friars began their work in the Southeast during the 1520s. Throughout much of Georgia and Florida over the next 180 years, they established more than 100 mission centers and outstations (where a friar or two lived in a Native village), and they moved as needed to accommodate the migratory lifeways of the Native Peoples. In the 1600s, they began building churches in about 50 Pueblo villages in the Southwest, followed by mission centers in Texas. Finally, Spanish settlement extended into California during the late 1700s, when 21 mission communities were established on a northern route from San Diego.

El Rancho de las Golondrinas

SEE MAP PAGE 21, LOCATION #27

Santa Fe vicinity (south), New Mexico
Phone: (505) 471-2261
http://www.golondrinas.org

▲ In early Spanish American homes, the courtyard was the center of activity, and all rooms opened onto it. Here buckets of water were drawn from the well, loaves of bread were baked, various labors were accomplished, farm animals roamed and children played.

▶ Interior elegance didn't require glitz and glamour imported from Spain. Beautiful natural materials could be obtained from the local environment. Rugs and table coverings could be woven from the farm's own wool. A variety of decorative items could be made from recycled items, such as tin boxes.

▶ Knowing how to preserve food was essential in early America. Vegetables, grains and herbs were constantly harvested and dried for later use.

During the 1700s and 1800s, Las Golondrinas was a welcomed stopping place on the El Camino Real, which linked the Spanish capitals of Mexico City and Santa Fe. Here at this self-sufficient rancho, horseback riders and ox carts filled with supplies began and ended their journeys. Here too Juan Bautista de Anza, Governor of New Mexico, rested overnight with his men while seeking a direct route to Arizpe in Sonora, Mexico.

Today, 200 acres of "The Ranch of the Swallows" have been restored, and interpreters dressed in period clothing provide an in-depth look at what life was like when a rural farming valley was an integral part of Spanish and Mexican rule. In addition to period buildings and Living History demonstrations, special festivals and theme weekends enable you to experience much of the music, dance and lifestyle which comprise our nation's Spanish American heritage.

Stroll along the dirt footpath to more than 60 featured sites and learn first-hand how people once lived in fortress-like protection and later spread out into the countryside as concerns about safety diminished. Visit the ranch kitchen, with its stone cooking fireplace, clay pots, metate for grinding corn and simple, rough-hewn

furnishings. Walk through the bedrooms, guest rooms and other living quarters. See old looms used to make not only clothing but also blankets for horses, rugs for floors and coverings for furniture. Step into the fully furnished schoolhouse, which includes a one-room apartment for the teacher. Learn about the many home crafts. Watch molasses being made from sorghum cane at the old mill. Stop by the water-powered gristmill where grinding stones make flour, a staple in the Spanish diet. See the many varied uses for animal hides,

and marvel at what had to be done to make something as soft and supple as a leather jacket. Finally, visit the chapel, where homemade items remind us all how important faith was to early settlers trying to survive and make a living in this harsh, arid environment.

You don't need to imagine what life was like for these people. You can see it all around you at Las Golondrinas. Everyday people were remarkably inventive, self-sufficient and able to grow, recycle, find and trade whatever they needed.

Located 15 minutes south of downtown Santa Fe, NM. Take I-25 exit 276 to 334 Los Pinos Road. Open Wednesday-Sunday from June-September; tours by appointment April, May, October. Admission charged.

Historic St. Augustine

SEE MAP PAGE 15, LOCATION #8

St. Augustine, Florida
Phone: (904) 829-5681 (Chamber of Commerce)
http://www.oldcity.com

Although the explorer Juan Ponce de Leon claimed the east coast of Florida for Spain in 1513, establishment of a permanent settlement was delayed until 1565, when St. Augustine was founded. This was 42 years before the English landed at Jamestown, Virginia, and 55 years before the founding of Plymouth, Massachusetts. St. Augustine is the oldest continuously inhabited European settlement in America.

Remarkably, much of its early history has survived for us to enjoy today. In addition to the Castillo de

San Marcos and Colonial Spanish Quarter described on the following pages, we recommend exploring the surrounding historic district. The Government House museum at 48 King Street showcases St. Augustine's

UNRELENTING POWER PLAYS

Once the Spanish gained control of Florida, they spent much of the next 250 years trying to hold onto their territory and win over the Indians to strengthen their position. Meanwhile, British colonists established settlements to the North, and France started colonies in the Midwest. Wars broke out between them, and Spain was caught in the crossfire. In the 1760s, British forces captured Havana, Cuba, a port too valuable for Spain to lose; so Spain gave Florida to Britain in exchange for Havana. British control of Florida lasted until Spanish forces took advantage of the American Revolution to regain their former territory. Still, the Spanish hold over Florida was tenuous – America was now a threat. During the War of 1812 between America and Great Britain, Spain took sides, letting Britain use Pensacola as a naval base. That was a serious mistake. American troops stormed into Florida and seized Pensacola. They later lost Pensacola but then took control again. Finally, in 1821, Spain gave up and permanently relinquished Florida to America.

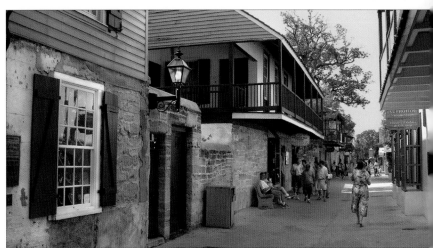

cultural, economic, architectural and archaeological history. The Herbarium, a colonial military hospital located at 3 Aviles Street, provides insight into the life of a patient in 1791 – including how drugs were "prescribed" by the apothecary, how records were kept in the Administrative Office, and how locally grown herbs were used to heal wounds. Just down the street, the Ximenez-Fatio House at 20 Aviles still has much of its colonial ambience and provides interesting insight into the life of a tourist in early St. Augustine. The González-Alvarez House at 14 St. Francis Street is the oldest dwelling, with much to show about its nearly 400 years in America. Nearby Old St. Augustine Village at 246 St. George Street provides a fine overview of village life as it evolved over the centuries, with buildings original to the site dating from 1790 to 1910.

Located just southwest of coastal fortification of Castillo de San Marcos in St. Augustine, FL. Open most days. Admission charged at individual sites.

▲ Narrow streets with overhanging balconies have retained their sixteenth-century charm in St. Augustine. Free of cars, they enable visitors to capture some of the spirit of the past.

◀ This opulent Murat House parlor in Old St. Augustine Village is authentically furnished in the Empire style of the early 1800s.

▼ One of the few early careers available to single women was the operation of a boarding house. Florida's first hotel, the Ximenez-Fatio House (circa 1798), is a fine example. Beginning in the 1820s, its female proprietor catered to visitors and new arrivals, accommodating up to 24 guests at a time.

Castillo de San Marcos National Monument

SEE MAP PAGE 15, LOCATION #8
St. Augustine, Florida
Phone: (904) 829-6506, ext. 234
http://www.nps.gov/casa

▲ In a hit-and-run attack, English pirates sacked St. Augustine in 1668. Then in 1670, the English settled in Charleston, showing a clear trend toward southern movement. Highly fortified Castillo de San Marcos was built in response. Spain was taking no chances in protecting its empire.

▶ English invaders underestimated the strength and artillery power of Castillo de San Marcos, and they were never able to take it by force. The Castillo was renamed Fort Marion when Spain finally relinquished Florida to the United States.

In the mid-1600s, the Spanish were shipping treasures from the Americas by way of Florida. They were not alone in their desire for wealth and power in the region. Pirates attacked mercilessly, and the English were a threat to the north. Castillo de San Marcos (circa 1672) was the tenth fort on this site. Unlike its predecessors, which were built of wood, this fort was constructed of coquina, a local shellrock. It was skirted on three sides by a moat, had massive diamond-shaped bastions at its four corners, and held 60 to 70 cannons on the gundeck. What's more, the rock walls were 14 feet thick at the base, nine feet thick at the top and 33 feet high. Formidable!

Understandably, although the Castillo was attacked a number of times, it was never taken by force. However, it did change hands through military agreements and political treaties. Among the flags which have flown here: the Spanish (1695-1763), the British (1763-1784), the Spanish again (1784-1821), the United States (1821-1861), the Confederate States of America (1861-March of 1862), and finally the United States again (1862-1900).

Castillo de San Marcos is a fascinating place to visit. There is no visitor center or guided tour, but museum exhibits provide a very good overview of the Castillo's illustrious history. Each exhibit focuses on a different theme or time period, such as construction of the fortress, military battles, the Castillo's powerful artillery and local Native Peoples. Some of the rooms have been furnished to represent Spanish barracks, British barracks and a storeroom.

Part of the "Cubo Line," a palisaded city wall, has been rebuilt, and a stairway leads to the gundeck, where impressive Spanish iron and bronze artillery are exhibited. Be sure to look at the view while there – the gundeck overlooks the Old City Gate, quaint streets and Matanzas Bay.

Adding to the visitor pleasures, special Living History events are scheduled throughout the year. Among the past offerings: Flight to Freedom (a black history event), Cannon School, Spanish Nightwatch, Change of Flags, Spanish Heritage Day, Musket School, Siege of 1702, and British Nightwatch. In addition, the cannons are fired on Fridays, Saturdays and Sundays.

Located at Castillo Drive and Avenida Menéndez along the bay in downtown St. Augustine, FL. Open daily except December 25. Admission charged.

SURPRISINGLY DURABLE

As you tour the fort, note the millions of tiny shells that comprise the coquina (coh-KEY-nah) used as building material. Bonded together with the passage of time, these shells formed a type of limestone which was quarried from Anastasia Island across the bay and ferried to the construction site. Mortar used between the blocks was made on-site by baking oyster shells in kilns until they fell apart into a fine white powder (lime), which was then mixed with sand and fresh water. Castillo de San Marcos had its first real test when British forces laid siege to St. Augustine in late 1702. More than 1,200 civilians and 300 soldiers crowded into the fort and remained safe for almost two months, until a relief fleet arrived from Havana. The British cannons had little effect upon the coquina walls, which easily absorbed the shock of many hits and suffered minimal damage. More than 300 years later, these walls remain standing, with the mortar intact.

Colonial Spanish Quarter

SEE MAP PAGE 15, LOCATION #8

St. Augustine, Florida
Phone: (904) 825-6830
http://www.historicstaugustine.com/csq/history.html

With its coastal location, St. Augustine was both strategically positioned and vulnerable. But despite repeated attacks by pirates and the English, determined soldiers managed to maintain their foothold. The Colonial Spanish Quarter – a restored and reconstructed village with costumed interpreters – recalls those early days as a remote outpost serving the Spanish Empire.

As you walk around, you are witness to the sights and sounds that once comprised everyday life in the 1740s. Village merchants and craftsmen go about their jobs – scribing, woodworking, blacksmithing, leatherworking, making buckets and repairing barrels. Soldiers and militiamen keep order. Farmers tend their

few livestock and raise poultry. Wives may work outside the home but also care for their garden, cook for their family, dip candles, make clothing and keep house. Ask them about the life of children in the mid-1700s. Many of the games and toys were similar to ours: leapfrog, marbles, hopscotch, kites, dolls, teeter-totter, jump rope, swings, blind man's bluff. Also ask them about the rights of Spanish women. What you hear may surprise you.

Located at 52 St. George Street in St. Augustine, FL. Take I-95 exit 95. Travel east on State Road 16 to US 1, then south to Castillo Drive and east to the Visitors Information Center and parking. Pass through the Old City Gate to the Spanish Quarter Village entrance. Open daily except December 25. Admission charged.

▲ Busy St. George Street is just beyond the garden wall. Centuries ago, one's home was also a business center. Residents made sure they had a comfortable porch for relaxing and visiting with customers.

◀ Few people could read or write in old St. Augustine. So the church scribe played a particularly important role. In his hands was the responsibility for not only church and legal documents but also personal letters. Typically, his payment was in goods and services, not money.

◀ Unlike the fireplace-style cooking hearths common in English settlements, Spanish Colonial kitchens had tabletop-high cooking areas (back of room). These produced less heat and allowed slow cooking.

MAKING ENDS MEET

Life in early St. Augustine was a challenge under the best of circumstances. A yearly government subsidy, the "situado," did provide a meager salary for the soldiers and their families. But it was not dependable: the payment from the Spanish-Mexican treasury often came late or not at all because of bad weather, pirates or even privateers. When the situado did not arrive, soldiers were often paid with food or goods, such as bolts of cloth, which could then be bartered for at least some necessities. In addition, husbands and wives traded homemade goods or offered to do odd jobs in exchange for whatever else was needed. The women performed various chores outside the home, including laundry and mending; many also ran shops and taverns. A number of the soldiers used skills such as woodworking to obtain more bartered goods. In addition, their house might serve as an outlet for selling merchandise, although the family did not own the goods. (The owner was someone of wealth who did not want to be known as a merchant.)

THE FRENCH

Fort de Chartres State Historic Site

SEE MAP PAGE 17, LOCATION #8

Prairie du Rocher, Illinois
Phone: (618) 284-7230
http://www.ftdechartres.com

▶ After two wooden stockades decayed beside the Mississippi River, the French rebuilt Fort de Chartres as a massive limestone fortress. But even this structure was not safe from the river's erosion. In 1772, the south wall and bastions collapsed into the Mississippi. After the fort was abandoned, settlers scavenged the stone and timber for their own structures. Today, much has been rebuilt.

France wanted a share of the riches Spain was gaining in the New World. So in 1562, explorers representing the king ventured to Florida, intending to create a commercial settlement. They sailed up the coast and built Charlesfort in South Carolina. All but 27 men then sailed back to France to resupply. However, their country was in the midst of a religious civil war; the expedition was stopped; and their American colony failed. In 1564, the French tried again, this time building Fort Caroline in Florida and broadening their goals to provide a refuge for Huguenots (French Protestants). Still, success eluded them. A series of bad choices led to major problems. Food became scarce, tempers flared and at least two mutinies occurred. One band of dissatisfied men seized a privateer's vessel, hoping

they could not compete against the Spanish

to profit by raiding Spanish ships in the West Indies. The end came when the Spanish founded St. Augustine and attacked the French colony.

In their third attempt at colonization, the French headed far north, to what is now Canada. They established Quebec in 1608 and soon spread out into other settlements in the region. There, a thriving fur trade made the difference. The French had wisely given European goods as gifts to the Indians – kettles, knives and other items that would make a difference in their lives. These gifts stimulated appetites for more goods and prompted the Indians to trade pelts with the French. Since European demand for fur was significant, the French-Canadian colonies benefited handsomely. Beaver was especially prized. Mink, marten, fox and otter also were in demand.

Nearly 100 years passed before the French made a major play for America. Focused on the center of the continent, they founded Biloxi, Mississippi, in 1699; Mobile, Alabama, in 1702; and New Orleans, Louisiana, in 1718. They amassed vast holdings along the St. Lawrence River, around the Great Lakes and in the Mississippi River Valley. Still, as so often happened, a series of wars erupted. The French lost their lands to the English and Spanish. They briefly regained some possessions from Spain during the Napoleonic Era. Then in 1803, they sold Louisiana Territory to America to prevent Great Britain from taking it. This one event, more than any other, set the stage for our nation's westward expansion.

▶ Although their focus was on fur trading, not the religious conversion of Native Peoples, French forts included a priest's quarters and a formal chapel, such as this one re-created at Fort de Chartres. Many French colonists were devout Catholics.

Following their success in Canada, the French hoped to gain a rich source of American furs and precious metals when they lay claim to Illinois Country in 1673. The region extended from Lake Michigan and Lake Superior to the Ohio and Missouri rivers, and it ultimately became part of the Louisiana Territory. Here in the 1700s, Fort de Chartres became important enough to be the last French possession surrendered to the English after the French and Indian War. Although time and the Mississippi River took their toll, the fort has been partially reconstructed. The north wall is complete with its bastions, musket ports, cannon embrasures and gatehouse. The guardhouse, storehouse and powder magazine are fully outfitted.

This is an ideal setting for the June Rendezvous, when costumed re-enactors in hundreds of encampments bring back to life an eighteenth-century fur trapper's gathering. You'll enjoy a wide variety of history-based activities – such as musket, cannon and archery competitions, military drills, music, dancing, Native craftwork, cooking, and old-style goods for sale. It is one of the largest such events in our nation!

Located 4 miles west of Prairie du Rocher, IL, on SR 155, south of East St. Louis, IL. Open Wednesday-Sunday except major holidays. Donations appreciated.

Old Fort Niagara

SEE MAP PAGE 11, LOCATION #9
Youngstown, New York
Phone: (716) 745-7611
https://oldfortniagara.org

The point of land jutting into Lake Ontario at the mouth of the Niagara River was strategically important. Controlling it meant controlling access to the Great Lakes and the westward route to the heartland of the continent. The French saw its significance and claimed the site by building Fort Conti in 1679 and Fort Denonville in 1687. Embroiled in conflict from the beginning, neither fort survived. Then came Fort Niagara in 1726. Although it was a strong, permanent foothold, later nicknamed "the French Castle," it fell into English hands during the French and Indian War.

The English held onto Fort Niagara throughout the American Revolution, yielded it to our new nation in 1796, recaptured it during the War of 1812 and ceded it again to America in 1815. With the completion of the Erie Canal in 1825, the strategic value of Fort Niagara diminished. However, it remained active as a training station and military barracks during both World Wars. The last army units were withdrawn in 1963.

Fort Niagara is an exceptional visitor attraction. Most of the buildings are original and were erected between 1726 and 1872. Although the first gate is a reconstruction, look at the system of stones, wheels and pulleys for the drawbridge. Inside the fort walls, 16 points of interest await you. Among them are the massive land defenses (1755-1872), Dauphin Battery and main gate (1756), Powder Magazine (1757), Provisions Storehouse (1762), Bakehouse (1762), South Redoubt (1770) and North Redoubt (1771). Most extraordinary is the French Castle (1726), which was built to resemble a large trading house – its purpose was to attract Indian business while also defending the region. Explore at your leisure. There's much to see and much Living History to enjoy.

The orientation film and museum displays are very good. Drills and ceremonies are presented daily, July-Labor Day. Special events are held March-September.

Located near Youngstown, NY. From Niagara Falls, travel north for 18 miles on Robert Moses Parkway. Open daily except some major holidays. Admission charged.

⬆ A massive French Castle is the fascinating centerpiece of Old Fort Niagara. It is fully outfitted as it might have been during the French occupation, with the guard room, chapel, powder room, trading room, large meeting room, commandant's dining room, commandant's bed chamber, and other quarters. The smaller building to the left is the Bakehouse.

◀ Although the post was remote and often cool and damp, the French commandant lived comfortably within the Castle in plush if not spacious quarters. His bed chamber doubled as an office, and his dining room was shared with officers, but he could worship privately in the chapel next door.

FRENCH INGENUITY

Originally the "Castle" was the only structure at Fort Niagara. Designed to look imposing but not intimidating, it was actually a citadel capable of resisting Indian attack. Within its stone walls was everything needed for a garrison of about 60 officers and men – even a deep well. There were storerooms, meeting rooms, the powder magazine and a guardhouse. Living quarters for both officers and soldiers were on the second floor, across the vestibule from a chapel. On the attic level, overhanging dormers provided defensive positions for muskets and light cannon. (Years later, during the War of 1812, the wooden roof was replaced by earthen ramparts, and cannon were positioned on the attic floor.) One of the most important features of the Castle was its ground floor Trade Room, where Indians came to exchange furs for manufactured goods. All of this is visible today, expertly restored to its 1727 appearance. It is so well outfitted that you will feel as though you have entered a working fort in the eighteenth-century.

Historic Natchitoches

SEE MAP PAGE 17, LOCATION #6
Natchitoches and vicinity (south), Louisiana
Phone: (318) 352-8072 or toll-free (800) 259-1714 (Convention & Visitors Bureau)
http://historicnatchitoches.com

▲ Facing a lake that was once a river, downtown Natchitoches retains its French Colonial ambience with iron filigree, carriage lights and brick streets.

▶ Melrose Plantation has a great story to tell. Here you can enjoy a unique glimpse into eighteenth-century plantation life and also see an outstanding collection of paintings and murals by Louisiana's most celebrated primitive artist, Clementine Hunter.

Established in 1714, Natchitoches (NAK-uh-tish) is one of the oldest permanent European settlements in the 13-state territory that comprised the Louisiana Purchase. This French community had two purposes: to promote trade with both the local Indians and Mexico, and to deter Spanish advances into Louisiana. It flourished until about 1825, when the military removed a long-established log jam in the Red River, unwittingly causing the river channel to retreat five miles east and turning the Cane River tributary into a long lake.

Downtown Historic District

Fronting Cane River Lake, this 33-block section of Natchitoches includes more than 50 centuries-old buildings. It is a charming mixture of Queen Anne and Victorian architecture, Creole-style cottages and beautifully landscaped gardens. Many of the mercantile buildings and houses have cast iron grillwork reminiscent of the old river port. The townhouses once served as second homes for the down-river planters. Major annual events are held in the district.

Cane River National Heritage Area

Beginning just south of Natchitoches, this largely rural area is known for its unique blend of French, Spanish, African, Native American and Creole cultures. While much is privately owned, several sites are open to the public. Fort St. Jean Baptiste State Historic Site is a full-scale replica of a 1732 French fort, with its trading warehouse, powder magazine, church, slave quarters, commandant's house, barracks, guardhouse, bastions and assorted huts. The American-built Fort Jesup has its original kitchen, furnished as it would have been in the 1840s, and a reconstructed officers' quarters. Melrose Plantation, built by the son of a French merchant and his ex-slave wife, provides a unique glimpse into a creative world that became a haven for artists and writers. The sizable Cane River Creole National Historical Park, which consists of Oakland Plantation and the outbuildings of Magnolia Plantation, captures the grace and elegance of French Creole society as well as the daily life of a Louisiana cotton plantation.

Located northeast of Alexandria, LA, just off I-49 exit 138. Open most days. Admission charged at individual sites.

THE CREOLE PEOPLE

Originally, "creole" simply meant "born in the colony" from 1714-1803, before the Louisiana Purchase. In the early 1700s, white Creoles were thought to be socially inferior to European immigrants, whereas black Creole slaves were generally regarded as more valuable than imported African slaves. Later, both white Creoles and free black Creoles became leaders in the social aristocracy of Louisiana. The most ambitious had beautiful homes, productive plantations and an active social life. Today, Creole Americans are typically the mixed-blood descendants of Native and colonial peoples, including French, Spanish and Africans. They have become world-famous for their lively Zydeco music and "special" cuisine – such as Trout Meunière, Oysters Rockefeller and praline candy.

Village of Sainte Genevieve

SEE MAP PAGE 19, LOCATION #14

Ste. Genevieve, Missouri
Phone: (573) 883-3686
http://www.ste-genevieve.com

If you were traveling through the Mississippi River Valley back in the 1700s, you most likely would have stopped in Ste. Genevieve for food, supplies and overnight accommodations. The village, established around 1735, once rivaled St. Louis in size and importance.

The Ste. Genevieve of today is a quiet, charming town. It is also a place where you can recapture some of America's French connection. This community has the largest concentration of original French Colonial buildings in all of North America. When we visited, we delighted in its uniqueness, even with the downtown's necessary transition into visitor-oriented services and shops. Consider spending a day or two exploring and absorbing. Also take day trips to French Colonial attractions in nearby Illinois – including Fort de Chartres (see page 68), the Courthouse in Cohokia, Pierre Menard House in Ellis Grove and Fort Kashaskia.

We suggest that you begin your visit at the Great River Road Interpretive Center and Tourist Information Office, 66 South Main Street, where you can obtain information about the self-guided walking tour. Several of the historic houses in Ste. Genevieve are open to the public. Just a few doors down Main Street are the Bolduc House (c. 1785) and Bolduc-LeMeilleur House

(c. 1820). At Fourth and Merchant Streets is La Maison de Guibourd-Vallé (c. 1806), and on the corner of Second and Merchant Streets is the Felix Vallé House State Historic Site, restored and furnished to the 1830s.

Located an hour south of St. Louis, MO. Take I-55 exit 154 east; right on US 61; left on Market Street to Main Street. Seasons vary. Admission charged at individual sites.

▲ The Bolduc House (left) and the Bolduc-LeMeilleur House (right) are representative of the unique French American architecture in Sainte Genevieve. They also show the dramatic lifestyle changes that occurred here within a single generation.

◄ The Bequette-Ribault House on St. Mary Road is a good example of French Creole construction, with vertical posts set in the ground and no foundation.

◄ The Felix Vallé House was both a home and a business. Here natural riches of the Missouri territory, such as furs and lead ore, were traded for manufactured goods.

LOUISIANA PURCHASE

Textbooks tell us how President Jefferson doubled the size of America in 1803 by purchasing the Louisiana Territory from France for $15 million. In fact, France did not own the territory; it was merely selling its claim to the land. Not that this was unusual – before the twentieth century most land sales, including those among whites, covered primarily the right to use and develop property. Undeveloped private land was considered public and often accessible to everyone. In the Louisiana Territory, however, far more Indians than French were using the land; so technically they had a greater claim to it and a prior right to engage in any sale. Yet, no one consulted the Indians about the Louisiana Purchase, and most of them did not know about it until years later. Naturally, when the American presence began to be felt, the Indians asserted their rights, and as a result, more than 50 Indian wars were fought. Our nation ended up paying not only France but also Native American tribes for the land throughout most of the 1800s.

Historic New Orleans

SEE MAP PAGE 17, LOCATION #7
New Orleans, Louisiana
Phone: toll-free (800) 672-6124 (Convention & Visitors Bureau)
http://www.neworleanscvb.com

▲ As if standing guard over the French Quarter, St. Louis Cathedral is tall and majestic. Inside, painted and gilded columns divide the church into nave and side aisles, first floor and balcony. The ceiling is an ornate collection of paintings that are more decorative than devotional. Stained glass windows and a mural above the altar depict St. Louis, King of France (1226-1270), at various stages of his life and sainthood.

▶ Though it may seem cliché, taking a carriage ride in the French Quarter can be great fun. The drivers have lots to tell you, and the mules are remarkably patient. But keep in mind that the elaborate buildings are actually more Spanish than French. This is because Spain ruled Louisiana in the late 1700s, when much of the city was rebuilt after devastating fires.

The French Quarter remains New Orleans' most popular destination – a jewel despite suffering many severe disasters during its lifetime. While this sizable area is best known for fine dining, nightlife and Mardi Gras fun, it also has several terrific historic attractions.

For starters, visit St. Louis Cathedral. This remarkable church was constructed during Spanish and American rule but has managed to retain its French heritage. The original structure was completed in 1794, replacing a 1727 French Catholic church that was destroyed in a great fire which swept through New Orleans. It was substantially remodeled several times, most notably in 1851 when the triple steeples and Greek Revival portico were added. Despite its elegance, St. Louis Cathedral is the people's church, as its location so aptly proves. The Cathedral faces Jackson Square, a world-famous (and formerly infamous) attraction in the heart of the French Quarter. In the early days, Jackson Square was the place where captains of pirate ships sold their cargoes to local merchants, where narcotics dealers met their buyers, where sinister plots were conceived, where criminals were publicly hanged, and where ladies of the night met their customers. Today, it is a pleasant place to stroll, picnic or just sit on a bench, people-watching.

Within an easy walk are a number of other historic attractions. At 514 Chartres Street is the New Orleans Pharmacy Museum, which was built in 1823 by the nation's first licensed pharmacist; it has a top-quality collection of apothecary items and medical equipment. At 820 St. Louis Street is the Hermann-Grima House, a restored 1831 Georgian-style mansion. At 1112 Chartres Street is the 1750s Old Ursuline Convent, where Catholic nuns cared for the indigent and taught school. These and many other sites attest to the wonderful, enduring history that makes New Orleans such a delight to visit.

Located within a 90-block area extending from the Mississippi River in New Orleans, LA. Most attractions are between Decatur and Bourbon Streets, Canal and Dumaine Streets. Admission charged at some sites.

REMARKABLE URSULINE NUNS

When Louisiana was just a fledgling colony, its governor requested that Ursuline Sisters come from France to nurse and educate its people. Under the auspices of King Louis XV, 12 courageous nuns took the strenuous five-month trip by sea and arrived in mid-1727. During the ensuing years, they established the first Catholic charitable institutions in America – an orphanage, girls' school and hospital. You can tour their lovely second convent, which survives to this day at 1112 Chartres Street, and learn about their remarkable history. Built in the early 1750s by royal troops of the New Orleans garrison, the Old Ursuline Convent is the oldest building in the French Quarter and the Mississippi Valley. The nuns occupied it until 1824, after which bishops and archbishops took up residence. Just inside the entrance is the clock that the nuns brought with them in 1727. Nearby is America's oldest self-supporting staircase, dating back to the first convent built on this site in 1734.

Vermilionville

SEE MAP PAGE 17, LOCATION #5
Lafayette, Louisiana
Phone: (337) 233-4077 or toll-free (866) 99BAYOU
http://www.vermilionville.org

In 1755, during the French and Indian War, French-speaking Acadians were expelled from what is now Nova Scotia, Canada, for refusing to pledge allegiance to the British Crown and Anglican Church. They wandered for years, unable to find a permanent home until the King of Spain invited them to South Louisiana. These Acadians – or Cajuns as they came to be known – settled along the bayous and across the prairies, farming land granted to them by the French and Spanish. One of the bayous was Bayou Vermilion, and one of their towns was Vermilionville, the site of present-day Lafayette. Settling with them

CAJUN CULTURE

The 700,000 Acadians who currently live in southern Louisiana are descendants of some of the first white people to settle in North America. Their ancestors came from Brittany, Poitou, Normandy and elsewhere across France to what is now Nova Scotia, Canada, in 1604 – three years before the English founded their first successful colony in Jamestown, Virginia. A century and a half later, when they were forced by the British to leave their Canadian homes during the French and Indian War, these Acadians moved far south, blending their culture with others they came to know along the way – Spanish, Germans, Native Americans, Blacks. Their spicy cuisine, lively music and energetic dancing harken back to a variety of old traditions. Still, the French influence remains strong. While many young Cajuns don't speak French, their grandparents probably do. There are a few Cajun Protestants, but most spring from Catholic roots. And even those who live in big cities tend to have some traditional French values and rural ways.

were Creoles, who were the descendants of African, West Indian and European pioneers. Together, these Cajuns and Creoles established one of the most culturally rich regions of America.

The Vermilionville heritage and folklife park faithfully portrays this segment of American culture, which never quite merged into our nation's great "melting pot." With its eighteenth-century French Bayou atmosphere, costumed interpreters and 23 park-like acres, it is a unique and enjoyable place to visit. Self-guided tours include six of the original homes and 13 reconstructed buildings containing period furnishings and artifacts. Among the interesting features are Anglo-American gable roofs adapted by Acadians to provide a large attic space. (Many have hand-cut shingles that extend well beyond the peak to add weather protection.) The largest and oldest surviving structure is the Amand Broussard House (c. 1790). Constructed of traditional colombage and bousillage, it has hand-wrought rams-horn hinges, French chandeliers and a hand-powered dining room fan. Vermilionville also includes a performance center where you can enjoy Cajun and Zydeco music, a "cooking school" where you can learn about Cajun-Creole foods, a Petite Bayou with ferry crossing, and special programs throughout the year.

Located in Lafayette, LA. Take I-10 exit 103A onto SR 167 (Evangeline Highway); drive south about 5 miles; exit at Surrey Street, heading east toward the airport, to 300 Fisher Road. Open Tuesday-Sunday except major holidays. Admission charged.

▲ Vermilionville provides a pleasant walking environment for exploring the homes, eating the food and hearing the music of early Cajuns.

◀ Le Magasin is a fine replica of an Acadian storehouse or barn. Here an interpreter dressed in period clothing has a wealth of stories to share about boat building, net and trap making, and decoy carving – all critical survival skills for people living near the bayous.

THE ENGLISH

While Spanish and French settlements were formed primarily to protect the commercial and territorial interests of their European monarchs, English colonies were designed to be "transplantations" of English society. (Hence, the term "plantation" later used to describe these settlements.) Many were religious communities; others were business ventures. Initially, all were more responsible to their church leaders, stockholders or private sponsors than to the English government, which took little interest in them during the early years. As a result, they were accustomed to feeling relatively free to make choices that were best for their group. Sometimes, without realizing it, they even began to develop political and social institutions that were quite different from those in England. The New World forced them to adjust constantly to ever-changing situations. Out of these adjustments came the beginnings of a distinctively American culture.

When they first arrived, the English settlers must have seemed extraordinarily naive and helpless to the local Indians. They believed in English superiority and in their "God given" mission to create a New World; yet many of them had much to learn about caring for themselves here. They tended to be strong-willed, self-centered and demanding, apparently determined to take rather than share the resources at hand. They viewed the land as a wilderness and did not see that it supported a highly successful Native economy. They witnessed the seasonal movements of Indians and did not recognize that these were meticulously planned to take advantage of regional bounty. They believed in God but did not feel that the spirit of nature could also be a divine source of inspiration. Even on a personal level, they had problems: the settlers were generally dirty and smelly. They thought baths were dangerous, whereas Native Peoples believed that frequent bathing was vital to purifying body and soul. Whether basic in nature or broader in scope, the differences were unresolvable.

Nevertheless, the English persevered. By the 1730s, the Original Thirteen Colonies were thriving, and by the start of the Revolutionary War in 1775, their combined populations totaled 2 1/2 million. (Note: England was growing overseas too. Having united with Scotland and Wales early in the century, it was now Great Britain.)

European Territorial Claims in the Early 1700s

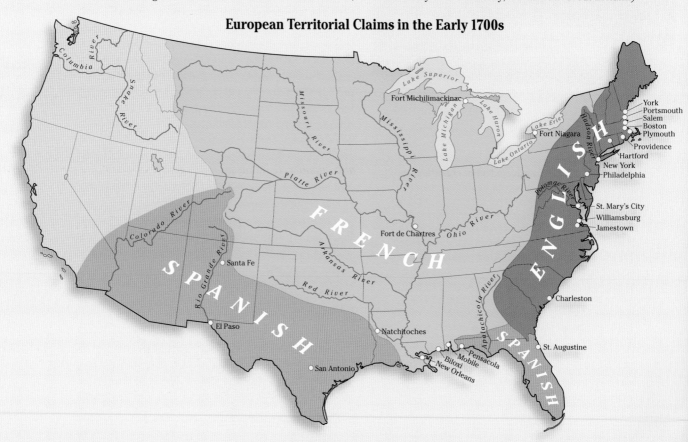

Historic Jamestowne *(the original site)*

SEE MAP PAGE 15, LOCATION #11B
Williamsburg vicinity (south), Virginia
Phone: (757) 229-1733 or (757) 898-2410
http://www.historicjamestowne.org
http://www.nps.gov/archive/colo/Jamestwn/jamestown.htm

The founding of England's first permanent settlement in North America began as a story of intense struggle and the constant threat of failure. The "promised land" settled in 1607 proved to be swampy much of the year and a breeding ground for disease. Highly stressed, the colonists fought among themselves and soon managed to anger local Indians who had tried to befriend them. What's more, the worst drought in 770 years destroyed their crops. Although hundreds came from across the Atlantic, only 60 had survived here by the spring of 1610. Such was the "birthplace of America."

How could Jamestown have survived? Remarkably, it did; ultimately, it even prospered. For over 90 years,

Jamestown served as the English colonial capital. But in 1698, its statehouse burned. After that, the capital was moved to nearby Middle Plantation, soon to be known as Williamsburg.

This is a fascinating place to visit. Significant parts of the original fort — including wells, interior buildings, a warehouse and several pits — have been identified. Archaeologists are still working at the site, and hundreds of the more

than 2 million artifacts discovered to date are displayed at the new Visitor Center and at the Archaearium exhibition center. Near the park entrance are the remains of a 1608 furnace used in a failed attempt to make glass. Close by is Jamestown Glasshouse, where master craftsmen today produce glass objects using seventeenth-century techniques. At the fort site itself, the church's brick tower is still standing, now part of the Jamestown Memorial Church. Portions of the palisade have been re-constructed where the original posts stood 400 years ago. And, of course, talks by costumed interpreters and park rangers heighten the experience.

Located in the Colonial National Historical Park in VA, at the southwest end of the Colonial Parkway, reached via I-64 and SR 199. Open daily except December 25 and January 1. Admission charged. Individual and combination tickets available for various Jamestown, Yorktown and Williamsburg attractions.

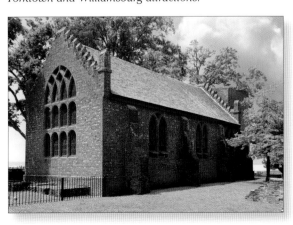

▲ After many years of searching, archaeologists finally identified the location of James Fort and its protective palisade. Portions are now under water in the James River. You might think today's reconstructed wall and archaeological digs are small, but that was the reality 400 years ago!

◄ Blown glass items were useful to the local colonists. More importantly, they were a commodity that workers hoped could be traded for goods from Mother England.

◄ Inside this 1907 church are the brick and cobblestone foundations of the 1617 and 1639 Jamestown churches. At one end is the only surviving seventeenth-century structure at Jamestown and one of the oldest English-built edifices in America – a 1680s brick tower that was built as an addition to the previous church.

TWIST OF FATE

Jamestown needed to make a profit in order to survive. Without the gold and jewels settlers had hoped to find in the New World, they explored other opportunities: harvesting natural resources, such as fish, lumber and furs, and developing industries, such as glass blowing. For years, however, commercial success eluded them. Ironically one of today's banes, tobacco, saved the colony from economic disaster. Introduced as a cash crop by Captain John Rolfe, the settler who married Chief Powhatan's daughter Pocahontas, it flourished in American soil. By the late 1600s, Jamestown was exporting over 20 million pounds of tobacco per year, and by the mid-1700s, the expanding Virginia Colony had become the wealthiest of England's thirteen colonies. Sadly, with this success came slave labor from Africa and the race-based system which became one of the most fateful aspects of pre-Civil War America. In 1763, about half the population of Virginia Colony – 170,000 people – were African slaves.

Jamestown Settlement

SEE MAP PAGE 15, LOCATION #11B
Williamsburg vicinity (south), Virginia
Phone: (757) 253-4838 or toll-free (888) 593-4682
http://www.historyisfun.org

⚠ When Jamestown became an established settlement in the early 1600s, the colonists created an environment that reminded them of their native England.

▶ A matchlock musket was the primary firearm used by colonists. It held a slow-burning cord "match," which touched off a flash that ignited the powder in the barrel, firing the bullet. Soldiers wore a string of pre-filled vials of gunpowder to avoid handling too much explosive near the match. But they could not so easily solve other problems: the match would not stay lit in heavy rain, and it glowed in the dark, giving away the musketeer's position.

Initially, Jamestown was a private commercial venture, sponsored by the Virginia Company. Its stockholders hoped to profit from the natural resources of the New World, but they also supported English goals – counterbalancing Spanish colonization, spreading Christianity among the Native Peoples, and finding a northwest passage to the Orient. Extreme hardships and Indian battles took their toll though, and in 1624, control of Virginia passed to the crown of England. Interestingly, as a royal colony Jamestown finally was able to enter a period of relative peace and prosperity. In succeeding years, it even became a land of opportunity for the English poor who signed on as indentured servants, bound by contracts to work for several years in return for their passage to America. When their contracts expired, many were able to purchase land at a low cost and begin working their own farms.

The Jamestown Settlement of today is a Living History museum, built to commemorate these important early years. For young and old, it offers much to enjoy. Begin your visit in the expansive indoor museum complex, where a film presents an overview of Jamestown's origins in England and its first 20 years as a colony. Exhibit galleries combine artifacts from the period with graphics and reproductions to expand on the Jamestown story.

After this orientation, step outside to explore four representative Living History sites populated by interpreters in period clothing. Seventeenth-century activities and special events bring Jamestown back to life.

Powhatan Indian Village

Exploring the Powhatan way of life, this area includes Native dwellings, a garden and ceremonial dance circle. See *America's Native Peoples*, page 50, for details

James Fort

Immediately upon arriving in the New World, the Jamestown colonists focused on ways to avoid the mistakes made at ill-fated Roanoke Island (England's first two attempts at colonization). The site they chose for settlement was low and swampy but highly defensible from both land and sea. They divided into three groups: one to build a fort, another to clear the land for crops and then plant the  seeds they had brought, and a third to explore the river upstream for a possible passage west to the Orient. (Clearly, they didn't realize that the coveted Orient was well beyond reach.) The hope was that Jamestown would become a "factory-fort"

INTERNAL STRIFE

While there are many reasons to admire the Jamestown settlers, remember that these were head-strong, independent people and very difficult to govern. By 1676, long-standing tensions between the colony's elite and its small farmers escalated to the breaking point. Economic problems had emerged, sparked by declining tobacco prices, devastatingly bad weather and rising costs for English goods. Apparently to vent their frustrations, some colonists began battling with the Virginia Indians. Governor William Berkeley's attempts to bring the situation under control only worsened matters and created a power struggle between him and Nathaniel Bacon, a prosperous planter. When Governor Berkeley refused to support raids on the Indians, Bacon's armed insurrection plunged the colony into turmoil, and Jamestown was burned. In the end, "Bacon's Rebellion" collapsed when its leader died of the "bloody flux" (probably dysentery) and 23 other rebellious leaders were hanged.

(trading post), able to effectively protect itself and be self-sustaining. It was a very humble beginning.

James Fort played an important role until the mid-1620s, when the colony expanded into a "New Town" to the east. While the fort fell to ruin, it was not lost forever. Here at Jamestown Settlement, you can visit an extraordinary representation based on eye witness accounts, a sketch from the period, educated guesswork and information emerging from remains of the original fort being unearthed just a mile away at Historic James-towne. Inside the wooden palisade are thatch-roofed, wattle-and-daub structures approximating the colony's church, storehouse, homes and armory. Jamestown interpreters in period clothing are busy working around the fort, engaged in the daily activities typical of the early 1600s, including gardening, cooking, carpentry, blacksmithing and military matters such as musket practice.

Susan Constant, Godspeed & Discovery

Three merchant ships loaded with passengers and cargo had embarked on the voyage from England to Virginia on December 20, 1606. Destined to set the course of American history were many gentlemen, a blacksmith, four carpenters, two bricklayers, a barber, a minister and some general laborers. They endured 4 1/2 grueling months at sea, wracked by storms and illness. And yet, of the 144 people on board – all men and boys – only one died during the voyage.

Roughly a month after Jamestown was founded, the *Susan Constant* and *Godspeed* returned to England with 39 crew members, leaving 104 courageous settlers to build a viable colony in an alien land. The smaller ship, *Discovery*, stayed behind and was used

Photo Courtesy of Jamestown Settlement

by Captain John Smith to trade goods with Indian villages along the Chesapeake Bay and Tidewater rivers. It also was used to chart the Cape Cod area of Massachusetts and to obtain fish from northern waters for the Virginia colony.

Today, you can board full-scale replicas of these three English vessels and talk with costumed interpreters about the spirit of adventure that motivated the early colonists. The barque-rigged *Susan Constant* is especially beautiful. Re-created at Jamestown Settlement, she was commissioned in 1991 and now periodically plies the waters of Virginia and Chesapeake Bay as a goodwill ambassador vessel.

Riverfront Discovery Area

At discovery stations along a winding pathway, historical interpreters provide a wealth of information about colonial life in America. They highlight the role of waterways in seventeenth-century travel, commerce and cultural exchange from the perspective of Powhatan Indian, European and African traditions.

Located at the Colonial Parkway and SR 31 in James City County, VA, near Historic Jamestowne. (See page 75.) Open daily except December 25 and January 1. Admission charged. Tickets available for Jamestown Settlement alone or in combination with Yorktown Victory Center. (See Road to Independence, page 155.)

▲ Climb aboard these vessels. Learn about the long, treacherous voyage from England. And see demonstrations of seventeenth-century piloting and navigation.

◄ Authentic building construction of wattle and daub (interwoven sticks covered with mud) requires almost constant maintenance. Yet it is true to the period and adds much to the visitor experience at Jamestown Settlement.

Plimoth Plantation

SEE MAP PAGE 11, LOCATION #4A

Plymouth, Massachusetts
Phone: (508) 746-1622
http://www.plimoth.org

▲ Although only about 50 colonists survived the first winter of 1620-1621, friends and family joined them in the ensuing years. By 1627, the colony had grown to approximately 160 people, including about 30 families and 20 single men. In addition, the community hosted a group of shipwrecked English and Irish people, who left for Virginia in late summer.

▶ You are welcomed into replica homes of this English village. Take time to chat with the "inhabitants." They achieve a remarkable authenticity – from their hearth cooking and other daily chores, to their clothing and mannerisms. Even their way of speaking belongs to another time. You have entered 1627.

1627 Pilgrim Village

A visit to this historically authentic English settlement feels very much like a trip to a foreign country, not just an exploration into the past. All of the interpreters talk with a strange accent; and although they speak English, many of their phrases are like nothing we hear today. What's more, no one will discuss their lives from a modern perspective – it is always 1627 in "New Plymouth," just seven years after  the arrival of the *Mayflower*. You have entered an incomparable world of Living History, where first person and interpretive artisan programs represent a lifetime you might have only imagined.

Here, you will meet the "original" Plymouth inhabitants, visit their homes, see their gardens and learn about the social and cultural life of their remarkable settlement. The activities, all appropriate to the changing seasons, are carried out in the seventeenth-century manner by museum re-enactors dressed in period fashions. On any given day, you may meet Elizabeth Tilley, who arrived as a child and lost her parents the first winter; her husband John Howland, who came as an indentured servant but was freed of his debt when his masters died; Governor William Bradford, whose first wife drowned before the colonists landed; military commander Miles Standish, whose first wife died the winter of 1620-1621; Samuel Fuller, surgeon to the colony, who arrived in 1620 and was joined by his wife in 1623; and many others. Their households contain reproductions of the furniture, tools and cooking equipment listed in the old village inventories. Even the farm animals come from heritage seventeenth-century stock.

Take a moment to go into the Fort that dominates the hillside on which the village is located. It provides a terrific view from the upper gundeck overlooking the village farms, gardens, cow houses, hay houses, outdoor ovens and double row of thatched and clapboarded homes. Also visit the Crafts Center, where you can watch modern-day artisans fashion the period furnishings and clothing used in the village; and stop by the Nye Barn to learn about the museum's rare and heritage-breed livestock.

THE "FIRST THANKSGIVING"

Our modern American harvest celebration dates back to 1863 when Abraham Lincoln declared a national holiday to stir up patriotism during the Civil War. Not mentioned were the people who later became popularly known as "Pilgrims." Writings from Plymouth (*Mourts Relation,* 1622) referenced their harvest celebration, but this event had been all but forgotten. Here is what happened: Chief Massasoit of the Wampanoag tribe and more than 90 of his warriors were honored guests at the colony's autumn harvest celebration in 1621. They brought five deer and other local bounty, and the generous feast lasted for days. In the early 1900s, information about this event re-emerged at a time when America was worried about rising foreign immigration and the difficulties of integrating new arrivals into the mainstream. The Thanksgiving image of dissimilar ethnic groups coming together in celebration was irresistible. By 1920, with the 300th anniversary of Plymouth Colony, the Pilgrims became fixed in the American psyche as our "spiritual ancestors" and icons of our autumn holiday.

Mayflower II

SEE MAP PAGE 11, LOCATION #4A
Plymouth, Massachusetts
Phone: (508) 746-1622
http://www.plimoth.org/visit/what/mayflower2.asp

Wampanoag Homesite

Soon after Plymouth was settled, an important Wampanoag (wahm-puh-NOH-ahg) Indian came as an ambassador of Chief Massasoit and stayed to serve as the colony's interpreter, guide and advisor on Native affairs. His name was Hobbamock, and he and his family lived adjacent to the colonists from 1621 until his death around 1641. The re-created homesite at Plimoth Plantation includes buildings, a garden area,

outdoor cooking arbor and artifacts which a man of Hobbamock's stature might have possessed. Despite close interactions with the English, his Wampanoag lifestyle and culture remained very different from that of the colonists. Reinforcing this difference, interpreters at the homesite share a modern viewpoint with you through conversation, craft activities and storytelling. Native American staff wear the deerskin and trade cloth garments of their ancestors.

Enter the two fully furnished houses (wetuash). The insides are lined with fine bulrush mats to provide both decoration and insulation. Along the walls are convenient built-in sleeping platforms covered with animal hides. You will also see many Native objects used by the Wampanoag as well as a few European trade goods, such as iron pots and tools. Outside, the interpreters are working – making a dugout canoe or constructing a house; crafting pottery or creating finger-woven storage bags; processing fish or cooking a meal over an open fire; and planting or cultivating corn, beans and squash in a traditional garden.

Located 3 miles south of Plymouth, MA. Take SR 3A. Or take SR 3 south, exit 4 (Plimoth Plantation Highway). Open daily April-November. Admission charged.

In the nearby harbor is a full-scale replica of the ship which carried approximately 100 colonists to America in 1620. On board are role-playing "passengers" and a modern-day crew, all of whom have much to share.

The three-masted, 106-foot *Mayflower II* was built in England with historically accurate materials and sailed to America in 1957. Moored alongside is the 33-foot *Mayflower Shallop*, a reproduction of the workboat that was transported in pieces on the original *Mayflower* and assembled on the beach at Cape Cod Harbor. In addition, you will see a 21-foot ship's boat, or longboat, typically carried on a ship of the *Mayflower's* size back in 1620.

Step aboard. On the Main Deck, the "helmsman" talks about seventeenth-century navigation. Under orders from the conning officer on the Half Deck above, he would have controlled the Whipstaff, a long lever used to move the tiller and then the rudder to steer the ship. Nearby are the Mate's Cabin, where the ship's progress was plotted, and the Great Cabin, which housed the commander. Be sure to talk with the "colonists," who typically are below deck. They "lived" on board for seven to nine months (depending on when they joined the voyage and debarked for shelter on land). Like other ships of the time, the *Mayflower* was a merchant vessel, not meant to carry passengers; so the colonists had "cabins" in a windowless space along the hull. They shared this deck with family pets, goats and poultry. Stowed further below were their building and farming tools, cooking equipment, furniture, muskets and provisions to survive and build a colony.

Located 3 miles north of Plimoth Plantation's Eel River site near Plymouth Rock. Open daily April-November. Tickets available for Mayflower II alone or in combination with a visit to Plimoth Plantation.

▲ On the *Mayflower II*, you will meet modern-day staff and crew as well as role-playing actors who will tell you about the original sailing ship, early navigation techniques and the amazing trip across the sea.

◄ Chief Massasoit, a nearby Wampanoag leader, had a treaty of mutual alliance with the English colonists. To help ensure good relations, he sent an ambassador to live among the colonists.

Colonial Williamsburg Historic Area

SEE MAP PAGE 15, LOCATION #10B
Williamsburg, Virginia
Phone: (804) 229-1000
http://www.colonialwilliamsburg.com

▲ From 1699 to 1780, Williamsburg was the political, cultural and educational center of Virginia – the largest and most influential English colony in America.

▶ Dozens of historic buildings and sites are open to visitors in Colonial Williamsburg. With the addition of authentic period furnishings, costumed interpreters and role-players, their lively pasts gain meaning.

In the late seventeenth century, when Virginia needed a new capital, planners looked to Middle Plantation. This spot, located five miles from Jamestown, had been settled in 1633 as a defensive outpost against the Indians. It was an inviting environment and the ideal "blank slate" for building a city that would become one of the wealthiest and most populous in Colonial America. In 1699, it became the official capital of Virginia Colony and was renamed Williamsburg in honor of King William III. The city was organized according to traditional English concepts and designed to function as the center of education, religion and government. While it never had more than 2,000 permanent residents at one time, Williamsburg swelled when the courts met and the lawyers, witnesses, plaintiffs and defendants came to town. Taverns provided fine dining, dancing and games of chance. Retail shops offered finely handcrafted local products as well as fashionable imports from Britain. Gentlemen came from the surrounding plantations to conduct business and enjoy good times with their wives. Many important people were educated at the College of William and Mary.

Today, you can experience much of what made this city great. Colonial Williamsburg has more than 500 restored and reconstructed buildings and a staff of 3,500 archaeologists, researchers, historians and historical interpreters. Every day, craftspeople are hard at work. Among them: the silversmith, blacksmith, harness and saddlemaker, gunsmith, cabinet maker, shoemaker, wigmaker and printer.

Watch. Learn. Ask questions. Citizens go about their lives in the personas of former residents – visit their homes and see how they lived. Famous men walk the streets – perhaps you'll meet Thomas Jefferson, who studied law here, or another patriot leader, such as George Washington or Patrick Henry. Stop at the courthouse – you might be the defendant, a witness or a justice in a staged trial. Learn about the African American culture, and hear the slave stories from re-enactors. See the Capitol building, where fundamental liberties were debated and a new

OUR ENGLISH HERITAGE

While many nationalities took interest in North America, the English had the most far-reaching impact. Our American spirit of independence showed itself for the first time when the English colonized Jamestown, and our separate cultural identity evolved under English rule in towns like Williamsburg. The settlers brought with them generations of English traditions. Their standards of living, working trades and strategies for barter and commerce were all modeled after English life and customs. Fundamentally, these men and women agreed with their European monarchy about various socioeconomic and political objectives. So in Williamsburg, as elsewhere, they accepted their British overseers and believed in the freedom to pursue private interests. Their self-confidence was steadfast until the Mother Country taxed them heavily to help recoup its expenses, sparking public protests that dramatically changed our nation's destiny.

government was created. Enter the Magazine, which contains an impressive collection of colonial weaponry. Tour the Governor's Palace, the elegant and imposing residence of seven royal governors. Enjoy refreshments at various taverns. Spend a day or two or three.

Living History Dining

An important part of the Williamsburg experience is dining in one of the Living History restaurants located within the historic area. All expect casual attire, though some provide an elegant atmosphere. Among them are Christiana Campbell's Tavern, said to have been George Washington's personal favorite; The King's Arm, a genteel colonial tavern which catered to Virginia's gentry and political statesmen; Shields, which operates in the spirit of an eighteenth-century coffeehouse; and Chowning's, which has a traditional-style Pit barbecue and casual menu emphasizing quick fare. You'll be served by costumed staff in a comfortable eighteenth-century environment that feels very Old America. Of course, Williamsburg also has conventional, modern eateries as well as the elegant Regency Room at the Williamsburg Inn (which requires dinner attire in the evening and suggests making reservations).

Colonial Gardens

Williamsburg is known for its wonderful green spaces, which combine historic native plants and exotics that tolerate the hot, humid summers in Virginia. As you walk around, you'll enjoy tidy colonial flower gardens, big shade trees, formal English-style gardens and fenced pastures. Don't be surprised if you find yourself taking lots of photographs as keepsakes.

Colonial Music

Music was an important part of Revolutionary War America, especially rousing music that "stirred men's souls" and raised their spirits on the road to battle. When Virginia Colony enlisted soldiers for its military, it also trained fifers and drummers – typically boys ages 10 to 18 – who worked with soldiers in the field. This tradition continues, with crowd-pleasing performances by the Colonial Williamsburg Fifes and Drums.

Williamsburg Shopping

We don't normally mention shopping at Living History places, but Williamsburg does have some very attractive selections for those of you who can't leave without a good souvenir or gifts for family and friends. Included are not only the expected modern goods but also many historically accurate reproductions. So bring a little extra money with you – just in case.

Encompassing a 1 1/2 mile wide historic district located in Williamsburg, VA, midway between Richmond and Norfolk. Take I-64 exit 238, and follow the green and white signs to the Visitor Center. Open daily. Shuttle bus service included in admission fee.

▲ On the steps of the Courthouse, the high sounds of the fifes and the thundering beat of the drums stir the spirit just as they did long ago.

◀ Williamsburg's gardens are lovely. This one located behind the Governor's Palace would have provided pleasing color and necessary vegetables, herbs and spices for colonial tables.

Historic St. Mary's City

SEE MAP PAGE 15, LOCATION #9
St. Mary's City, Maryland
Phone: (240) 895-4960 or toll-free (800) 762-1634
http://www.stmaryscity.org

▶ The *Maryland Dove* commemorates the founding of the fourth permanent settlement in British America – Maryland colony. It is a replica of a late 1600s trading vessel that plied the coastal waters between British colonies and sometimes traveled back across the Atlantic.

▶ When St. Mary's founders arrived, they made a special point of befriending local Indians. (They had learned from the mistakes of others.) The Indians helped them build "witchotts" like their own homes, to provide shelter while the land was cleared, trees were cut and "proper," English-style housing was constructed.

▶ St. Mary's City was dominated by two large buildings: the Maryland State House and the Roman Catholic Chapel. Both structures have been rebuilt based on archaeological findings. Shown here is the Chapel under construction using seventeenth-century techniques. Even the scaffolding is believed to be authentic, with lashed-together tree trunks and hand-operated winches to raise bricks and mortar to the workmen.

St. Mary's City was colonized in 1634 with the support of Roman Catholic investors. Although some were seeking religious freedom, the focus here was not on religion but on tolerance. St. Mary's City thrived on government and legal business, serving as Maryland's capital for 60 years. But after 1695, when the capital was moved to Annapolis, the city began a steady decline. Most people in the surrounding area lived on tobacco plantations and had little need for city services and amenities. By 1720, St. Mary's City ceased to exist.

Thankfully, archaeological findings have enabled the old city to be reborn. Today you will find several Living History attractions plus 800 acres of Tidewater landscape along St. Mary's River. The square-rigged *Maryland Dove* is docked at the waterfront. This 76-foot sailing ship represents the smaller of two vessels that brought the colonists to America. On board, sailors share tales about the tobacco trade and immigration. Nearby, the Woodland Indian Hamlet provides insight into the lives of local Native Peoples and the ways in which they interfaced with settlers. Godiah Spray Plantation re-enacts the day-to-day activities of a successful tobacco farmer, his family and indentured servants. The Town Center includes Cordea's Hope, a storehouse; Smith's Ordinary, an inn typical of Maryland

in the late seventeenth century; and the 1676 State House, where most government and court business took place. It's easy to imagine the paths colonists trod 370 years ago. Portions of the original village have been reconstructed as authentically as possible, based on historical and archaeological research.

Historic St. Mary's City is recognized as one of America's best-preserved colonial archaeological sites, with excavations and partial reconstructions visible across the landscape. Costumed interpreters in the re-created seventeenth-century settings illustrate and talk

about colonial times. During our visit, one of the most interesting spectator attractions was the reconstruction of the brick Chapel using seventeenth-century tools and techniques. Special weekend events offer unique opportunities to work alongside archaeologists and also participate in a wide range of history-based activities. The best time to visit is mid-June to late September.

Godiah Spray Tobacco Plantation

Tobacco was a very labor-intensive crop during colonial times, requiring the plantation family to work alongside indentured servants and (later) enslaved peoples. Indentured servants required a smaller investment than slaves and thus were the first choice as laborers. As a result, more than three quarters of Maryland's settlers in the seventeenth century worked as indentured servants in exchange for transportation to the colonies. Bound to a master for four to five years or more, they labored up to 14 hours a day, six days a week. Food, clothing and shelter were provided. At the conclusion of the contract, by law, they received a new suit of clothes, one axe, two hoes, three barrels of corn, and rights to 50 acres of land. Regrettably, they still needed to hire out for wages or become a tenant farmer before finally having the resources to finance their own farm.

First-person portrayals of the "plantation owner," "family" and "servants" provide an in-depth understanding of plantation life in 1661.

Located near St. Mary's College of Maryland, along SR 5 in St. Mary's City, MD. Open mid-March to late November – from Tuesday-Saturday in spring and fall; Wednesday-Sunday in summer. Admission charged.

Old York

SEE MAP PAGE 11, LOCATION #8
York, Maine
Phone: (207) 363-4974
http://www.oldyork.org

York was founded in 1630 by an English nobleman – Sir Ferdinando Gorges – who never traveled to America but dreamed of having a city here. His representatives led a group of aristocratic Englishmen to the coastal site and established the first chartered city on this continent. It was initially named Bristol and then Gorgeana; but after Gorges' death, it became part of Massachusetts Bay Colony and was renamed to honor the Puritan capture of York, England, during the English Civil War.

The Old York Historical Society has preserved an intimate view of the city's past through a variety of restored historic buildings. You can explore the circa 1719 Old Gaol – it includes the quarters of the jailer and his family, as well as cells outfitted as they would have been for various types of prisoners. You can visit the waterfront warehouse co-owned by John Hancock from 1787-1793 – it is outfitted with wharf and fishing items that might have been stored there. (In later years, the building served as the Customs House.) In addition, you can tour the 1754 Jefferds' Tavern displaying dining room, kitchen and bedroom settings; the 1740 Emerson-Wilcox House containing period rooms from 1750-1850; and several other historic buildings.

Buy the Walking Tour Guide at Jefferds' Tavern for a more comprehensive view of this pretty town.

Located in the center of York, ME. Guided tours begin at Jefferds' Tavern, on the corner of York Street (Route 1A) and Lindsay Road. Open daily from early June to mid-October. Admission charged.

▲ In York, you can tour the oldest remaining British Colonial public building in America – a jail. In addition to exhibits on crime and punishment, it has the home of the jailer and a variety of prisoner cells.

◀ As was true on virtually all early plantations, the house occupied by Godiah Spray and his family also provided sleeping space for his servants and field workers. Note the use of clapboards on the roof instead of the more typical thatch or shingles.

Strawbery Banke

SEE MAP PAGE 11, LOCATION #5
Portsmouth, New Hampshire
Phone: (603) 433-1100
http://www.strawberybanke.org

▶ This lovely Living History neighborhood enchants visitors with an interesting cast of characters. We visited with "Mrs. Ichabod Goodwin" in her elegant mansion and chatted about her "husband," a prominent New Hampshire politician who became the state's governor in 1859.

▼ Although clay or iron water pipes were not available, Strawbery Banke managed to have running water in its homes and businesses by the early 1800s. The water was piped through hollowed-out logs, buried deep underground and linked to a nearby reservoir. Original water pipes can still be seen today.

The English settlers who came up the northeast coast to the Piscataqua River in 1630 had been sent by a group of London merchants intent on establishing a commercial colony in the New World. Harvesting lumber was clearly a good possibility – trees along the Piscataqua were plentiful and top quality. The men named their settlement Strawbery Banke, inspired by the wild berries growing along the river's edge.

Although the fledgling community had all the makings for success, the London sponsors seem to have overextended themselves. They went bankrupt in 1638, leaving the colonists on their own. Luckily, the growing Massachusetts Bay Colony to the south reached out to include Strawbery Banke in 1641 and helped transform the colony into an economically diverse trading port. In 1653, the town's name was changed to Portsmouth in recognition of its fine position at the river's mouth. Then in 1679, New Hampshire was established as a separate royal province, and Portsmouth became its capital. Over the ensuing years, the town's history continued to be one of growth and prosperity, ebbing and flowing with the changes that swept over America. At the same time, as was true throughout our nation, its historic old buildings were being torn down to make way for new structures.

In 1958, history-minded citizens took protective action. Through a plan of urban renewal and historic preservation, the district along the old waterfront took on a new look and an old name. Memorable houses that once belonged to sea captains and artisans were renovated. Other historic buildings were brought in from elsewhere in the city. Ultimately, about 45 buildings dating from 1695 to 1955 were included, many furnished to depict their time period and others set up with museum displays. Pretty heritage vegetable, herb and flower gardens were added for color and authenticity. Well-informed docents, role-playing actors and traditional craftspeople and artisans were hired to educate and entertain the public. Boat builders came to work on-site part-time, representing the town's

earliest industry. Finally in 1965, the "new" Strawbery Banke opened. It remains today as a very interesting, very enjoyable Living History museum.

Located in Portsmouth, NH, at Marcy and Hancock Streets, an hour north of Boston, MA, and an hour south of Portland, ME. Open year-round – daily May-October; Saturday-Sunday November-April. Admission charged.

TIMBER & SHIPPING ECONOMY

Whatever wood products were needed – ship masts, boat oars, small boats, boards, house frames, furniture, wagon spokes, barrel parts – Portsmouth made them and profited handsomely. In 1800, when the Federal Government established Portsmouth Navy Yard, the town became a shipbuilding center. From here came the 74-gun man-of-war *Washington*, launched in 1814; the *USS Portsmouth*, instrumental in the annexation of California in 1846; and the *Kearsarge*, which achieved Civil War fame by sinking the Confederate raider *Alabama* in 1864. Clipper ships also emerged from local shipyards. By the 1900s, with the forests depleted, Portsmouth's maritime days had waned. However, World War II brought the Navy Yard back to life – 75 submarines were constructed here – and, later, nuclear submarine technology created another resurgence.

Shirley Plantation

SEE MAP PAGE 15, LOCATION #6B
Charles City vicinity (west), Virginia
Phone: toll-free (800) 232-1613
http://www.shirleyplantation.com

Nearby Attractions

Buy a Walking Tour Guide from the Chamber of Commerce at 500 Market Street. Several striking Portsmouth homes are tourable. To name a few:

Governor John Langdon House (1784)

This impressive mansion was built for a prosperous merchant, shipbuilder, signer of the U.S. Constitution and three-term state governor. Grand reception rooms, ornamented with elaborate rococo-style wood carvings, are among the highlights. At 143 Pleasant St. http://www.historicnewengland.org/visit/homes/langdon.htm

John Paul Jones House (1758)

Displaying rich and diverse museum collections, this stately house was built for a ship captain to impress his socialite bride. Ironically, she had to take in borders after his death to survive financially. Among them: John Paul Jones, who later became a naval hero. At 43 Middle Street. http://portsmouthhistory.org/jpjhouse.html

Rundlet-May House (1807)

Known for its technological advances, this was the home of a wealthy merchant. It has most of its original furnishings and innovations. At 364 Middle Street. http://www.historicnewengland.org/visit/homes/rundlet.htm

Wentworth-Gardner House (1760)

Formerly owned by famed collector Wallace Nutting and the NY Metropolitan Museum, this exceptional Georgian home was scheduled to be moved to Central Park before Portsmouth citizens intervened. It was built as a wedding gift to showcase family wealth. At 50 Mechanic Street. http://seacoastnh.com/wentworth

Colonial peoples must have been in awe of antebellum southern homes such as Shirley Plantation. Even today, such luxury is startling. This stately manor and its surrounding agricultural fields represent the oldest plantation in Virginia and the oldest family-owned business in North America (extending back eleven generations to 1638). Close relatives and descendants of the family include three signers of the Declaration of Independence (Carter Braxton, Thomas Nelson Jr. and Benjamin Harrison); two United States Presidents (William Henry Harrison and Benjamin Harrison); Confederate General Robert E. Lee (whose grandparents owned Shirley Plantation and whose mother was born here); a Supreme Court Justice; and eight Governors of Virginia.

Enjoy a guided tour of the circa 1723 mansion. It has beautiful hand-carved woodwork and a "floating" staircase as well as family portraits, silver and furniture passed down through the generations. Also take time for a self-guided tour of the grounds and outbuildings.

▲ Shirley Plantation offers a perfect opportunity to view American history through the eyes of "the rich and famous." The mansion and several outbuildings form a Queen Anne-style courtyard unique in America.

◀ The pineapple (a colonial symbol of hospitality) is featured in hand-carved woodwork inside the house and as a 3 ½-foot-tall finial on the rooftop.

Located on SR 5 about 10 miles west of Charles City, VA, and 15 miles east of Richmond. Open daily except Thanksgiving and December 25. Admission charged.

Historic Salem

SEE MAP PAGE 11, LOCATION #6A
Salem, Massachusetts
Phone: {978} 740-0444
http://www.essexheritage.org/visiting/placestovisit/housemuseums/index.shtml

▲ Built for John Gardner, son of a prosperous merchant, this elegant 1804 Federal-style house is widely recognized as an architectural gem. The beautiful wood ornamentation, which complements lavish furnishings, was designed by Samuel McIntire, Salem's master builder and carver.

▶ What is now famous as The House of the Seven Gables was built by Captain John Turner, an early merchant who owned a number of ships and made a fortune trading in the West Indies. The house has undergone several renovations since its construction 340 years ago. Some of them are quite curious, such as adding and removing gables and installing a hidden staircase.

Salem, Massachusetts, played a pivotal role in early American history. Today it provides unique insight into that past. The following are a few of the better attractions.

Peabody Essex Museum

Primarily an exhibit center of art, architecture and culture, the internationally acclaimed Peabody Essex covers three city blocks. It is a pleasure to visit. But from a Living History perspective, what matters most are the tourable historic landmarks that span three centuries of New England life. They include the circa 1684 John Ward House, circa 1727 Crowninshield-Bentley House and circa 1804 Gardner-Pingree House. Guided tours begin at the museum on New Liberty Street, East India Square. http://www.pem.org/collections/architecture.php

REPRESSIVE ATMOSPHERE

The Puritans, who were English Protestant reformists, were said to have come to the New World seeking religious freedom. Actually, what they wanted could not be called "freedom" today. Dictating that all political power be limited to fellow believers, they established Massachusetts Bay Colony as a theocracy (governed by religious principles and religious officials). Roger Williams, a Puritan pastor in Salem and Plymouth Colony, questioned this approach. The church and state should be separate, he contended, declaring that "forced worship stinks in God's nostrils." For his beliefs, Williams was convicted of heresy in 1636 and banished from the colony. Later that year, he founded Providence Plantations (now Providence, Rhode Island). A number of families joined Williams, agreeing to be governed by majority rule and by the tenet that no one was compelled to attend church or honor the Sabbath. They could worship as their conscience dictated. Finally, true religious freedom!

Jonathan Corwin House ("Witch House")

This is Salem's only building with direct ties to the witchcraft trials of 1692. Around 350 years old, it is a high-end example of First Period, or Post-Medieval, construction – the earliest architectural style in New England. Even more interesting: its namesake was heir to a sizable Puritan fortune and served as a judge in the most famous witch hunt in American history. At 310 Essex Street. http://www.corwinhouse.org

The House of the Seven Gables

The Turner-Ingersoll Mansion, built in 1668 by a trader/merchant, was made famous by Nathaniel Hawthorne, author of *The Scarlet Letter* and *The House of the Seven Gables*. Although it has changed substantially with the passage of time, the house is interesting to tour. Also on the grounds are Hawthorne's birthplace (c. 1750), seaside period gardens and a panoramic view of Salem Harbor. At 54 Turner Street. http://www.7gables.org

Derby Street Historic District

A wonderful place for a walking tour, this district was prominent in foreign commerce from the 1760s through 1820s, when Salem served as one of America's leading ports of entry. It runs from Herbert Street north to Blockhouse Square and includes The House of the Seven Gables. Learn about Salem's maritime history by visiting Derby Wharf and also touring the sailing ship and buildings encompassed by Salem Maritime National Historic Site. (See *Our New Nation*, page 188.)

Located off of SR 128, exit 25. Go southeast on SR 114 into downtown Salem, MA. Admission charged at sites.

Fort King George State Historic Site

SEE MAP PAGE 15, LOCATION #7

Darien, Georgia
Phone: (912) 437-4770
http://www.cr.nps.gov/goldcres/sites/ftkg.htm

As so often happens when visiting early settlement sites, we marvel at the ordeals American ancestors endured for the sake of others. Here in southeastern Georgia, the English hoped to create a buffer zone against the French and Spanish; so they built Fort King George in 1721 along the Altamaha River. The location may have been strategically good for England, but it was a serious problem for the occupying soldiers. In just one-third of an acre, the men built a blockhouse, soldiers' barracks, officers' quarters and guard houses. Surrounded by land that could not produce crops, they were forced to eat "salt provisions" year-round. Their barracks flooded with the spring tide. The swampy conditions bred terrible diseases that killed in large numbers. The nearest settlement was 150 miles away, and friendly contact with outsiders was rare. Added to all this was the constant threat of invasion. The men became unruly, fought among themselves and apparently mutinied. When the fort mysteriously burned down – probably due to arsonist soldiers – it was rebuilt. Not until 1727 was Fort King George finally evacuated.

In its place came the colony of Georgia in 1733, which was founded near present-day Savannah by James Oglethorpe, a member of Parliament. Regardless of the cost, Britain needed to protect its interests. Oglethorpe brought with him 35 families, including not only English people but also German and Swiss Protestants fleeing religious persecution. During his leadership, Spanish invaders were defeated, and the British territory was protected with the aid of Scottish Highlanders.

Based on old records and drawings, Fort King George has been reconstructed at its original location. The remains of three sawmills and tabby ruins are still visible within the historic site – rare examples of early colonial industry. In addition, a museum and film tell fascinating tales about local Native Peoples, the English, the Spanish, the Scottish Highlanders, and prosperous nineteenth-century sawmills. Cannon firings occur on some weekends. Re-enactments are held throughout the year. Other enjoyable activities include nature walks, canoe excursions and special programs.

Located in Darien, GA, 60 miles south of Savannah. From I-95, take exit 10, and head south on US 17 to downtown Darien. Follow the signs. Open Tuesday-Sunday except major holidays. Admission charged.

▲ Seen from the corner guardhouse, Fort King George is a compact arrangement of buildings surrounded by protective ramparts and ditches.

◀ As was true long ago, this English fort is perched on a knoll in the middle of a swamp.

◀ The coastal wetland, teeming with wildlife, was a natural deterrent to attacks. Toothy defenders in the water could be more dangerous than cannons on the ramparts.

The Fort At No. 4

SEE MAP PAGE 11, LOCATION #3
Charlestown, New Hampshire
Phone: (603) 826-5700
http://www.fortat4.com

▲ Civilian frontier forts often grew from a single building, with structures added as more and more settlers arrived in the area and needed protection. Each house was owned and occupied by a single family. Additional structures were built to provide temporary quarters for groups of people living outside the fort walls.

▶ Bedrooms were as good a place as any to store a cannon. Essentially useless as a weapon on the open frontier, the fort's cannon served primarily as a signal gun.

▶ Fort at No. 4 had two particularly valuable features. The first was a palisade of spaced-out posts that protected against the buildup of snow, which would have allowed attackers to merely walk over the stockade during wintertime. The second was a tall lookout tower that provided an unobstructed view of the surrounding countryside.

This authentic reconstruction of a fortified village sits near the Connecticut River, flying the red ensign flag of a British colony and representing frontier life during King George's War. The time is 1744-1760, when France, Spain and their Indian allies joined forces against Great Britain. Despite political uncertainties, the General Court of Massachusetts had chartered settlements along the Upper Connecticut River Valley in what is now Vermont and New Hampshire. Charlestown was the fourth "plantation" sold to land speculators and settlers.

In this beautiful but hostile territory, the people soon learned: survival on the frontier was physically arduous; the Mother Country was too consumed by war to provide more than a few soldiers; and the only safe haven was within fortified walls. Determined to stay, the settlers pulled together five existing houses, added a sixth, and then connected them with six lean-tos and a two-story defensive building. These were protected by a palisade of more than 700 posts, spaced four to

five inches apart in order to prevent snow from drifting up against the stockade walls. Six families lived in the houses. Others lived outside the stockade and used the lean-tos as temporary housing during times of strife.

Today's Fort at No. 4 is based on detailed drawings made in 1746. It is a remarkably complete and entertaining place to visit. Living History interpreters re-create Fort life and share a wealth of knowledge. In addition, special fairs and other events explore such topics as women in the wilderness; social and recreational life on the frontier; the lifestyle of Native Peoples; military matters (including fort construction, drills and musket/cannon firings); the French and Indian War; the Revolutionary War; and various handcrafts such as coopering, blacksmithing, harness and broom making, basket weaving, and tinsmithing.

Located in Charlestown, NH, on SR 11 just ¹/₂ mile east of I-91 exit 7. Open Wednesday-Sunday from late May to mid-October. Admission charged.

BIG CONTRASTS

Modern Americans take for granted what only the privileged few enjoyed in colonial homes – finished walls and ceilings (painted, plastered or wallpapered), windows with glass and curtains, rugs on floors, decorative items on walls and shelves, separate rooms for sleeping, cooking and entertaining. Visitors peek into slave quarters and think how humble they were, but the fact is: the average early Euro-American home was not much better. Before frame houses could be built, wattle-and-daub structures were the norm in the 1600s-1700s, especially in New England, and log or sod houses were commonplace on the frontier in the 1800s. Most had one room and perhaps a loft, rough walls and open-beam ceilings, window cutouts that could be covered with wood or animal hides, dirt or bare wood floors, a bed for some and mattresses rolled out on the floor for others, and few if any decorations. Many famous Americans including at least five Presidents – Jackson, Polk, Buchanan, Lincoln and Garfield – were born in such humble dwellings.

Saugus Iron Works National Historic Site

SEE MAP PAGE 11, LOCATION #7A
Saugus, Massachusetts
Phone: (781) 233-0050
http://www.nps.gov/sair

Saugus Iron Works played a key role in the colonies from 1646-1668, providing the local iron essential for everyday living. It was a busy, noisy place. One of seven waterwheels rumbled beside the blast furnace, powering 18-foot bellows which heated the furnace to 3,000 degrees Fahrenheit. Liquid metal, collected at the bottom of the furnace, was converted into bars of cast

iron (commonly called "pig iron"). Most of the pig iron was transferred to the forge, where a heavy hammer worked it into long wrought iron "merchant bars," which could be made into tools or used for building materials. Close by was the rolling and slitting mill, one of only a dozen in the world at that time. Here, a pair of rollers flattened wrought iron into sheets used to make wheel rims and barrel hoops. A pair of slitters cut thin strips of rod to be used for making nails.

This fully integrated complex became a center for technology and innovation. It also provided

the basis for what would become America's iron and steel industry. Today, it is a very interesting National Historic Site with reconstructed blast furnace, working waterwheels, forge, and rolling and slitting mill. Also on the site is a timber-framed 1680s mansion house with several rooms open to the public. Archaeological artifacts, including early ironworks products and an original 500-pound hammer head, are on display.

Located at 244 Central Street in Saugus, MA. Open daily except some major holidays. Self-guided tours year-round; guided tours April-October. Free.

Old Fort Western

SEE MAP PAGE 11, LOCATION #2
Augusta, Maine
Phone: (207) 626-2385
http://www.oldfortwestern.org

Old Fort Western is America's oldest surviving wooden fort. Built in 1754, it was originally part of the British Colonial effort to take over all of North America. After our Revolutionary War squelched those plans, the enterprising former garrison captain, James Howard, purchased the fort for his own use. With the aid of his sons (who also had been stationed here), he transformed the barracks into a comfortable home and then opened a store. For the next 50 years, James Howard's store was a centerpiece of trade between settlers in the Kennebec Valley and people in Massachusetts, New Foundland and the West Indies. The merchandise was all-inclusive – farming and forestry tools; ceramics, crockery and tableware; andirons, shovels, tongs and fishhooks; homespun and factory cloth; leather for shoes; feathers for bedding; window glass; casks, boxes and barrels of food. Now 250 years later, costumed interpreters and special programs bring this unique heritage site back to life.

Located at 16 Cony Street in Augusta, ME. Open daily from early May to mid-October and the first Sunday of each month from December-April. Admission charged.

▲ Located high on the banks of the Kennebec River, Fort Western was originally part of a system of forts built by the British to control northern trade and keep out the French.

◀ Saugus Iron Works is an exceptional reconstruction of early American industry, with historically authentic buildings and functioning equipment.

◀ Even when frontier structures were not highly refined, the addition of a few luxuries such as fine furniture made life more enjoyable. The chairs shown here were custom made for the Howard family parlor in the mid-1700s.

◀ It is impossible to appreciate the power of the 500-pound Saugus hammer unless you are standing nearby as it goes into action. The floor shakes and your body vibrates when the waterwheel throws it into the air and lets it drop to beat pig iron into wrought iron. Cover your ears!

▲ Tranquil environments were great attractions to European settlers seeking "religious freedom." They wanted to feel thousands of miles away from the rest of the world.

▶ Known for its hard work, quality and integrity, Hancock Shaker Village, MA, attracted numerous outsiders. Some visitors came just to purchase goods and services. Others were so impressed that they converted to the Shaker religion.

▲ Heritage Village in Salt Lake City, UT, will open your eyes to a highly productive world created by Mormon settlers.

◀ California's Spanish missions, such as San Diego de Alcalá, are immediately recognizable by their unique bell towers and bell walls.

RELIGIOUS & SECULAR GROUPS

We think of America as "the land of the free." And yet, the freedom we live by today was considered a bad thing in colonial times, typically associated with "the work of the devil." Even though a substantial portion of European settlers came to the New World seeking freedom to worship in their own way, few had any intention of granting liberties to themselves or anyone else. For the most part, they came to fulfill strict religious ideals and establish utopian communities where their own views would prevail and others would be excluded. To live among them was a privilege, not a right. And conformity was required in all aspects of life, from religious practices and social behavior to work, education and family life. This is a fascinating part of America's history and a major contributor to our nation's evolution. But freedom, as we know it, came later.

HISTORICAL PERSPECTIVE:
RELIGIOUS & SECULAR GROUPS

▶ While education was a high priority for religious and utopian groups, the Harmony Society took it to a new level. This group's natural history museum in what is now "Old Economy," PA, was among the first of its kind. It was open to the general public, for a 10¢ entry fee, and provided insights that had not been seen before outside of major cities.

Although commercial interests motivated much of the European colonization, America's early growth and development is largely a story of religious settlement and church-dictated lifestyles. The Pilgrims who landed in 1620 at Plymouth, Massachusetts, were Protestants, and roughly two-thirds were members of a Puritan sect known as Separatists, who rejected many tenants of the Church of England. They came to America intent on maintaining an independent congregation that could worship freely according to its own beliefs. The more-conforming Puritan groups which emigrated to Massachusetts Bay Colony in the 1630s were part of the Church of England, but they too wanted changes and were guided by strong religious convictions. They built a "city on a hill" (now Boston), expecting to serve as a model of godly living for not only Church members but also the general populace. Non-Puritans were allowed to reside in the colony but were forbidden to participate in the government.

those who disagreed with the ruling church were usually banished

Between 1630 and 1640, an estimated 20,000 English men, women and children emigrated to New England, and their numbers kept rising. They settled in closely bound villages most often guided by Puritan principles. Colonists who disagreed with their community's ruling Church were usually labeled "heretics" and banished. Such was the case for Roger Williams, a preacher who founded Rhode Island, and Anne Hutchinson, a midwife and religious teacher who became influential

in both Rhode Island and New York. Non-Puritans, were generally viewed with suspicion and even hatred. (Baptists and Quakers, especially, suffered from cruel laws directed against them.) Perhaps this made sense when day-to-day survival was an enormous challenge, but matters got out of hand. The 1692 Salem witchcraft trials tore apart Massachusetts Bay Colony with accusations and fear. Ironically, the shame of these trials *reduced* the repressive atmosphere.

Widespread Influence

While New England was their stronghold, the Puritans inspired powerful religious impulses in all colonies north of Virginia. In a way, they were role models. They proved that it was possible to successfully build communities based on common beliefs, far from the harassment and outright persecution of "non-believers." Thus, thousands of like-minded people came together in early America. Spanish-Portuguese Jews formed their first American congregation in 1654 when they found a safe haven in New Amsterdam (now New York). French Huguenots also successfully settled in New York, establishing New Paltz in 1677. English Quakers settled in Pennsylvania beginning in 1681. They were followed by several groups from Germany, including the Quakers and Mennonites in 1683, the Amish in the 1720s-1730s, and the Moravians in the 1730s. In the late 1700s, Shakers from England founded at least 19 northern settlements based on their own unique religious expression. Many other utopian groups emerged during

▶ During the early years of our country, agriculture was the primary source of income for most people. Large, well-built barns erected by the more cooperative and communal groups, such as the Amish and Shakers, attest to the success they enjoyed. This impressive barn is at Yoder's Amish Home, Millersburg, OH.

the mid-1700s to early 1800s. Among them: the Amana Colonies in eastern Iowa, the Harmony Society in western Pennsylvania, the Ephrata Cloister in eastern Pennsylvania and the Zoarites in eastern Ohio.

In stark contrast to these spiritually motivated communities were movements of people who may have been highly religious but who were more interested in commercial success. They saw the potential for selling a

vast array of American products overseas and opening up new markets here for trade goods from Europe and the Far East. English Catholics backed settlement in Maryland, and radical Anglicans concentrated on Virginia. Many others who were loyal to the Church of England migrated in large numbers to the South and to areas around New York City. Across the Southeast and Southwest, Spanish settlers built Catholic missions and then surrounded them with prosperous communities. Through all of this, few anywhere strayed far from a life guided by religious principles.

Power Shift

How did the people ever separate colonial government from church rule? A major turning point came in the 1690s, after the dominant English crown merged its Plymouth, Maine and Massachusetts Bay colonies. The new regime, ruled by non-sectarian professionals from London, put an end to theocracy in the Northeast.

Of course, this wasn't the end of the religious fervor. During the 1730s-1760s, the Great Awakening swept through English-speaking Europe and into the American colonies, invigorating even as it divided the churches. Major supporters of the Awakening and its evangelical focus – Presbyterians, Baptists and Methodists – grew into the largest American Protestant denominations. Opponents of the Awakening or those split by it – especially the Anglicans, Quakers and Congregationalists – lost ground. Surprisingly democratic in spirit, the Great Awakening was the first intercolonial cultural movement. Although it waned with the approach of the American Revolution, allowing further separation of church and state, a Second Great Awakening followed in the 1820s-1830s. It emphasized personal improvement, avoidance of sin and dedication to hard work. As such, it also set the stage for reforms related to temperance, abolition of slavery, moral justice, public education and philanthropy.

Changing Focus

Industrial, economic and political advances opened up opportunities that were too tantalizing to ignore. Over time, the American focus shifted to the creation of a more comfortable life. Most religious and commercially oriented communities changed accordingly or ceased to exist. Nevertheless, many of their early achievements remain – fascinating windows into a remarkable past.

▲ Historic Nauvoo, IL, is surprisingly well preserved. This was where Joseph Smith, founder of the Mormon religion, built a thriving community and hoped to find peace from religious intolerance. His dream did not last.

◀ Missionaries took it upon themselves to educate Native Peoples in European religions and lifeways, and many stressed the importance of music. Catholic padres in California not only led choirs but also provided training on orchestral instruments (including violins, violas, cellos, flutes, oboes and horns). Manuscripts of religious music, such as this one at Mission San Diego de Alcalá, CA, were brought from Spain and Mexico or produced at the missions.

THE HUGUENOTS

▲ The gracefully pointed arches that define the sanctuary of the Huguenot Church in Charleston, SC, reflect the influence of classic French Gothic cathedrals such as Notre Dame and Sainte Chapelle in Paris.

▶ In contrast to the elegant church in Charleston, this small reconstructed worship center in New Paltz, NY, shows the more humble beginnings of Huguenot worship in America.

Huguenots (HYOO-guh-nots) were at the center of political and religious quarrels in France during the 1500s and 1600s. Like the Puritans of England, they were followers of Protestant John Calvin and believed that the people – not just kings and bishops – should share in policy making. Surprisingly, several kings allowed them to become a large and influential group. But over time, life in France became very dangerous.

In 1564, 300 French settlers arrived in America. They sought a new life for themselves but sadly were doomed to fail from the start. The people were a disparate, difficult-to-manage population – rich noblemen and former criminals, artisans and laborers, single men and women, some families, mostly Huguenots but also a few Catholics and agnostics. They built their settlement – Fort Caroline – near Jacksonville, Florida, in an area that threatened Spanish interests. Members staged at least two mutinies after realizing the settlement barely had enough food to survive and only a slim chance of finding wealth (the lure for many). In a desperate move, they attacked a local Indian tribe and captured the chief, hoping to obtain food in return for his release.

Supply ships did finally arrive from France, but to no avail. By mid-1565, the colony was lost. Spanish soldiers, taking the territory they believed rightfully belonged to

Spain, attacked; they spared only women and children. Frenchmen from the supply ships joined the battle, but most of them perished too.

Still, the Huguenots needed a place to call their own. In mostly Catholic France, they were caught in the middle of a religious civil war. And even though the 1598 Edict of Nantes gave them certain freedoms, a 1628 royal decree barred them from settling in New France (Canada, Acadia and Louisiana). It was only a matter of time before the Edict of Nantes was repealed. When that day came in 1685, an estimated 200,000 Huguenots had to flee France, fearing imprisonment and death.

America offered these Protestants safety and hope. Among the possible places for settlement was New York, where a few Huguenots had successfully founded New Paltz in 1677. South Carolina also welcomed them. In fact, the French proprietors of one Carolina colony published a series of pamphlets and distributed them

to the Huguenots, guaranteeing freedom of religion with the hope of attracting much-needed settlers to their struggling venture. The colony wanted the hard-working, highly skilled craft workers from France. So the Huguenots came, and they brought prosperity to the places they settled.

LOOKING GOOD

Protestant John Wesley, founder of Methodism, noted in a sermon that "cleanliness is indeed next to godliness." Whether he coined a popular phrase or simply drew upon long-held religious teachings, this practical preacher was making an important point. While European settlers bathed infrequently, they were expected to look clean. Even in early colonial days, soap was a necessity. A person could wish for the superior French soaps made with olive oil, but Americans got what they could afford – typically English soaps made with tallow (beef fat). When time permitted, they made their own soap. An excellent example of colonial recycling, the recipe was simple but time-consuming: 1) Make lye by pouring water through wood ash saved from hearth fires. 2) Melt and render (clean) waste cooking grease plus fat collected from butchered animals. 3) Mix the liquid lye and fat together. 4) Boil the mixture for several hours. The result was a yellow-brown jelly-like glop. Hard soap could be made by adding common salt at the end of the boiling process.

New Paltz

SEE MAP PAGE 11, LOCATION #21
New Paltz, New York
Phone: (845) 255-1660
http://www.hhs-newpaltz.org

In 1677, twelve French Huguenot families purchased 40,000 acres from the local Esopus Indians and created a home for themselves in a region inhabited primarily by the Dutch. They decided to name their village after die Pfaltz, Germany, where they had found refuge before journeying across the Atlantic.

Today on Huguenot Street, six of their original stone homes plus a reconstructed French church can be toured with a guide. The interesting Bevier-Elting, Jean Hasbrouck and Abraham Hasbrouck Houses are furnished and interpreted much as they appeared in the early 1700s. The three other homes reflect 300 years of changing styles. The 1799 LeFevre House is a Federal design. The Deyo House is an 1894 renovation of a colonial home, with Queen Anne-style architecture and decor. Similarly, the Freer House, remodeled in the 1940s, reflects Colonial Revival tastes. Delightful!

Located on Huguenot Street, a village road open to the public, in New Paltz, NY. Owned and operated by the Huguenot Historical Society. Guided tours from Visitor Center at historic DuBois Fort on Tuesday-Sunday from May-October. Admission charged.

Huguenot Church

SEE MAP PAGE 15, LOCATION #12
Charleston, South Carolina
Phone: (843) 722-4385
http://www.frenchhuguenotchurch.org

This stucco-over-brick building is the only remaining independent Huguenot Church in America. Services were conducted here in French for 150 years before being switched to the English language in the nineteenth century. It is a striking example of Gothic Revival architecture, unaltered from its original 1845 construction, and a pleasure to visit. Among the

unusual features are decorative iron details on the exterior – alternatives to carved stonework, which was difficult to obtain during the antebellum period. In addition, unlike many other Christian churches, it has clear glass windows.

Two previous Huguenot churches stood on this site. The first was built in 1687 but regrettably was detonated in 1796 to create a fire break against a raging neighborhood blaze. The second, built in 1800, timed its services to coincide with the tides in nearby Charleston Bay, where boats arrived carrying worshippers from the surrounding plantations. It was later torn down to make way for the current church in 1845, which contains a beautiful mid-1800s "tracker" organ carved in the style and shape of a Gothic chapel.

Located at 136 Church on the corner of Queen Street near downtown Charleston, SC. Open for self-guided tours Monday-Thursday from March-June and September-November. Visitors welcome to attend Sunday services.

◀ While their heritage was French, Huguenots in New Paltz built in the Dutch style of their neighbors. Some of their houses had Dutch doors, massive ceiling beams and jambless fireplaces. As they prospered, stone became the preferred building material, and putting one's "best face forward" meant having a red brick façade like the one on the LeFevre house.

◀ Just inside the door to the Huguenot Church in Charleston is a plaque that lists the names of more than 20 U.S. Presidents who have Huguenot ancestry. The first is George Washington.

◀ While leaving one's homeland behind often meant leaving all that was familiar, a few family heirlooms usually made the trip to America. At the Bevier-Elting House in New Paltz, you'll see this charming brass lamp and inlaid table.

THE QUAKERS

▶ Entertaining overnight guests was a common practice for influential men such as William Penn. The custom was to provide the best you had to offer. Of the many finely furnished rooms to be seen at Pennsbury Manor, PA, the guest bedroom is the showiest.

Printed courtesy of Pennsylvania Historical and Museum Commission

Some would say that the Quakers had a profound influence on the whole religious movement in America, causing people to look inward and question closed-mindedness. In many ways, this may be true. Quakers showed a degree of charity that was extraordinary for the seventeenth and eighteenth centuries, stressing religious tolerance and giving sanctuary to many religious rebels. They believed in a loving God who speaks directly to each penitent soul and offers salvation freely. They emphasized religious experience over cold tradition, argued for an egalitarian form of church rule, and were determined to reduce the power of ordained clerics.

At the same time, the "Society of Friends," as they called themselves, exercised substantial non-religious influence. Pennsylvania Colony was governed by an elected assembly, with the principle of tolerance written into the Great Law and an assembly bill that required freedom of conscience. The colonial capital, Philadelphia, was conceived as a place of equality and a refuge for the persecuted.

Quakers took strong stands on equality, consensus building and social justice

Outspoken activists, Quakers took strong stands on equality, consensus building and social justice. They also aggressively advocated prison reform, education, women's rights, temperance, abolition of slavery, and decent care for all people regardless of class, race or economic situation. In the 1800s, many Quakers risked their lives in the "underground railroad," hiding slaves in their homes and helping them attain freedom.

Settling first in Pennsylvania and New Jersey and branching out into Virginia and North Carolina, the Quakers who arrived during the 1680s were determined to spread their influence, rather than keep to themselves. Within 70 years, an estimated 50,000 Quakers lived in the English colonies. They were especially prominent in Philadelphia, where by the early 1800s, according to one estimate, 13 percent of the Quakers were considered to be "gentlemen," and 45 percent were merchants, businessmen or professionals. They were less successful in the southern colonies, where their pacifist view of war and their belief in abolition ultimately caused them to lose their evangelistic appeal and political presence. Unable to overcome established traditions, many southern Quakers moved to the Midwest, where the Northwest Ordinance promised a land free of slavery. By 1850, Indiana had the fourth largest concentration of Quakers in the world. While their numbers have dwindled over time, there are still over 100,000 Quakers in America.

INNOVATIVE LEADERSHIP

The original capital of our nation – Philadelphia – was founded by William Penn, the Quaker son of an English admiral. Penn had received the charter for colonization from Charles II as payment for a debt owed to his family. He was a well-educated man, determined to establish an efficient, productive city. This meant implementing a new kind of government based on equality and social justice, a government which prompted Thomas Jefferson to call Penn "the greatest law-giver the world has produced." Penn also believed in creating a well-organized plan for the city's growth and development. At a time when most cities grew up around crossroads and cow paths, he plotted the building of businesses and houses according to a rectangular grid with town squares. It was a design that set the pattern of American urban planning. In subsequent years, many other "firsts" occurred in Philadelphia, including America's first public school, hospital, medical college, fire company, stock exchange, bank, paper mill and sugar refinery.

Historic Fallsington

SEE MAP PAGE 11, LOCATION #16B

Fallsington, Pennsylvania
Phone: (215) 295-6567
http://www.historicfallsington.org

This 300-year-old village is a living testament to Quaker peacefulness and an architectural heritage that is strikingly American. Founded in 1682, Fallsington was a religious, social and market center as well as a stagecoach stopover on the "King's Road" from

Philadelphia to New York and areas north. In the late 1700s, Congress considered nearby Morrisville for development as our national capital. Happily for us, political compromises required a southern location, and this area was able to keep its country charm.

Over 90 historic buildings remain from the late-1600s settlement period through the mid-1800s Victorian era. Guided walking tours are offered in picturesque Meetinghouse Square. Here is your chance to step inside three very interesting, well-preserved buildings: a 200 year-old settler's log house; the elegant former home of a village doctor; and a stagecoach tavern which operated from 1799 until Prohibition. Three Quaker Meeting Houses are located within the square.

Begin at Historic Fallsington, Inc., 4 Yardley Avenue in Fallsington, PA. (Take Tyburn Road to South Main to corner of Yardley and Lower Morrisville.) Tours offered daily mid-May to mid-October; weekdays only November-April; closed major holidays. Fee charged for tours.

Pennsbury Manor

SEE MAP PAGE 11, LOCATION #18B

Morrisville, Pennsylvania
Phone: (215) 946-0400
http://www.pennsburymanor.org

Printed courtesy of Pennsylvania Historical and Museum Commission

William Penn, a highly influential Quaker and proprietor of three colonies in America, built his residence in 1682-84 just three miles from Fallsington, preferring a rural estate to a home in bustling Philadelphia. In the countryside, he wrote, "we see the works of God, but in cities little else but the works of man." After Penn's death, his plantation fell into disrepair and eventually was covered by nineteenth-century buildings. In the 1930s, however, the land was donated to the Commonwealth of Pennsylvania, and this remarkable place was reconstructed based on archaeological findings and Penn's original instructions for its design. Take the guided tour to enter the house. Marvelous!

Located at 400 Pennsbury Memorial Road in Morrisville, PA. Open Tuesday-Sunday except major holidays. Admission charged.

KEEPING PEACE

Fallsington kept its Quaker ways for an unusually long time; even the excesses of Victorian architectural style left little impression. In the 1860s and 1870s, when other religious influences emerged, Fallsington had a population of around 340. There were two general stores, both of which housed the post office at one time or another, depending on the political party in power. Other local businesses included one hotel, two doctor's offices, three blacksmith shops, three wheelwrights, three shoemaking shops, a shoe store, a carriage-trimming and harness-making shop, a tinsmith and a paint store. While new businesses have replaced the old many times, the peacefulness of this place has remained.

▲ Overlooking the Delaware River, this remarkably complete reconstruction of William Penn's rural home includes not only the beautiful Manor House and outbuildings but also sizable portions of the farm, vineyard, orchard, kitchen garden and formal gardens.

◀ Meetinghouse Square in Fallsington appears much as it did almost 200 years ago. The tree-lined streets include three historic Quaker meeting houses as well as Federal and Victorian buildings. You can tour the original 1799 Stagecoach Tavern, furnished in period.

◀ The hand-hewn Moon-Williamson Log House is believed to be the oldest home in Pennsylvania remaining on its original site. Near the entrance are two huge sycamores, the "bride and groom" trees, planted when the earliest occupants were newly married.

THE SHAKERS

▶ Separate but equal was the motto for the sexes, even in the design of hallways and stairwells. In this beautiful second-floor area at Shaker Village of Pleasant Hill, KY, the men walked up "their" stairs into "their" set of rooms, while the women took the other stairs and entered the other set of rooms. They could meet in the middle but could not cross over to the opposite side.

During the 1740s, the Quakers changed their process of worship, eliminating the frenetic trembling and quaking for which they were named. One group in Manchester, England, refused to change and split into a separate religious movement in 1747. Members formed the United Society of Believers in Christ's Second Appearing, commonly known as the "Shaking Quakers," or "Shakers." Traveling to the New World in 1774, a small group of Shakers settled in New York and established the spiritual foundation for a relatively small sect which, quite remarkably, was destined to contribute significantly to American culture and business. Success came at a high cost, however. Early Shakers were harassed, beaten, imprisoned and driven out of many American towns. In addition, their dynamic founder, "Mother" Ann Lee, died in 1784. Nevertheless, by the 1830s, at least 19 Shaker communities had been established in New York, Maine, Massachusetts, New Hampshire, Connecticut, Ohio, Kentucky and Indiana. Their religious movement peaked before the Civil War at about 6,000 members. Today only one active community remains – Sabbathday Lake in New Gloucester, Maine. (It has 18 buildings on 1,800 acres of land. True to their heritage, Shaker members engage in farming and make a variety of handcrafts. Visitors are welcomed.)

What made the Shakers so controversial to some people and so tantalizing to others? Like many religious societies, they lived a communal lifestyle in the countryside, far from the corrupting influences of city life. They tried to create "heaven on earth," seeking perfection by applying the virtues of simplicity, purity and devotion to God. They encouraged intellectual and artistic development along with hard work. They practiced celibacy, living and working separately as Brothers and Sisters while also sharing key communal roles. Although they did not practice procreation, they recognized the importance of young people and adopted children into their community. All these attributes were admired. But they also believed heavenly spirits came to earth, bringing visions to Shaker people, especially women, who danced, whirled, spoke in tongues and interpreted these visions for others. They believed that God is both mother and father, and that gender equality is therefore essential in all aspects of life. Furthermore, they insisted that to kill or harm others is unacceptable, even in time of war. Exempted from military service by President Lincoln, Shaker males were among the first conscientious objectors in American history.

SHAKER CONTRIBUTIONS

Practical farmers and business people, the Shakers were renown for their high quality goods and inventiveness. Thank them for the metal nibs on writing pens, the flat-sided broom, apple peeler/corer, rotisserie ovens, commercial clothes washer, waterproof and wrinkle-free cloth, a transom window over doorways to circulate indoor air, clothes pins, packaged vegetable and flower seeds, a metal chimney cap to block rain, and an improved plow. These advances first came out of Shaker workshops. But they only hint at the Shaker impact. The circular saw (invented by a Shaker woman in 1810) sparked changes in the production of wood products worldwide. The simple, graceful designs of Shaker furniture influenced not only American but also Japanese, Scandinavian and European furniture makers. A wooden ball-and-socket chair-tilter was the Shaker precursor of moving parts used in many chairs today. And Shaker buildings reflect the pioneering principles of form and function that were later advocated by noted architects and designers.

Ironically, the death knell for the Shakers was not so much religious as it was economic. As cheaper, machine-made goods became commonplace, Shaker income from handmade products fell sharply and could not support large groups of people. For a while, "Winter Shakers," who practiced their faith seasonally, joined the villages after the harvest and left before planting time; but even they could not afford to continue. Not to be forgotten, the Shaker spirit lives on today in the following 15 sites, which have been preserved and lovingly restored. The first nine are open to the public.

Alfred Shaker Historic District
Alfred, Maine

Canterbury Shaker Village
Canterbury, New Hampshire

Enfield Shaker Museum & Historic District
Enfield, New Hampshire

Hancock Shaker Village
Pittsfield, Massachusetts

Mount Lebanon Shaker Society
New Lebanon, New York

Shaker Museum & Historic District
South Union, Kentucky

Shaker Museum & Sabbathday Lake
New Gloucester, Maine

Shaker Village of Pleasant Hill
Harrodsburg, Kentucky

Watervliet Shaker Historic District
Albany, New York – Site of first Shaker settlement and burial place of Mother Ann Lee

Enfield Shakers Historic District
Enfield, Connecticut

Harvard Shaker Village Historic District
Harvard, Massachusetts

North Union Shaker Site
Cleveland, Ohio

Shirley Shaker Village
Shirley, Maine

Tyringham Shaker Historic District
Tyringham, Massachusetts

Whitewater Shaker Settlement
New Haven, Ohio

◀ The Shakers were widely respected as hard working, industrious people. In most of their communities, a thriving seed business helped to provide a sound financial foundation.

▼ Distinctive manufactured goods, ranging from boxes to bonnets and from handcrafted tools to top-quality furniture, also provided substantial income.

Shaker communities have remained places of harmony and peace. Their grand objective from inception was to provide a sense of balance and grace appropriate for an earthly paradise and devotion to Godly endeavors. Buildings used by both men and women, such as meetinghouses and dwellings, incorporate separate entrances and stairways for each sex, functioning as though they are split in half. In keeping with the Shaker focus on absolute equality, each half is a mirror image of the other. At Pleasant Hill, for instance, twin stairways in the Trustees' Office spiral together up three floors in a supreme achievement of artistic elegance. Of course, the Shakers were not always separated. Their meetinghouses have an uninterrupted, shared space for religious "dancing." At Mount Lebanon, an ingenious arched roof, or "rainbow roof," spans the dance floor. Many Shaker buildings were also very large, to prevent overcrowding and allow for growth. The Great Stone Dwellinghouse (c. 1837) in Enfield, New Hampshire, is six stories tall, measures 100 feet long by 58 feet wide, and has 200 windows. It was built of white granite hauled by oxen over frozen Lake Mascoma and, despite its size, is light and airy.

Hancock Shaker Village

SEE MAP PAGE 11, LOCATION #23

Pittsfield, Massachusetts
Phone: toll-free (800) 817-1137
http://www.hancockshakervillage.org

▲ The Shakers adopted progressive agricultural practices. At Hancock, they built a number of innovative features into the round barn in order to efficiently stable and milk up to 52 dairy cows per day.

▶ Orphans and children of the poor were very welcomed additions to the Village, cared for by the Shakers and given a well-rounded classroom education. When the children reached adulthood, they could make the choice to officially become a Shaker or move on.

Situated in the scenic Berkshire Hills of western Massachusetts, Hancock Shaker Village was considered the center of Shaker authority in America from 1787 until 1947. Today, it is a 1,200-acre Living History museum. This village offers a terrific opportunity to expand one's understanding of the Shakers and their place within a broader American society. In addition to 20 original buildings, an historic working farm and an heirloom garden, you can enjoy a number of hands-on activities and first-person portrayals of Shakers from the past.

Take a walk through the Village. An impressive five-story brick dwelling – formerly home to nearly 100 Sisters and Brothers – is furnished with one of the nation's finest collections of Shaker furniture and artifacts. The remarkable 1826 Round Stone Barn reflects the best of Shaker inventiveness. The Trustees Office and Store, built in 1813 as a simple rectangular structure, shows off its 1895 Victorian transformation – including bay and Palladian windows, a tower, bracketed porches, wallpapered rooms and "worldly" furnishings apparently intended to show outsiders that

this Shaker community was up-to-date. The gambrel-roof meetinghouse, with its unadorned but dramatic dance/worship room, was central to the Shaker lifestyle. Members worshipped here – "laboring" or dancing, singing a cappella and giving testimonies to God and fellow believers. Although identical to the original Hancock building, this meetinghouse was moved to the Village from Shirley, Massachusetts.

The Brethren's Workshop and the Sisters' Dairy and Weave Shop (both c. 1795) are still a hub of domestic trades. Here, museum staff and volunteers use traditional Shaker tools and techniques to make chairs, rag carpets, oval boxes, baskets, brooms, linen towels and other hand-made items. The Tan House (c. 1835) has demonstrations of Shaker blacksmithing and cabinetmaking. The Laundry/Machine Shop (c. 1790) displays a working reproduction of an 1858 water turbine. Presentations on the Shaker lifestyle, religion, music, technology, cooking and agriculture are offered throughout the day. In addition, Hancock Shaker Village has two fine exhibition galleries. Displays include a rare collection of Shaker gift drawings.

Located at the junction of Routes 20 and 41, about 5 miles west of downtown Pittsfield, MA. Open daily except major holidays. Admission charged.

INGENIOUS CONSTRUCTION

Barns are visually dominant buildings in all Shaker communities. Even so, the Round Stone Barn at Hancock Shaker Village is exceptional. In its day, it was a model of efficiency. It was also a curiosity to "the world's people," including not only farmers but also progressive thinkers such as Nathaniel Hawthorne and Herman Melville. In fact, its design was so unique that building plans published in a nationally circulated farm journal sparked the construction of approximately 24 similar barns in Vermont. Built into an artificial hillside, it allowed ground-level access on three floors. Hay and grain were stored on the top floor, in a space 95 feet in diameter. A herd of 50 or more dairy cows were milked and fed on the next level down, held in place for easy handling by a circular series of stanchions radiating from a central manger. Trap doors placed at intervals behind the stanchions allowed clean-up into a bottom-floor pit accessible by wagon.

Shaker Village of Pleasant Hill

SEE MAP PAGE 17, LOCATION #9
Harrodsburg vicinity (northeast), Kentucky
Phone: toll-free (800) 734-5611
http://www.shakervillageky.org

This wonderfully tranquil environment in the heart of Kentucky Bluegrass country provides a one-of-a-kind Living History experience, complete with meticulously restored buildings, costumed interpreters, an array of nineteenth-century activities and workshops, a riverboat excursion, hiking and horseback riding, shopping for Shaker goods, family-style dining, and lodging in the original buildings. Whether you visit for a few hours or a few days, you are likely to feel the magic of the Shaker lifestyle which brought converts to this spot nearly two centuries ago.

Pleasant Hill flourished through the 1850s, peaking at 490 members. Highly productive, it had thousands of acres of farmland, extensive gardens, vast fruit orchards and herds of farm animals. In addition, about 260 buildings were constructed to serve community needs. Today 34 of those structures remain (14 can be visited), and 2,900 acres of land are maintained in historic fashion by a non-profit, educational organization. Surrounding all of this are miles of picket and plank fences as well as handsome fieldstone walls.

The 40-room stone Centre Family Dwelling is the highlight of Pleasant Hill, widely admired for its architectural details and its extensive collection of original Shaker furniture and household items. The refined symmetry of this dwelling beautifully reflects the

EXCEPTIONAL FARMERS

The agricultural success at Pleasant Hill was renowned. Here were thousands of acres of wheat, rye, oats, flax, Indian corn, broom corn and potatoes. Here, too, were large flower gardens and huge fruit orchards with up to 800 trees. Their products included seeds, which were sold in convenient-to-use packets rather than in bulk containers. In addition, the Village's devotion to excellence led Shaker Brothers to purchase the best livestock available and to develop improved breeds. Most notable among them were the Percheron horses, Bakewell and Leicester sheep, several varieties of poultry, and one of the nation's largest herds of registered Durham Shorthorn milking cattle. As a result, Pleasant Hill became a leading agricultural experimental station. Brothers served as cattle judges at Kentucky's first state fair, and they wrote agricultural pamphlets distributed by the U.S. government. Today, the farm program at Pleasant Hill is working to preserve livestock breeds that are significant to both Shaker and Kentucky history.

Shaker lifestyle: order, utility and complete equality of the sexes. Nearby are four original workshops where skilled artisans perform nineteenth-century trades, including broom making, coopering, woodworking, spinning and weaving. The Shakers wrote thousands of hymns, and their music is performed frequently by a soloist in the 1820 Meeting House. Adding to the authenticity, interpreters in period clothing engage in domestic chores, farm work and heirloom gardening throughout the Village. Other visitor attractions include hiking and horseback riding trails that reveal old mill remains, former bridge sites, old stone fences and the Chinn-Poe Nature Preserve. At Shaker Landing, the *Dixie Belle* sternwheeler takes visitors on an excursion through the Kentucky River palisades where the Shakers once gathered building materials, chiseling great blocks of limestone from the cliff walls and harvesting virgin timber from the forested shoreline.

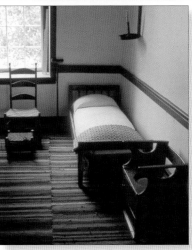

▲ Famous for its elegant simplicity and perfect symmetry, the Centre Family Dwelling provides a fascinating introduction to the rich legacy of Pleasant Hill.

▲ While the Shakers lived a simple life, they believed in aesthetic quality and balance in all things, even their bedroom furnishings.

Located 7 miles northeast of Harrodsburg, KY, on US 68. Open daily except December 24-25. Nearby Dixie Belle river excursions are offered daily from late-April through October. Admission charged.

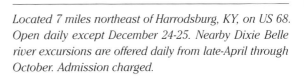

Canterbury Shaker Village

SEE MAP PAGE 11, LOCATION #13
Canterbury vicinity (northeast), New Hampshire
Phone: (603) 783-9511
http://www.shakers.org

▲ At the Village's peak in 1840, about 300 people lived, worked and worshipped in 100 buildings. The Dwelling House was the largest structure at Canterbury Shaker Village and could house and feed 80-100 Brothers and Sisters on its four floors. The innovative bakery in the basement could bake 60 loaves of bread at one time.

▶ Always practical, the Shakers were known for their elegantly simple architecture. Still, as the years went by, they moved beyond pure functionalism and began to adopt elements of Victorian style on some of their buildings. They also chose to add some color. The fire station, for example, was red. (Note the tower.) The nearby school was gray-green, and the hospital was a light purple.

The seventh Shaker settlement in America, Canterbury is not only one of the oldest but also one of the most completely preserved of the communal villages. Here 25 of the original buildings and three reconstructed structures house a fascinating collection of Shaker innovations. Among them are the only intact first-generation Meeting House (c. 1792) and Dwelling House (c. 1793), both of which can be seen on narrated tours. Other interesting buildings include the Laundry, School House, North Shop, Dry House, Syrup Shop, Bee House, Carriage House and Ministry Shop. We also suggest taking a stroll to the organic vegetable, flower and medicinal herb gardens. The Shakers made good use of their land.

Just as important to your visit, Canterbury Shaker Village has numerous educational activities. Craft demonstrations, which vary from day to day, provide an ideal opportunity to see first-hand the processes that made Shaker industries widely respected and highly successful. Learn from skilled woodworkers about the construction of Shaker furniture (including woodturning and dovetailing). Chat with weavers and spinners about the Shaker textile industry, and see their skills at work in Shaker-style dressmaking, knitting, rugmaking and embroidering. Watch basket weavers, oval box makers and broom makers use nineteenth-century innovations to make their old-style tasks easier. Appreciate the craftsmanship involved in making Shaker poplarware, a process by which split, cured wood is woven into small boxes, trays and needle cases.

Also hear about the Shaker printing industry at Canterbury, which was once a center for published materials used by most Shakers.

For a more in-depth experience, try your hand at some of the do-it-yourself projects. Throughout the season, special workshops are offered on subjects as varied as basket making, broom making, printing, herbal medicines, watercolor painting, woodworking and traditional crafts. Be sure to register in advance.

Located northeast of Canterbury, NH. Take I-93 exit 18. From town, go east on Baptist Road and north on Shaker Road. Open May-December – daily May-October; Friday-Sunday November-December. Admission charged.

ECSTATIC FORM OF WORSHIP

Many nineteenth-century Christians were shocked by Shaker religious practices. To them, it was a sacrilege to bring dancing, whirling and clapping into a house of worship and elevate this behavior above the word of God spoken by an ordained minister. It was almost as "bad" to turn a religious service into a show. In actuality, while the Shakers invited outsiders to watch them – and even built benches for that purpose along meetinghouse walls – they had good reasons for their openness. They believed in direct communication with God. They believed in the ability to find and give voice to an Inner Light. And they sought to express a communal, not individual, relationship with God in their "meetings" by singing, stamping their feet while dancing, and working up a frenzy when the spirit moved them. Although spontaneous dancing was replaced by choreographed dancing in the early 1800s, it was reintroduced around the 1840s. In the 1900s, however, more sedate worship services became the norm.

THE AMISH

Amish roots date back to sixteenth-century German-Swiss Christians who believed that the Bible's call to "repent and be baptized" applied to persons old enough to understand and make a choice. They stopped the standard practice of baptizing children, and they rebaptized adults. Called "Anabaptists" (rebaptizers), this fairly large group included former Catholic priests. They might have been tolerated within the general population had they not held a number of very unpopular views. Most "dangerous" was their belief in a separation of church and state, with Christ's teachings placed above adherence to common laws and traditions. Both Catholics and Protestants objected,

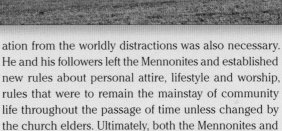

Labeled as heretics, the Anabaptists were fiercely persecuted. Nevertheless, many were able to gather together in communal societies. Among them were the Mennonites, who believed in a personal spiritual responsibility and strict obedience to the Scriptures. In the late 1600s, Jacob Amman, a Swiss Mennonite bishop, concluded that separation from the worldly distractions was also necessary. He and his followers left the Mennonites and established new rules about personal attire, lifestyle and worship, rules that were to remain the mainstay of community life throughout the passage of time unless changed by the church elders. Ultimately, both the Mennonites and Amish left Europe for the New World.

Today, 23 states and parts of Canada have Amish communities. The largest American settlements are in Ohio, Pennsylvania and Indiana, where you can enjoy a delightful variety of Amish shops, restaurants and local sights. In central Ohio, tour the counties of Holmes, Tuscarawas and Wayne. In southeastern Pennsylvania, visit Lancaster and surrounding towns. In northern Indiana, wander through Nappanee, Shipshewana and other nearby communities. The Amish live among "the English" (those who are not Amish) but keep their links to a minimum. You will recognize their homes by the lack of modern trappings – there are no cars, no electrical lines, no TV antennas, no phone cables.

◢ In Pennsylvania, take a drive into the country east of Lancaster and north of Highway 30. You will find idyllic landscapes with broad fields punctuated by tidy, prosperous-looking farms. Along the way, you are likely to see horse-drawn black buggies parked in front of homes or traveling on the roadway.

◢ At first glance, the inside of an Amish house looks much like any other rural home. However, no matter how close it is to electrical or gas lines, the household operates "off the grid." As you will learn at the Amish Farm and House in Lancaster, PA, appliances are typically powered by propane or gas generators.

OLD ORDER AMISH

The Amish have many "Orders," or branches, which vary in their adherence to the strict standards of their European ancestors. Among the strictest are the Old Order Amish, but even they vary significantly. Some accept semi-modern conveniences; others maintain a theology and lifestyle practiced in the 1800s or earlier. All have an overriding determination to protect their members from the problems of modern life. From their perspective, God wants them to stay true to their heritage and not give in to external pressures; so they live self-sufficient lives and forego most (or all) technological advances. Their lifestyle is a deliberate way of maintaining humility, family harmony and community ties. Asked why they do not use modern conveniences, many Amish might say: "Such things have no place in a holy life and would link us too closely to the world of man rather than the kingdom of God." Less strict Amish do use some modern appliances, such as refrigerators, stoves and clothes washers – as long as these conveniences operate without commercial power. Some may even ride in cars driven by others and use phones outside their homes.

Yoder's Amish Home

SEE MAP PAGE 17, LOCATION #11
Millersburg, Ohio
Phone: (330) 893-2541
http://www.yodersamishhome.com

▲ These family homes represent two generations and two very different Amish lifestyles.

▶ Silos are essential on Amish farms. They store fodder (chopped ears of corn and hay), a staple food for livestock. This silo is 10 x 40 feet. We have seen others as large as 24 x 70 feet.

▶ Old Order Amish take responsibility for holding group services in their homes rather than attend formal churches. About once a year, each family in turn clears their furniture from the front room and sets up benches. After the service, the women serve lunch.

▶ Most Amish believe in practical technological improvements. These two sewing machines are decades apart in age, and both use foot-power instead of electricity; but the range of capabilities expanded significantly with the newer model (right).

Holmes County in east-central Ohio is believed to have the largest population of Amish anywhere in the world. Here on a designated scenic byway, you will find an authentic 116-acre Amish farm that is open to the public. No longer occupied by the owners, it enables you to gain an exceptional inside look at the Amish culture and people. Guided tours take visitors through two original homes to see the lifestyle of different Orders and learn how Amish ways can vary significantly – from very strict and traditional to more open and modern. Stop by the barn afterwards, especially in late spring and early summer when you can enjoy many newborn farm animals. If time permits, also take a ride around the property in a classic Amish buggy.

Located at 6050 SR 515 between the towns of Trail and Walnut Creek in Millersburg, OH. Open Monday-Saturday, mid-April through October. Admission charged.

Amish Farm & House

SEE MAP PAGE 11, LOCATION #17B
Lancaster vicinity (east), Pennsylvania
Phone (717) 394-6185
http://www.800padutch.com/z/amishfarm&house.htm

This 15-acre farm/museum provides a close-up look at the Old Order Amish simple, wholesome way of living. Guided tours are offered inside the 1805 farmhouse, where you will learn how the furnishings, clothing, kitchen and even the Christian door all symbolize

important aspects of the Amish culture and beliefs. The Front Room has been readied for a typical worship service which will usually last longer than three hours and will have as many as seven preachers and bishops. The kitchen is surprisingly modern, but appliances are powered by propane and/or a generator. Upstairs, you will see simple bedrooms with colorful bed quilts and Amish clothing.

Equally interesting is the farm itself, which has everything an Amish family needs. You are free to wander. So investigate the barns, water wheel, windmill,

lime kiln, spring house and one-room schoolhouse. See the crops and animals that support the farm in multiple ways – grains, vegetables, cows, pigs, horses, sheep and chickens. Also take a buggy ride.

Located 5 miles east of Lancaster, PA, on Route 30. Open daily except Thanksgiving, December 25 and January 1. Admission charged.

The Amish Village

SEE MAP PAGE 11, LOCATION #25B

Strasburg, Pennsylvania
Phone: (717) 687-8511
http://www.800padutch.com/avillage.html

Past and present intermingle at this interesting attraction, providing a broad perspective about the history and customs of the 24,000 Amish living in Lancaster County today. Your visit begins with a guided tour of the authentically furnished Old Order Amish farmhouse, which dates back to 1840. Afterwards, you can wander around the property, seeing a blacksmith shop, one-room schoolhouse, barn and farm animals,

buggies and wagons, waterwheel and windmill. Stop by the smokehouse, too, which is stocked with traditional "Pennsylvania Dutch" foods available for purchase.

Be aware that "Dutch" in this context is a misnomer. Usually not of Dutch heritage, the Amish came from German-speaking areas throughout Europe. These areas were once broadly defined as "Dutch," presumably because the people spoke a dialect referred to as "Deitsch" (spelled Deutsche). Even today, the Amish will call themselves "Dutch," in keeping with the old tradition.

Located on Route 896, about 2 miles north of Strasburg, PA. From Lancaster, take US 30 east 5 miles; turn south onto Route 896. Open year-round – daily March-December; weekends January-February; closed Thanksgiving and December 25. Admission charged.

Amish Acres

SEE MAP PAGE 17, LOCATION #12

Nappanee, Indiana
Phone: (575) 773-4188 or toll-free (800) 800-4942
http://www.amishacres.com

Once the Stahly-Nissley-Kuhns farmstead, this reconstructed village provides a unique Living History experience. The original 12-room house, which displays many family furnishings, was built in 1874 in the distinctive Germanic style. The 1876 Sweitzer bank barn is reminiscent of structures seen in the foothills of Switzerland. Numerous other historic buildings, moved from the surrounding countryside, also draw their character from the Old World. Together they represent the lifestyle and domestic industries practiced by pioneering Amish families in northern Indiana.

Depending on the season, maple syrup, apple butter, cider, sorghum molasses, dried foods and lye soap are produced here just as they were in the 1800s. Colorful Amish quilts are hand-stitched by skilled craftswomen. Brooms are made the "old way"; rugs are woven; candles are dipped; bread is baked in an outdoor oven. Rotating documentary films are shown in the Meeting House. And just for fun, a Broadway musical is performed frequently on the Amish Acres stage.

Located a mile west of Nappanee, IN, at 1600 West Market Street (on US 6). Open on weekends in March and daily April-December; closed December 24-25. Admission charged.

▲ Three related generations lived at the Stahly-Nissley-Kuhns farmstead. Their life-styles and homes have been restored thanks to oral traditions within the family.

◀ This round barn was built in 1911. Its 60-foot-high, self-supported dome provides excellent acoustics for the shows it now hosts.

◀ Since the 1930s, some Amish have adapted their lives by adding such modern technologies as lights and turn signals on their buggies. They allow telephones in the their shops, though not in their homes. And indoor bathrooms have all but replaced the traditional outhouses.

◀ Quilting will always be a creative way for Amish women to transform sewing scraps into colorful bed covers for personal use and for sale.

THE MORAVIANS

▲ The Home Moravian Church in Winston-Salem, NC, is located on the northeast corner of Salem Square in the restored Moravian town now called Old Salem. Its sanctuary has been in continuous use, except during times of renovation, since 1800.

▶ Schoenbrunn Village was founded in 1772 at the invitation of a Delaware Indian leader. This Moravian Mission was home to more than 300 Delaware until dangers associated with the Revolutionary War and the encroachment of American frontiersmen became too great. Many of the buildings have been reconstructed on the original site in New Philadelphia, OH.

Among the earliest Christians to separate from the Roman Catholic church were followers of John Hus, a Czech reformer, professor of philosophy and rector at the University of Prague. Although Hus was condemned as a heretic and burned at the stake, his spirit continued through the Moravian Church, or *Unitas Fratrum* (the Unity of Brethren). The church's ministry was formalized in 1467, 100 years before the Anglican Church was established in England and 60 years before Martin Luther's reformation movement began in Germany.

The Moravian Church quickly flourished in Bohemia and Moravia (both now part of the Czech Republic). By 1517, it had at least 200,000 members in over 400 parishes. Nevertheless, as happened to many other religious groups who protested against the Roman Catholic clergy and hierarchy of that time, the Moravians suffered bitter persecution. Although they spread to Poland, they could not avoid the counter-reformation movement that took hold throughout Europe. With the added impact of the Thirty Years War (1618-1648), the Moravian Church nearly died out.

In the early 1700s, under the patronage of a German Count, Moravians found a new home in Saxony. As their community grew, they began once again to spread their ministry. Missionaries traveled to America in 1735 and attempted to settle in Savannah, Georgia. Here, however, they found themselves in the midst of colonial strife between warring Spain and England. Undeterred, they gave up their Georgia settlement, moved to Pennsylvania and in the 1740s established two new communities: Bethlehem and Nazareth. From there, they spread out to New Jersey and Maryland, creating frontier centers for their ministry, with particular emphasis on service to the Native Peoples. In the 1750s and 1760s, they established their first North Carolina settlements – Bethabara, Bethania and the main "Wachovia" town of Salem (now Winston-Salem). Then, as now, they stressed simple worship and Christian goodness, with the Bible as their rule of faith. The basic Moravian motto: "In essentials, unity; in nonessentials, liberty; and in all things, love."

Despite many trying times, the end result was significant. Widely admired for their piety and simplicity of life, the Moravians helped shape modern Protestantism. What started out as a small contingency in the New World now numbers 50,000 church members in 16 American states and two Canadian provinces.

DEDICATED MISSIONARIES

In the winter of 1752-1753, an expedition of Brethren from the Moravian Church set out from Pennsylvania to establish a new colony in a new region, North Carolina. Never mind that the season was cold, wet and probably quite snowy. Their goals took priority. They intended to expand the church's reach and to minister to the Native population. For their faith to be genuine, the Brethren believed, it must be "a faith that works," finding expression in day-to-day Christian deeds. The first North Carolina arrivals built a small village and farming community called Bethabara (meaning "house of passage" in Hebrew). Since the church intended to have a number of small settlements rather than one large one, Bethabara was just the beginning. Many in the group would continue on to found a series of new cities, conducting missionary work and expanding their numbers by setting an example for others to follow.

Old Salem Museums & Gardens

SEE MAP PAGE 15, LOCATION #14

Winston-Salem, North Carolina
Phone: toll-free (888) 653-7253
http://www.oldsalem.org

Both Europeans and enslaved African Americans once lived in this eighteenth-century Moravian town, centering their lives around work and worship. Their initial structures were simple half-timbered houses referred to as the First, Second, Third, Fourth and Fifth Houses. Single-family homes were added later along

with trade shops and community buildings such as the *Gemein Haus* (the Congregation House). A tavern was built on the outskirts of town so that "strangers" (non-Moravians) could be kept at a distance but still enjoy this peaceful haven and buy its handcrafted goods.

Salem, North Carolina, was the designated commercial and religious center of the Moravian region, Wachovia. Dating back to 1766, it was laid out in a grid pattern typical of other Moravian towns, with many of the key buildings situated around a central square. The gardens here were models of practicality and beauty. While they had to provide enough food for the household, each also expressed aesthetic sensibilities, with flowers tucked among the vegetables and herbs. Salem added a gravity-fed water system in 1778.

In 1950, when encroaching commercial growth threatened Salem's roots, a not-for-profit corporation was formed. Today, the historic district, which occupies 14 city blocks, has been restored to represent the period

from 1766 to the mid-1800s. Heritage plants are grown exclusively in more than 30 gardens. Majestic trees and fruit orchards reflect historic times. Even the streets and lighting are as authentic as possible to the period. While most of the nearly 100 restored buildings are private residences, 15 can be toured at your leisure. Costumed interpreters describe the life of Moravians and demonstrate the original trades, domestic activities and crafts. Spring, summer and holidays are especially busy with interesting visitor activities.

Be sure to also make time to explore the Museum of Early Southern Decorative Arts, the Old Salem Toy Museum and the Old Salem Children's Museum (a special history-oriented play place for children).

Visitor Center located at 900 Old Salem Road south of downtown Winston-Salem, NC. Open daily except major holidays. Admission charged.

▲ The 1769 Single Brothers' House (left), provided lodging and trade shops for single men in the community. On a tour, you can see the workshops, the large kitchen and dining room, the chapel (with its 1798 pipe organ built by David Tannenberg) and the business manager's quarters. Craftsmen work here today, demonstrating the original techniques of the potter, tinsmith, cabinetmaker and tailor.

◀ The bakery in Old Salem is always a favorite stopping place for visitors. Enjoy the smell of fresh-baked loaves of bread and buy a few tasty delights.

AFRICAN AMERICAN HISTORY IN SALEM

A self-guided walking tour brings to light Old Salem's complex history of enslaved African Americans, providing better documentation than is typical elsewhere. Like many of their Christian contemporaries in the eighteenth century, white Moravians believed slavery was an institution ordained by God. In the 1760s and 1770s, they began buying enslaved Africans to help build their community and practice various trades. Although these slaves comprised a small segment of the population, they contributed substantially to building the town even as they struggled to maintain lives of coherence and dignity. They converted to Christianity, were baptized into the Moravian Church and upon their deaths were buried side-by-side with whites in God's Acre, the Moravian graveyard. Things changed in the early 1800s when white Moravians began to adopt the racial viewpoints of their southern neighbors and to institute segregation. By 1816, African Americans had a separate cemetery at the edge of town and, in 1823, a small log church. In 1861, a large brick structure was completed next door. It would eventually be called St. Philips Church and serve its African American congregation until 1952. Today visitors can tour the cemetery, reconstructed log church and restored brick church.

THE CATHOLICS

While Protestants were actively colonizing the eastern side of the continent, Spanish Catholics were focused on creating mission communities in the southern regions, from Florida to California, and French Catholics were building churches wherever their people could finally settle. In contrast, English Catholics kept a

▶ Dating from the mid-1700s, a few mission frescos (paintings made in wet plaster) have survived. The intriguing depiction of the sun shown here can be seen on the convento ceiling at Nuestra Señora de la Purísima Concepción de Acuña (Mission Concepción) in San Antonio, TX.

relatively low profile at first, wanting to avoid the anti-Catholic sentiment that flourished in Britain. Ironically, the mainstream of Catholic life in America emerged from the minority Catholics residing in English colonies, rather than from the Spanish or French. Undoubtedly, an important factor was the election of John Carroll from Maryland as the first Roman Catholic bishop of the United States in 1789 and as archbishop in 1808.

Spanish Missions of the Southeast

The first known Spanish missions in America were founded in Florida and Georgia beginning in the 1520s. Most were little more than a church in a Native village, but a few were large mission communities. Among them was impressive Mission San Luis de Apalachee in what

is now Tallahassee, Florida. Built in the mid-1600s, it was part of a powerful Spanish-Indian alliance involving about 7,500 people. It was burned in 1704 as inhabitants fled an English raid. However, the church, Council House and other structures have been reconstructed. See http://www.missionsanluis.org

Spanish Missions of Texas

During the 1600s and 1700s, Franciscan friars founded a network of missions in Texas. Some are now mere ruins or have disappeared completely, their locations remembered by historical markers. Others, such as three missions in El Paso, have been changed.

San Antonio had the largest concentration of missions in America, and the five clustered here are relatively well preserved National Historic Landmarks. Created primarily to strengthen Spain's influence and secure vast land claims, the following were established along the San Antonio River:

San Antonio de Valero (The Alamo) – 1718
300 Alamo Plaza, across from Rivercenter Mall

San José y San Miguel de Aguayo – 1720
6701 San Jose Drive, east of Mission Parkway

Nuestra Señora de la Purísima Concepción de Acuña – 1731
807 Mission Road, south of I-10

San Juan Capistrano – 1731
9101 Graf Road, north of I-410, west of I-37

San Francisco de la Espada – 1731
10040 Espada Road, south of I-410

These missions flourished for decades and then declined as inadequate military support, disease and Indian hostilities took their toll. The Alamo became a

---

MISSION INDIANS

Wherever one hears about Spanish missions – California, New Mexico, Texas, Georgia, Florida – questions arise. Why did the Franciscans give their lives to bring Catholicism and Spanish culture to the Native Peoples? Did they truly want to save Indian souls? Or were they, like so many others, seeking power? Religious conversion of indigenous peoples was very challenging. Although it is true that some missions were happy places, others were not. The Pueblo Indians in New Mexico staged a revolt, killing several missionaries and forcing others to flee, before finally accepting the presence of Catholic churches. Texas Indians apparently joined the missions voluntarily but soon became disillusioned; a number ran away and were forcibly returned or came back because the missions provided much-needed food. The California Indians were particularly resistant. Many who disobeyed mission rules were publicly humiliated; the most difficult were flogged, jailed or even executed; those who escaped were hunted down, captured and returned. By the 1790s, some California missions actually needed military might to persuade new "converts" to participate in mission life.

shrine after the Texas war for independence. The other four became part of San Antonio Missions National Historical Park, along with Rancho de las Cabras (the Mission Espada ranch outside of Floresville, Texas).

Spanish Missions of California

In the 1760s, religious leaders in Spain insisted that the California Indians needed to be instructed in the Catholic faith. The King agreed – not because of his religious faith but because he could use Catholic missions as a power play in Europe, demonstrating his intentions to make California a bastion of Spanish authority and influence. In July 1769, Father Junipero Serra and his contingent began establishing a series of 21 California mission communities on a northern route from San Diego, one long day's walk apart.

Theirs was not an easy task. They had traveled about 2,000 miles to California, suffering major hardships along the way. Shortly after arriving, they were attacked by Native Peoples. They moved to another location, but Native relations remained poor. Not a single Indian was

baptized during the first year. In addition, malnutrition and starvation threatened Spanish survival. But finally, local Indians agreed to be Christianized. Under the direction of the padres, they built unique and beautiful church complexes and devoted their lives to creating the prosperous economy at the center of mission life.

Little did the Catholics or their king realize that in just 65 years, Spanish authority would be gone from California, and the mission system would pass out of existence. Much of what remains from this time has been restored, at least in part. In geographic order, the

California missions include the following:

San Diego de Alcalá in northeast San Diego – 1769

San Luis, Rey de Francia on a hill in San Luis Rey – 1798

San Juan Capistrano in San Juan Capistrano – 1776

San Gabriel Arcángel in San Gabriel – 1771

San Fernando, Rey de España in San Fernando – 1797

San Buenaventura in Ventura – 1782

Santa Bárbara, Virgen y Mártir in Santa Barbara – 1786

Santa Inés, Virgen y Mártir in Solvang – 1804

La Purísima Concepción northeast of Lompoc – 1787

San Luis, Obispo de Tolosa in San Luis Obispo – 1772

San Miguel Arcángel north of Paso Robles – 1797

San Antonio de Padua southwest of King City – 1771

Nuestra Señora de la Soledad south of Soledad – 1791

San Carlos Borroméo de Carmelo in Carmel – 1770

San Juan Bautista in San Juan Bautista – 1797

Santa Cruz (half-size replica only) in Santa Cruz – 1791

Santa Clara de Asís in Santa Clara – 1777

San José in Fremont – 1797

San Francisco de Asís (Mission Dolores) San Francisco – 1776

San Rafael Arcángel in San Rafael – 1817

San Francisco Solano in Sonoma – 1823

▲ The restored altar at La Purísima Concepción has retained its early California authenticity. Striking folk art designs and faux marble textures showcase three exceptional statues.

◄ San Antonio de Padua was a particularly successful mission. By 1830, it reportedly had 8,000 cattle and 12,000 sheep; large crop harvests; and thriving wine and basket-making industries. To see the restored mission, take Jolon Road (G14) about 1½ miles west of King City, CA. Travel 18 miles south to Mission Creek Road, through Fort Hunter Liggett Military Reservation, and follow the signs.

Mission San José y San Miguel de Aguayo

SEE MAP PAGE 19, LOCATION #18

San Antonio, Texas
Phone: (210) 932-1001
http://www.nps.gov/saan/visit/MissionSanJose.htm

in the 1920s and 1930s. As a result, you will find much to enjoy. The sculpted "Rose Window," circa 1780, is considered to be one of the finest examples of Spanish Colonial ornamentation in America. Other carved stonework, especially around the church entryway, also is impressive. What's more, you can see the buttress-supported granary, reconstructed grist mill, defensive walls and Indian quarters. The restorations were thoughtful, and much was left alone, enabling visitors to feel the magic of the past. Be sure to explore the museum, with its authentic and replicated artifacts. Take advantage of guided tours, movies and demonstrations as well as the Junior Ranger Program for children.

Located at 6701 San Jose Drive in San Antonio, TX. Open daily except Thanksgiving, Dec. 25 and Jan. 1. Free.

▲ A priest describing Mission San José wrote in 1778: "It is, in truth, the first mission in America...in point of beauty, plan, and strength...there is not a presidio along the entire frontier line that can compare with it." Amidst such beauty, local Indians trained to become Spanish Catholic citizens.

▶ The famous sacristy Rose Window has no stained glass. It is remarkable for its ornate, easily viewed exterior carvings.

▶ Many of the stone artworks, including this restored detail near the front door, remain as a testimony to the talent and skill of the Spanish artisans and their Indian apprentices.

With its 12,000-square-foot visitor center and exceptional structures, Mission San José is the major orientation point for visiting the San Antonio Missions National Historical Park. We highly recommend visiting all four historic missions – San José, Concepción, San Juan and Espada. You might also take a tour of Rancho de las Cabras near Floresville (first Saturday of each month).

Mission San José was a major social and cultural center founded by Spanish padres in 1720. At its height, 300 Indians were receiving instruction here, not only in the Catholic faith but also in European lifeways, with the goal of becoming Spanish citizens. Together with the missionary, they built a rich community sustained by vast farm fields and sizable livestock herds. San José was a model among Texas missions.

After Spain relinquished its Texas territory to Mexico in 1821, the mission period ended here, and San José fell into ruin. Thankfully, though, the San Antonio Conservation Society and our Federal Government, among others, stepped in to restore portions of the mission

MISSION MILL AND ACEQUIA

The first grist mill in Texas was built at Mission San José in the 1790s, as part of an effort to expand the maize-based Indian diet to include wheat. Serving the surrounding Spanish settlements as well, it helped to establish Mission San José as an important contributor to the community's growth and prosperity. The acequia (irrigation ditch) provided water to power the mill wheel that turned the grinding stone. Today, recycled water is used to operate the mill, which was rebuilt on the Spanish Colonial site in the 1930s. (A remnant of the original 270-year-old acequia, with its dam and aqueduct, can be seen a few miles away at Mission Espada.)

The Alamo

SEE MAP PAGE 19, LOCATION #18
San Antonio, Texas
Phone: (210) 225-1391
http://www.thealamo.org

The legend of The Alamo has been burned into our childhood memories, made famous in numerous songs, books and films. A group of 189 men – primarily frontier settlers and native Texians – stood strong inside the mission walls, holding out for 13 days against Mexican General Antonio López de Santa Anna and an estimated 4,000-5,000 soldiers. From February 23 to March 6, 1836, the Texian force led by Colonel William Travis and Colonel James Bowie defended their position despite low supplies and limited ammunition. In the end, all the men were killed, including the famous frontiersman and congressman from Tennessee, Davy Crockett. But their heroic resistance galvanized Texians. Six weeks later, led by General Sam Houston and shouting "Remember The Alamo," they surprised and quickly defeated General Santa Anna's troops in the last important battle for Texas' independence from Mexico.

To modern Texans and non-Texans alike, the Alamo symbolizes the courage and sacrifice necessary to achieve liberty and independence. Regrettably, however, little of the original mission-fort has survived to this day.

Only the chapel and the Long Barrack remain relatively intact. During the battle, the mission (now referred to as The Shrine) was used as the officer's quarters, powder magazine and artillery position. Earthen ramps were built to raise the cannon to window level. The Long Barrack served as infantry and artillery quarters. The remainder of the mission deteriorated and is now covered by modern Alamo Plaza and Alamo Street.

If you are like millions of other people from around the world, you will want to visit The Alamo. Interpreters are stationed throughout the site, eager to share information and tell the legendary tales of this powerful place. It is a moving experience.

Located at 300 Alamo Plaza in the heart of San Antonio, TX, near the famous River Walk gardens, shops and restaurants. Open daily except major holidays. Donations appreciated.

▲ Undoubtedly the most famous former mission in America, The Alamo stands as a major symbol of the struggle for independence.

◀ The Alamo façade still boasts the rich carvings which were so characteristic of Texas missions. Highly skilled artisans came from Spain to create such classic beauty.

THE SPIRIT LIVES ON

Spurred by events at The Alamo, the new Lone Star Republic of Texas was formed in 1836. General Sam Houston became its President, having received 80 percent of the 6,000 votes cast. Because Houston was an old friend of Andrew Jackson, then President of the United States of America, speculation ran high that Texas would not be alone for long. Yet, it existed as a country from 1836 to 1845 and became the nation's twenty-eighth state only with great effort. The annexation of Texas was a highly contentious subject. The South wanted Texas to join America, but the North and East bitterly objected because Texas allowed slavery. Across the seas, France and Britain also wanted Texas to remain on its own, fearing that annexation would increase America's power and enable it to soon control the Southwest. Texas had its own concerns, beset by serious money problems, the threat of another Mexican war, and fears that its alliance with England might dissolve at a critical time. Skilled political action and foreign diplomacy somehow turned the tide.

Presidio La Bahia

SEE MAP PAGE 19, LOCATION #16
Goliad, Texas
Phone: (361) 645-3752
http://www.presidiolabahia.org

▲ A cannon believed to have been used during the Texas Revolution of 1835-1836 was excavated from the grounds of Presidio La Bahia and returned to its rightful place on the fort wall in the mid-1930s.

Established in 1749, Presidio La Bahia and its nearby mission complex is one of the few remaining examples of the partnership which existed between the Spanish Crown and the Catholic Church during the colonization of the New World. While supporting Catholic settlement, the fort had a more critical role: guarding the Spanish interests from Indian and French attacks.

Strategically located, Presidio La Bahia was the most fought over fort in Texas history. Spanish, Mexican and Texian soldiers all garrisoned within its fortified walls, and nine flags flew overhead at different times. Also known as Fort Defiance, the Presidio is an important part of both Texas and Catholic heritage. It is managed by the Catholic Diocese of Victoria, Texas, and has been restored to its 1836 appearance based on historic documents and archaeological evidence.

Our Lady of Loreto Chapel, erected in the quadrangle of the fort in 1779, is one of the oldest churches in America and one of the few which still has its "groin vaulted" ceiling. The Chapel was built for use by soldiers and Spanish settlers living in the nearby town of La Bahia. It became the place where the first Declaration of Texas Independence was signed. It also served as a private residence for a short while. Today, the exterior is authentic, but much of the interior has changed. In a niche above the entrance, you can see a statue of Our Lady of Loreto created by Lincoln Borglum, one of the key sculptors of Mount Rushmore.

The museum complex, with its original rock construction and high wall, consists of the officer's quarters, Chapel and enlisted men's barracks. Special annual events include the Goliad Massacre-Fort Defiance Living History Program which re-enacts the 1836 "Battle of Coleto Creek" fought by Texians under Colonel James W. Fannin's command against Mexicans led by General José de Urrea. It relives the sad but heroic tale of over 300 Texians who surrendered, were held captive for several days in Our Lady of Loreto Chapel and, except for a few who managed to escape, were executed. Re-enactors, faithful to the period, bring these important events back to life.

Located a mile south of Goliad, TX, on US 77A/183. Open daily except major holidays. Admission charged.

MISSION ESPÍRITU SANTO

As part of a larger plan to colonize the Texas frontier, two Catholic complexes were built near Presidio La Bahia. The first was Mission Nuestra Señora del Espíritu Santo de Zúñiga, which was protected by a high wall and two manned cannons. Established in 1749, this mission brought numerous Native Peoples into its fold and trained them in the ways of Mexican vaqueros. As a result, it was able to raise 15,000 head of cattle in one three-year period to feed not only its own people but also Spanish forces as far away as Louisiana. The second complex was Mission Nuestra Señora del Rosario, apparently constructed to separate out the Karankawa Indians, whose cultural independence made them more difficult converts. Today, Mission Rosario is largely undisturbed ruins. Mission Espíritu Santo was restored in the 1930s by the Civilian Conservation Corps and refurbished by the Texas Parks and Wildlife Department in the 1970s. It is now the centerpiece of Goliad State Park, about a mile down the road from Presidio La Bahia.

Mission San Juan Capistrano

SEE MAP PAGE 23, LOCATION #20
San Juan Capistrano, California
Phone: (949) 234-1300
http://www.missionsjc.com

Probably the most famous of the Franciscan settlements in the West, "The Jewel of the Missions" was the seventh Spanish mission built in California. Its flower gardens and Moorish-influenced courtyard are exceptionally beautiful. In addition, the mission is the spring home for thousands of swallows which have migrated to the area in mid-March since long before the padres' arrival. Their return is celebrated March 19, the Feast of St. Joseph.

San Juan Capistrano has the distinction of being twice-founded. Originally dedicated on October 30, 1775, the site was abandoned eight days later, when word arrived that Mission San Diego de Alcalá had suffered a massive Indian attack. Leaving the Mission cross in place and burying the church bells for safe keeping, the Franciscans returned to San Diego to help restore order and rebuild that Mission. A year passed before the second founding, when Father Junipero Serra and his group arrived on November 1, 1776, the Feast of All Saints.

Sadly, natural disaster took its toll in 1812, when the earthquake that destroyed La Purísima Concepción (see page 115) wreaked havoc here as well. Forty neophytes were killed, and the huge church which had taken many years to build was leveled in minutes. The missionaries did not rebuild. By 1833, when the Mission system was secularized, San Juan Capistrano seemed destined to fall into total ruin. But then in 1865,

President Abraham Lincoln signed documents which returned Mission ownership to the Catholic Church. It was one of his last acts as President.

San Juan Capistrano was finally restored to its present glory beginning in the early 1900s. It has had three churches: the Great Stone Church, in ruins but still showing a section of wall and a single dome; the relatively new seven-domed parish church, built in the style of the fallen church, with its 104-foot bell tower; and the 1778 Serra's Chapel, where Father Serra said Mass. A self-guided tour of the 10-acre mission site is an exciting opportunity to see numerous artifacts and interesting buildings. Museum rooms feature the Native American, Spanish and Mexican periods of mission history. Living History days are held on the second Saturday of each month. In addition, the mission has a number of art events, lectures and re-enactments.

Located in San Juan Capistrano, CA, off of I-5, just 2 blocks west of the SR 74 junction, on Ortega Highway. Open daily except major holidays. Admission charged.

▲ In the late 1700s, when San Juan Capistrano was a thriving mission, the grounds were used for housing animals, growing crops and doing craftwork. As you can see, things have changed since then. Regardless, the flowers now grown here are spectacular and make visiting the mission a special treat.

◄ The chapel's Baroque altar, shipped from Barcelona in about 1806, dates to the seventeenth or eighteenth century. The reredos located behind the altar is comprised of 196 parts, houses five handsome statues and is spectacularly covered with gold leaf.

MISSION ARCHITECTURE

What began as simple structures ultimately became unique expressions of the resident Franciscans. In contrast to the Texas complexes, California missions were made of adobe bricks and stone, whitewashed inside and out, and the roofs were hewn timber covered with thatch or clay tiles. Roman arches lined many arcades. Fountains graced many courtyards and gardens. Artisans added colorful embellishments, and the Catholic Church contributed fine religious articles. Some missions had bell towers; others had bell walls. At Santa Barbara, the church façade was reminiscent of an ancient Latin temple. At San Carlos Borroméo de Carmelo, a Moorish dome topped the church, and a Moorish doorway led to the mortuary chapel. At San Juan Capistrano, the ceiling of the Great Stone Church had six domes. At San Gabriel Arcángel, the church had a mosque-like appearance. So distinctive were the 21 missions, they inspired the California Mission architectural style of home building, which flourished from 1890-1920.

Mission San Fernando, Rey de España

SEE MAP PAGE 23, LOCATION #16
San Fernando, California
Phone: (818) 361-0186
http://www.missionsofcalifornia.org/missions/mission17.html

▲ The reconstructed church remains true to its Spanish heritage but is no longer the simple place of worship it once was. The exterior is a replica of the original 1806 building. The gold-leafed altar, carved in Spain in 1687, replaced a modest one in 1991.

▶ Old building techniques were used for the reconstruction. The adobe church walls, for example, are seven feet thick at the base and taper to five feet at the top. The nearby fountain is a copy of the original (in the park across the street).

▶ The convento was restored to represent the early 1800s. The large reception room shown here still has its original hand-forged door locks and bolts as well as its iron window gratings.

This was a mission for travelers. Built in 1797, it was specifically situated to relieve the long journey between Mission San Gabriel and Mission San Buenaventura. By 1822, it had a two-story convento – 243 feet long and 50 feet wide – which served as a hospice, or hotel, as well as the missionary quarters. Fronted by a colonnade with 21 arches, this was a beautiful, peaceful place to stay.

Even the Native Peoples seemed happy at Mission San Fernando. Nearly 1,000 neophytes (Christianized Indians) were housed here, and many others came to work from nearby villages. While learning both Spanish and Catholic lifeways, they kept busy crafting shoes and other leather items, weaving cloth and blankets, making tallow and soap, working the fields, producing wine and olive oil, caring for the livestock, and building a complex of sturdy adobe buildings with red-tile roofs. At one time, San Fernando had 30,000 grapevines and nearly 22,000 head of cattle, sheep and horses. It became wealthy satisfying the needs of travelers, surrounding settlements and other California missions.

After secularization, however, the mission complex fell prey to careless outsiders. Roof tiles were removed by locals for use in their buildings, leaving the adobe walls unprotected. (Only the tall convento was spared.) Vandals, following a rumor that the padres had prospected for gold, dug up the church floor looking for buried treasure. The church and hospice became a warehouse and stable; the central quadrangle became

a hog farm. Yet, somehow enough survived to allow San Fernando to become a church again in 1923. Since then, it has been restored to much of its early California glory.

The convento, located outside the quadrangle, is especially interesting, with its fully restored and finely furnished quarters and a museum of historic and replica artifacts. Ask about viewing the films depicting early mission life, which are shown in the theatre. Also cross the street to pretty Brand Park, where you can see the old soap works, original mission fountain (moved 30 feet from its first location) and water reservoir for the mission complex.

When planning your trip, keep in mind that Mission San Fernando is a very popular place for weddings. During summer months, you might prefer a weekday visit.

Located at 15151 San Fernando Mission Blvd. in Mission Hills, CA, within the triangle formed by I-5, I-405 and the Simi Valley Freeway (SR 118) north of Los Angeles. Take Sepulveda Blvd. north; turn right at San Fernando Mission Blvd. Open daily except Thanksgiving and December 25. Admission charged.

La Purísima Mission State Historic Park

SEE MAP PAGE 23, LOCATION #13

Lompoc vicinity (northeast), California
Phone: (805) 733-3713
http://www.lapurisimamission.org

La Purísima Concepción was founded in December 1787 but destroyed by an earthquake 25 years later. Determined to build an even grander replacement, the Franciscan padres gathered their then-homeless band of neophytes and moved to a new site four miles to the northeast. Here, they built a huge mission complex. Designed to resist future earthquakes, the adobe walls were 4 ½ feet thick, and the southwest wall (which

the missionaries believed might be particularly vulnerable) was reinforced with a stone buttress. This mission also had several small courtyards rather than the large quadrangle that was typical of other Catholic missions. Water was brought from springs in the hills three miles away via a large irrigation system of aqueducts, clay pipes, reservoirs and dams.

Life here was good until 1824, when word reached the neophytes that one of their fellow Indians had been killed and another had been flogged at Mission Santa Inés. Furious, the La Purísima Indians

revolted, took over their own mission and held it captive for almost a month. The Mexican Governor sent more than 100 soldiers from Monterey to recapture La Purísima Concepción. This force succeeded, but 17 Indians died in the battle, several of their leaders were later put to death, and others were imprisoned. Afterwards, as if nothing had gone wrong, the mission returned to its accustomed routine, focused on religion and managing productive ranch lands.

Approximately 1,000 Chumash Indian neophytes lived on the mission property, taking care of as many as 20,000 cattle and sheep as well as hundreds of horses, mules, burros and other livestock. When secularization brought an end to the mission system in 1833, the Indians left, and the mission fell into ruin.

Still, that wasn't the end of the story. Much of La Purísima Concepción was restored to its former splendor by the CCC. Visitors are welcome to tour the authentic, fully furnished buildings and gardens. Volunteer docents, assuming the roles of mission inhabitants of the 1820s, gladly share the mission's history, tend the gardens and practice a variety of traditional crafts. In addition, special visitor activities are held throughout the year – including Mission Life, Mountain Men, Purísima's People, Village Days, Garden Tours, Candlelight Tours and more.

▲ All around the grounds are signs of everyday mission life. Among them are carts for hauling produce, outdoor cooking areas used to render animal fat, an olive press and corrals holding a variety of farm animals.

◄ A military presence was necessary to keep the mission secure. Several rooms are fully outfitted to depict the Spartan life of mission soldiers.

REMARKABLE RESTORATION

In 1935 at La Purísima Concepción, the Civilian Conservation Corps (CCC) began one of the most complete mission restorations. Their work was based on painstaking research and incorporated the ruins of the old mission complex into the new structures. The monastery building alone required the molding of 110,000 adobe bricks, 32,000 roof tiles and 10,000 floor tiles. Encompassing 1,928 acres, La Purísima is now part of California's state parks system and is a pleasure to visit. Ten buildings and part of the water system, including an historic aqueduct, have been restored. A five-acre garden shows native and domestic plants typical of a mission. Burros, horses, longhorn cattle, sheep and goats are corralled nearby. This re-created environment represents the most important portion of the original 300,000-acre La Purísima Concepción property.

Located about 2 miles northeast of Lompoc, CA, near Highway 246 at Mission Gate and Purísima Road. Open daily except major holidays. Small admission charged.

Mission San Juan Bautista

SEE MAP PAGE 23, LOCATION #19

San Juan Bautista, California
Phone: (831) 623-2127
http://www.oldmissionsjb.org

▲ Mission Indians were very fond of music. At San Juan Bautista, Fray Estevan Tapis created music sheets with color-coded notes to guide choirs of Native singers. In addition, a barrel organ, which played a few songs when the handle was turned, was brought outside to enchant the Indians and help inspire their conversion.

▶ The 40-inch stone baptismal font (larger one in back) was sculpted by California Indians from a huge block of sandstone. Like its replacement (in front), it is worn smooth on the rim – testament to the thousands of Indians baptized in the mission whose patron saint is John the Baptist.

The seemingly zealous determination of Catholic padres in 1797 California is at times baffling. While these highly religious men unknowingly founded Mission San Juan Bautista on a great earthquake fault, one would think that the frequency of the quakes – sometimes as many as six per day during that unusually active period – would have led them to relocate. Big cracks appeared in the ground, and some of the adobe walls of their new buildings split from top to bottom. Yet, the padres ignored these hazards and began building their church on this site a few years later. Theirs came to be the largest church in the California chain of missions, but it was doomed to be damaged by earthquakes and partially abandoned after the violent 1906 quake which overwhelmed much of central California. Somehow, it survived and has since been restored. The church also has been partially reinforced for seismic protection.

Like other mission churches in California, San Juan Bautista was secularized in the 1830s but later returned to the Catholics by federal decree. It remains an active Parish; so time your visit accordingly. You will want to enter the church and Guadalupe Chapel as well as the furnished period rooms and the convent wing, which contains relics, artifacts and manuscripts. Still visible in the church are the footprints of animals who walked on newly made floor tiles as they dried in the sun long ago. The original baptismal font sculpted out of native sandstone is still here, measuring nearly four feet in diameter. Behind the altar is the dramatic reredos designed and built by Fray Estevan Tapis and Felipe Arroyo del la Cuesta. (It was decorated by a Boston sailor who jumped ship on the California coast in 1816.) Wonderful old statues and Spanish Colonial paintings have

been restored. You will even see a little hole in the blue side door of Guadalupe Chapel, where cats entered to catch mice. Another door leads to the cemetery, where over 4,000 Indians and Europeans were buried.

Located in downtown San Juan Bautista, CA, just off State Highway 156, about 3 miles east of US 101. Open daily except major holidays. Admission charged.

SAN JUAN BAUTISTA STATE HISTORICAL PARK

The property surrounding the mission is a California State Historical Park. It preserves a number of interesting structures, each with exhibits or vignettes depicting early California history. Included are the Plaza Hotel, Plaza Hall (home of Angelo Zanetta), livery stable with a large collection of carriages, blacksmith shop, Settler's Cabin, San Juan Jail, Castro-Breen Adobe (once the headquarters of José Castro, governor of Alta California, and later the home of the Patrick Breen family) and several gardens. On the first Saturday of each month, early California comes alive with Living History, and the Hotel bar is open for a cold root beer or sarsaparilla. On Father's Day weekend in June, the park holds an Early Day Celebration and Victorian Ball.

THE JEWS

Jewish immigration to Colonial America was a gradual process. Neither coordinated nor on a grand scale, it occurred as opportunities presented themselves to individuals or small groups of people living in Europe, South America and the Caribbean. When they arrived, Jews tended to settle in cosmopolitan port cities where people of diverse backgrounds lived side-by-side. As their numbers grew, they formed synagogue-communities – first in New York, New York, and in Newport, Rhode Island. Similar synagogue-communities followed in Savannah, Georgia; Charleston, South Carolina; Philadelphia, Pennsylvania; and other major American cities. Here, people of the Jewish faith could come together and enjoy both freedom of religious expression and economic opportunity. This is not to say that life in America was free of prejudice. Like numerous others, Jews still had to fight for their rights on many levels – social, political and economic as well as religious. The real turning point came after the American Revolution, when the new nation committed itself definitively to the principles of freedom, especially religious freedom, and the separation of church and state.

The beginning of Jewish community life in America dates back to 1654 when a boatload of 23 Jews arrived, after a series of mishaps, in what was then the Dutch port of New Amsterdam (later the English colony of New York). They came from Recife, Brazil, a Dutch

ETHNIC OR RELIGIOUS?

Jewish Americans came to America from all over the world. Yet, they tend to be viewed as an ethnic group rather than a religious group. It's an easy conclusion – many have established close-knit communities; they practice similar customs and celebrate common holidays; and they are united by their history and social practices. Furthermore, they consider one nation to be their spiritual homeland: Israel. And their religion, Judaism, is the religion of only one people: the Jews. But we shouldn't be misled. From a cultural perspective, people of Jewish faith differ significantly. Most Ashkenazi Jews trace their origins to central and eastern Europe, and several of their religious traditions are unique to them. Sephardic Jews have origins that vary widely from Spain and Portugal, to Arabia and Persia, to the Middle East and northern Africa. Other groups are descended from Jewish communities in Ethiopia and India. At the same time, Jewish Americans follow differing branches of Judaism – Orthodox, Reform, Conservative.

colony which had just been captured by the Portuguese. Four years later, the first Jews arrived in Newport, Rhode Island. They sent favorable reports to other Jews, who apparently had been living in Curaçao in the West Indies. Soon, 15 families joined them. The third Jewish congregation began in Savannah, Georgia, where 42 Jews arrived in 1733 primarily from Portugal, which was suffering through the last stages of the Spanish Inquisition, and also from Germany.

In those early years, Jews worshipped in private homes or rented quarters, restricted by colonial rules and their own modest means to keep their faith to themselves. Not until 1730 was the first Jewish house of worship permitted to be built in America. Known then as the Spanish and Portuguese Synagogue of New York City – the Mill Street Synagogue – it has been replaced several times by grander structures and is today known as Shearith Israel. Regrettably, the original historic site, all but forgotten, is now a parking garage.

In general, Jewish settlement in America continued slowly. The city of Portsmouth, New Hampshire, is an interesting example. The first two Jews arrived from Prussia around 1780; but for several decades thereafter, apparently no others came. By the late 1880s, a nucleus of about 16 Jewish families lived in Portsmouth, and by 1912, the total had grown to about 38 families. Today, Strawbery Banke recaptures part of that past through Living History. (See *European Colonization*, page 84.)

▲ The Shapiro House at Strawbery Banke in Portsmouth, NH, was the home of Russian-Jewish immigrants. While it interprets Jewish life in the 1919s, it provides an interesting overview of how Jewish people historically blended into communities, setting up businesses, conducting religious services in private homes and, in this case, establishing their first synagogue in 1912 – in a building that was formerly a Methodist Church.

Touro Synagogue National Historic Site

SEE MAP PAGE 11, LOCATION #22

Newport, Rhode Island
Phone: (401) 847-4794
http://www.tourosynagogue.org

▲ In many ways, Touro Synagogue reflects the international character of America. The small but imposing Georgian-influenced structure was built of brick imported from England, in a style reminiscent of a synagogue in Holland but with added features from synagogues in Spain and Portugal. It was designed by the preeminent colonial architect Peter Harrison, who was not Jewish.

▶ Around the corner from the Synagogue you will find the Colony House, which once served as Rhode Island's cultural and political center. This is where the Declaration of Independence was read aloud to rebellious citizens...where the British established a barrack while occupying Newport during the Revolutionary War... and where our French allies created a war hospital after helping to liberate the city.

For over 100 years, Jews in the New England seaport community of Newport, Rhode Island, worshipped in private homes. Their means were limited, and their congregation was relatively small. Finally in 1763, with funds contributed not only by their own members but also by Jewish congregations as far away as Amsterdam and London, they managed to construct one of the most distinguished buildings of eighteenth-century America. Today, their Touro Synagogue is the oldest Jewish house of worship in our nation.

Set at an angle to the street, the building is positioned so that the congregation faces Jerusalem. Its quiet exterior gives little hint of the elegance that awaits inside. So make time for the half-hour interpretive tour. Unescorted visitors are not allowed to enter Touro.

The synagogue chamber is a work of art. Ionic columns support a mezzanine gallery, and Corinthian columns rise above them to support the domed ceiling. Massive brass candelabra glisten overhead. Everywhere, the woodwork is extraordinary. At the east end is the Holy Ark containing the hand-lettered Torah Scrolls, which record the Five Books of Moses, the source of Jewish faith. In the center of the room is an elevated platform where the Rabbi reads the Torah.

Located at 85 Touro Street near Washington Square in downtown Newport, RI. Visitor information at gift shop on corner of Spring and Touro streets. Guided tours offered Sunday-Friday from May-October; Friday and Sunday rest of year. No tours on Saturday or Jewish holidays. Proper dress is required. Fee for tours.

Other Historic Hill Attractions

To better understand the multi-cultural Newport where many Jewish settlers lived, stroll through Historic Hill. Excellent signage points out key landmarks, including Georgian mansions and public buildings as well as the homes of colonial working people and African American entrepreneurs. In Newport, as was true elsewhere, the Jewish people blended into the community. Many of them were merchants with access to worldwide trade networks. Along with a sizable population of Quakers, they helped transform Newport from an agricultural outpost to a cosmopolitan city.

Several guided tours are available. For details, see http://www.newporthistorical.org/tours.htm or call the Museum of Newport History at (401) 841-8770.

ONE MAN'S IMPACT

Beginning in the late 1200s, when tolerance of non-Catholics reached a low in Europe, a law forbade Jews from living on English lands. This continued for hundreds of years. Then, in a twist of fate during the 1650s, a Rabbi in Holland took exception to the law. His argument was persuasive. If there were no Jews in England or its colonies, the Messiah could not come. (According to Biblical teachings, this cosmic event requires the spread of Jewish people throughout the world.) The Dutch Rabbi petitioned Oliver Cromwell, lord protector of England, to cancel the anti-Jewish law and readmit Jews to English lands. Whether Cromwell was persuaded by the religious argument or was more mindful of the economic value of Anglo-Jewish relations, he softened his position. No official decree was issued, but the doors were opened, and Jewish immigration to the "New World" increased. Today, nearly half of all Jews live in America.

THE MORMONS

What is commonly called the Mormon faith is actually a group of roughly 200 sects spawned by the Latter Day Saint movement founded in 1830. Although these sects have their roots in the teachings of prophet Joseph Smith Jr., their doctrines, practices and cultures vary enough that some do not accept the designation "Mormon." An estimated 13 million worldwide are members of the Church of Jesus Christ of Latter-day Saints, or "LDS Church," headquartered in Salt Lake City, Utah. Another 250,000 worldwide are members of the Community of Christ, formerly known as the Reorganized Church of Jesus Christ of Latter-day Saints or "RLDS Church," headquartered in Independence, Missouri. These are the largest organizations. Many of the smaller denominations operate separately.

Mormonism began in western New York when Joseph Smith Jr. was a teenager. According to Smith, he experienced a series of religious visions telling him that the original teachings of God had been lost or greatly altered by other Christians. In several of those visions, an angel showed him an ancient religious history and charged him to translate it by revelation. In 1830, he published the Book of Mormon and began to actively preach a new Christianity. The views he shared were both persuasive and highly controversial in a nation filled with Protestants and Catholics convinced of the righteousness of their own Christian beliefs.

Smith and his followers left New York when a revelation instructed them to "go to the Ohio," where new converts had been baptized. From there, they traveled to Missouri but were forced by unfriendly neighbors to move. In 1839, they founded the city of Nauvoo, Illinois, and made it the Mormon headquarters. Here, for a brief period, both the city and church were able to flourish. American converts flocked to Nauvoo,

and an estimated 4,000 others joined them from England, Ireland and Wales. However, rapid population growth, outsider fears of political domination by the LDS Church and misunderstandings about Mormon beliefs sparked intense hostility among non-Mormons living nearby. In 1844, Smith was murdered.

A long period of disorganization and dispersion followed Smith's death, and the body of the church fragmented into a number of denominations. Two main branches finally emerged. They included the LDS members who traveled over a thousand miles to what is now Utah, led by Brigham Young, plus a large group which remained in the Midwest and eventually branched off into the RLDS, led by Joseph Smith's son.

▲ Heritage Village, built on a hillside overlooking Salt Lake City, gives visitors a very real sense of what life must have been like in early Utah. Located in This is the Place Heritage Park, it is comprised of historic and replica buildings and populated by interpreters wearing mid-1800s attire.

SALT LAKE BOUND

Brigham Young and his followers left Nauvoo, Illinois, in early 1846, seeking a location remote enough to afford them sanctuary from a society which seemed unable to accept their different religious perspective. The group got no farther than Council Bluffs, Iowa, where they were met by U.S. Army officers. Our nation was at war with Mexico, and America needed recruits in California. A contract was negotiated, and 500 of the youngest, most capable men headed off to the battlefield. Their fellow Latter-day pioneers would suffer through a harsh winter without them, and the men would arrive in southern California too late to fight. Most families and friends ultimately did manage to reunite. In the meantime, on July 23, 1847, a small vanguard from the main group of settlers entered the Salt Lake Valley. They were home at last! Within two hours, they began plowing and irrigating the land. Five acres were plowed that day; potatoes and other seeds were planted the next morning. Later that same day, July 24, 1847, Brigham Young and the remaining 147 settlers arrived – an event now celebrated as Pioneer Day. By winter, 1,700 Mormons had settled in Salt Lake City.

Kirtland Historic Sites

SEE MAP PAGE 17, LOCATION #10

Kirtland, Ohio
Historic Kirtland – Phone: (440) 256-9805
http://www.lds.org/placestovisit/location/0,10634,3986-1-1-1,00.html
Kirtland Temple – Phone: (440) 256-1830
http://www.kirtlandtemple.org

▲ Kirtland Temple stood at the center of village life, serving more than 2,000 believers by 1838. Within a year, however, all but 100 church members had moved away with Joseph Smith Jr., seeking a community where they could worship in peace, free of anti-Mormon hostilities.

▶ The Whitneys, who were converts, offered several rooms in their store to serve as the home of Joseph Smith and his family. Here Smith received about 20 divine revelations that became part of the church's Doctrine and Covenants.

▶ At the reconstructed Kirtland ashery, you can learn how the nineteenth-century chemical plant produced a highly useful commodity from ordinary wood ash.

completely stocked Newel K. Whitney general store (where Smith lived), the furnished Whitney home, an operating sawmill, a schoolhouse, the only restored ashery in America and the John Johnson Inn (now an exhibit area). There's much to learn and enjoy here.

Kirtland Temple

Built from 1833 to 1836, this handsome building was the first house of worship for believers of Mormonism. Among its most noteworthy features: both the main floor worship hall and second floor education center have two sets of richly carved pulpits, at the front and rear. In the pews, seat backs can be shifted forward or backward to face either set of pulpits. The Visitor Center includes museum exhibits and a video presentation.

One of the best ways to understand both The Church of Jesus Christ of Latter-day Saints and the Community of Christ is to visit the city of Kirtland, Ohio, where Joseph Smith Jr. first settled after leaving New York.

Historic Kirtland

Recalling the period from 1831-1838, this meticulously restored and reconstructed portion of the original village includes an exceptional introductory film and a guided tour of the

Located in Kirtland, OH, just east of Cleveland. Take I-90 to SR 306. Visitor Center for Historic Kirtland at 7800 Kirtland-Chardon Road. Open daily year-round. Visitor Center for Kirtland Temple at 7809 Joseph Street. Open year-round – daily from Mar.-Dec.; weekends Jan.-Feb. Both closed major holidays. No admission charged. Small preservation fee for Temple tour.

POTASH AND PEARL ASH

What we so blithely throw away today from our home fires – wood ash – was once a prized trade item. From it came potash (a dry lye) and pearl ash (baked, purified potash). Both were used in producing glass, soap and saltpeter (for gunpowder). With the Industrial Revolution, their biggest application was in textile manufacturing. Companies known as asheries dotted the countryside, making pearl ash from potash supplied by homesteads or from ash made in their own kilns. So important was this pearl ash that England refused to allow Colonial America to sell it outside of the British realm. After America gained its independence, pearl ash remained a chief export item well into the 1800s. Even the U.S. Patent Office wanted to protect this commodity, awarding its very first patent to a new method of making pearl ash. Only when sodium hydroxide, also known as lye or caustic soda, became available did the need for potash and pearl ash decrease.

Historic Nauvoo

SEE MAP PAGE 17, LOCATION #13

Nauvoo, Illinois
Phone: toll-free (888) 453-6434
http://www.historicnauvoo.net

Nauvoo, which means "beautiful place" in Hebrew, was the Mormon headquarters for roughly seven years. After thousands left for Salt Lake City, it was re-settled by the French, German and Swiss, who planted the area with extensive vineyards and produced fine wines. In the mid-1900s, descendants of the early Mormons returned to Nauvoo to restore their ancestral community and rebuild their vandalized Temple. Over two dozen historic sites have been returned to their former stature and refurbished with period furnishings. Many are

staffed with volunteer guides, dressed in representative costumes, who gladly share a wealth of interesting facts. Other sites offer demonstrations of pioneer activities such as brick making, printing, blacksmithing, coopering, weaving and candle making. The following are just a few of the buildings you can tour:

EARLY POSTAL SERVICE

In the 1840s, letter writers went to great lengths to keep their postal costs down. The price was based on the number of pages sent as well as the distance traveled. This prompted many in Nauvoo to use a style known as "cross-writing," in which they wrote the first page in the normal fashion, from top to bottom, then rotated the paper sideways and wrote over their previous words – getting two pages for the price of one. There was also the question of who paid for the letter: the sender or the receiver. If payment was made in advance, there was no guarantee the letter would be delivered. If the recipient was responsible, the postman would deliver the letter in anticipation of payment. The recipient could decline the letter and not pay, but such a decision was difficult since no return address was shown. Prophet Joseph Smith liked receiving mail but stopped paying for deliveries when he began receiving criticisms from anti-Mormons – he saw no point in paying to be insulted.

▓ Mansion House, where Prophet Joseph Smith and his family lived and entertained guests.

▓ Brigham Young home, where the second president of the LDS Church lived very comfortably with his first wife, Mary Ann and their six children.

▓ Wilford Woodruff home, furnished with original belongings. After the Mormons moved to Utah, Woodruff became the fourth president of the LDS Church.

▓ Jonathan Browning Home and Gun Shop, which displays rifles, handguns and shotguns from the 1800s as well as modern counterparts made and sold by the now-worldwide Browning Arms Corporation.

▓ Riser Home and Boot Shop, where you can learn about the craft of an 1840s shoemaker.

▓ Webb Blacksmith Shop. Here you can see the vital techniques of wagon making and blacksmithing that enabled early Mormons to transport most of their belongings on the long and arduous journey from Nauvoo to Salt Lake City, Utah.

▓ John Taylor Home, Post Office and Printing Office. Taylor, a convert from Canada, served as editor of weekly and semimonthly Mormon publications that were widely read by members of the faith.

▓ Stoddard Home and Tin Shop, including a demonstration of 1840s tinsmithing. Stoddard's tinware included lanterns and kitchenware, as well as stoves and pipes for Nauvoo buildings.

The Visitor Center at Main and Young Streets in Nauvoo, IL, is a good starting point. Open daily. Many sites have seasonal activities and events. Free to the public.

▲ Brigham Young, second president of the Mormon Church, built this imposing home for his family. After Prophet Joseph Smith was murdered in nearby Carthage, Young added an east wing to accommodate his church responsibilities. It is an interesting look into a great man's life.

◀ Mansion House was built by Prophet Joseph Smith in 1843 and later expanded with a hotel wing to accommodate early Nauvoo visitors. The hotel wing has been removed, but you can view the fine rooms used by Joseph and Emma and hear about their home life. Across the street you can also visit their first Nauvoo home, a humble log cabin by the river.

Heritage Village at This is the Place Heritage Park

SEE MAP PAGE 21, LOCATION #30
Salt Lake City, Utah
Phone: (801) 582-1847
http://www.thisistheplace.org

▲ Heritage Village is not an amusement park but an authentic re-creation of a mid-1800s Utah community. Original buildings moved to the site and interpreters in period clothing bring to life a unique and interesting history.

▼ Imagine limiting yourself to a few personal belongings, piled into a wooden cart shared by four other people. Imagine pulling that cart, now weighing several hundred pounds, with your own hands across America – over hills and across rivers; through rocky terrain, desert sand and mud; under the scorching sun, pelting rain and freezing snow. For poor Mormons on their way to Salt Lake City, there was no other choice.

This painstakingly re-created mid-1800s village presents a comprehensive slice of Utah's pioneer era, from roughly 1847-1869. Located within the 430-acre This is The Place Heritage Park, its homes, businesses and outbuildings are a combination of relocated original structures and replica reconstructions.

Today, 38 of the 46 buildings are open to the public. They are an interesting mix. The John Gardner cabin (c. 1864), where ten children were raised, has one lower room and a loft accessible only by an outside ladder. The Charles Rich home (c. 1850s) accommodated two wives by having a private room for each wife on opposite ends of the building and a shared room in the center. The Niels O. Anderson home is a beautiful replica of the one built by Scandinavian immigrants. The John B. Fairbanks home (c. 1850s) is an adobe structure with ornamental details reflecting the upper-class status of the family. These are just a sample of the many dwellings at Heritage Village.

Pioneer activities are demonstrated at various Village businesses. Stop at the Tithing Office to see

where in-kind tithing donations were received, and spend time at the cabinet and furniture shop, where a skilled craftsman uses traditional tools to make fine pioneer furniture. Other interesting attractions include the shaving parlor, bank, blacksmith shop, general store, hotel, print shop and schoolhouse.

Heritage Village is alive with activity as "citizens" dressed in period clothing perform the everyday tasks of pioneer life and make you feel a part of it all. While having fun, you'll discover how early Utahans lived and prospered in a hot, dry place that many others believed was uninhabitable. During the visitor season, you can ride a horse-drawn wagon through the Village or simply stroll at your leisure, stopping at various homes and businesses. On holidays and special-event days, role-playing actors represent historical figures such as Brigham Young and Mark Twain. Special Living History events include Brigham Young's Birthday in June, Liberty Days and the Pioneer Festival in July, Halloween-oriented activities in October and a Candlelight Christmas in December.

Located in This is the Place Heritage Park, across the street from Hogle Zoo in eastern Salt Lake City, UT. Open Monday-Saturday from Memorial Day-Labor Day and post-season for special events. Admission charged.

MORMON HANDCART TRAIL

It's a story not often told outside the Mormon religion but important for us all to know. From 1856 to 1860, nearly 3,000 members of The Church of Jesus Christ of Latter-day Saints made a 1,000-1,300 mile journey overland to Salt Lake Valley by pushing and pulling their possessions in two-wheeled handcarts (giant wheelbarrows). This was all the Mormons could afford. Most were converts from England, Scotland, Wales and Denmark. Two early groups – over 1,000 men, women and children – met disaster in 1856 because of a late start and an early winter. They trekked through mud and snow; food ran out; cattle died; the snow deepened; people froze; and in Wyoming, they could go no further. Brigham Young sent rescuers from Utah, but despite heroic efforts over 200 people died, and dozens more were maimed by frostbite. It was the worst disaster in western overland travel. Still, the handcart groups kept coming. You can learn about their amazing adventures at the Mormon Handcart Visitors Center and Martin's Cove northeast of Muddy Gap, WY.

THE AMANAS

Numerous experiments in communal living dot the landscape of American history. Among the longest-lasting is the Community of True Inspiration known as the Amana Society. Like many other religious societies, the Amanas sought out isolated, sparsely populated areas in which to establish their communities. They also made sure they had adequate economic opportunities and good land for an agriculturally based lifestyle. As was true of the Amish, they spoke German and dressed in uniformly outdated styles. As was true of the Shakers, they focused on hard work and industry, with both men and women laboring. What seems to have been particularly unusual, aside from their religious beliefs, was their willingness to adapt to changing times.

Their beginnings date back to the early 1700s, when Inspirationists emerged as part of the Pietist and Spiritualist movement within the Lutheran Church in Germany. Inspirationists believed in divine revelation through inspired prophets. They also emphasized developing and nurturing one's Inner Life. In 1842, 800 Inspirationists sailed across the Atlantic Ocean and settled near Buffalo, New York, seeking religious autonomy and freedom from persecution. Twelve years later, for economic and spiritual reasons, they purchased land in Iowa and moved west, forming a village along the Iowa River. They called their new home "Amana," an Old Testament word meaning "to remain faithful." Eventually, 26,000 acres were purchased and six more villages were settled in the surrounding area. All land and buildings were owned by the community. Families had separate living quarters, and each person of working age was assigned tasks in the kitchens, fields, factories or shops.

The Amanas have progressed successfully into the twenty-first century by modifying their system into two distinct organizations, one secular and one spiritual. Outside of the church, they have relaxed their ways, discontinuing their communal society in 1932 and gradually eliminating strict regulations about dress and lifestyle. The Amana Church Society now directs matters related to their faith, and the Amana Society, Inc. oversees their commercial and farming operations. Today, many of the Amana businesses are independently owned and operated. Church life itself remains relatively unchanged, however, with its simple form of worship in unadorned meeting houses. Unique cultural traditions also remain today, affirmed and passed on from generation to generation.

▲ Although residents in the seven Amana Colonies now live relatively conventional lifestyles, their world still feels quite different. Handcrafts and boutique businesses are the norm. Restaurant meals are served family style. Neighborhood streets are quiet places for a leisurely stroll.

◄ The rich brown local stone lends a uniquely warm and cozy feeling to the homes on tree-lined streets in many Amana villages.

COMMUNAL LIFESTYLE

What was life like for the Amanas? Members chose their own spouses but had to obtain final approval from the Council of Elders and wait a full year before marrying (to improve their chances of a happy life together). Job assignments were made along traditional gender lines, and work was considered to be both a religious act and an economic necessity. Six agents traveled the country selling and promoting goods produced by the Amanas. Children entered Kinderschule at the age of 2, and their education usually stopped at the age of 14. The villagers frowned on frivolity but indulged in some diversions, such as Pelznickel (one of the many nineteenth-century versions of Santa Claus), Easter-egg hunts, group songfests and the music of violins, zithers and accordions. Their German-style food was cooked in communal kitchens and eaten communally – no home had a kitchen. Beer and wine-making were allowed. The German language was used for all communications, except when English was necessary in order to interface with the outside world.

Amana Colonies

SEE MAP PAGE 19, LOCATION #15
Amana, Iowa
Phone: toll-free (800) 579-2294
http://amanacolonies.com

▲ West Amana has some of the prettiest old homes in the Amana Colonies as well as arts and crafts businesses. Stop by the wood shop to see the giant 11-foot-tall rocking chair. It'll make you feel like a kid again.

▶ The main colony, Amana, has many shops and restaurants, as well as Living History sites. Among the top attractions are the woolen mill with its old weaving machines, the furniture and clock shop with its highly skilled woodworkers, and the heritage museum with its informative displays (including the Noé House shown here).

The Amana Colonies have long been a popular destination for people interested in buying Old World crafts and learning more about communal life. Here are seven quaint and closely united villages: Amana, East Amana, High Amana, Homestead, Middle Amana, South Amana and West Amana. The ideals of hard work and quality craftsmanship were passed down through the generations and can be seen today in their products. In addition, the sights are both charming and distinctive.

The village of Amana is the largest community and a good starting point for your explorations. In many cases, you will have the opportunity to watch artisans at work. Visit the furniture and clock shop, woolen mill, broom and basket shop, candle works, cutlery and ironworks, plus general craft shops. Enjoy a traditional German family-style meal at one of the delightful restaurants. Buy a local wine or beer from downtown tasting rooms. Also satisfy your sweet tooth at the old-time bakeries.

Much of the pleasure of Amana Colonies comes from the Old World ambience. We recommend that you drive through the countryside and observe the imprint that the early Amanas made on their landscape.

There are old groves of trees called Schulwalds and a seven-mile canal dug long ago to provide water power for the woolen mill. Barns and agricultural buildings are clustered together at the edge of each village. You can tour the Communal Kitchen and the Cooper Shop in Middle Amana; the Homestead Store; the Communal Agricultural Museum in South Amana; the Industrial Machine Shop in Amana; and even the Mini-Americana Barn Museum of miniature replicas in South Amana. Of course, the focus of the colonists' lives was their religion – services were held 11 times a week. At the Amana Community Church Museum in Homestead, you can visit one of Amana's original churches.

Located in the rolling hills of east-central Iowa, off of I-80 exit 225. Stores and craft shops open year-round. Most historic sites open daily beginning in May. Some close for the season in September; others in October or December. Admission charged at historic sites.

THE GREAT CHANGE

Disaster struck the Amana Colonies in 1923 when a fire destroyed the flour and woolen mills, causing severe economic loss. Then the worldwide Great Depression came, and orders for Amana products dried up. Three years into the Depression, the Society reorganized in order to survive. The people became stockholders in the communal businesses. Some founded their own companies, while others began to work for wages. They purchased cars and other items needed for a non-communal lifestyle. They added kitchens to their homes and began cooking their own meals. Several of the community kitchens, which once fed 1,500 or more villagers, became homes; others became the Amana restaurants of today. The changes were major, but the Amanas adapted. Approximately 475 historic buildings and sites remain today, along with a still-small population. They have enabled the Amana Colonies to keep their Old World charm and quiet way of life. Visitors feel very welcomed.

OTHER GROUPS – RELIGIOUS & SECULAR

Americans developed a significant interest in social and religious experimentation. This was especially true between the early 1700s and early 1800s, when many immigrants had escaped serious oppression and economic hardship in Europe. The New World opened the door to a better life, and it was easy for some to envision taking the next steps toward creating what they viewed as utopias, or perfect societies. America was not yet "the land of the free," but the continent was large and sparsely populated. Experimentation could take place in self-contained communities, where unconventional ideas could be put to the test relatively undisturbed by nosey neighbors. So, along with the major religious movements, more than 100 utopian communities established themselves in America before 1860.

The most successful were built on a solid foundation of religious practices. They also had the added strength of a social structure based on hard work and industry. Ephrata Cloister, Zoar Village and "Oekonomie" (Old Economy) were fine examples of single-village religious

▲ Life in some utopian communities, such as Ephrata Cloister, PA, could be peaceful but very busy. An important opportunity for social-izing came with the time spent spinning and weaving flax for the community's clothing.

◀ Innovation was common among communal societies. Isolated as they were, members had to rely on themselves to meet day-to-day needs; so they invented labor- and space-saving devices to help. Sometimes it was the simplest of things that made a big difference – like this wood-storage box under a stove at Zoar Village, OH.

groups. Others tried to create a "heaven on earth" that placed communal business practices ahead of faith. While their socialism-cum-religion approach often seemed sound, success required individual members to put the group's common financial goals ahead of personal self-interests. That was a lot to expect when there was little underlying religious motivation. (Success seemed to require a deep and abiding faith.)

Among the more influential social reformers was Robert Owen, a Welsh-born businessman. He had tried without success in England to convince business and government leaders that society would benefit from improving the welfare of employees and educating working children. Owen wanted to create "villages of cooperation," where all members were treated as important contributors. His ideas are not unusual today, but Owen was very much ahead of his time. Hoping to prove his point in America, he purchased New Harmony, Indiana, in 1825 and, under a son's leadership, transformed the former religious settlement into his grand experiment. The effort failed, probably due to a lack of commitment by members, but it did spawn other "Owenite" communities. Among them was Nashoba, an agricultural cooperative in Tennessee, which hoped to teach former slaves how to lead independent, productive lives. Another Owenite inspiration was Brook Farm, founded by transcendentalists seeking a union between intellectual and manual labor. Inhabitants included writer Nathaniel Hawthorne, who called Brook Farm "a daydream, and yet a fact." None of these communities remained intact.

BECOMING CORPORATIONS

Several major American businesses have their roots in communal societies. Amana Company, now owned by Maytag, was a workshop where beverage coolers were made in the Amana Colonies, Iowa. It patented frost-free refrigeration technology, developed innovations in microwave technology, and grew into one of our nation's leaders in home appliances and heating/cooling products. Oneida Corporation – known today for its high-quality silverware – began life as a collective, not a business. Founded in 1848 in New York, it was focused on eliminating sin and achieving happiness though "Perfectionism." The society ultimately prospered by manufacturing silver knives, forks and spoons, dropped its social controls in 1880 and became a corporation. And the next time you buy seeds for your vegetable garden, remember that America's commercial garden seed industry is an outgrowth of Shaker ingenuity. This society grew seeds commercially and is generally considered the first to sell seeds in paper packets.

Ephrata Cloister

SEE MAP PAGE 11, LOCATION #15B

Ephrata, Pennsylvania
Phone: (717) 733-6600, ext. 3001
http://www.ephratacloister.org

▲ The buildings at Ephrata Cloister mirror European architectural styles, with steep roofs, dormer windows, low doorways and scattered window placements. Many were made of squared logs notched at the corners. Others were wood-framed, with stone and mud filling the spaces and siding covering exterior walls.

▶ The community's scriptorium was well known for its illuminated music manuscripts and large posters of Bible verses. These were created by the Ephrata Sisters using formal German Fraktar (Gothic script).

This devout Protestant community thrived on the spirit of one man, Conrad Beissel, who believed in an intensely personal union with God and also stressed the importance of music for both body and soul. Beissel became one of America's earliest composers of hymns and anthems, as well as the publisher of America's first book of original compositions, *Turtel-Taube*. Initially a preacher for the German Baptist Brethren in Germantown, Pennsylvania, he had left the Brethren to pursue his own form of spiritual mysticism in 1732. Many Brethren, attracted by his magnetic personality, joined him at Ephrata (EH-frah-tah) Cloister.

Beissel and his followers shared a life characterized by strict discipline and intense self-denial in preparation for Christ's return to earth. Though many were married, celibacy was viewed as ideal for achieving a reliable channel of communication with God. Living quarters were small and austere, typically with a wood bench for a bed and a wood block for a pillow. Idleness was frowned upon; so the days were very busy. Assigned individuals tended the gardens, orchards and grain fields; manufactured cloth from Cloister-grown flax; made and mended clothes; worked in the sawmill, gristmill or paper mill; produced books and hymnals in the printing shop; created poetry, music or decorative writing called Fraktur; and, of course, prepared meals and took care of all other community needs. When the chores were done, their focus turned to religious activities such as evening choral singing and communion.

Stimulated by Beissel's devotion to his cause, the Cloister prospered. By 1750, it had about 300 members. Sadly, after Beissel's death in 1768, the community began to dissolve. In 1770, only 135 members remained. And yet, after all were gone, their unique world was protected by others, simply because they cared. Today much of what Ephrata Cloister created remains for the world to see and ponder. Ten of the original buildings have been restored

and furnished to re-create the atmosphere of this eighteenth-century communal village. Fascinating!

Following an introductory film in the Visitor Center, tours are conducted by costumed guides. Special events are held throughout the year.

Located at 632 West Main Street in Ephrata, PA. Take I-76 west to exit 21, Route 222 south to Ephrata and then Route 322 west for about 2 miles. Open daily except major holidays. Admission charged.

REJECTING LIBERAL VIEWS

Most members of the Ephrata Cloister had once been members of the German Baptist Brethren, itself a new religious group founded in 1708. The Brethren had separated from the Lutheran and Reformed churches in Germany, unhappy about the liberties taken with the teachings of the Scriptures. Striving for a high level of piety, they blended a renewed emphasis on spirituality and discipline with the Anabaptist focus on outward expression of faith. The Brethren were especially influenced by the Mennonites, with whom they had a close interaction, and to a lesser extent by the Amish. But unlike the Mennonites and Amish – who interpreted the Old Testament through the eyes of the New Testament – the German Baptist Brethren held the New Testament to be their only creed. Doctrinal conflicts haunted them and led to defections. Today there are a number of different Brethren groups in America, Canada and Europe.

Zoar Village

SEE MAP PAGE 17, LOCATION #16

Zoar, Ohio
Phone: toll-free (800) 262-6195
http://www.ohiohistory.org/places/zoar
http://www.zca.org

A group of about 200 German Separatists founded this Ohio village along the Tuscarawas River in 1817 as a refuge from the religious persecution they had suffered in their homeland. Naming their settlement Zoar (zohr), after the Biblical town where Lot sought refuge from Sodom, they came full of hope and determination. As too often happened in early America, they also came unprepared for the financial burden associated with establishing a new life. Two years after their arrival, out of economic necessity, the village became a communal society called "The Society of Separatists of Zoar."

By combining their resources and working for the good of all, the Zoarites found the road to success – relatively quickly, in fact, although not in the usual ways. The Ohio & Erie Canal was being built, and the Zoarites contracted to dig the seven miles which passed through their land. The pay was good, enabling them to completely erase their substantial debt. More importantly, the canal opened up their area to commerce, and the Zoarites became entrepreneurs, operating canal boats, attracting tourists and selling a variety of products to outsiders. The result was staggering: by the mid-1800s, this small group of religious dissenters had accumulated assets worth over one million dollars. In 1898, the Society finally was dissolved by membership vote; the property was divided; and Zoar became just another small country town where residents worked for their own reward.

OHIO & ERIE CANAL

When Ohio became a state in 1803, its main industry was agriculture, and the fertile soil produced bumper crops. Yet, with no reliable way to move products to eastern markets, Ohio farmers struggled to make a living. The solution came between 1827 and 1832 with the opening of the Ohio and Erie Canal – 309 miles of waterways extending from Portsmouth on the Ohio River to Cleveland on Lake Erie. In a remarkable turn of fortunes, Ohio farmers were able to sell their crops for huge profits – wheat, for instance, sold in the big markets for ten times the at-home price. What's more, Ohioans could finally afford imported goods. Even coffee, which had been a Sunday treat, was theirs to enjoy daily, replacing a beverage made from burnt wheat. One of the poorest states had become one of the richest. Today, a towpath of the former canal is part of the Ohio & Erie Canal National Heritage Corridor near Zoar.

Photos printed courtesy of Ohio Historical Society

Thankfully, most of the historic buildings have survived as unique reminders of a very interesting past. While many are now private residences and businesses, ten are managed by the Ohio Historical Society and showcase various aspects of Zoarite life. They include Number One House (which was the home of leader Joseph Baumeler and two other families), the Greenhouse and Gardener's Residence and Kitchen/Laundry/Magazine Complex, plus the Blacksmith Shop, Wagon Shop, Tinshop, Zoar Store, Bakery, Dairy and, last but not least, Bimeler House Museum (representing the commune's final decade). Plan on a leisurely visit and guided tour. The buildings are exceptionally varied and well appointed.

▲ The Zoar community garden was an important place to walk and contemplate. Geometrically patterned, it symbolized the Zoarite vision of Jerusalem. It still has a tree of life at the center and 12 radiating pathways representing the tribes of Israel. The guided tour takes you into the Greenhouse and attached Gardener's Residence shown here.

◀ This complex-looking and fully functional piece of equipment was developed at Zoar to streamline the process for making cheese, a commercial product and staple in the Zoarite diet.

Located on SR 212 about 3 miles southeast of I-77 in Zoar, OH. Take I-77 exit 93 to 198 Main Street. Open April-October – weekends April-Memorial Day; Wednesday-Sunday Memorial Day-Labor Day; weekends after Labor Day to October 31. Admission charged.

Old Economy Village

SEE MAP PAGE 11, LOCATION #12

Ambridge, Pennsylvania
Phone: (724) 266-4500
http://www.oldeconomyvillage.org

▲ Behind leader George Rapp's house, a flower-lined path leads to a peaceful retreat of trees and flowers. This lovely spot includes an elegant Pavilion and reflecting pond as well as a straw-roofed grotto. Seen from here is the church steeple towering in the background. When the Society dissolved in 1905, the church building was sold to the Lutherans – ironically, the denomination Rapp had separated from in Germany.

▶ Though they lived simply and had few personal belongings, the Harmonists fully appreciated nice things. They often crafted everyday furniture in decorative styles. For public rooms, they also purchased fine furniture and religious art such as this expert copy of the Benjamin West painting *Christ Healing the Sick in the Temple*.

In 1804, nearly 800 followers of the Separatist George Rapp emigrated from Germany, seeking religious and economic freedom. They built their first home in Harmony, Pennsylvania, stayed for ten years, and then built New Harmony, Indiana. After ten more years, they moved back to Pennsylvania, this time to establish "Oekonomie," now known as Old Economy. It was here that the Harmony Society found its final home.

Known worldwide for its religious dedication, social organization and economic prosperity, this communal experiment was based upon a simple, pious life guided by the teachings of early Christianity. Members turned over all of their personal possessions to the Society and worked for the common good. In return, they received only what they needed to live comfortably. They practiced celibacy in order to purify themselves for Christ's Second Coming, which was expected at any moment, and they were pacifists.

Perhaps the Harmony Society's greatest achievements were in adapting to new and innovative technologies. By 1826, their textile factories were powered and heated by steam engines. Their silk was so fine it received gold medals at textile exhibitions in Boston and New York. Society members established a steam laundry and community dairy. In addition,

individuals developed into skilled craftsmen – blacksmiths, tanners, hatters, wagon makers, potters, woodworkers, linen weavers, tinsmiths. They even set up a sizable Natural History Museum to educate and enlighten not only members but also visitors. Still, like other communal groups, their numbers diminished over time, and their economic vitality waned. In 1905, the Harmony Society disbanded, and the town became part of Ambridge.

Six acres of the Society's original holdings, including 17 historic structures, are open to the public through guided tours. Among them are the Cabinet Shop containing original Harmonist tools, benches and lathes; the Mechanics Building which houses the Tailor Shop, Shoe Shop and Print Shop; the homes of joint leaders George and Frederick Rapp; a worker's home; and the Natural History Museum. Other restored structures include the Community Kitchen, Granary, Warehouse, Store and Wine Cellar. You will also find a neatly laid out vintage garden. Very interesting and enjoyable!

Located in the historic district of Ambridge, PA, next to Route 65. Visitor Center at 270 Sixteenth Street. Open Tuesday-Sunday except most major holidays. Admission charged.

TRADING PLACES

When the Harmonists returned to Pennsylvania, they left behind a sizable town in Indiana, where they had developed a flourishing market for their products. Robert Owen, the wealthy industrialist from England, saw this as a great opportunity to try out his own version of communal living. He purchased everything from George Rapp and attracted 900 new residents by promising them an earthly utopia (perfect society). Owens' idea was to establish community ownership and equality of work and profit, with no religious underpinnings. New Harmony became famous under Owen, and it attracted innovators in education, geology and women's suffrage whose contributions achieved national importance. Yet, this community, like the others, was far from perfect. The people split into factions, and Owen abandoned the effort. Some of the historic Harmonist and Owenite buildings have been restored and can be enjoyed today on guided walking tours in New Harmony, Indiana.

Mission Houses Museum

SEE MAP PAGE 23, LOCATION #11
Honolulu, island of O'ahu, Hawai'i
Phone: (808) 531-0481
http://www.missionhouses.org

The most remarkable Protestant story took place in Hawai'i. It began when two crucial events converged: the rise to power of Kamehameha the Great's favorite wife, Kaahumanu, after his death in 1819 and the arrival of New England missionaries in 1820. Kaahumanu had convinced the new king, Kamehameha II, to eliminate the Hawaiian taboo against women dining with men. When the gods did not punish the new behavior, other long-held traditions came under question. The people wondered: By what right did the King rule? Why were women forbidden to eat certain foods? Why couldn't commoners own land?

Christianity offered an alternative code of behavior that was very appealing to the Hawaiians. So with the arrival of Protestants, profound changes – changes which took hundreds of years to evolve elsewhere – happened in rapid succession. Most important was education. The missionaries developed a written form of the Native language, printed a Hawaiian translation of the bible, and taught reading and writing. By the mid-1800s, Hawai'i was one of the most literate nations in the world. At the same time, the missionaries introduced modern medicine, became business leaders and inserted themselves into island politics. These Protestants are credited with guiding efforts to maintain Hawaiian independence at a time when the islands were ripe for colonization.

Mission Houses Museum shares this dramatic tale with exhibits in its Visitor Center and tours of historic buildings from the 1820-1863 "missionary period." The Hale La'au wood-frame house, pre-cut and shipped around Cape Horn in 1820, is reputedly the oldest building in the state. It became the home of missionary Hiram Bingham, physician Dr. Gerrit Judd, printer Elisha Loomis and their families. On display are clothing, furnishings, books and other items belonging to the missionary families. The re-created Printing Office has an operating reproduction of a nineteenth-century press. The 1831 Chamberlain House, built entirely of coral blocks, was both a home and storehouse.

Across the street is Kawaiaha'o Church, which was built by Hawaiians in 1842 with 14,000 bricks of coral quarried by hand from reefs 10 to 20 feet under water.

Located at 553 South King Street in Honolulu, island of O'ahu, HI. Guided tours Tuesday-Saturday except holidays. Admission charged. Just down the street is 'Iolani Palace, residence of the last monarchs of Hawai'i. (See America's Native Peoples, page 57.)

▲ Initially, missionary Hiram Bingham and his company – including a farmer, a printer, two teachers, wives and children – were only allowed to build thatched houses. Finally King Kamehameha III allowed them to build American-style homes. At the Mission Houses Museum, you can tour the missionary buildings and, depending on the season, enjoy scholarly lectures, workshops and Living History demonstrations.

HOLDING STRONG

When Captain James Cook and his men discovered Hawai'i – then called the Sandwich Islands – England and America were at war; France had recently joined America's fight for independence; and other world powers were preoccupied with their own affairs. Response to the 1778 discovery was therefore relatively low key. Religious missionaries were actually among the first to show an intense interest in the lush Hawaiian paradise and its inhabitants. With the arrival of multiple faiths, the threat of colonization became serious. In 1842, the French demanded broad powers for the Catholics. In 1843, the English raised a flag over Native lands. The United States provided protection to the Hawaiian government but then followed up in 1854 with an envoy sent to explore the possibility of Hawaiian annexation. King Kamehameha III, the reigning monarch, was most receptive to the Americans but also cautious. It took 44 years for the Republic of Hawai'i to finally become a United States territory. In 1959, it became our nation's fiftieth state.

▲ The vast, rolling meadows and lush forests of historic battlefields hide the evidence of their military days, but they still have much to tell you.

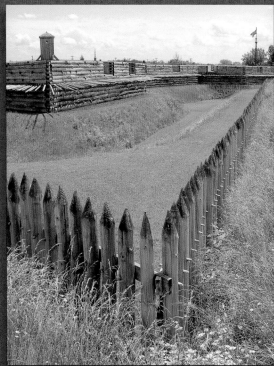

▶ Fort Stanwix, NY, was state-of-the-art for its time. Attackers could not easily cross the deep moat edged with sharp posts or climb past the pointed logs protruding from fort walls.

▶ Exciting, well-executed battle re-enactments are staged at many of our nation's forts. Most are held in the summer. Check fort websites for schedules.

▶ Placid and lovely in summer, the Delaware can be fierce in winter. Yet General Washington and his troops crossed here one snowy Christmas night and very likely changed the course of history.

ROAD TO INDEPENDENCE

The emergence of American anger and indignation was startling.

How could anyone have known it would ignite a revolution?

In the early 1760s, most colonists of English heritage were

happy enough with British imperialism and its many benefits.

They enjoyed international trade, military protection, a stable

political system, and a shared history and lifestyle. What's more,

they expressed an almost delirious pride in 1763 when

Britain took over most of France's colonial empire along with

Spanish Florida at the close of Europe's Seven Years War.

Little did colonists realize the full extent of Britain's tremendous

financial burden – not only from its wars in both Europe and

America but also from its expanding role in colonial affairs.

Little could Americans predict the impact of their rage when

Britain "unfairly" taxed them to help refill its coffers.

HISTORICAL PERSPECTIVE:
ROAD TO INDEPENDENCE

Seeds of self-determination took root early in the English colonies. Because England was preoccupied with other matters both here and in Europe, the Crown and Parliament focused on expanding and defending colonial holdings rather than managing them. Representatives were placed in powerful positions in America, but the colonies still had enough autonomy to develop culturally, intellectually and politically into societies that differed markedly from Mother England. Americans had a rebellious attitude about their freedom – it was an absolute right not subject to the whims of Parliament. They also had an inflated sense of their own importance. Thus the colonial assemblies, which London officials considered to be minor governing bodies, were viewed by Americans as centers of vital authority. And the power to levy taxes, which Great Britain took for itself, was considered by Americans to be a local prerogative.

"the cause of America is in great measure the cause of all mankind"

▶ Thomas Jefferson wrote the Declaration of Independence in rented lodgings on the outskirts of Philadelphia, PA. The private home, now called Declaration House, has been reconstructed on its original site, and Jefferson's two rooms have been re-created with period and reproduction furnishings.

▶ With few exceptions, the men who signed the Declaration of Independence came to their decision with reluctance. Franklin, for example, was slow to agree to revolution. But when it came time to sign the Constitution, he and most others did so with confidence and conviction. At National Constitution Center in Philadelphia, PA, life-size statues re-create the final, momentous hours of discussion.

Collision Course

As long as Great Britain left America alone, these fundamental differences were overlooked. But with the end of the Seven Years War (or the French and Indian War, as Americans knew it), the situation changed.

King George III, who assumed the British throne in 1760, believed that his government had the right and obligation to expand its involvement in the colonies. The English-American relationship unraveled beyond repair when Britain levied a series of taxes, hoping to rebuild its dwindling financial resources. The first effort at taxation was the Stamp Act of 1765, which sparked united colonial action against Great Britain. Parliament ultimately repealed it but two years later passed the Townshend Acts, once again attempting to raise revenues. After the bloody clash between British troops and American protesters known as the Boston Massacre, these Acts were partially repealed. Still, over the next few years, Parliament continued to pass laws and set policies that sparked outrage among Americans. Seeking solutions, twelve of the colonies came together in the First Continental Congress; but their efforts could not alter British actions. In fact, Parliament declared Massachusetts to be in a state of rebellion. When it sent British troops to take control, the colonists had reached the breaking point. War erupted in April 1775.

Despite major military battles, the colonies tried for a year to avoid a full-scale revolution. In January 1776, political firebrand Thomas Paine persuasively laid out the realities in his pamphlet *Common Sense*: "it is not in the power of Britain to do this continent justice…To be always running three or four thousand miles with a tale or a petition, waiting four or five months for an answer, which when obtained requires five or six more to explain it in, will in a few years be looked upon as folly and childishness – There was a time when it was proper, and there is a proper time for it to cease." He was adamant: "A government of our own is our natural right: And when a man seriously reflects on the precariousness of human affairs, he will become convinced, that it is infinitely wiser and safer, to form a constitution of our own in a cool deliberate manner, while we have it in our power, than to trust such an interesting event to time and chance." He was also passionate: "the cause of America is in a great measure the cause of all mankind...Every spot of the old world is overrun with oppression. Freedom hath been hunted round the globe. Asia, and Africa, have long expelled her – Europe regards her like a stranger, and England hath given her warning to depart." Anything less than rebellion was unacceptable according to Paine. George Washington, along with many other American leaders, lauded his "sound doctrine and unanswerable reasoning." On July 4, 1776, America finally declared war.

Making of a Nation

Few outside observers believed the American people could win against Britain. Our ancestors were fighting the greatest military power in the world, and American soldiers were for the most part farmers, not military professionals. In addition, the colonies were only loosely united by a confederation that had little central authority. Not surprisingly, the American cause seemed at times to be on the verge of collapse. Finally, though, a succession of British blunders and American successes turned the tide. After eight long and difficult years, a peace treaty confirmed the existence of our new nation.

That was just the beginning. Still ahead was the design of a new political system and the assignment of national versus state powers. The Articles of Confederation adopted during war had set up a national Congress, consisting of delegates from all thirteen colonies. But it limited Congressional powers primarily to the declaration of war and peace, the maintenance of an army, and the coinage of money. There was no national executive and no supreme court. As a result, the colonies acted independently, according to their own interests, and held tightly to their independence.

With no other choice, the Constitutional Convention met secretly in 1787. Fifty-five delegates deliberated for four months, presided over by George Washington, and they finally came to a solution which has guided our nation ever since. The U.S. Constitution went into effect in 1789, establishing our national government and defining the rights and liberties of the American people. It was a remarkable achievement, but it was also flawed. In order to agree on its final wording, the delegates set aside divisive issues, most notably slavery and women's rights. The future would have to take care of itself.

▲ Independence Hall in Philadelphia, PA, stands tall and proud. In this building, the Second Continental Congress adopted the Declaration of Independence...the Constitutional Convention drafted the "law of the land"...and the Liberty Bell rang out to commemorate events.

◀ Family names such as Adams are widely recognized, but many lesser-known names also played key roles. At Middleton Place, SC, you will learn about Henry Middleton, a member of the first Continental Congress, and his son Arthur, who signed the Declaration of Independence.

Claude Moore Colonial Farm

SEE MAP PAGE 15, LOCATION #20A
McLean, Virginia
Phone: (703) 442-7557
http://www.nps.gov/clmo
http://www.1771.org

▲ Chimneys on the houses of lower-class colonial Virginians were most often made of wood and mud, just like the houses themselves. Wood provided the structure and shape of the chimney; mud was caked on the inside for a degree of fire protection. Even so, families needed to be very careful not to set their chimneys – and their houses – on fire!

▶ Once harvested, the tobacco crop was hung to dry, initially in a shady spot outside and then in a drying barn that had open spaces between the logs to allow air to flow through and moisture to escape. Farmers wanted a leathery soft, not crisp and dry, product for market.

Part of the George Washington Memorial Parkway in Virginia, this privately operated National Park enables Living History travelers to step into the life of a typical low-income farmer and his family just prior to the Revolutionary War. Park staff and volunteers, dressed in period clothing, work 12 acres of land and greet visitors in first-person portrayals. The year is 1771.

Imagine yourself in this time period. "Home" is a one-room log and clapboard house built by the family from nearby trees and situated between the apple orchard and the kitchen garden. Small fields of corn, tobacco, wheat, flax and rye are tilled, planted and cultivated with a hoe. The corn field provides the family's staple grain, which is ground into cornmeal for the daily bread, Johnny cakes. Hogs root around the tobacco field; chickens, turkeys and geese roam the yard; and cattle graze in the meadow. Split rail fences keep the livestock out of the orchard and crop fields.

Oronoco tobacco was the main cash crop in eighteenth-century Virginia. Starting with tiny seeds, a man would grow and harvest this tender plant with extra care, cure it in his tobacco barn, and then take it to the nearest warehouse for sale. He received his payment in tobacco notes, which were tradeable as money. If he were a tenant farmer, with no land of his own, he would pay his landlord with tobacco notes. If any of the notes were left, he would use them to buy items he couldn't make himself: metal tools, fabrics, pottery and imported items

Photo courtesy of Katie Jackson

such as spices and sugar. He might obtain additional goods from neighbors and acquaintances by bartering grains he raised, eggs his children collected, fresh and pickled vegetables his wife produced, plus butter and cheese she made from the cow's milk.

Located east of McLean, VA. Take I-495 exit 44. Drive east on SR 193 (Georgetown Pike) about 2 1/2 miles to Colonial Farm Road. Open Wednesday-Sunday from April to mid-December; closed Thanksgiving. Part of the National Park system but operated by a private foundation. Admission charged.

WHAT A LIFE!

In colonial times, self-sufficiency was essential. Even when store-bought goods were available, most folks could not afford them. Need sewing thread? Grow, process and spin flax. Need a warm pair of stockings? Raise and sheer sheep, clean the wool, spin the yarn, knit the garment. Want meat for your meals? Raise hogs; let them forage for food; leave corn nearby to keep them close to the farm; capture, kill and butcher the hogs when their time comes; salt the meat and hang it for long-term use. Raise geese for food and feathers, chickens for eggs, cows for milk, corn as your primary grain, and herbs for medicinal purposes. Render animal fat and use it to make candles. Pour water through wood ashes; slowly cook the resulting liquid lye; add rendered fat and continue cooking to make soap. Grow tobacco and wheat for sale, using the wheat for yourselves only when cornmeal is unsuitable (such as for pie crusts). Buy cloth to make into clothing and buy tools to maintain your farm. Barter for most other necessities. Forget about vacations; put your children to work when they are old enough to help; and pray you don't get sick or lose your spouse. Surviving alone was almost impossible.

Historic Deerfield

SEE MAP PAGE 11, LOCATION #29
Deerfield, Massachusetts
Phone: (413) 774-5581
http://www.historic-deerfield.org

In eighteenth-century New England, many farmers chose to live in communities rather than on their farmland – there was safety in numbers. Such was the case in Deerfield, where today thirteen historic homes and businesses beckon you to discover the past. Some buildings can only be explored on guided tours; others allow you to wander at your leisure; all have unusual furnishings and interesting stories to share. Down the street and around a corner is The Flynt Center of Early New England Life, itself filled with museum treasures.

The following are a few key sites to include in your visit. You can enjoy much more if your time permits. Admission includes an orientation program and guided walking tour, as well as several 30-minute house tours.

Wells-Thorn House (1746/47)

The rooms in this unique house are time capsules of colonial life, each representing a different period. Your

first stop interprets the early frontier days, when light and heat came only from cooking fires; furniture was scarce; and stuffed sacks served as beds. As you walk through 125 years of history, you see how life became easier: the rooms are brighter and decorated; furniture is stylish and comfortable; rugs cover floors; lamps grace tables.

Barnard Tavern (1795)

This stagecoach stop was once the center of village life for men – a place where they could drink, enjoy com-

panionship, share the latest news. Proper eighteenth-century women only ventured upstairs to attend gala events in the ballroom. The tavern connects to the Frary House, which dates back to the 1760s. While not authentic to the period, this home is quite interesting, thanks to the contributions of preservationist Charlotte Alice Baker.

Hinsdale & Anna Williams House (1816/17)

Hinsdale Williams was a wealthy landowner and farmer. The Federal-style house he shared with his wife was built in the mid-1700s and remodeled in the early 1800s. Noteworthy features include beautiful furnishings, wallpapers, an early cook stove and a clothes washer.

Located just off US 5 and SR 10 in Deerfield, MA. Open daily April-December; Flynt Center museum also open January-March, on weekends. Admission charged.

THE GREAT DEERFIELD RAID

Native Peoples and African slaves were not the only ones in America to have been rounded up and marched off to a far-away land. In 1704, the people of Deerfield, Massachusetts, were attacked by French troops and their Indian allies, caught by surprise at night in the depth of winter. The raid was an extension of hostilities in Europe, where France and England were fighting each other for control of the Spanish throne. Deerfield was the most northwestern settlement of New England and, by its presence, irritating to the French. Of the 260 residents in Deerfield on that fateful night, approximately 50 were killed. More than 100 others were captured and forced to march 300 miles to Canada; more than 20 died along the way. Once in Canada, the captives became the subject of intense bargaining between the French and English. Finally, many were purchased outright or traded for prisoners held by the English. Some voluntarily remained in Canada, living with Indian or French families.

▲ The largest home in town, the Hinsdale & Anna Williams House shows the best of what Deerfield had to offer 190 years ago.

◀ Over the centuries, many of the houses have been expanded and remodeled. A tour of the Wells-Thorn House will open your eyes to the dramatic progress over time.

◀ Originally built as a family home, this structure was doubled in size 30 years later to include a tavern. While not entirely true to period, it has many interesting features plus a few surprises.

Peter Wentz Farmstead

SEE MAP PAGE 11, LOCATION #35B
Philadelphia vicinity (north), Pennsylvania
Phone: (610) 584-5104
http://www.peterwentzfarmsteadsociety.org

This Pennsylvania German farmstead holds a special place in history. It served as the headquarters for General Washington during the fall of 1777, while he was planning the Battle of Germantown – and yes, he slept here! Still, the real reason for stopping at Peter

▲ The distinctive Georgian-style stone house (above) and barn (below) reflect the German heritage of Peter and Rosanna Wentz. Both have been restored to their Revolutionary War era appearance when Washington was headquartered here.

▶ Colonial Pennsylvania Plantation is an ideal setting for special re-enactments held seasonally. Among them: the French and Indian War, Revolutionary War and Civil War.

▶ The plantation kitchen is well outfitted with sturdy everyday ware that is used by the museum staff. With the aroma of pies baking and pots steaming, visitors feel as though they've simply entered someone's home and caught them in the midst of daily chores.

Wentz Farmstead has more to do with Living History. It re-creates late-1770s life on a 90-acre estate.

Although modern farm techniques would make life much easier, historic authenticity prevails here. Interpreters are raising heritage farm animals. The gardens, orchards and fields are cultivated as they would have been in the period. And the 1758 German-Georgian manor house has eighteenth-century furnishings and an eighteenth-century kitchen.

If possible, try to schedule your visit during special exhibits and seasonal events, such as the spring sheep shearing and fall harvesting. You'll gain a more complete understanding of early American farm life.

Located near Philadelphia, PA, in Worcester. Take Route 363/Valley Forge Road; east on Route 73/Shippack Pike; drive ¼ mile; turn left on Shearer Road. Open Tuesday-Sunday except major holidays. Donations appreciated.

Colonial Pennsylvania Plantation

SEE MAP PAGE 11, LOCATION #37B
Philadelphia vicinity (west), Pennsylvania
Phone: (610) 566-1725
http://www.colonialplantation.org

Perhaps you could not imagine yourself as an ordinary citizen during the time just before and after our revolution. For most people, life was defined by survival needs back then, and individual responsibilities were clearly set. Men focused on maintaining fences, caring for farm animals and working in the fields, pasture and orchard. Women took care of the household, processed textiles, made clothing, tended a garden and preserved food. Children too had a number of regular chores.

Colonial Pennsylvania Plantation makes all this work surprisingly interesting. True to the 1700s, the farmstead includes a stone farmhouse with its period furnishings, a privy, a springhouse and separate wagon and stable barns. Interpreters re-create all aspects of eighteenth-century farm life, and visitors are welcome to participate. You might try dipping candles, drop-spinning yarn, making cheese,  sawing wood "the old way" or repairing a fence. On weekends, spring through fall, youth-oriented activities enable the entire family to learn together.

Located 16 miles west of Philadelphia in Ridley Creek State Park, Media, PA. Park entrance is on SR 3, 2½ miles west of Newtown Square. Open weekends only, April-November. Admission charged.

Middleton Place House

SEE MAP PAGE 15, LOCATION #15

Charleston vicinity (northwest), South Carolina
Phone: (843) 556-6020 or toll-free (800) 782-3608
http://www.middletonplace.org

Gunston Hall Plantation

SEE MAP PAGE 15, LOCATION #18A

Lorton, Virginia
Phone: (703) 550-9220
http://www.gunstonhall.org

The estates of wealthy Americans provide valuable perspective on the mentality that guided our rebellion against Mother England. Middleton Place is especially insightful – even though only the south dependency was left standing after this lovely estate was burned during the Civil War and devastated by an 1886 earthquake. The House Museum, which was originally built as guest quarters by Henry Middleton in 1755, contains an outstanding collection of family treasures. Among

them: furniture, silver, paintings, books, important documents and a rare silk copy of the Declaration of Independence. (The original was signed by Henry's son, Arthur.) Guided tours introduce visitors to the people who made Middleton Place their home.

The gardens, renowned for their grandeur, were created with precision and balance over perhaps ten years by 100 hard-working slaves. Today you can enjoy 65 acres of landscaped terraces, flower-lined footpaths, ornamental ponds and garden rooms. Azaleas bloom in spring, magnolias in early summer, perennials from summer to fall, and camellias in winter.

At the Plantation Stableyards, costumed interpreters and craftspeople re-create the life of African Americans who labored at Middleton Place and other southern plantations during the 1700s and 1800s. Their breadth of knowledge extends to domestic life at a freedman's cabin, labor at the rice mill and spring house, religion and spirituality at the slave chapel and cemetery.

Located on SR 61 approximately 14 miles northwest of Charleston, SC, and the junction US 17. Open daily except major holidays. Admission charged.

Have you heard about George Mason? He was one of a handful of men at the Constitutional Convention who refused to sign the final draft of the U.S. Constitution. (He believed it did not adequately protect the rights and liberties of individuals.) A great political leader, Mason had crafted the Virginia Declaration of Rights and Virginia Constitution in 1776. Both were models for similar documents prepared by other colonies. More importantly, the Virginia Declaration of Rights served as the basis for our nation's Bill of Rights (the first ten Amendments to the Constitution).

Gunston Hall was his home. Although Mason had complained about "the etiquette and nonsense" in

Philadelphia, this house reflects the beauty and grace you would expect from a man of taste. Enjoy your tour!

Located 20 miles south of Washington, DC, via I-95 exit 163; left on Lorton Road; right on Gunston Cove Road. Open daily except Thanksgiving, December 25 and January 1. Admission charged.

▲ Carpenter/joiner William Buckland, an indentured servant from England, is believed to have been the primary designer of Gunston Hall (circa 1755-1759). The building's external balance and simplicity contrast beautifully with an elegant interior.

◀ When you stroll through the gardens at Middleton Place, remember the vital contribution of slave labor. According to a 1783 tax assessment, Henry Middleton had 266 slaves on multiple rice plantations totaling 27,871 acres. Today, Living History interpreters provide a rare glimpse into their challenging lives.

◀ William Bernard Sears, an indentured servant, is credited with creating the elaborate carvings and fine woodwork seen throughout Gunston Hall. His decorative embellishments are quite exceptional, even by today's standards.

FRENCH & INDIAN WAR

> ▶ Not in the best of locations, tiny Fort Necessity stood on low ground surrounded by a forest. Taking advantage of this situation, the French did not fight in the expected line formation, out in the open, but instead fired from behind the trees. Washington and his men had no choice but to abandon their trenches and crowd together inside the fort.

The French & Indian War (1754-1763) was the last and most important conflict in America before the Revolutionary War. It began as a dispute over land claims in America and spread across the Atlantic, becoming part of Europe's Seven Years' War.

Igniting the conflicts were rival French-Canadian and British-American claims to the vast region along the Ohio River between the Appalachian Mountains and the Mississippi River. This region was important both economically and strategically. When the governor of Virginia learned that the French had built forts in territory claimed by his colony, he sent an eight-man diplomatic expedition under George Washington (then only 21 years old) to demand that the French leave. Of course, the French refused.

What followed was a series of bloody battles involving not only European and colonial rivals but also Native Peoples – especially Huron and Algonquin tribes who allied with the French, and the Six Nations (Iroquois) who allied with the English. For several years, France was the stronger force. Among the significant early events: General Braddock died and his troops were defeated at Fort Duquesne in 1755. The English forts of Oswego and George were destroyed, and General Webb gave up the Mohawk Valley in 1756. Fort William Henry was captured and burned in 1757. Worst of all, General Abercromby suffered a miserable defeat at Fort Carillon in 1758 and had to be removed from authority. In the meantime, the Cherokees waged their own war in the Southern colonies (1758-1761).

France gave up almost all of its lands in North America

The tide finally turned in mid-1758 when British forces captured Louisbourg, Fort Frontenac and Fort Duquesne (renamed Fort Pitt). In 1759, they took Forts Niagara, Carillon (renamed Fort Ticonderoga) and St. Frederic. Also in 1759, Quebec (New France) fell to the British. When the battles finally ended in 1763, both in America and in Europe, France had lost much. It relinquished most of its lands in North America to Britain, including Canada and territory east of the Mississippi River (except New Orleans), as well as its empire in India. Spain, France's ally under a mutual protection agreement, gave up Florida to Britain but received New Orleans and lands west of the Mississippi from France as compensation. There were no territorial changes in Europe.

Fort Necessity National Battlefield

SEE MAP PAGE 11, LOCATION #44
Uniontown vicinity (east), Pennsylvania
Phone: (724) 329-5512
http://www.nps.gov/fone

What began as a campaign to build a military road for British Colonial troops turned into the opening battle of the French and Indian War. As fate would have it, young George Washington was at the heart of it all. He and Virginia frontiersmen were working their way westward when French troops confiscated a new British fort at the forks of the Ohio River. Hearing the news, Washington decided to establish a base camp at what was then known as the Great Meadows. A few days later, he and 40 of his men engaged in a battle with French soldiers nearby, killing 13 and capturing 21 others.

Expecting a retaliation, the Virginians hastily built Fort Necessity and were joined by reinforcements. On July 3, 1754, they were attacked. Although they fought valiantly, they had to quit by day's end, overwhelmed by heavy rain, flooded trenches and impossible odds. This was the first major event in Washington's military career and the only time he surrendered to an enemy. Today the site is a National Park with three outdoor units, including the reconstructed fort and battleground.

Located southeast of Pittsburgh, PA. Take US 51 south to Uniontown and then US 40 east for 11 miles. Open daily except major holidays. Admission charged.

MOUNT WASHINGTON TAVERN

Near the site of Fort Necessity, this circa 1830 tavern catered to stagecoach travelers on the National Road (our first federally constructed highway). Take a tour. Visit the barroom and ladies' parlor. Step into the dining room where up to 72 travelers took turns eating family-style. Enter the kitchen where food was prepared in an open hearth. See where strangers bedded down together for the night.

Fort Frederick State Park

SEE MAP PAGE 15, LOCATION #17
Hagerstown vicinity (west), Maryland
Phone: (301) 842-2155
http://www.dnr.state.md.us/publiclands/western/
fortfrederick.html

Fort Frederick was built in 1756 to protect British settlers in the Maryland frontier from attack during the French and Indian War. It was one of the largest British fortifications in North America, and while most other forts were enclosed by wood and earth, this one was protected by a 20-foot-high stone wall. It conformed to the style developed by a French military engineer considered to be the father of modern fortification.

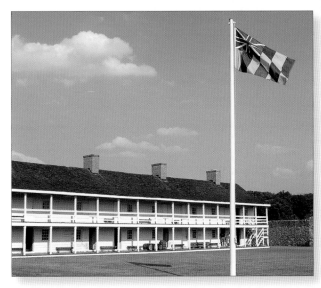

Fort Frederick never saw military action, but it did serve as a valuable staging area and supply base for British-American campaigns. Among the troops garrisoned here were the Maryland Forces, a spirited group accustomed to frontier-style warfare. Later, the Fort served as a prison camp during the American Revolution, a Union infantry station during the Civil War and, in a surprising change of fate, the farm of an African American family well into the twentieth century. Today, the stone wall and two barracks have been restored to their 1758 appearance. Daily Living History programs are presented from Memorial Day through Labor Day. Military re-enactments and other special events are staged annually.

Located 18 miles west of Hagerstown, MD, and a mile south of I-70 near Big Pool (Route 56, exit 12) – about 1 1/2 hours northwest of Washington, DC, and Baltimore, MD. The state park lands adjoin the Potomac River, and a section of the Chesapeake and Ohio Canal passes through park acreage. Open daily except major holidays. Admission charged.

Fort Loudoun State Historic Area

SEE MAP PAGE 17, LOCATION #18
Vonore, Tennessee
Phone: (423) 884-6217
http://www.fortloudoun.com

In 1756, the British Colony of South Carolina garrisoned here to protect trade interests with the Overhill Cherokee Nation. This effort helped to ally the Cherokees against the French, but relations eventually broke down. In 1760, the Cherokees burned Fort Loudoun.

The current fort is a nearly complete reconstruction based on archaeological evidence. Built on a hillside, it provides interesting perspective on colonial military life. Take advantage of tours and talks offered by costumed interpreters. Also try to time your visit with one of the Living History events held almost monthly. Garrison Weekends re-create British military life, and the 18th Century Trade Faire is a fun way to see how British soldiers and civilians came together with traders, French soldiers and Indians.

Across from Fort Loudoun is the Sequoyah Birthplace Museum, where you can learn about the Cherokee people and their unique written language.

Located at 338 Fort Loudoun Road near Vonore, TN, about 30 miles south of Knoxville. From I-75, take Highway 72 (Loudon exit); go east 20 miles to Highway 411; take 411 north through Vonore; turn onto 360 south, and follow the signs to the park. Open daily except December 25. Free except during special events.

▲ The tall palisade of pointed logs, the sharp barricades of woven sticks, and the troops hidden behind earth-works...all must have been intimidating. But perhaps the most fear-some line of defence at Fort Loudoun was the dense hedge of locust bushes. It was full of long, very sharp thorns that would rip through a person's skin.

◀ The flag flying over Fort Frederick combines two elements: the black and yellow design of the family flag of George Calvert (the first Lord Baltimore who owned Maryland in 1629) and the heraldic imagery from the British Union Flag.

◀ Looking like tools of torture, eighteenth-century surgical instruments were frightening enough to make even strong-hearted men avoid doctors. Yet they enabled medical officers to accomplish remarkable feats, as the interpreter explains.

Fort Ticonderoga

SEE MAP PAGE 11, LOCATION #41
Ticonderoga, New York
Phone: (518) 585-2821
http://www.fort-ticonderoga.org

The fort finally did fall to the British in 1759 and was renamed "Ticonderoga," a Mohawk word meaning "the land between two waters." Its capture enabled the British to construct a fleet of war ships on Lake Champlain and build a major new fortress at Crown Point. Fort Ticonderoga later became a stronghold for both the British and the Americans during the Revolutionary War.

▲ Perched on a hill and surrounded by massive stone walls studded with cannons, Fort Ti would have presented a daunting sight to attackers.

▶ Inside the fort, restored buildings house an extensive museum displaying artifacts found on the site as well as items related to the fort's time in history. The powder horn collection is particularly noteworthy. Works of art, many of the horns belonged to soldiers garrisoned here.

▶ Fort Ti played a key role in not only the French and Indian War but also the Revolutionary War. In 1775, Ethan Allen and Benedict Arnold stormed up the stairway of the Officers' Barracks (right-hand building) to demand the fort's surrender in America's first major victory of the Revolution. Two years later, the fort changed hands again.

Situated above the narrow choke-point between Lake Champlain and Lake George, this star-shaped fort was built by the French in 1755-1758 and was first named Fort Carillon. Its purpose was to guard the portage between the two lakes and serve as a defensive position against British forces advancing toward French Canada. As such, it interfered with commonly used British-American trade routes between the Hudson River Valley and the French-controlled Saint Lawrence River Valley.

In July 1758, a British army of 16,000 attacked. Surprisingly, the French force of 3,200 prevailed. While we would like to credit French defensive works quickly built in the path of the enemy, we cannot ignore British blunders. It was a bloody battle, with combined casualties totaling nearly 2,500 men. Over 1,900 in the British force were killed or wounded, including 350 American provincials and 490 men from the 42nd Regiment of Foot (the Highlanders or "Black Watch"). For them, it was a failure of command, communication and coordination. General Abercromby was relieved of his duties.

Important as it was, "Fort Ti" was not destined to remain intact. The French blew up the powder magazine and set fire to the warehouse when they left in 1759. Although the British immediately made repairs, they too blew up the fort two decades later, rather than allow its use by American rebels. Locals and visitors then carried off building stones. When the restoration began in 1908, most of the walls were only knee-high. Still, the fort's "footprint" was clear, and the two-story Officers' Barracks was complete to nearly its eaves. Through private philanthropy by the William Ferris Pell family, an impressive rebuilding program brought back the fort's grandeur. This was the earliest commitment – private or public – to historic preservation in America.

Today you'll find much to enjoy: guided and self-guided tours, interpreters in period clothing, a truly world-class museum, military demonstrations, and special events such as a French and Indian War re-enactment.

Located in Ticonderoga in northeastern NY. Take SR 22 south to SR 74 east and follow the signs. Open daily from mid-May to mid-October. Admission charged.

Fort Ligonier

SEE MAP PAGE 11, LOCATION #31
Ligonier, Pennsylvania
Phone: (724) 238-9701
http://www.fortligonier.org

When Great Britain and France went to war over ownership of the immense inner basin of North America, British general John Forbes was told to seize France's Fort Duquesne (du-KANE) at the forks of the Ohio River (in Pittsburgh). This meant hacking out a wagon road across Pennsylvania and constructing a chain of fortifications to secure the region. The last post to be built was Fort Ligonier (lee-gun-EAR), and it was a formidable structure. The French attacked this fort twice in October 1758 while it was still under construction, recognizing they were in serious jeopardy.

But it stood strong and soon became a supply depot and staging area for 5,000 British and American troops. Now outnumbered, the French made a practical decision: they destroyed Fort Duquesne and left. The British took over the site the next day and built Fort Pitt.

For the remainder of the French and Indian War, Fort Ligonier continued to serve as a strategically placed garrison. It later became a vital link in British communication and supply lines during Pontiac's War of 1763. When no longer needed, this stronghold was decommissioned in 1766 and then quietly fell into ruin.

Today's Fort Ligonier is an extraordinary, full-scale reconstruction standing on its original hilltop site in the beautiful Laurel Highlands of Pennsylvania. Noteworthy in many respects, it contains a sizable collection of artillery and a fascinating array of eighteenth-century military defenses. You will see the 1,600-foot-long outer retrenchment; the daunting fraise (a slanted rampart of pointed stakes); the Chevaux de Frise (giant structures of crossed spears guarding entryways); the cannon battery moat and fascines (bundled branches creating a difficult-to-climb wall in the dry moat); and a second, inner wall of sharp planks that stand like centurions. Inside the fort defenses are seven outfitted buildings. Outside are a number of other structures that were important for supporting garrisoned troops. Be sure to explore the Visitor Center museum as well. On display are the exquisite pistols presented to George Washington by his ally and protégé the Marquis de Lafayette.

Numerous Living History events and special programs bring the fort to life. Most popular is the annual Fort Ligonier Days held the second weekend in October, typically during the height of fall foliage.

Located on US 30 and SR 711 in Ligonier, PA, about 50 miles east of Pittsburgh and about 3 miles from the Compass Inn in Laughlintown. (See Our New Nation, page 178.) Open daily May-October. Admission charged.

▲ In front of the fort is an extensive collection of reproduction British artillery equipment – mortars, field pieces, Howitzers, powder carts, ammunition wagons, a sling cart and a tumbrel cart.

◄ To breach the fort, attackers had to get past the first barrier: eight courses of stakes, inclined and pointed on top. They would then face this dry moat protected by a column of sharpened posts and lined with bundled branches, almost impossible to scale.

◄ Outfitted buildings, peopled by realistic-looking mannikins, include the officers' quarters, officers' mess, soldiers' barracks, commissary, quartermaster supply room (shown here), armory, powder magazine, hospital, and home of ailing General Forbes. Outside the fort walls are the smokehouse, sawmill, forge, bake ovens and dwelling for non-military personnel.

AMERICAN REVOLUTION

▲ Imagine this view at Yorktown Battlefield as a relatively flat field. In preparation for their defense, British troops had cleared away the trees and large bushes to provide an unobstructed view. They had also created batteries and redoubts (raised, man-made, earthen battlements) where cannon would have a clear shot with minimum exposure to enemy fire.

Try as they will, history books and historical movies can barely prepare a person for the graphic reality of standing within a major battlefield of the American Revolution. Often, you are not out in a field; you are in the middle of a town. You are not surrounded by military barracks; you are surrounded by people's homes, farms and businesses. That's the way it was back then. Men fought hard on their own land to defend not only their property but also their rights from what they perceived as a tyrannical superpower. Many died beside their neighbors and within sight of their wives.

An historic interpreter in a tavern across from the Lexington Green points to a bullet hole in his door. "It happened on April 19, 1775," he says. Earlier that year, the British Parliament had found Massachusetts to be in open rebellion and gave troops the legal right to shoot troublemakers. During the night of April 18, British soldiers marched from Boston toward Concord on what they believed was a secret mission to capture or destroy the colonial arms and gunpowder stored in Concord and potentially take key leaders as prisoners. Joseph Warren, a Bostonian, discovered that the British were on the march. In the now-famous ride on horseback, three speedy couriers – William Dawes, Paul Revere and Dr. Samuel Prescott – rode by separate routes to warn the people of Concord and nearby Lexington.

When the British arrived in Lexington near dawn on April 19, the colonists were prepared. Volunteer soldiers called Minutemen met the Redcoats on the village Green. Shots were fired. Eight of the Minutemen fell dead, and ten were wounded. A single British soldier was

hurt. Importantly, the rebel leaders Samuel Adams and John Hancock had escaped.

The British force continued on, meeting more Minutemen at North Bridge just outside of Concord. Here, three British soldiers and two Minutemen were killed, but the colonists were able to spirit away most of their battle supplies and evacuate Concord. Unable to complete their mission, the British turned back toward Boston.

That could have been the end of the skirmishing. Instead, the British were met on a country road by the colonial militia, now 3,500 strong. In a running fight that continued all the way to Boston, the British faced heavy fire from men who took cover behind buildings, trees, bushes and fences. Despite 1,000 reinforcements, they could not win. The weary British straggled into Boston, dispirited by the unexpected fury of colonial rebels and the fierceness of the fighting. Their dead, wounded and missing totaled about 270; rebel losses were about 90. The American discontent over British taxation and the shouting about colonial rights had ended. April 19, 1775, was the first day of a very real war. There was no turning back.

FIGHTING FORCES

Apparently believing the old adage "might makes right," the British expected an easy victory in America. The Redcoats were well-trained professional soldiers, totaling about 50,000 at their peak. In contrast, the rebel forces under General Washington rarely numbered over 15,000 and were frequently far fewer; the majority of their training came from hard experience. The Americans were primarily citizen-soldiers between the ages of 16 and 60, who could be called upon to serve only a few days to a few months. With overriding responsibilities to their farms and businesses, most preferred serving in local militias and supporting the war effort when the danger was close to home. Adding to American problems, many of our military leaders were less experienced and less assured than their British counterparts. They did, however, have a major strategic advantage: the British military leaders were cautious in their battle plans, while the Americans were willing to take chances. In the long run, daring leadership and unorthodox fighting tactics, along with support from key enemies of Britain (especially France but also Spain), put the odds in American hands.

Historic Lexington

SEE MAP PAGE 11, LOCATION #30A
Lexington, Massachusetts
Phone: (781) 862-1450
http://www.lexingtonhistory.org/houses_2002.html
http://www.libertyride.us/historic.html

When the first musket fired April 19, 1775, on the Lexington Green in Massachusetts, was it British or Patriot? Was it intentional or the act of a nervous trigger finger? No one knew for certain; it didn't matter. A ferocious skirmish followed.

From the Redcoats' perspective, this was not supposed to happen. Their force of 700 men was on a "secret" mission to destroy or take the American military provisions in nearby Concord and diffuse colonial resistance. They didn't expect their job to be an easy one, but they had been confident of success. In Lexington, at what is now the junction of Massachusetts Avenue and Bedford Street, they were surprised by 77 brave Minutemen (colonial volunteers ready to fight at a minute's notice). The rebels raised their weapons against a column of British Regulars and, although heavily outnumbered, refused to back down.

Buckman Tavern

The headquarters for the Minutemen was Buckman Tavern. Built around 1710, the tavern had long been a popular gathering place for churchgoers during their Sunday "nooning" and for drovers moving their herds to market. The interior appears today very much as it did in 1775 when the Minutemen waited here for the British troops. Historic items include the original taproom fireplace, the bar, the old front door with its bullet hole from a British musket ball, and a portrait of John Buckman, the proprietor. Located at 1 Bedford Street.

Munroe Tavern

Needing a safe haven after the battles of Lexington and Concord, the British occupied Munroe Tavern for

an hour-and-a-half, using the dining room as a field hospital. Fourteen years later, President Washington dined here when he stopped to see the Lexington battlefield. Many period items are on display, including an eighteenth-century tavern sign, a fine tricorn hat box and personal articles used by the proprietor and his family. Here, too, are documents and a table associated with Washington's visit. The tavern building dates to the early 1700s. Located at 1332 Massachusetts Avenue.

Hancock-Clarke House

Samuel Adams and John Hancock were spending the night in Lexington when Paul Revere arrived from Boston to warn about the advancing British. The early 1700s residence recalls that time beautifully. In addition to period furnishings and interesting portraits, it has the drum William Diamond played and the pistols Major Pitcairn used during the clash with British troops. Located at 36 Hancock Street.

Visitor Center is across from the Battle Green at 1875 Massachusetts Avenue in Lexington, MA. Open daily except major holidays. The three pre-Revolutionary buildings are open April-October – daily from June 15 and at varying times earlier in the season. Admission charged. Patriots Day re-enactments held every April.

◁ Munroe Tavern became the unwilling host of the retreating British, who needed to nurse their wounded and take sustenance. Presumably, the officers were unaware that the proprietor was an orderly sergeant with the Minutemen.

◁ Paul Revere was captured by the British on his way from Lexington to Concord. Apparently his horse was taken, but he was released. On foot, he returned to Lexington and the Buckman Tavern, where he helped remove a trunk full of papers belonging to John Hancock.

▽ This was the family home of two ministers who served Lexington during a 105-year period. A frequent visitor was Reverend Hancock's grandson, John, who became the first signer of the Declaration of Independence.

Minute Man National Historical Park

SEE MAP PAGE 11, LOCATION #28A

Concord, Lincoln and Lexington, Massachusetts
Phone: (978) 369-6993
http://www.nps.gov/mima

Located 18 miles from Boston, in the towns of Lexington, Lincoln and Concord, MA. From I-95, take exit 30B (Route 2A west) to main Visitor Center in Lexington. Open daily April-November. The North Bridge Visitor Center is located at 174 Liberty Street, Concord. Open daily year-round. Hartwell Tavern is located in Hartwell Historic Area, Route 2A, Lincoln. Open Memorial Day-October. The Wayside is located at 455 Lexington Road, Concord. Open Memorial Day-October. Entry into the National Historical Park is free. Admission charged at The Wayside.

▲ The reconstructed North Bridge arches gracefully over the Concord River, much as it did when the British and Minutemen faced off in April 1775.

▶ Hartwell Tavern, built in the 1730s, was located on the Battle Road. Anyone inside would have witnessed the British advance to Lexington and their retreat back toward Boston with the local Minutemen in pursuit.

▶ This famous statue was created in the 1870s by 23-year-old Daniel Chester French, whose talent and inspiration more than made up for his limited experience at the time. Years later, French sculpted the seated Abraham Lincoln at the Lincoln Memorial in Washington, DC.

Located along the actual Battle Road of April 19, 1775, Minute Man National Historical Park preserves, protects and interprets significant historic sites and landscapes tied to the opening days of the American Revolution. Dramatically personalized, freedom takes on new meaning here. Try to imagine yourself in the shoes of Patriots. How determined they were to gain their liberty! How much they were willing to sacrifice for American rights, for cultural independence, for individual responsibility!

Begin at the Visitor Center in Lexington with a multi-media theatre program, "The Road to Revolution," and a variety of informative exhibits. Then walk or bike the wheelchair accessible Battle Road Trail, which connects to historic sites such as Hartwell Tavern. Alternatively, drive through the park, stopping at designated areas. Also visit The Wayside, a typical 1700s two-story, wood-frame farmhouse. And, of course, walk across North Bridge, site of "the shot heard 'round the world." You'll find daily interpretive programs at Hartwell Tavern, The Wayside and North Bridge. In addition, special events and re-enactments are held from April to December.

FIGHTING TACTICS

Contrary to popular myth, the Americans did not win the war by hiding behind trees and rocks, easily shooting the "dumb" British who were standing out in open ranks. Once the local militias were trained in the "Army way," American troops learned that some form of linear tactic was usually more effective than guerilla warfare. There were exceptions, of course. At the start of the war in Lexington and Concord, using cover added the element of surprise. Mostly though, the troops would stand side-by-side in lines two or three deep across the battlefield. The front line would fire, sending a mass of musket balls toward the enemy, and reload while the next line of men fired. By shooting in volleys, the soldiers were able to compensate for the notorious inaccuracy of muskets, which after 50 yards made a man-sized target very difficult to hit deliberately. The objective was to break up the enemies' organized lines and then charge forward with bayonets at the ready.

Washington Crossing

SEE MAP PAGE 11, LOCATION #45B, #43B

Pennsylvania side:
Washington Crossing - Phone: (215) 493-4076
http://www.ushistory.org/washingtoncrossing
New Jersey side:
Trenton vicinity (northwest) - Phone: (609) 737-0623
http://www.state.nj.us/dep/parksandforests/parks/washcros.html

The war did not go well for us in the early years. By the close of 1776, American troops were staggering under a succession of defeats. Morale was falling fast, and enlistments were expiring. General George Washington could see disaster looming. From his camp on the Pennsylvania side of the Delaware River, he took a desperate chance on the night of December 25: he had General Glover's 14th regiment row him and his men across the ice-choked river through sleet and snow. Their objective was to launch a surprise attack on British-hired Hessians (Germans) at Trenton. The 2,400 Americans – their bodies near-frozen and their feet,

lacking good shoes, wrapped in blood-stained rags – assembled on the New Jersey shore, marched about ten miles downstream, and routed 1,200 Hessians in a battle lasting less than two hours. About 100 enemy were killed, and over 900 were captured; but American casualties were light. Still outnumbered by enemy troops in the area, the Americans recrossed the river to safety that afternoon. It was a brilliant, much-needed success, reinvigorating their cause for freedom.

Two states justifiably lay claim to this great triumph. The Pennsylvania side of the Delaware River is now an historic park. The New Jersey side is a state park and recreational area.

Washington Crossing Historic Park

In Pennsylvania, this picturesque 500-acre park is divided into two sections. The Visitor Center in the Washington Crossing section has several houses and work buildings that represent Pennsylvania industry and home life in the 1700s and 1800s, as well as replicas of the troops' Durham boats. The Thompson-Neely House in the upper park functioned as a regimental hospital during the time of Washington's encampment. It has an original gristmill and restored officers quarters.

Located near the town of Washington Crossing, PA. The McConkey's Ferry section is in town on SR 32 (River Road), north of SR 532. The Thompson's Mill section is 5 miles further north on SR 32. Open Tuesday-Sunday except major holidays. Admission charged.

Washington Crossing State Park

Connected by a bridge to the Pennsylvania park is Johnson's Ferry, the New Jersey landing site for George Washington and his men. Visitor Center galleries explore many facets of the Revolutionary War, with emphasis on "The Ten Crucial Days." In addition, tours are offered at the Johnson Ferry House, which most likely was used by General Washington as he waited for his troops to finish crossing the Delaware. The keeping room, bedchamber and textile room are furnished with period pieces. Every year at 1 p.m. on Christmas Day, hundreds of re-enactors, dressed as the Continental Army, cross the river in replica Durham boats.

Located in Titusville, 8 miles northwest of Trenton, NJ. From I-95, take Route 29 north; follow signs. Visitor Center open daily. Johnson Ferry House open Wednesday-Sunday. Summer parking fee on weekends and holidays.

◁ The McConkey Inn was ideally located at a narrow spot on the Pennsylvania side of the Delaware River. General Washington and his officers used it to make their final plans for the crossing and attack on Trenton, NJ.

▽ The only surviving period structure from the New Jersey side of the river is the Johnson Ferry House, a charming eighteenth-century farmhouse and tavern which offers weekend tours.

◁ Replicas of the Durham boats used by Washington and his men can be seen in the boathouse at the Pennsylvania park. Durhams, which could be as long as 65 feet, were built to haul cargo up and down the river.

Old Barracks Museum

SEE MAP PAGE 11, LOCATION #42B
Trenton, New Jersey
Phone: (609) 396-1776 or (609)777-3599 (weekends)
http://www.barracks.org

▲ At one time, citizens were forced to quarter British troops in their homes. Old Barracks was built in 1758 in response to demands for alternative housing. After the battle of Trenton, it was taken over by American troops and became an Army hospital.

On December 28, 1776, General Washington and his men crossed the Delaware a second time near Trenton. Their goal was to surprise the enemy again, this time at Princeton. It was like a cat-and-mouse game. Learning about the Americans, the British marched on Trenton. But Washington's troops knew about back roads. So they left their campfires tended by a few militiamen and quietly stole off into the night. Proceeding on foot to Princeton, they routed the unsuspecting British rearguard. In just ten days, virtually all of New Jersey had been retaken by the Continental Army.

Old Barracks Museum is an important addition to a visit to Washington Crossing. (See page 145.) It presents the personal side of both the first and second battles of Trenton – the human foibles, prejudices and misunderstandings that give dimension to any war effort. This cultural history museum was established in the only surviving British Colonial barracks in America. Constructed in 1758, it became an Army hospital after the Battles of Trenton and was assigned to inoculate soldiers against smallpox using methods that became the foundation of modern vaccinations. Today you can take a guided tour of the well-appointed officer's quarters, soldier's barracks and hospital room where Living History interpreters dramatically recount an extraordinary period in American history.

Located on Barrack Street in downtown Trenton, NJ. Take I-95 to Route 29 North to Calhoun Street exit; right onto West State Street; right unto Barrack Street. At traffic light just past the museum, turn right into the Capitol Complex Parking Area and obtain a pass at the Guard's shack. Open daily except major holidays. Admission charged.

Stony Point Battlefield State Historic Site

SEE MAP PAGE 11, LOCATION #40
Stony Point, New York
Phone: (845) 786-2521
http://nysparks.state.ny.us/sites/info.asp?siteID=29

Another daring attack by the Americans took place in July 1779, when Brigadier General Anthony Wayne commanded a midnight assault on the fort at Stony Point, a peninsula on the Hudson River. The infantry was using a strategy crafted by General Washington and altered somewhat by Wayne to meet his own needs.

▶ Separate from its strategic importance in history, Stony Point offers a beautiful place to relax and picnic amidst picturesque forest scenery and panoramic views. The British soldiers who were camped here, high on the hill above the Hudson River, had plenty of time to enjoy the view – until one fateful night.

With an attack force that was double the size of the British garrison, the men moved stealthily under the cover of darkness. They had no artillery support and no loaded weapons, just fixed bayonets. One column of soldiers proceeded around the south end of the peninsula, a second moved around the north, and a third column positioned itself in the center. Their path was hilly and rugged; little was visible in the darkness. To avoid confusion during the attack, the men wore pieces of white paper in their hats. They struck, and in just one hour, the British surrendered. A few days later, after taking valuable supplies and armaments, the Americans destroyed the fort that had been a staging ground for British raids on the Connecticut coast.

Today you can enjoy a self-guided tour of the well-marked battlefield. The park has weekend demonstrations of military weapons and eighteenth-century camp life as well as a museum and many seasonal events. A restored 1826 lighthouse stands atop the hill.

Located 25 miles north of Manhattan in Stony Point, NY. Take Palisades Interstate Parkway exit 15; follow signs to Route 106/210 (east); turn onto Route 9W (north) and in a mile turn right on Park Road; stay to left at bottom of hill. Grounds open daily. Museum open Wednesday-Sunday mid-April to October. Parking fee on weekends.

Saratoga National Historical Park

SEE MAP PAGE 11, LOCATION #39

Stillwater, New York
Phone: (518) 664-9821
http://www.nps.gov/sara

In mid-1777, British general John Burgoyne launched a four-month campaign to cut a wedge in our nation between New England and the Middle States. His troops included 4,200 British regulars, 4,000 German allies, and several hundred Canadians and Indians. These enemy soldiers achieved a number of early successes, including a sweeping victory at Fort Ticonderoga on Lake Champlain; but time and the tide of events began to run against them. Finally in October, Burgoyne's campaign collapsed after he and his troops were outwitted and outnumbered in two hotly contested battles at Saratoga. Unable to overcome an American force of nearly 15,000 men, Burgoyne surrendered.

Many historians rank this American victory among the most important battles in world history. It was more than a decisive military win, ending British hopes of dividing the colonies. It changed France's opinion about America's struggle for independence and ultimately led to the signing of two French-American treaties, one establishing amity and commerce, and the other forming a strategic alliance against Britain, with vital financial and military aid to our infantry. Without this, democracy as we know it might never have happened.

In several units, Saratoga National Park tells the amazing stories of this critical time. Among the most remarkable were the feats of General Benedict Arnold, whose military tactics and enormous courage were pivotal to our success. (How ironic that he would become an embittered man and a traitor to America three years later!) Be sure to see the introductory film and Visitor Center fiberoptic map of the battles.

Located in Stillwater, NY, 40 miles north of Albany and 15 miles southeast of Saratoga Springs. Take I-87 exit 12, and follow park signs. Visitor Center open daily except some holidays. Battlefield Tour Road usually open April to mid-November depending upon weather conditions. Schuyler House, Neilson House (on Battlefield) and Saratoga Monument open Wednesday-Sunday from Memorial Day to Labor Day. Admission charged to drive the Battlefield Road loop. Other sites free.

▲ The battlefield road covers nine miles and has ten tour stops, several of which include audio recountings of various events. In 1777, the area was primarily farmland. Only one building remains: the red-painted home of John and Lydia Neilson.

◀ Seven miles north of the battlefield on US 4 is the country estate of General Philip Schuyler (SKY-ler). It offers an intriguing peek into the life of a wealthy landowner who contributed much behind the scenes to our success at Saratoga.

FROM ENEMIES TO FRIENDS

What a difference a few years made! We fought on the side of England against France during the French and Indian War (1754-1763). But when we declared our independence from England, many French people were sympathetic to our cause. French soldiers, as individuals, joined us on the battlefields. The most notable among them was the Marquis de Lafayette, who left his wife, fortune and high social position in 1777 to serve under General Washington. (He played an important part in the defeat of British General Cornwallis during the final campaign of the Revolution.) Beginning in 1778, the King of France (Louis XVI) openly provided substantial support to America, including a fleet of ships, armies of fighting men, military supplies and money. On the most basic level, he authorized large quantities of muskets with bayonets, gunpowder, cartridge boxes, uniforms and other military accoutrements, alleviating serious American shortages. Could America have won independence without its French allies? Benjamin Franklin didn't think so.

Fort Stanwix National Monument

SEE MAP PAGE 11, LOCATION #38

Rome, New York
Phone: (315) 338-7730
http://www.nps.gov/fost

▲ Today's Fort Stanwix is a remarkable achievement. The city of Rome, NY, cleared away several blocks of nineteenth-century buildings to make this reconstruction possible on the original footprint. It is based on fort plans retrieved from English archives.

▶ As is true at any fort, the staff room at Fort Stanwix was the hub of all long-range planning and daily activities. What makes this one unique today are the replicas of colonial and regimental flags hanging on the walls. Fort Stanwix may have been the first place to fly a red-and-white striped flag with white stars on a blue field.

▶ Medicine in the 1700s was as much art as science. Frontier doctors, who had no apothecary nearby, needed to acquire their own knowledge of medicinal plants and other ingredients in order to make pills and poultices by hand.

This is a place to learn the major lessons of history: what can happen when one's focus is too narrow, when the ramifications of individual actions are miscalculated, when too many things are tackled at one time. Fort Stanwix was at the heart of conflict from its beginnings.

The British built this impressive fort in 1758 along a vital Indian trade route between the Atlantic Ocean and Lake Ontario. Favorably received by the Six Nations (the Iroquois), its location secured the region during the French and Indian War. However, many Native Peoples viewed the fort as an example of white encroachment into Indian territory. While a 1763 Royal Proclamation restricted further settlement west of the Appalachians, it could not ease the frustrations that led to Pontiac's Rebellion. Then in late 1768, a treaty signed at Fort Stanwix with the Six Nations opened up lands east and south of the Ohio River for British settlement – without the consent of some tribes who lived and hunted there. This set the stage for future conflicts.

Next came the American Revolution. The British had previously abandoned Fort Stanwix but in mid-1777 decided to reclaim it, only to find Continental soldiers

garrisoned there. They lay siege to the fort, along with Indian allies and Loyalists, and soon became embroiled in a second battle by ambushing an American relief column. Patriot soldiers at the fort took advantage of the turmoil, stealing off to destroy enemy camps and cart off

21 wagonloads of supplies. Unable to reoccupy the fort, the British and their allies withdrew.

In 1784, old problems repeated themselves when Fort Stanwix was the site of American treaty negotiations with the Six Nations. Indian representatives ceded lands in western Pennsylvania and Ohio without proper authority. The questionable legality of the treaty, along with westward expansion, led to major Indian wars.

Of course, Fort Stanwix was the site of many more-positive times as well. Today's re-creation is a fascinating monument to all sides of the story. The buildings are faithfully reconstructed, fully outfitted and populated with well-informed interpreters. Numerous special events further enhance the experience.

Located in downtown Rome, NY. From New York Thru-way, take exit 32 at Westmoreland to Route 233 north and then Route 69 west into Rome. Fort open daily April-November (except Thanksgiving) and during special December events. Visitor Center open year-round. Free.

NATIVE AMERICAN SOLDIERS

Initially, both Loyalists and Patriots urged Indians to be neutral during American-British disputes, claiming that the conflicts were a family quarrel. But that was a short-lived position. Even before full-scale war broke out, George Washington had recruited gunmen from Eastern tribes, and by the fall of 1775, General Gage solicited warriors for the British side. Most Indians, frustrated by American settlement on their lands, sided with the British or moved out of the battle region. The results were disastrous. When the Mohawk, Onondaga, Cayuga and Seneca joined the British fight, against the wishes of the Oneida and Tuscarora, the Great Peace that had lasted for centuries among the Six Nations was shattered. Powerful southern Indians – the Cherokees, Choctaws, Creeks and Chickasaws – suffered similar factional strife. Then, after the Revolutionary War was over, American negotiators reproached numerous Indian nations, claiming that they were now conquered peoples since so many had sided with the losers.

Morristown National Historical Park

SEE MAP PAGE 11, LOCATION #32
Morristown, New Jersey
Phone: (908) 766-8215
http://www.nps.gov/morr

This was our nation's first national historical park, created by an Act of Congress in 1933 to mark the site where General Washington and his Continental Army spent the harsh winters of 1777 and 1779-1780. You will come away from here with renewed pride and respect for the man who became America's first President.

General Washington twice chose Morristown as his winter headquarters. He had several reasons: its close proximity to New York City and important communication routes, its defensible terrain within reach of critical resources (including a local gunpowder mill), and a supportive nearby community where his wife Martha could join him. But the weather was nearly unbearable during the second encampment. Reportedly 28 merciless blizzards hit the estimated 10,000 men, causing them to suffer from serious food shortages, inadequate clothing and poor log shelters. How Washington was able to keep his men alive and together is a marvel. Today, this time of struggle and determination is remembered at four key locations.

Jockey Hollow

Most of the Continental Army sites at Morristown are located within Jockey Hollow. Among them is the furnished, staffed Wick House and Farm near the Visitor Center. Once owned by a relatively prosperous farmer,

it served as the headquarters of General Arthur St. Clair in 1779-1780. Be sure to spend time at the Visitor Center. It has excellent exhibits about the soldiers – ordinary folks from every occupation and social class, brought together as equals in a common cause. You can walk from here to five reconstructed solders' huts at an encampment site or drive to the trail center parking.

Ford Mansion

Mrs. Jacob Ford Jr., a widow with four children, generously allowed General Washington to use this handsome house as his headquarters and home for six months in 1779-1780. Her husband was a colonel in the New Jersey militia before his death in 1777; so she was especially supportive of Washington's efforts.

Fort Nonsense

An earthen redoubt was constructed in 1777 on a ridge above the town, ostensibly to serve as a refuge for the regiment detailed to guard military stores. According to legend, its name comes from Washington's intent to prevent both idleness and desertion by keeping his troops busy. Not much remains, other than a great view.

New Jersey Brigade area

Four regiments totaling about 900 men camped here during 1779-1780. They spent Christmas building their log huts. Today you can enjoy the Cross Estate Gardens.

Located via I-287 exit 36 in Morristown, NJ. Open daily except major holidays. Admission charged.

◀ Over 1,000 huts such as these were built by Washington's troops in Jockey Hollow. Their size, spacing and alignment were prescribed by Continental Army rules.

▲ This gracious, well-appointed home feels as though it was recently occupied by George and Martha Washington. Their bedroom has been re-created with period items and has at least one piece of the original furniture.

◀ With a folding canopy bed, folding camp stool, portable writing desk and borrowed table and chairs, General St. Clair and his staff made themselves at home in the Wick House.

Fort Boonesborough State Park

SEE MAP PAGE 17, LOCATION #17
Richmond vicinity (north), Kentucky
Phone: (859) 527-3131
http://parks.ky.gov/stateparks/fb

▲ Construction of the original fort progressed slowly over three years. The men were more concerned about staking their own land claims, planting, hunting and exploring. They were not alone in their enthusiasm. By the early 1800s, an estimated 200,000-300,000 settlers had made their homes in Kentucky and the Midwest.

▶ Boone must have had a good upbringing in his boyhood home. Among his many accomplishments, he was elected to three terms in the Virginia General Assembly.

▶ There were few luxuries and much hard work on the Kentucky frontier. Grinding grain could mean using a wooden mortar with the wooden pestle hanging from a spring pole.

▶ Boone worked as a surveyor and merchant after the war but went deep into debt as a land speculator. Overcome by legal problems resulting from his Kentucky land claims, he resettled in Missouri, where he lived to be nearly 86.

While the American Revolution was raging in the East, the time was right for migration to the West. The Transylvania Company, founded in 1775, purchased Cherokee land extending from the northern Ohio-Kentucky River to the most southwesterly branch of the Cumberland River. Eager to settle here, frontiersman Daniel Boone and several axmen built a protective fortification of one-story log cabins and corner blockhouses.

The Revolutionary War intruded from the beginning, primarily as battles between settlers and British-allied Indians. The worst attack came in August 1778, when the Shawnee and their French-Canadian companions launched a full-scale assault instigated by British officers. Boone learned about the battle plans while a captive of the Shawnee and escaped – purportedly barefoot, wearing Indian leggings and sporting a scalp-lock haircut – in time to alert his friends. The settlers proved to be strong opponents, and the attackers withdrew.

Fort Boonesborough has been reconstructed as a working fort complete with cabins, blockhouses and furnishings. Resident artisans and many special Living History events give modern-day visitors a true sense of what life was like for Daniel Boone and other pioneers in Kentucky.

Located north of Richmond, KY. From I-75, take exit 95 to KY 627; from I-64, exit at Winchester to KY 627. Open for tours April-October. Admission charged.

Other Boone Attractions

For a more complete understanding of Daniel Boone, visit the homes where he was born and lived out his life:

Daniel Boone Homestead

This was the legendary pioneer's Pennsylvania birthplace in 1734. Only the log foundation and cellar with a spring are original to the one-room, one-story log house built by Daniel's father in 1730. The rest was altered by subsequent owners (includ-

ing a Boone relative). It is nevertheless a very enjoyable place, surrounded by six other eighteenth-century structures, 579 acres of land and a lake. Many special events. Open Tuesday-Sunday except certain holidays. At 400 Daniel Boone Road, Birdsboro, PA. Phone (610) 582-4900. www.danielboonehomestead.org

Daniel Boone Home and Boonesfield Village

Built on a hilltop by Daniel and his son Nathan in 1799, this Georgian-style mansion is actually four stories tall on the downhill side – including a kitchen and dining room in what might be considered the basement. Actually owned by Nathan, it had seven fire-

places, and a ballroom once occupied the top floor. Daniel lived the last 20 years of his life here, proud to be a family man with 10 children, 70 grandchildren and the first of what would be 250+ great-grandchildren. Nearby is a village of relocated nineteenth-century structures, including an 1830s school house, milliner's shop, porter's workshop, general store, grist mill and several homes. Open daily except certain holidays. At 1868 Highway F, Defiance, MO. Phone (636) 798-2005. www.lindenwood.edu/boone

York County Heritage Trust Colonial Complex

SEE MAP PAGE **11**, LOCATION **#46**

York, Pennsylvania
Phone: (717) 848-1587
http://www.yorkheritage.org

Our nation had eight temporary capitals before settling on Washington, DC. The town of York was the fourth – after Philadelphia, Baltimore and Lancaster. (Subsequent capitals, interspersed with repeated use of Philadelphia, were Princeton, Annapolis, Trenton, New York and finally Washington.) At the time, York was on the edge of the Pennsylvania frontier, but it was relatively safe. The Continental Congress met here from September 30, 1777, to June 27, 1778, endorsing the Articles of Confederation and ratifying treaties that guaranteed French military and financial aid.

The York County Heritage Trust provides a window into this vital past at the Colonial Complex. Here you can visit four buildings. The circa 1741 Golden Plough Tavern, built in the German tradition, was a popular place for sharing news and ideas. The circa 1751 English-style General Gates House appears much as it did when General Horatio Gates, hero of the Battle of Saratoga, stayed in York; its second floor features an unusual hinged wall which allowed two bedrooms to be turned into a banquet room for special occasions. The Barnett Bobb Log House is a representative example of homes built in York during the early 1800s. The Colonial Court House, which has been reconstructed, is furnished to recall the nine-month period when the Continental Congress was headquartered in York.

Located at 157 West Market Street in downtown York, PA. Open Tuesday-Saturday mid-April to mid-December except major holidays. Guided tours only. Buy tickets at York County Heritage Trust, 250 East Market.

Hugh Mercer Apothecary

SEE MAP PAGE **15**, LOCATION **#16**

Fredericksburg, Virginia
Phone: (540) 373-1776 or toll-free (800) 678-4748
http://www.apva.org/hughmercerapothecary

A friend to George Washington and a doctor to his mother Mary, Dr. Hugh Mercer practiced medicine for 15 years in Fredericksburg. Then in 1776, he closed his shop to join the Continental Army as a Brigadier General. Dr. Mercer died during the Revolutionary War in the Battle of Princeton.

Today, costumed tour guides present a vivid Living History interpretation of the ins and outs of colonial

medical practices – not only the grisly details behind certain treatments but also the popular solution to a lady's hysteria and a medicine so potent it would "cheer a man suffering with a bad wife." Opium, the only anesthesia at the time, was very costly; so people in the waiting room were asked to help hold down patients who could not afford pain relief during treatments such as tooth extractions.

Items on display include silver-plated pills and large, hand-blown glass jars with striking artwork painted on the insides. A physic garden of lavender, thyme and other medicinal herbs adjoins the building.

Located at 1020 Caroline Street in Fredericksburg, VA. Open daily except major holidays. Admission charged.

◀ According to local legend, the General Gates House was the scene of a 1778 toast to General George Washington by the Marquis de Lafayette. This show of support apparently prevented the Conway Cabal from succeeding in its suspected attempt to replace Washington with Gates as commander of the Continental Army.

◀ Descriptions of medical practices in the 1700s may make us squirm. Yet, one day our modern practice of using needles to deliver medications will seem equally barbaric.

◀ A good herb garden was a valuable asset to pharmacists in the 1700s and 1800s, augmenting what was imported. Then, as now, many medical cures and remedies came from plants and flowers.

Historic Brattonsville

SEE MAP PAGE 15, LOCATION #19
McConnells, South Carolina
Phone: (803) 684-2327
http://www.chmuseums.org/ourmuseums/hb

▲ The Brattons, for whom the village was named, were a family of cotton planters, merchants and physicians. Their large homestead, built in the 1820s, has many interesting features, including a detached brick dining room used for special occasions such as dinners, dances and music recitals.

▶ Costumed interpreters talk about the lives of 139 African American slaves who were owned by the Brattons. Slaves worked in the Big House and in the fields. They lived with their families in humble cabins that you can visit today.

▶ The original log Bratton House had one room downstairs and one room upstairs. In 1839, it was remodeled and expanded to serve as a school and teacher's home. Academic subjects, art, music and needlework were taught to local girls in this classroom.

Most of the back-country conflicts during the war were not between the Continental and British armies, but between Americans – the Patriots/Whigs and the Loyalists/Tories. They pitted family members, friends and neighbors against one another in a manner more akin to a civil war than a revolution. Brattonsville, a small country town, was the site of one such battle: Huck's Defeat. Unwilling to forget, Historic Brattonsville holds a major, two-day Living History re-enactment each July commemorating the 1780 confrontation of Patriots and Loyalists near the original battlefield site.

Huck was a Philadelphia lawyer and staunch Loyalist who particularly disliked the Scotch-Irish Presbyterians in the Carolina back country, most of whom were anti-British. He led a military force intent on capturing Colonel William Bratton. Surprised by the local militia, Huck died during the ensuing battle along with many of his men. In military terms, this was not a big engagement. But for the rebels, it marked a turning point in public opinion: the enemy was not invincible. The Patriots could win.

From today's perspective, Historic Brattonsville is much more than the site of a Revolutionary War battle. This 775-acre Living History village features 36 historic structures, some original to the site and others moved here from nearby towns. Most of them are furnished true to the period and are open to visitors. The re-created community is authentic enough to have been a site for the filming of the Revolutionary War movie, *The Patriot*, starring Mel Gibson.

Living History programs chronicle developments in the Carolina back country from the 1770s to 1840s. They are scheduled every Saturday from March through November. In addition, an award-winning heritage farm program preserves several rare breeds of farm animals, including Gulf Coast sheep, red Devon cattle, long-snout Ossabaw Island hogs and Dominique chickens.

Located at 1444 Brattonsville Road in McConnells, SC. Take I-77 exit 82-B in Rock Hill; south through Rock Hill on Cherry Road, which becomes SR 322. Follow highway approximately 10 miles to Brattonsville Road. Open daily except major holidays. Admission charged.

SMALL BATTLE; BIG CONSEQUENCES

When the British prepared to invade the South, they banked on having large numbers of Tories helping them against a few upstart Whigs. On February 20, 1776, a force of 1,600 Tories – mostly Scottish Highlanders wielding broadswords – did indeed set out to join the British forces. They were carrying only about 500 firearms, expecting to meet little resistance along the way. Seven days later, they arrived at Moore's Creek Bridge near Wilmington, North Carolina. Over 1,000 Patriots/Whigs were waiting for them with muskets and cannons. The battle was over in minutes; 30 Tories were dead, including their leaders; and in the days following, 850 Tories were captured along with wagons, weapons and a treasury of British sterling. Elsewhere, British forces were waiting for the Tories, who would never arrive. This turn of events demonstrated the surprising strength of rebels in the countryside. It discouraged Loyalist sentiment in the Carolinas, spurred North Carolina's declaration of independence, and later caused British forces (lacking the expected aid) to be defeated in their bid for South Carolina.

Valley Forge National Historical Park

SEE MAP PAGE 11, LOCATION #36B
Philadelphia vicinity (northwest), Pennsylvania
Phone: (610) 783-1077
http://www.nps.gov/vafo

Valley Forge is not a valley but a series of small hills, and while some claimed it was a bleak terrain in the winter of 1777-1778, it certainly is a beautiful place now. During our visit, we stood in front of a series of reconstructed log cabins, remembering from childhood that George Washington had written a distressing letter to Congress in February 1778, describing the soldiers as "naked and starving." We recalled too what a ranger recently said to us: "Don't take those words too literally. Washington was trying to get additional funding from Congress to make life more comfortable for his troops. His words were meant to prompt action. So think of them as political persuasion, referring to the few, not the many."

The fact is: life was pretty good at Valley Forge, considering the times – except for the North Carolinians, whose food and clothing were a long time coming from their state. The weather was warmer than in past years. Food was available, although it was often monotonous. And while one in ten are said to have died, that number is heavily skewed by the regiment from North Carolina, which lost nearly 20 percent of its men.

The most remarkable story about Valley Forge is that the winter was relatively uneventful. While the colonies were at war with Great Britain, no battles were fought for six months – from December 1777 to June 1778. The Americans stayed at their winter encampment, learning how to be better soldiers, and the British stayed in Philadelphia. How different from today's wars!

Valley Forge National Historical Park has 18 miles of trails, including six miles of paved biking and walking paths. It also has a 10-mile, self-guided automobile tour, with a number of interesting stops along the way. Be sure to include a visit to Washington's Headquarters, three miles west of the Welcome Center on SR 23W. Also known as the Potts House, it is furnished in period and has well-informed costumed interpreters. Throughout the park, there's much to see and enjoy.

Located 18 miles northwest of Philadelphia, PA. Take I-76 to US 422 north; then SR 23 to the park. Open daily except Thanksgiving, December 25 and January 1. Free.

▲ Valley Forge has many points of interest. Shown here are replicas of the cabins that American soldiers built for themselves. Some are expertly made while others are relatively crude. Such was the case in the winter of 1777-1778. Not everyone had the skills to properly care for themselves.

◀ The Isaac Potts House served as Washington's headquarters, and many nearby homes were used by other officers. Nevertheless, while supportive of the troops, the local populace was divided on its political feelings. Many wanted to be free of the conflict with England.

BARON VON STEUBEN

Warfare in eighteenth-century America was comparatively simple. Individual battles generally consisted of mass-fire musket melees followed by hand-to-hand combat with bayonets. Success depended on speed, and speed depended on the methods and commands of maneuver. During the first years of the war, Americans fought too much as individuals. Standardization and discipline were needed. So when Baron von Steuben, a former Prussian military officer, volunteered to work with the Continental Army, he was sent to Valley Forge to teach the Americans how to fight like an army. He knew how to increase speed – drill until the motions of loading and firing are automatic; drill using the same exact procedure each and every time; drill in rhythm, with eight counts and fifteen motions. There was only one way: the Army way. When it was time to return to battle, our military had been reorganized, and our troops were following a uniform system. They were far more efficient and a better match for the well-trained British soldiers.

Washington's Headquarters State Historic Site

SEE MAP PAGE 11, LOCATION #33
Newburgh, New York
Phone: (845) 562-1195
http://nysparks.state.ny.us/sites/info.asp?siteID=32

▲ Reflecting the temporary nature of Washington's stay, the Hasbrouck House has an unusual mixture of utilitarian folding furniture and elegant appointments. The Visitor Center museum displays a Badge of Military Merit conceived here. It also has part of a log boom that stretched across the Hudson River to block enemy ships.

▶ Raised earthen battlements such as the British Redoubt 9 were protected against infantry assaults by deep ditches and rows of spiked stakes. The Gatinais regimental flag indicates that French troops assaulted and captured this defensive position.

▶ Cannon were placed on earthworks at key strategic points on the Yorktown Battlefield.

Needing to be safe but close to his fighting forces, General Washington established temporary headquarters in strategically located private residences during much of the war. From April 1782 until August 1783, he and his aids lived and worked in the home of Tryntje Hasbrouck, the widow of Colonel Jonathan Hasbrouck. Martha Washington joined her husband for most of his stay in the eight-room fieldstone farmhouse. From this vantage point, 12 miles north of the forts at West Point, Washington was able to oversee protection of the Hudson Valley while managing other critical matters. He could also keep tabs on the British in New York City.

Furnished much as it was 225 years ago, the sturdy home feels important even today. One can imagine Washington here, rejecting the suggestion that America become a monarchy; calming angry officers who threatened mutiny over delayed back pay and pensions; conceiving the Badge of Military Merit, forerunner of the Purple Heart; and preparing for the "cessation of hostilities" to end the Revolutionary War.

Located at corner of Liberty and Washington Streets in Newburgh, NY. From I-87 (Thruway), take exit 17 for Newburgh; follow Route 17K east (Broadway) for 2 3/4 miles; turn right on Liberty Street. Open Wednesday-Sunday, mid-April through October. Admission charged.

Yorktown Battlefield

SEE MAP PAGE 15, LOCATION #21B
Yorktown, Virginia
Phone: (757) 898-2410
http://www.nps.gov/colo

In a bit of historic irony, the last major battle of the Revolutionary War was waged at Yorktown, Virginia, about 20 miles from the site of the first permanent English settlement in America, Jamestown. From September 28 to October 19, 1781, General Washington and his 17,600 American and French troops surrounded General

Cornwallis and his 8,300 British, German and American Loyalist forces. Meanwhile, the French fleet blockaded the British at sea. Besieged and unable to receive aid, Cornwallis surrendered. Although limited fighting continued for two more years, the war was essentially won at Yorktown. As a result of the battle, a new group of British ministers came to power early in 1782 and began peace talks to end the war. Two self-guided auto tours traverse the battlefield and encampment areas.

Make a point to visit the city of Yorktown as well. It was occupied by the British during the siege. Nine buildings have survived from this period.

Located in Colonial National Historical Park. Drive to Yorktown Visitor Center on Colonial Parkway, VA. Open daily except major holidays. Admission charged.

Yorktown Victory Center

SEE MAP PAGE 15, LOCATION #21B

Yorktown, Virginia
Phone: (757) 253-4838 or toll-free (888) 593-4682
http://www.historyisfun.org

Exceptional on many levels, Yorktown Victory Center provides a broad overview and a highly personalized perspective on America's road to independence. It begins at the beginning of the story, with an entrance path that leads you through a timeline of major events which made war seemingly inevitable. At the end of the path, an evocative film and several exhibition galleries await you, chronicling the lives of ordinary Americans, the impact of our revolution and the Siege of Yorktown. This part of your visit can be as in-depth or as general as you wish. The first time we visited, we breezed through it but were sorry. The next time, we saw everything. There's much to absorb – and it's all very enlightening!

In "Witnesses to Revolution," read the eyewitness accounts of ten individuals who lived during this turbulent period of American history. In "Converging on Yorktown," discover the nature of multinational forces that came together to do battle. In "Yorktown's Sunken Fleet," explore the story of how British ships were scuttled and sunk in the nearby York River during the 1781 siege. Lastly, learn about the people from many different cultures who shaped a new society and took

the final steps in America's journey to nationhood, with the first-of-its kind Constitution and first ten amendments (the Bill of Rights). If you are traveling with children, stop by the hands-on discovery room. If you have particular adult interests, visit the resource room, which has computer stations and reference materials.

With this background, the stage is set for a wonderful Living History experience. Step outside and meet two

groups of people most affected by the Revolutionary War. On one side of the exhibition building is a re-created Continental Army encampment. Here you will learn about soldiers who had no choice but to fight not only the British but also Loyalist friends and neighbors. On the other side of the building is a 1780s farm. It highlights the struggle of most Americans to rebuild their lives after the war had ended. Daily Living History activities and demonstrations by costumed interpreters bring past realities back to life.

Located near Colonial Parkway in Yorktown, VA, off I-64 exit 247 on Route 1020. Open daily except December 25 and January 1. Admission charged.

▲ Cannon firings, military drills and musket demonstrations are just part of the Continental Army encampment. Here interpreters will also tell you about military medical practices, the quartermaster's role in managing army supplies, and how troops dealt with everyday needs such as cooking meals.

◀ The Continental Army encampment depicts the soldiers' life during the final year of war. Explore everything, even the tents. Ask interpreters about their weapons, clothing and personal items.

◀ The 1780s farm presents a different side of the story: what happened when the war was over. Enjoy the seasonal cycles of work at the farmhouse, separate kitchen, fields, gardens, chicken coop and tobacco barn.

Boston National Historical Park

SEE MAP PAGE 11, LOCATION #27A
Boston, Massachusetts
Phone: (617) 242-5642
http://www.nps.gov/bost

▲ Old State House, built in 1713, is the oldest public building in Boston. In the days preceding the American Revolution, it was one of the most important places in the colonies – the seat of the colonial Royal Government; the meeting place for the Massachusetts Assembly; and the home of the Massachusetts Supreme Judicial Court, the longest-seated court in America.

▶ Christ Church, the "Old North Church," is famous for its role in warning colonists about the advance of British troops on April 18,1775. Two lanterns held briefly in the steeple window signaled that the British were crossing the Charles River. Colonists across the river were thus forewarned, and Paul Revere began his famous midnight ride to alert Lexington and Concord. Built in 1723, this pretty structure is the oldest church building in Boston and boasts the tallest steeple (191 feet high).

Boston blazed a trail through American history, from colonialism to independence, and it played a pivotal role in the formation of our national ideals about freedom of speech, religion, government and self-determination. Perhaps this was inevitable. As far back as 1630, when a fleet of 11 ships sailed into Massachusetts Bay bearing 700 passengers, 40 cows and 60 horses, early Bostonians had big plans. "We shall be as a City upon a Hill," their governor said. "The eyes of all people are upon us." To those deeply religious Puritan settlers, America was a Promised Land, and they were a chosen people.

Boston was the largest town in Colonial America and one of the busiest ports. After Great Britain attempted to levy taxes on America in the mid-1760s, it also was at the heart of protests. A series of skirmishes led to disaster when the Redcoats fired on an angry mob. Shrewd colonial leaders exploited the incident, calling it the "Boston Massacre" and using it as an example of British injustice. Although a quiet period followed, resentment grew and tempers were quick to flare. When the Tea Act was imposed on the colonies, a group of Bostonians boarded ships laden with English tea and dumped their cargoes into the harbor amidst the cheers of onlookers. This "Boston Tea Party" brought harsh British reprisals. Then, when the Revolutionary War broke out, Bostonians engaged in one of the earliest and bloodiest fights – the "Battle of Bunker Hill."

After the war ended, Boston underwent a make-over, transforming itself from a haphazard seaport into a relatively refined community. New public buildings were constructed, and old ones were renovated. Prestigious residential neighborhoods, such as those in beautiful Beacon Hill, began to appear. Boston's population changed too. A flood of Irish immigrants arrived in the late 1840s, seeking relief from the potato famine; Italians formed a sizable settlement; and others came from southern and eastern Europe. To accommodate this growth, landfill projects increased the size of the peninsula on which the city was built.

Today, in the midst of modern Boston, you will find a remarkable National Historical Park recalling the early days.

Battle Monuments

Visit two monuments: The Battle of Bunker Hill obelisk honoring the heroism of June 1775, and the tower on Dorchester Heights commemorating a March 1776 victory. Park rangers are stationed at the Bunker Hill Monument (actually located on Breed's Hill) and have much to share.

AMERICA'S FIRST NEWSPAPER
Information is power, and Boston has a long history of keeping people informed. *Publick Occurrences* emerged in 1690 Boston as the first newspaper in the colonies. Outraging public officials with "reflections of a very high order," it was immediately suppressed. The weekly *Boston News-Letter* was more successful in 1704, probably because its news came mostly from the *London Gazette*. Along with reporting the intrigues of English politics and European wars, it told colonists about deaths, sermons, storms, fires, accidents, and ship arrivals and departures. Even back then, there was advertising too. As the first issue stated: "all persons who have any lands, houses, tenements, farms, ships, vessels, goods, wares or merchandise to be sold or lett; or servants runaway, or goods Stoll, or lost, may have the same inserted at a reasonable rate..." In 1719, the *Boston Gazette* became a competitor. It was followed in 1721 by the *New England Courant*.

Freedom Trail

Take the 2 ¹/₂ mile red-line walking path which cuts across downtown Boston, through shopping areas, the financial district and the North End to Charlestown. Free tours are available from the park Visitor Center, but you can also tour on your own. This is a wonderful way to see Boston. You might want to split the walk into two or three days, to have plenty of time. Markers identify historic stops. Special programs include first-person re-enactments. Among them: the only female soldier in the Revolutionary War; farmers, printers and tailors who defended Boston Harbor; Paul and Rachel Revere who have a house full of memories; and Abigail Adams, wife of our second president, John Adams, and mother of our sixth president, John Quincy Adams. Be sure to visit the following attractions in particular:

Old South Meeting House

On December 16, 1773, a restless crowd of several thousand came together at this religious and political gathering place to protest the British tea tax. Many dressed as Mohawk Indians (fierce warriors when angered) and staged the Boston Tea Party.

Old State House

Here was the center of political life and discourse in the colonies. The Boston Massacre occurred in front in 1770. Our Declaration of Independence was read aloud from the balcony in 1776. John Hancock was inaugurated here in 1780 as the first governor of Massachusetts.

Faneuil Hall

Today's Faneuil Hall Marketplace is so enjoyable as a modern attraction, its rich history is often overlooked. Five buildings are crowded with restaurants, boutiques, produce stands, retail push carts and street performers. Look at the buildings too. The central complex is listed on the National Register of Historic Places. The hall, used by the British when they occupied Boston, has a military museum and paintings of notable battles.

Paul Revere House

Built around 1680, this is the oldest house in downtown Boston and was owned by Paul Revere from 1770-1800. It contains period furnishings and memorabilia including some of the famous Revere silver and a Revere-made bell. You'll see a colonial herb garden too.

Old North Church

On the night of April 18, 1775, sexton Robert Newman secretly climbed the 14-story steeple in total darkness. At the top, he lit and held up two lanterns, signaling to fellow colonists that the British were headed their way.

USS Constitution

This historic Navy frigate never lost a battle. It earned the nickname "Old Ironsides" in 1812 when shots from a British warship bounced off its thick oak hull. Today, active-duty sailors in 1812 dress uniforms lead tours.

Black Heritage Trail

Not part of the Boston National Historical Park but a valuable addition to any Boston visit, the Black Heritage Trail explores the North Slope of Beacon Hill associated with the struggle for equal rights. Time your visit to see the 1806 African Meeting House and 1834 Abiel Smith School. http://www.nps.gov/boaf/

◀ The Paul Revere House was remodeled several times in the century after Revere owned it. In 1908 his great-grandson restored it and opened the house as one of the first house museums. Ninety percent of the structure is original.

▼ Built in 1797, this 44-gun frigate served in many conflicts until 1815. In 1830, the Constitution was scheduled to be scrapped, but the poem "Old Ironsides" by Oliver Wendell Holmes, Sr. rallied public sentiment to save it.

Visitor Center for Boston National Historical Park located at 15 State Street in downtown Boston, MA. Visitor Center for USS Constitution located on the Freedom Trail near Gate 1 of the Navy Yard. Open daily except major holidays. Fees collected at the privately owned sites, including Old South Meeting House, Old State House and Paul Revere House. No fee at the federally owned sites.

Independence National Historical Park

SEE MAP PAGE 11, LOCATION #34

Philadelphia, Pennsylvania
Phone: (215) 965-2305 or toll-free (800) 537-7676
http://www.nps.gov/inde

▲ Representatives of each colony (except Georgia) met for the first time in Carpenters' Hall. Here they realized the importance of working together to resist the unfair laws and taxes imposed by the British Parliament.

▶ Congress Hall, next door to Independence Hall, served as a Capitol for the new republic. The 65 delegates of the first House of Representatives met in this first-floor chamber until 1800, when the nation's capital moved to Washington, DC.

Many call Philadelphia the birthplace of the United States of America. This title seems indisputable. While Boston was the place that fermented our rebellion, Philadelphia was the place that shaped our government. The First Continental Congress convened at Carpenters' Hall in September 1774 and adopted the Declaration of Rights and Grievances sent to King George III of Great Britain. When the king and his government failed to satisfy American complaints, a Second Continental Congress met in May 1775 at the Pennsylvania State House, known today as Independence Hall. The situation was dire: armed conflict had broken out between British and Americans in Massachusetts, and Congress had the unwelcome task of directing a war. The delegates appointed George Washington commander of the Continental Army, responsible for defending American liberty. But they continued to seek diplomatic solutions for another year, hoping to avoid a full-scale revolution. Finally, rallied by the Virginian Richard Henry Lee, Congress conceded the inevitable. On July 4, 1776, delegates adopted the Declaration of Independence. Soon after, they began to frame our first constitution, the Articles of Confederation.

Conveniently located between the northern and southern colonies, Philadelphia was the ideal city for all these activities. It might have become the permanent seat of our government, except for the appearance of mutinous Pennsylvania soldiers who surrounded the State House in 1783 demanding back pay. This caused a nervous Congress to move to Princeton, then Annapolis, Trenton and finally New York City. Philadelphia managed to win back the national government in 1790, but only for one decade while a new Federal city – Washington, DC – was being prepared. During that time, our fledgling government welcomed the first new States (Vermont, Tennessee and Kentucky), established the United States Mint and the First Bank of the United States, overcame the first internal threat to national authority (Whiskey Rebellion of 1794), and faced its first challenges from major foreign powers (France and England). When Philadelphia ceased to be our nation's capital in 1800, America was well on its way to becoming a strong and influential nation both at home and abroad.

Independence National Historical Park includes the buildings in Independence Square as well as others throughout Philadelphia that are associated

PAPER MONEY

Where did our leaders get the money to finance a revolution? They printed it – $242 million in nearly five years. The artwork on these notes promoted the cause of liberty. An $8 Continental featured a thirteen-string harp, representing the thirteen colonies, and the motto "the large Colonies and the small Colonies are in harmony." A $20 note had a drawing of wind blowing on waves with the motto "driven by force." And a $60 note featured a quote from Psalm 97: "God reigns, let the earth rejoice." Congress asked the states to levy taxes to cover these notes, but states printed their own paper money instead, putting another $210 million into circulation without the backing of silver or gold. Private individuals and the British counterfeited millions more. The resulting hyperinflation made it all virtually worthless by 1780. Taxes were finally levied and used to retire substantial amounts of currency; but it was too little, too late. A depression followed America's independence.

with Colonial America, the founding of our nation and Philadelphia's early role as the capital. The best place to start is at the Visitor Center, where a 30-minute film, "Independence," is presented throughout the day. You can also enjoy daily talks about Thomas Jefferson, Benjamin Franklin, Paths of the Founders, A Soldier's Life, the Liberty Bell and other topics. Be sure to stop at the Visitor Center desk well in advance of your sightseeing to obtain site tickets. Sometimes entry is by ticket only (free) at assigned times.

Independence Hall

This World Heritage Site was at the center of everything important in our early government. Here George Washington was appointed Commander-in-Chief of the Continental Army; the Declaration of Independence was adopted; the design of the American flag was agreed upon; the Articles of Confederation were adopted; and the U. S. Constitution was drafted. The Georgian-style structure has been restored to its eighteenth-century appearance and has period furnishings including the "rising sun" chair used by Washington during the Constitutional Convention.

Liberty Bell Center

This symbolic voice of freedom is displayed at eye level, almost close enough to touch. It rang out many times during the 80 years before being cracked, despite the irritation of pre-Revolution Philadelphians who petitioned to have it muted in 1772. It also toured our nation after the Civil War, helping to remind all Americans of our common bond and the need to heal the wounds of internal strife.

Congress Hall

Major events which took place in this setting included the Presidential inaugurations of George Washington (his second term) and John Adams; the establishment of the First Bank of the United States, U.S. Mint and Department of the Navy; and the ratification of Jay's Treaty with England. The building has been restored to its original appearance as the 1790-1800 U.S. Capitol. On the first floor is the chamber of the House of Representatives; upstairs is the Senate chamber.

Declaration House

When 33-year-old Thomas Jefferson drafted the Declaration of Independence in 1776, he chose to get away from the city. The setting for his inspiration was a rented second-floor bedchamber and sitting room in a private home surrounded by open fields. Now in the heart of Philadelphia, the dwelling has been reconstructed with period furnishings as well as reproductions of Jefferson's swivel chair and lap desk.

Bishop White & Todd Houses

These two restored buildings are interesting examples of late eighteenth-century Philadelphia, and both can be seen on guided tours. Rev. William White, Pennsylvania's first Episcopal bishop, lived in his house from 1787-1836; the dwelling reflects an upper-class lifestyle. Lawyer John Todd and his wife Dolley Payne lived in their middle class home from 1791-1793. After Todd died in the yellow fever epidemic of 1793, Dolley married James Madison, who was destined to become the fourth President of the United States.

Visitor Center located at Sixth and Market Streets in downtown Philadelphia, PA. Best access route is via I-676 or I-95. Entry to the main attractions is through a security entrance. (Ask at the Visitor Center for details.) Open daily except December 25. Free.

▲ Originally housing Pennsylvania's colonial government, Independence Hall was large and grand for its time and thus very suitable for our Founding Fathers. This is where members of the Second Continental Congress argued and struggled toward the difficult decision to declare independence from England.

◀ "Proclaim liberty throughout all the land, and to all the inhabitants thereof." Those words were cast on the bell long before thoughts of independence entered the American psyche. Still, the name "Liberty Bell" was not used until 1835, when the bell became a symbol in the antislavery movement.

▲ Some things are better left in the past. This bucolic scene at Hopewell Furnace, PA, would have been spoiled by smelly iron furnaces and loud manufacturing equipment operating here in the 1770s.

▶ Nowhere in our nation is Old Glory more significant than at Fort McHenry, MD, where our flag flew defiantly in 1814 and inspired Francis Scott Key to write "The Star-Spangled Banner."

▶ Cotton was king following the Industrial Revolution, but tobacco was still a viable cash crop, even for small farmers as far north as New Salem, IL.

▶ Maintaining law and order was haphazard at best in our new nation. Jails like this one in Old Bedford Village, PA, were run by local officials who followed their own rules. The first trained police force was not established until 1838 in Boston, MA.

OUR NEW NATION

While our political leaders wrangled over how to run

the new government of the United States of America,

"ordinary folks" focused on very different priorities. They

had suffered through a wrenching war that only one-third

of them supported. They had seen their lands ravaged,

cities burned, friends and family members pitted against one

another, personal fortunes lost and livelihoods diminished

or even destroyed. When the Revolutionary War was finally

over and America was free and independent of mighty England,

our people – like our national government – needed a

new beginning. "If we must start over," they seemed to say,

"let's make the most of this opportunity." So our nation

began to build and spread out and mature. It also became

part of a new revolution: the Industrial Revolution.

HISTORICAL PERSPECTIVE:
OUR NEW NATION

The world watched closely as our fledgling republic took form. America's independence represented more than just a shift in power.

Changing Population

Millions came from across the seas, drawn by the promise of their own new beginnings. In just ten years' time, from 1780 to 1790, the population in our first 13 states grew 60 percent, from an estimated two-and-a-half million to four million. The people came in a flood, primarily from throughout Europe, alarming our nation's early leaders who wondered how America could settle into its own identity if it kept changing its cultural mix. The taste of "freedom" was an elixir few could resist.

Of course, not everyone felt welcomed here. Approximately 100,000 Loyalists – a portion of those in America who had supported the British crown during the war – packed up and left. They settled in Canada, the Bahamas and other parts of the West Indies or traveled across the Atlantic. Among them were about 15,000 African Americans, some of whom helped to found the country of Sierra Leone in Africa.

Changing Landscape

While most people chose to live in relatively developed areas, tens of thousands wanted to break into new territory where life was an adventure and neighbors were miles away. Even before the Revolutionary War, they crossed over the long stretch of Appalachians – the initial barrier to westward movement – and settled between the mountains and Mississippi River, a seemingly endless space. Dense forests greeted them,

> **making way for them was the Indian Removal Act passed by Congress**

▶ With the war over, the private sector turned its attention to growth. Hundreds of miles of man-made waterways were built to speed the nation's goods to market. Entrepreneurs thrived on the new business opportunities, including those along the scenic Chesapeake & Ohio Canal in Potomac, MD.

▶ America did not start out as a wealthy nation. In fact, many of our early Presidents came from humble beginnings. John Adams was born in this farm house. His son John Quincy Adams was born in a smaller home just 75 feet away. Both houses can be seen today at Adams National Historical Park in Quincy, MA.

and they had to fell trees to bring in sunlight before they could even think about farming. In succeeding decades, they would travel farther west and face the vast, open prairie, red-rock lands, almost impenetrable mountains, huge, seemingly empty deserts, and even rain forests.

As major cities in the East continued to fill with people, they needed more land. Boston, which was built on a peninsula, commissioned landfill projects to literally create new ground. When New York City was selected as one of the nation's temporary capitals, this distinction stimulated not only a beautification program but also an extension of the shoreline through landfill. Other cities transformed marshes into usable land.

Mostly, though, America expanded through acquisitions. France sold the Louisiana Territory to our new nation in 1803, and Spain ceded Florida in 1819. By the 1830s, pioneers had pushed the frontier across the Mississippi River and into Iowa, Missouri, Arkansas and eastern Texas. Making way for them was the Indian Removal Act, passed by Congress in 1830, which forcibly moved potentially adversarial Native Peoples out of the Southeast. Tragically 4,000 Cherokee Indians died in 1838 on the "Trail of Tears" to the officially established Indian Territory, now modern-day Oklahoma.

Next, Texas declared war on Mexico, won its independence and in 1845 joined the United States. This action was followed by America's own war against Mexico (1846-1848), after which Mexico ceded the vast territories which now comprise California, Utah, Nevada and parts of New Mexico, Arizona and Wyoming. With little reason to maintain a foothold, Britain ceded its portion of Oregon Country in 1846. Our nation's land holdings virtually tripled in size in less than 45 years.

Changing Livelihood

As America grew, a network of new roads and improved waterways provided access to commercial markets nationwide, and the economy transformed itself with startling speed. More and more farmers began raising crops and livestock specifically to make a profit.

Southern farmers as far west as Texas grew huge quantities of cotton. Kentucky and Tennessee farmers prospered by growing tobacco. Midwestern ranchers raised cattle and other livestock, while distant neighbors produced corn and wheat. They were supplying both a growing nation and a demanding world. In the ten years between 1790 and 1800, American exports grew four-fold in value – and that was just the beginning. Cotton was the biggest money-maker, accounting for nearly half the value of all exports from 1816 to 1820 and even more in subsequent years. America had become the world's leading agricultural nation.

In addition, factories began replacing small shops and home craftworkers throughout New England and the Mid-Atlantic, producing a wide variety of products quickly and cost-effectively. The first American cotton spinning mill opened in 1793 Rhode Island, and the first textile factory with automated weaving machines opened in 1814 Massachusetts. In Connecticut, a firearms factory built by Eli Whitney began mass producing muskets in 1798 using standardized, interchangeable parts. Such progress was stimulated by other great advances, especially in the Pennsylvania iron industry. By 1840, manufacturing accounted for nearly one-fifth of all production in America.

Changing Culture

Farm life was still the "heart and soul" of our nation. In fact, 89 percent of Americans lived in rural areas in 1840. However, big cities and urban centers were rapidly increasing in importance. They provided key infrastructure and civilizing influences – the banks, stores and hotels; doctors, lawyers, schoolteachers,

clergy members and even human rights activists; newspapers and book publishers; plays, minstrel shows and other forms of entertainment; art, culture, private clubs and civic-minded organizations.

In the world's eyes, America also had developed a distinctive personality – straight-forward (to the point of seeming unsophisticated), driven by practicality and need (frequently associated with impatience), and entrepreneurial (because change was not only irresistible but necessary). Perhaps most representative of the American spirit was an innovative new style of construction: balloon framing. Rather than build walls in traditional ways – beginning with heavy hand-hewn posts and beams or solid stone/brick – many frontier builders chose to frame their structures with lighter, pre-cut two-by-four wood studs held together by factory-made nails. Much easier, cheaper and faster to erect, this balloon framing proved strong enough and flexible enough to remain a standard to this day. (The earliest known balloon-frame structure was the 1833 St. Mary's Catholic Church in Chicago.) Another example of American originality was the simple, no-nonsense furniture of the 1700s and 1800s. Often serving dual purposes, the craftsmanship was typically more functional than decorative – like the Shaker furniture, well-suited to frontier life and beautiful in its simplicity. At the same time, great American writers, philosophers and artists took their place on the international scene – Washington Irving, Herman Melville, Nathaniel Hawthorne, Henry David Thoreau, Ralph Waldo Emerson, Walt Whitman, Charles Willson Peale, Gilbert Stuart and many others.

Finally people could say "I'm an American," and the world would understand what that meant.

▲ From the selection of its first architect by George Washington, to its completion during the Civil War and its remodels in more recent times, the United States Capitol building in Washington, DC, stands as a symbol of our ongoing effort to be the best we can be as a nation.

Washington, DC

SEE MAP PAGE 15, LOCATION #33A
District of Columbia
Phone: (202) 789-7000 (Convention and Visitors Center)
http://www.washington.org

▲ While the "south lawn" of the White House is most often shown in historical photographs, the north side shown here is the actual entrance.

Congress made the decision in 1783 to have a national capital, but individual members could not agree where it should be located. Their compromise solution was the Residence Act of 1790, giving George Washington the power to select the site. The President's choice, made in 1791, was a 100-square-mile area near his Mount Vernon home. It encompassed land north of the Potomac belonging to the state of Maryland, including the port of Georgetown, and land south of the Potomac belonging to Virginia. The states relinquished their territorial rights, and individual landowners donated their properties. Then President Washington tackled the biggest part of his assignment: overseeing the development of a capital city in this new District of Columbia.

Considering the magnitude of the task, Washington, DC, was an astounding achievement. It was the first American city to be designed before it was built. Our visionary President hired a French engineer, who planned the physical layout. Two surveyors (a free African American scientist/mathematician and a Revolutionary War veteran) laid out the streets and lots. Three commissioners appointed by President Washington directed the construction and coordinated the city affairs. Nine years after the site was selected, our Federal Government moved to its new home.

Some might say the timing was too aggressive. John Adams, the first President to occupy the White House, chose to live there during the last weeks of his term, when not a single room was finished. The plaster was still damp on the walls, and some of the windows were open to the elements, making the indoors as cold as the outdoors. Furthermore, most of the district was swamp and farmland, and there was little in the way of lodging

for the members of Congress. Of course, homes, shops and taverns were under construction. Over time, the city grew to encompass the entire federal district, and "DC" became its nickname.

Washington is a city where every aspect of American history is represented in one form or another – museums, art galleries and performance centers; monuments, memorials and parks; historic districts and major seats of power; libraries and archives. The following four key government buildings are must-sees.

White House

Ironically, George Washington was the only President who never slept in the executive mansion, even though he approved its design. When finally completed, the White House was said to be magnificent. But its early glamour was short-lived. During the last stages of the War of 1812, the British invaded Washington, DC, and burned most of the public buildings, including the White House as well as the Capitol, Library of Congress and Navy Yard. First Lady Dolley Madison was forced to flee the executive mansion with just a carriage-load of priceless objects. The famous Gilbert Stuart portrait of George Washington, removed from its frame for easy

---

MAGNA CARTA

While this English charter does not directly relate to the United States, its impact on our nation's founders was substantial. Within the single page of text are the beginnings of democracy.

Members of the English aristocracy wrote the Magna Carta and forced their king to approve it in A.D. 1215. Basically, it was a list of commands for the benefit of the elite, but the rationale was important. The document placed England's sovereigns and magistrates within the rule of law and granted rights to people which could not be arbitrarily canceled by other laws. The conceptual debt in America is obvious: our Constitution is "the supreme Law of the Land."

As a model for democracy, the Magna Carta was broad in its impact. Among its 63 articles were stipulations that there could be no laws or taxation without the consent of the people's representatives; individuals had the right to a trial by jury; safeguards must be used to protect against unfair imprisonment; the church is separate and free from government interference. Such ideals were brought to America and included within the framework of our Constitution. Ultimately, they were broadened to include all people.

transport, is said to be the only object remaining from President Adams' short occupancy. Today's White House is a grand place for high government business, stately affairs and the First Family. Visitor Center information is at the southeast corner of E and 15th Streets. Scheduled self-guided tours are available Tuesday-Saturday but must be requested in advance through one's Member of Congress. Located at 1600 Pennsylvania Avenue, N.W. http://www.whitehouse.gov/history/tours

United States Capitol

First called the Congress House, the Capitol is situated in a beautiful 59-acre park on Capitol Hill. This is where the Senate and House of Representatives meet to make laws and conduct other federal business. In 1800, when our government moved to Washington, DC, only the Senate wing was complete. So in the early years, the Senate, House of Representatives and Supreme Court shared it. Seven years later, the House wing was ready for occupancy. The Supreme Court did not have its own building until 1935.

The Capitol was being expanded when our Civil War broke out. President Lincoln insisted that the construction continue, as evidence "that we intend the Union shall go on." The cast-iron, white-painted dome was finished in 1866 and decorated inside with a huge fresco, *The Apotheosis of George Washington.*

For the best view, see it with a splendid reflection in the National Mall pool. Guided tours are available Monday-Saturday except major holidays. In addition, the Capitol Visitor Center offers brief films about the House and Senate, as well as live feeds when Congress is in session. Tour tickets are free on a first-come, first-served basis at the Capitol Guide Service kiosk near the intersection of First Street S.W. and Independence Avenue. Phone (202) 225-6827 for general information about the tours. http://www.aoc.gov/cvc

◀ When designing the Supreme Court Building, the architect was inspired by the glory days of Rome to represent justice, order and mercy. The carved pediment (just below the roof line) was created using real people as models – chief justices, the architect and the sculptor himself.

◀ Enlarged and modified over the years, the Capitol building houses our national Congress. Its cast-iron dome, constructed in 1855-1866, stands out as one of the most awe-inspiring architectural sites in Washington, DC.

Supreme Court Building

Facing the Capitol between East Capitol Street N.E. and Maryland Avenue, this 1935 white marble edifice is home to the highest court in our nation. As specified by the Constitution (Article III), the Supreme Court has three functions: to oversee the federal judicial system, interpret federal laws and decide major constitutional questions. Ground floor visitor services include exhibits and a short film. On weekdays when the Supreme Court is hearing arguments or deliberating, the public is welcomed to observe the proceedings. When the Court is not in session, lectures are given in the courtroom. Phone (202) 479-3211 for details. http://www.supremecourtus.gov/visiting/visiting.html

National Archives

Preserving historic government records, this building is located on Pennsylvania Avenue between 7th and 9th Streets, N.W. It has an exciting, though relatively small, display vault that enables all people to see the Declaration of Independence, United States Constitution, Bill of Rights and other important documents. Free. Phone (866) 272-6272. http://www.archives.gov/national-archives-experience/visit/visit.html

First & Second Banks of the United States

SEE MAP PAGE 11, LOCATION #59B

Philadelphia, Pennsylvania
Phone: (215) 965-2305 or toll-free (800) 537-7676
http://www.nps.gov/inde/second-bank.html

Before and after Washington, DC, was transformed into our capital, Philadelphia continued to play a pivotal role in governmental operations. In 1791, the First Bank of the United States was established here

▲ The temple structure of the Second Bank of the United States is said to be one of the finest examples of Greek Revival architecture in America.

▶ The flags of all 50 states hang in the National Constitution Center. At the beginning is Delaware, which became the first state on December 7, 1787.

▶ You can almost hear the animated discussions, the final arguments and the ponderings as you walk among true-to-life statues of America's early leaders. With their signatures, they put into law a document they had struggled over for months, knowing it would rule long after they were gone.

to standardize our currency and implement a sound fiscal policy. Congress abandoned the bank in 1811, however, under a cloud of controversy over its questionable constitutionality. Five years later, Congress chartered the Second Bank of the United States. This became one of the world's most influential financial institutions but was besieged by major controversies here at home; it lasted only until 1836.

Both bank buildings are now part of Independence National Historical Park (page 158). The Second Bank is especially noteworthy. Considered an architectural treasure, it has been the standard-bearer for many American bank buildings since its completion in 1824. Most exciting for visitors is its barrel-vaulted banking room, which houses an extraordinary portrait gallery of colonial and American leaders, military officers, explorers and scientists. A substantial portion of the 100 works were painted by Charles Willson Peale, the foremost portrait artist of his day. Be sure to include this gallery as part of your journey to Philadelphia.

Located on Chestnut Street, between 4th and 5th streets, in Philadelphia, PA. Open Wednesday-Sunday. Free.

National Constitution Center

SEE MAP PAGE 11, LOCATION #59B

Philadelphia, Pennsylvania
Phone: (215) 409-6600
http://www.constitutioncenter.org

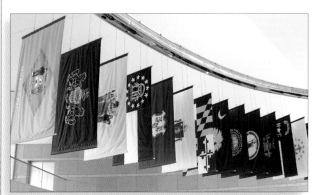

You may have thought you learned enough in school about the United States Constitution, but don't believe it. This one-of-a-kind 160,000-square-foot museum tells a story that should not be missed. Your visit begins with "Freedom Rising" in the Kimmel Theater, where a live actor uses film and video to review major themes that span 220 years of constitutional history. Afterwards, you are on your own to explore more than 100 interactive and multimedia exhibits, photographs, sculptures, texts, films and artifacts. Give yourself plenty of time.

National Constitution Center uses innovative ways to make learning both enlightening and fun. Here you will gain insight into the complex tug-of-war between the states, Presidential office, Congress and Supreme Court over interpretations of our Constitution

and claims of power. You will discover the impact on ordinary citizens and see how amendments are meant to clarify ambiguities and prevent problems. You will see changing displays at The Freedom Exhibit Gallery. And at the end, you will walk among remarkably lifelike, full-size statues of the 39 signers and three dissenters of the Constitution. It's a surprisingly moving experience!

Located on the third block of Independence Mall, at 525 Arch Street between 5th and 6th streets in Philadelphia, PA. Open daily; closed Thanksgiving and December 25. Admission charged.

Philadelphia's Historic Residential Districts

SEE MAP PAGE 11, LOCATION #59B

Philadelphia, Pennsylvania
Phone: (215) 636-3300 (Convention & Visitors Bureau)
http://www.philadelphiausa.travel/plan-your-visit-section.php?section=2

For the more personal side of history, explore Philadelphia's old neighborhoods where the rich and famous as well as "ordinary folks" shared their lives.

Elfreth's Alley

Quaint, modest brick houses were built by many Philadelphians during the early 1700s. Often they were only one room – but they were a very welcomed home nevertheless. Numerous examples line this narrow, cobblestone alley between Arch and Race streets. They comprise what is probably America's oldest street of continuously occupied homes. For information about tours, drop by Elfreth's Alley Museum, 126 Elfreth's Alley. Open year-round; closed major holidays.

Society Hill

One of Philadelphia's chief historic neighborhoods lies south of Independence National Historical Park, roughly from Walnut to South Streets, and Front to Eighth, just west of I-95. It includes Washington Square (with its Tomb of the Unknown Soldier of the American Revolution) and hundreds of restored 200-year-old row houses – a grand parade of Colonial America with hidden gardens and courtyards. You'll find several historic churches here as well: the 1763 St. Mary's Roman Catholic Church at 252 South 4th Street; the 1768 Old Pine Street Presbyterian Church at 412 Pine; and the 1818 Mother Bethel African Methodist Episcopal Church at 419 Richard Allen Avenue. Headhouse Square, bounded by Second, Pine, Front and Lombard Streets, was Society Hill's New Market when it opened in 1745 and is today a center for dining, shopping and business.

Fairmount Park Houses

Along the Schuylkill River, in what is now Fairmount Park, a group of eighteenth- and early nineteenth-century country estates were built by prominent Pennsylvania families. A number can be toured for a nominal entrance fee. They offer delightful opportunities to see what gentlemen-merchants considered rural retreats. Among them are Laurel Hill, Lemon Hill, Mount Pleasant, Strawberry Mansion, Sweetbriar Mansion and Woodford Mansion. Visiting days vary, but most are open April-December. Phone (215) 684-7926 or visit http://www.fairmountpark.org/Tours.asp. Also drive across the Schuylkill River to see the west Philadelphia neighborhood of Parkside, with its extraordinarily fanciful Victorian architecture.

▲ Named for the Free Society of Traders, an investment company which peaked in the late 1600s, Society Hill once boasted the rich and politically powerful among its residents. With its recent restorations, it is once again a sophisticated neighborhood.

◀ Jeremiah Elfreth built the first house on this famous alley in 1713. The last of the 33 surviving houses was built in 1836.

◀ The central portion of Strawberry Mansion dates back to 1789. Known then as Summerville, it was owned by Judge William Lewis, a Quaker who hosted such luminaries as George Washington and Alexander Hamilton. In 1821, Judge Joseph Hemphill purchased the house and added the Greek Revival wings, making it the largest home in Fairmount Park.

Van Cortlandt Manor

SEE MAP PAGE 11, LOCATION #52

Croton-on-Hudson, New York
Phone: (914) 271-8981
http://hudsonvalley.org/vancortlandt

▲ This eighteenth-century home began life as a hunting lodge and summer retreat, passed down from father to son. In the mid-1700s, it was expanded and remodeled; today it appears much as it did then. Upstairs are fine furnishings from the Colonial Georgian and later Federal periods. Downstairs is the colonial kitchen.

▶ Sloops, schooners and pirogues regularly moored at the Van Cortlandt dock near the confluence of the Hudson and Croton rivers. A ferry carried people and goods across the Croton. In addition, the river's energy was harnessed to power the Van Cortlandt sawmill and gristmill.

▶ The reconstructed tenant farm house and restored original ferry house provide an unusual look into "the other side of life" in our new nation. Both were occupied by renters who made their living on Van Cortlandt land.

While the Thirteen Original Colonies worked to unite as states between 1787 and 1790, the American people focused on making a living. Van Cortlandt Manor was a working estate in the New York countryside. It was big but not overbearing, elegant but not pretentious. Today it feels quite homey – perhaps because it contains primarily original objects and family furnishings. Heritage flowers, vegetables and herbs grow in the garden. Living History demonstrations range from blacksmithing and open-hearth cooking, to spinning, weaving and other period crafts. And three buildings can be toured: the manor house, a tenant farm house and the ferry house.

This was the frontier when Pierre Van Cortlandt moved his family from New York and left behind a four-

generation family dynasty of Manhattan merchants. He was determined to make his own fortune, serving markets not only in America but also in Europe and the West Indies. Believing diversification was the key to success, Pierre worked concurrently as a transportation agent, land developer, landlord, commercial farmer and

tavern owner. He had a sawmill to cut his own lumber, a gristmill to grind his grain into flour, a processing facility to prepare his beef for market. And he protected his interests by participating in politics. Pierre was a member of the New York Provincial Congress that ratified the American Declaration of Independence. He later became Lieutenant Governor of New York State and Acting Governor when the need arose.

Visiting Van Cortlandt Manor can be as leisurely as you wish. See the manor house with a guide. Wander on your own to the gardens. Visit the tenant farmhouse. Watch the black-smith. Walk down to the river to see the freight boat. Tour the ferry house and tavern. For a while, you're in the eighteenth century.

Located 30 miles north of New York City, NY, in village of Croton-on-Hudson. Take Route 9 to Croton Point Avenue exit; turn right off exit ramp; right at traffic light onto South Riverside Avenue; continue to the end. Open April-December – Wednesday-Monday April-October; weekends November-December. Admission charged.

HANDMADE BRICKS

Many of our nation's most admired historic buildings were constructed of handmade bricks. We enjoy the brick today, little realizing the chore involved in creating this essential building material. Pierre Van Cortlandt had a kiln built beside the Croton River for use in brick-making. Nearby, workers shoveled dense clay from the river bottom and mixed it with water in a horse-driven "pug mill." Out oozed slugs of soft clay. These slugs were broken to the proper size, coated with lubricating sand, hand-pressed into wooden box frames and set out to dry. Once hardened, the bricks were removed from their frames and stacked for more thorough air drying. Finally, they were baked in the wood-fueled beehive kiln. Workers needed about four days to bake the bricks, stoking the fire round-the-clock, plus three to four days to cool them. Whew! Today, handmade bricks are vital to the authentic restoration and repair of historic buildings nationwide. While the brick making process has improved, it is still very time-consuming.

Historic Alexandria

SEE MAP PAGE 15, LOCATION #22A
Alexandria, Virginia
Phone: (703) 838-4200
http://www.funside.com/things_to_do/attractions

Alexandria emerged in the mid-1700s as a seaport and soon became the business, social and political center for many prominent Virginians. George Washington served as one of the city's governing trustees, as well as its representative to the colonial Virginia

legislature. He was a vestryman at Christ Church and had a pew which still bears his name. In addition, he was the first Worshipful Master of the Alexandria Masonic Lodge under the Virginia charter. Today, many

of the lodge's original furnishings as well as Washington memorabilia are on display in The George Washington Masonic Memorial. At the end of his life, the Old Presbyterian Meeting House served as the site of Washington's memorial services.

Alexandria is a wonderfully historic city, best enjoyed by walking. Many of the local historic sites have interesting tales to tell. Gadsby's Tavern, in

particular, was "the place" to be in early Alexandria. It held an annual Birthnight Ball in Washington's honor and hosted several dazzling Presidential events, including Thomas Jefferson's inaugural banquet. Guided tours are available. Christ Church and the Old Presbyterian Meeting House are just a few blocks away.

In addition, Alexandria was the home of Revolutionary War general "Light Horse" Harry Lee and the boyhood home of his son Robert E. Lee. In fact, from 1785-1903, 37 members of the Lee family lived at what is now the Lee-Fendall House Museum in the historic district. A short walk away is the Palladian-style Carlyle House, which many viewed as the grandest home in mid-1700s Alexandria. Another nearby attraction is the Stabler-Leadbeater Apothecary Shop Museum, opened in 1792 and operated as a family business for 141 years. Remarkably, the shop still has thousands of its original healthcare items. At 221 King Street is Alexandria's visitor center – it is located in the Ramsey House, believed to have been built down-river around 1724 by a city founder and barged to its present site in 1749.

Located south of Washington, DC, across the Potomac River. Most attractions are open year-round, although the days vary; some are open only from April-September. A few charge admission; many are free.

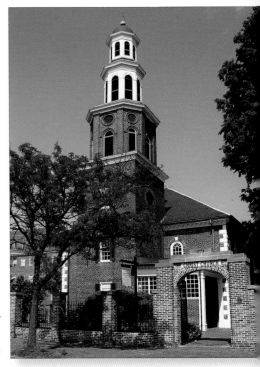

▲ George Washington and Robert E. Lee were regular worshippers at Christ Church. This imposing structure at 118 North Washington Street was designed by James Wren in the Colonial Georgian style and built in 1767-1773.

◀ "Old Town" is a revitalized waterfront area with colonial houses, churches, museums, shops and restaurants that are easily enjoyed on a casual walk.

◀ Stop for a tour at Gadsby's Tavern Museum, 134 N. Royal Street. It comprises the circa 1785 tavern and the 1792 City Tavern & Hotel. Furnished rooms recall lively times in our nation's history.

EVEN CHURCHES CHANGED

Did you know that the Episcopal Church in America was previously the Church of England and a dominant ruling body? In Virginia, for example, populated areas were divided into Church of England parishes under the domain of the British government. Each parish provided its own religious services, and its elected vestrymen handled civil and church business, including social and welfare services. In return, residents paid taxes to the church. When Alexandria was founded in 1749, it had a chapel-of-ease, or branch church, within a larger parish. When it became a thriving community, the parish was divided, and twin churches were built – Falls Church (in Falls Church) and Christ Church (in Alexandria). After our Revolutionary War, the Church of England in America separated from the British government and became the Episcopal Church. It is still part of the Anglican Communion, under the spiritual authority of the Archbishop of Canterbury.

Stratford Hall Plantation

SEE MAP PAGE 15, LOCATION #32
Stratford, Virginia
Phone: (804) 493-8038
http://www.stratfordhall.org

▲ Stratford Hall has many interesting architectural features, including oversized chimney clusters and walls of multi-color brick, arranged in patterns.

▶ Old Bedford Village has over 40 log, stone and frame buildings. Most of the structures were brought here to protect an important slice of Pennsylvania heritage and tell the story of early American life through Living History.

▶ The stables at Stratford Hall display several beautifully restored carriages as well as a collection of harnesses decorated with the family colors and squirrel emblem.

This "Great House," circa 1738, was the elegant home for prominent Virginia planter Thomas Lee and his wife, Hannah. Remaining in the Lee family until 1822, it was witness to an extraordinary lineage, including two signers of the Declaration of Independence, Richard Henry Lee and Francis Lightfoot Lee; two important diplomats, Arthur and William Lee; Revolutionary War hero "Light Horse Harry" Lee; and Civil War General Robert E. Lee. Meticulously preserved, it is a pleasure to visit. In addition to

taking the house tour, walk through the expansive gardens, enjoy the magnificent views of the Potomac, and explore the Visitor Center. Despite all we have seen in our travels, we discovered new things here. Among them: a copper still used to make medicinal drinks and an interesting clock made in the 1600s.

Located at 483 Great House Road in Stratford, VA, 42 miles southeast of Fredericksburg. Take Route 3 to Lerty; turn left onto Route 214; drive 2 miles. Open daily except major holidays. Admission charged.

Old Bedford Village

SEE MAP PAGE 11, LOCATION #47
Bedford, Pennsylvania
Phone: toll-free (800) 238-4347
http://www.oldbedfordvillage.com

The industrial base of our nation was to become an outgrowth of artisan skills. In the East, as elsewhere, people made what they could and traded with others before manufacturers found ways to mass-produce goods more cheaply. Living History at Old Bedford Village makes those days real for visitors. Not only can you see period skills practiced here in historic and re-created buildings; you also can learn the old crafts yourself by  taking one of the many classes offered throughout the season. There's lots to see and enjoy here!

Located 2 miles north of downtown Bedford, PA, on Business Route 220 just south of Pennsylvania Turnpike/I-76 exit 146. Open Memorial Day to late October – Thursday-Tuesday Memorial Day-Labor Day; Thursday-Sunday rest of season. Admission charged.

SUNDAY TOYS

Well into the 1800s, children were confined by strict prohibitions during the Sabbath. Forbidden to run, whistle, whittle or otherwise wile away the hours, many became restless and cranky on Sundays. Doting parents found a solution: "Sunday Toys." These were educational as well as amusing and based on religious themes. Among the favorites was Noah's Ark, a boat-shaped toy chest filled with small, removable wood carvings. From it, exotic jungle beasts paraded two by two, with barnyard cows and sheep, family pets, bugs, birds and whatever else the carver imagined. Jacob's Ladder helped recall Jacob's dream about angels moving up and down between heaven and earth. The board game Christian Endeavor demonstrated the rewards for virtue and the penalties for vice. The Pillars of Solomon, an illusion toy, recalled the Bible story about Solomon's Pillars connected by a chain. Other "nice, quiet toys" included building-block churches and the Wolf in Sheep's Clothing.

Historic Concord

SEE MAP PAGE 11, LOCATION #49A

Concord, Massachusetts
Phone: (978) 369-3120 (Chamber of Commerce)
http://www.concordchamberofcommerce.org

Concord has had an illustrious history, separate from its role as the target of British soldiers on the first day of the Revolutionary War. It began life in 1635 as a frontier outpost of the Massachusetts Bay Colony. Over the years, it grew into a charming town, developed a stately New England elegance and, in the mid-1800s, emerged as the home of some of America's greatest literary minds. Today Concord proudly fosters its rich heritage. We especially recommend the following attractions.

The Old Manse

Built in 1770 by the Reverend William Emerson, this historic house contains over 200 years of family furnishings. The Reverend's grandson, Ralph Waldo Emerson, drafted his 1836 essay "Nature" in The Old Manse.

Nathaniel Hawthorne and his bride, Sophia, lived here from 1842 to 1845. (You'll see his writing desk and a windowpane with her initials carved into it.) The surrounding landscape includes an heirloom vegetable garden similar to the one planted by Henry David Thoreau as a wedding gift to the Hawthornes. Located at 269 Monument Street, next to the North Bridge. http://www.thetrustees.org/pages/346_old_manse.cfm

Louisa May Alcott Orchard House

In early America, many buildings were moved from one place to another – that was cheaper and easier than starting over. Bronson Alcott, father of Louisa May Alcott, went one step further, purchasing two buildings and joining them together to create his family's home.

Louisa used the house as her setting for "Little Women" and wrote at a "shelf" desk built by her father. About 75% of the furnishings are original, and the rooms look much as they did during her lifetime. Located at 399 Lexington Road. http://www.louisamayalcott.org

Ralph Waldo Emerson House

A prolific writer, philosopher, lecturer and poet, Ralph Waldo Emerson was at the center of the American transcendental movement. His home from 1835-1882 was the place where friends and colleagues could spend long days talking about radical religious views and forward-looking social reforms. Amidst original furnishings and Emerson memorabilia, you will learn about a very interesting man and a very formative time. Located at 28 Cambridge Turnpike. http://www.rwe.org/emersonhouse

Walden Pond State Reservation

Many consider this the birthplace of the conservation movement. Henry David Thoreau lived at Walden Pond from July 1845 to September 1847 and used his experiences to write *Walden*. It is a lovely place in its own right, with undeveloped woods and a 102-foot-deep glacial kettle-hole lake. Special efforts have been made to maintain the unspoiled environment. Dogs, bicycles, flotation devices and picnic grills are prohibited. A replica of Thoreau's one-room log cabin is on display near the original location. Year-round interpretive programs and guided walks are offered. Walden Pond is located on SR 126 about ¹/₂ mile south of the Concord Turnpike. The parking lot is across the road. http://www.mass.gov/dcr/parks/northeast/wldn.htm

Visitor Center for these and other sites located at 58 Main Street in Concord, MA, just south of Monument Square. Take SR 2A (Lexington Road), which passes through Minute Man National Historical Park. Open daily. Admission charged at historic homes.

Balance and symmetry were hallmarks of the 1700s and early 1800s architecture. In virtually all of the houses and major buildings, including the three shown on this page, the front door was centered between matching sets of windows.

▲ Emerson's house, built in 1805, was particularly refined. Square-shaped and with four chimneys, it has matching symmetry on multiple sides.

◀ More typical examples of Georgian/Federal styles in America are The Old Manse, circa 1770, and Orchard House, a composite of two early 1700s homes.

Old Sturbridge Village

SEE MAP PAGE 11, LOCATION #62
Sturbridge, Massachusetts
Phone: toll-free (800) SEE-1830
http://www.osv.org

Located an hour west of Boston, MA. Take I-84 exit 2; turn west; follow signs to the main entrance. Open year-round – daily Memorial Day to late October; Tuesday-Sunday (plus Monday holidays) late October to Memorial Day; closed December 25. Admission charged.

▲ You will gain a broad understanding of 1800s village life at Old Sturbridge. Attractions range from in-town homes, shops, a tavern and the bank to rural farms and small-scale industrial operations.

▶ The blacksmith shop down the lane and the sawmill across the pond are picturesque reminders that in the early days of our young nation, villages had to be self-sufficient in most respects.

▶ For many of the interpreters, this is not just a place to share information. They rarely get to take a break at the farm, which keeps them busy tending the animals, laboring in the fields and doing household chores.

Old Sturbridge Village began life as a vision of the Wells brothers, three wealthy men who took up an avocation to preserve a vanishing past. Like other prominent American families who transformed their collections into open-air museums – Rockefeller (Colonial Williamsburg), Ford (Greenfield Village) and du Pont (Winterthur Museum) – they were concerned about protecting our past from the powerful currents of change. Although this specific village never existed, the buildings, exhibits and history-based activities are all authentic, dating back to the 1830s. Within the 200-acre rural landscape are more than 40 structures, including restored buildings brought from across New England as well as some period reconstructions. Heritage livestock are grown here, as are heirloom gardens (labeled with documented household, culinary and/or medicinal uses). Many visitors spend an entire day here or return for a second day. Truly enjoyable!

HERITAGE LIVESTOCK

American worries about endangered species tend to focus on wild animals and habitat destruction. All too often, the so-called "heritage" or "minor" domesticated farm animals are forgotten. Yet they, too, are endangered. On the surface of it, why should we care? After all, domesticated breeds are endangered because they have lost their value, have become unpopular or simply have been replaced by other breeds. The problem is: they represent much of the genetic diversity remaining in various livestock species. This includes disease and parasite resistance as well as increased longevity and foraging abilities – important qualities that are often diminished by modern selective breeding practices. Once heritage breeds die out, their lost characteristics can never be recovered. We need to encourage the preservation of rare breeds of farm animals – not only because they are a living part of our rural past, but also because they are a genetic resource that one day might prove vital to mankind's food supply.

The Farmers' Museum

SEE MAP PAGE 11, LOCATION #50
Cooperstown, New York
Phone: toll-free (888) 547-1450
http://www.farmersmuseum.org

Throughout our young nation, many small towns grew up specifically to serve the needs of local farmers. None were "ordinary." In fact, some were quite extraordinary. This restored 1845 village enables you to explore early rural life in New York State. It is a place for discovering things you won't find elsewhere.

One of your first stops is the American Paper-Staining Manufactory, which still serves customers. Artisans use the only block-press of its kind remaining in America to re-create the types of wallpaper that glamorized homes from the late 1700s to mid-1800s. (Remnants decorate matching personal items such as hat boxes.)

Nearby is a re-created 1800s Country Fair. Featuring colorful period tents, it will amuse and amaze you with the Cardiff Giant and other nineteenth-century hoaxes. Other attractions include the Biographic Picture Theatre, agricultural demonstrations and early games.

Wander down to the working farmstead, where you will see heritage animals and learn how New York once produced 90 percent of our nation's hops. More than giving flavor to beer, hop flowers were a vital preservative, enabling early America's leading beverage to last more than a day. Long before hops were a commercial crop, native and imported varieties

State Carousel. Enjoy several heritage gardens, ranging from the practical Kitchen and Physic gardens to the artful Downing Garden. Then walk uphill to the Seneca Log House, for a unique look at the Six Nations (Iroquois) culture 150 years ago. Also watch scheduled demonstrations throughout the museum complex.

Located at 5775 SR 80, a mile north of Cooperstown, NY, on the west side of Otsego Lake; 70 miles west of Albany. Open April-October – daily mid-May to Columbus Day; Tuesday-Sunday rest of season. Admission charged.

▲ Many of the distinctive buildings are populated by Living History interpreters and craftspeople. Down the lane, a working farmstead has heritage animals such as red Duroc pigs, Devon cattle, a draft horse, Narragansett turkeys, black Cayuga ducks, and of course several types of chickens.

◀ Stenciled patterns were a popular way for the less-affluent to decorate their homes when wallpaper was too costly.

◀ The tavern looks like a luxurious plantation home with its tall columns and long wagon barn. This was not a place for "common folk."

◀ The Seneca Log House shows how members of the Six Nations adapted to European building styles. But don't be misled. As the interpreter will tell you inside, the people remained faithful to their Native lifeways.

were common in settlers' gardens. Young hop shoots were a special treat in salads. The flowers were a good alternative to yeast in bread-making. A wax extracted from the tendrils made a reddish-brown vegetable dye. Hop fibers were used in textiles as a substitute for flax, and the stalks could be woven into baskets.

That is just the beginning of what you will discover at The Farmers' Museum. Also tour the various homes and businesses, chatting with the Living History interpreters and craftspeople. Ride the charming Empire

Historic Arkansas Museum

SEE MAP PAGE 19, LOCATION #20
Little Rock, Arkansas
Phone: (501) 324-9351
http://www.historicarkansas.org

▲ Behind this white picket fence is a pre-Civil War world waiting to be visited. Role-playing actors portray the original residents with cleverness and charm. Periodic Living History events add to the fun.

▶ These classic clapboard structures are deceptive. The custom of the day was to upgrade homes by hiding log cabins behind attractive siding.

▶ "Cobb family members" invite you into their home at Rocky Mount. Along with "friends" and "servants," they make your visit memorable, depicting life on the farm and sharing interesting bits of history.

Arkansas' largest history museum offers entertaining guided tours of four early nineteenth-century houses that highlight America's rich and complex cultural heritage. Here you will learn about a man of German descent who in 1826 constructed the Hinderliter Grog Shop as a business and eventual home for his wife and two slaves...

a Scottish stonemason who built the Brownlee House in 1848 but soon left to search for gold in California...a young New Yorker who moved to Arkansas to print the territory's first newspaper and operated his business at the Woodruff Print Shop from 1824-1827... and a Mexican War veteran who became the director of the state penitentiary and built the 1848 McVicar House. Interesting people. Interesting buildings.

Historic Arkansas also has a 51,000-square-foot exhibit building with fine and decorative arts, knife and firearms displays, a variety of hands-on experiences, changing historical exhibits and a contemporary Arkansas Artists' Gallery.

Located at 200 East Third Street in the heart of downtown Little Rock, AR. Take I-30 exit 141-A. Open daily except major holidays. Admission charged for guided tours. Museum center and galleries are free.

Rocky Mount Museum

SEE MAP PAGE 17, LOCATION #25
Piney Flats, Tennessee
Phone: toll-free (888) 538-1791
http://www.rockymountmuseum.com

In the Southwest Territory, the Cobb farmstead was the place to be in 1791. George Washington had appointed William Blount as Territorial Governor, and he chose to use Mr. and Mrs. Cobb's fine two-story log house as his residence and office until the Territorial capitol could be built in Knoxville. As you walk through the front door, you enter a topsy-turvy world, where a farmstead serves as a center for government business and a farm family

tries to conduct daily chores while important people come and go. First person interpretations familiarize you with their lifestyles, domestic and work skills, pioneer crafts, food, clothing, furnishings and games. You will "meet" Cobb family members, neighbors and servants. If your timing is right, you might get to taste culinary delights such as gingerbread or sausage muffins cooked over an open fire in the kitchen. You'll see edibles in the 1791 garden as well as medicinal and dye plants. At the weaving cabin, interpreters card, spin and weave flax and wool. The blacksmith shapes iron in his shop. And, of course, there are many special events such as Woolly Day in April (sheep shearing, music, storytelling, farm activities), Raid on the Watauga in July (battle re-enactment, Native Americans, European settlers, music, storytelling), Shape Note Singing in August, and Spirit of the Harvest in October.

Located at intersection of US 11E and Hyder Hill Road in Piney Flats, TN, between Johnson City and Bristol. Open Tuesday-Saturday from March to mid-December; by appointment January-February; closed major holidays. Admission charged.

Tryon Palace Historic Sites & Gardens

SEE MAP PAGE 15, LOCATION #30
New Bern, North Carolina
Phone: toll-free (800) 767-1560
http://www.tryonpalace.org

On many levels, this is an amazing place. In its day, Tryon (tree-ON) Palace was the colonial capitol of North Carolina and home of the Royalist governor. Yet, the most remarkable part of the story is not its place in history but its modern re-creation. All but one wing of the palace burned in a disastrous fire in 1798. Much of what remained was demolished in the early 1800s, and the property virtually disappeared as George Street extended over the foundations, new buildings filled the space and the Trent River bridge took over the riverfront.

In 1944, well over 100 years later, the almost-unbelievable occurred: Mrs. James Edwin Latham, a wealthy, civic-minded native of New Bern, challenged the state of North Carolina to join her in rebuilding the palace. The state agreed; Mrs. Latham established a trust to fund the project; and in the 1950s, work began. Their first challenge was to remove more than 50 buildings and reroute SR 70, including the bridge over Trent River. Their second challenge was to uncover the original Palace foundations and remove layers of stucco from the stable office, which was the only remaining part of the 1770 structure. Third challenge: reconstruct the Palace as precisely as possible according to the original architectural plans. Craftspeople from around the world came to do the work. Trips to England yielded appropriate furnishings, based on an inventory from 1798. Today, guides in period dress conduct tours of all major areas, and Living History interpreters bring the eighteenth century back to life. Stunning!

Still, this isn't all. Acres of gardens display three centuries of landscape history, including the eighteenth-century wilderness that greeted the first European colonists, the lush Victorian displays wealthy settlers created for their homes, and twentieth-century Colonial Revival interpretations. In addition, several original homes nearby are open for visits. Each has intriguing tales to tell about former residents and the lifestyles they led during the late 1700s and early 1800s.

If ever you find yourself thinking that Americans don't care enough about their national heritage, remember Tryon Palace and smile.

▲ If Tryon Palace reminds you of the Georgian manor houses of England, this may be because architect John Hawkes came from Britain to handle this project in the 1760s.

◀ The grounds include beautiful formal gardens such as this one, plus an extensive, well-labeled kitchen garden with a wide variety of fruits, vegetables and herbs.

Located at 610 Pollock Street near the intersection of Broad and George Streets in New Bern, NC. Open daily except major holidays. Admission charged.

Conner Prairie

SEE MAP PAGE 17, LOCATION #20
Fishers, Indiana
Phone: toll-free (800) 966-1836
http://www.connerprairie.org

▲ While most buildings at Conner Prairie are simple and functional in style, the Conner House is a mansion with elegant furnishings. Unusual features include a beehive oven built into the kitchen wall and extending out into the yard. (Note the bulge on the far left corner of the building.)

▶ The shelves of the general store are fully stocked with everything from rope to cones of sugar (wrapped in blue). The cast iron heating stove was common by the 1740s.

▶ Vegetable gardens were substantial and required hours of labor. As parents aged, their grown children often had to take on the biggest burden. Here, the adult "daughter" of the local cabinet maker is preparing the soil next to her "father's" shop.

This absorbing open-air museum, set within 860 acres of natural beauty, provides an opportunity to explore everyday life in Indiana Territory within the context of the evolving melting pot of multiple cultures. Four historically accurate lifestyles are presented at Conner Prairie, complete with costumed interpreters and period-specific activities. A fifth interpretive area lets adults and children experience crafts, skills and games common to the people and periods represented. As you will learn, life changed quickly as vast numbers of people came from the East and from across the Atlantic to homestead and make a new life for themselves.

In the beginning, there were the local Native Peoples and their small wigwam communities, represented by the 1816 Lenape Camp & McKinnen's Trading Post. In startling contrast came the sophisticated world of a successful white fur trader, entrepreneur and politician, William Conner. He built an estate for his family in 1823 and lived in a Federal-style brick home. In addition to taking a tour of his house, you can see old-time dyeing, spinning and weaving techniques demonstrated at a loom house on this property.

Soon, large groups of settlers were advancing into the Old Northwest Territory. A representative example is provided by the 1836 Prairietown, which is comprised of 29 historic buildings, including a restored schoolhouse and general store as well as blacksmith, carpentry and pottery shops. At this re-created village, a number of fictional residents re-enact elections, weddings and funerals. They also perform everyday village chores and crafts that increase visitor understanding of this period.

Just across the historic Cedar Chapel Covered Bridge is 1886 Liberty Corner, a rural crossroad hamlet. Here you will see the Hoosier world in transition. The Friends Meeting House provides insight into the continuing importance of religion, and the historic District #2 School shows how youngsters were educated. "Home" is the Zimmerman Farm, with

its large Victorian house, barns, livestock, crops and orchard. More stylish and spacious than the others, it reflects civilizing influences and, by its modern conveniences, signals the big changes that came to Indiana.

Located 6 miles north of Fishers, IN, on Allisonville Road. Open Tuesday-Sunday plus major holidays April-October. Admission charged.

Alabama Constitution Village

SEE MAP PAGE 17, LOCATION #21
Huntsville, Alabama
Phone: (256) 564-8100
http://www.earlyworks.com

Historic Saint Charles

SEE MAP PAGE 19, LOCATION #21
Saint Charles, Missouri
Phone: toll-free (800) 366-2427 (Convention and Visitors Bureau)
http://www.historicstcharles.com

Alabama had a rocky road to statehood. Settled by the French in 1702, it was split in two after the French and Indian War. The Mobile area became a British holding but later fell to the Spanish. The rest became part of the Illinois country and joined America in 1795. During the War of 1812, the Mobile area was captured by American troops. Yet even then, there were battles to be fought – the Creek Indians refused to surrender their lands. Alabama finally became a state in 1819, and Huntsville was its first capital.

Alabama Constitution Village commemorates that point in time when statehood was finally achieved. It also recalls the enormous diversity once present in any one part of Huntsville. Although the circa 1805-1819

buildings are reconstructions, they were built on the original sites according to old records. Among them are the Walker Allen cabinet shop (now called Constitution Hall), the Clay law office, urban slave quarters (better than their rural counterparts), apprentice quarters for young white men learning a trade, the post rider's stable and home, the Boardman Building newspaper office, Huntsville's first public library, and private residences. Guides in period dress lead visitors on tours, stopping at the various buildings where interpreters re-create daily tasks of the Old South. This is an enjoyable opportunity to explore the heritage and hospitality of nineteenth-century Alabama. Among the varying Living History activities are old-style cabinet-making, news printing, blacksmithing, weaving, heritage herb and vegetable gardening, spinning, butter churning and candle dipping.

Located off of US 565 in Huntsville, AL. Take exit 19 toward downtown; drive south to 109 Gates Avenue. Open March-December – Wednesday-Saturday March-October; less often November-December; closed Thanksgiving and December 24-25. Admission charged.

Founded in 1769 by French-Canadian farmers and fur traders, St. Charles was an important supply point for explorers and pioneers. Lewis and Clark began their epic journey in St. Charles, as did the majority of early settlers heading west. Although downtown South Main Street has necessarily transformed itself into a shopping/dining area, it remains a beautifully preserved historic district. Among the attractions are the First Missouri State Capitol; Haviland China exhibit in the Newbill-McElhiney House; reconstructed St. Charles Borromeo Church (with its vertical log, poteaux en terre construction); and Lewis & Clark Boat House and Nature Center, with its handcrafted replicas of the keelboat and

pirogues. Be sure to take your walking tour using the guide of historic buildings available at the Convention and Visitors Bureau, 230 South Main.

Located just 30 minutes west of downtown St. Louis, MO, off of I-70. To reach the downtown historic district, take exit 229 (Fifth Street) heading north; turn right on Boone's Lick Road and follow it to Main Street. Most stores and historic sites are open daily. The Haviland Museum offers tours Tuesday and Thursday. Admission charged at some locations.

▲ "Stone Row," extending from 318 to 330 South Main Street, was built in the 1820s. The stone used to construct these buildings was quarried from within this city block.

◄ A vacant Huntsville cabinetmaker's shop, now called Constitution Hall, was the only structure large enough to accommodate 44 delegates at Alabama's Constitutional Convention in 1819.

◄ Missouri's first Capitol was in Saint Charles. It is furnished much as it appeared in 1821, when legislators began the task of transforming a territorial government into a state system. This structure is actually two buildings. The ground floors were the home and store of brothers Ruluff and Charles Peck as well as the home of carpenter Chauncey Shepard. The second floors became the state's Great Assembly Hall, Governor's office and committee rooms.

COMMERCE & INDUSTRY

Compass Inn

SEE MAP PAGE 11, LOCATION #56

Laughlintown, Pennsylvania
Phone: (724) 238-4983
http://www.compassinn.com

▶ Just a few steps from the dining table at the Compass Inn, alcoholic beverages were served. When the proprietor left or decided that patrons had had enough to drink, the overhead barricade dropped down and the "bar" was closed. While times have changed, the name remains.

In the mid-1700s, most machines were made of wood and were powered by hand, animals or water wheels. But over the period of just a few decades, the unimaginable happened. Steam power proved to be safe and effective. High-quality iron became cheap enough to be used for factory machinery and innovative agricultural equipment. Time-consuming jobs were taken out of the home and out of the workshop to be handled in more efficient factories. Goods of all types became available in larger quantities at cheaper prices, and items which the middle class and working class had only dreamed about before were now easily obtainable.

manufacturing was taken out of the home and out of the workshop

With these advances, American livelihoods and lifestyles were forever altered. Some workers were displaced by machines and floundered for a while. Others found jobs working in factories, not only as equipment operators and engineers, but also as clerks, managers and other professionals. Farmers felt the changes too – beginning with the commercialization of the cotton gin and the availability of cast-iron plows. Of course, there were many people who lamented the loss of a simple life. Yet, the benefits of industrialization could not be denied. Life was, for the most part, easier and more enjoyable.

The Industrial Revolution began in Great Britain, which had ready supplies of iron for making machinery and coal for producing steam power. By the early 1800s, it had spread to other parts of Europe and across the Atlantic. In America, the "early adopters" were in New England, particularly in the textiles, small arms and light metals manufacturing sectors. But progress soon spread to other areas, stimulated by the demands of a rapidly growing population.

With the Industrial Revolution came many other revolutions as well. Key among them were advances in transportation – initially through the creation of artificial waterways – as demand for raw materials and finished goods extended over great distances. Banking prospered too, as businesses borrowed large sums for building and required a well-managed flow of money. In the midst of all this, an unexpected new industry also emerged: gold mining. America had become the "land of plenty."

▶ The rear of the Compass Inn clearly shows the structural additions made over time. As the business grew, building styles changed. The log section came first, then the stone and finally the clapboard.

Completion of the Philadelphia-Pittsburgh Turnpike in 1817 brought travelers to the Compass Inn on a regular basis until 1862, when trains and canal boats became the primary modes of long-distance travel. Today at this authentically restored stagecoach stop, costumed docents tell stories of travel and everyday life in the early 1800s. The tour visits seven rooms at the Inn, including the "common" room, kitchen, ladies' parlor and four bedrooms, plus the reconstructed cookhouse, blacksmith's shop, carpenter's shop and barn. Living History Weekends are held mid-month during summer, and a Halloween story-telling event is held in late October.

Located on Route 30 in Laughlintown, PA, 3 miles from Fort Ligonier (Road to Independence, page 141). Take Pennsylvania Turnpike exit 9 at Donegal Interchange; turn left on Route 31; take 711 north 12 miles; turn right on Route 30; drive 3 miles east. Open Tuesday-Sunday, plus Monday holidays, mid-April to Oct. Weekend Candlelight Tours, Nov. to mid-Dec. Admission charged.

Rising Sun Tavern

SEE MAP PAGE 15, LOCATION #27

Fredericksburg, Virginia

Phone: (540) 373-1776 or toll-free (800) 678-4748

http://www.apva.org/risingsuntavern

Charles Washington, the youngest brother of George Washington, purchased two lots in a section of Fredericksburg laid out by his brother-in-law, Fielding Lewis. Here in the 1760s, Charles built what would be his home for the next 20 years. After his departure,

the house took on a different purpose, as so often happened in past times. It was transformed into the Golden Eagle Tavern and later the Rising Sun Tavern, and then it changed again, back to being a private residence. Its life as the Rising Sun Tavern seems to have been the most memorable. This was, after all, the only "proper" tavern in the bustling port city on the Rappahannock River.

The Rising Sun no longer serves food, but its costumed wenches do provide a lively interpretation of eighteenth-century tavern life. You are welcomed into the past as an upper-class visitor and quickly feel as though you just stepped off a stagecoach in the late 1700s. Of particular interest are the Tap Room bar cage (a reconstruction); the fine collection of English and American pewter; the ladies' parlor which was off-limits to men; and the Great Room where the men preferred to eat, drink, smoke, play games, talk politics and skip a good night's sleep.

Located at 1304 Caroline Street in Fredericksburg, VA. Open daily except major holidays. Admission charged.

Michie Tavern

SEE MAP PAGE 15, LOCATION #25

Charlottesville, Virginia

Phone: (434) 977-1234

http://www.michietavern.com

Whether you take a guided tour or stop to dine, the 1784 Michie (MICK-ee) Tavern will make you feel right at home in the eighteenth century. Little has changed other than its location, which was 17 miles away until 1927. The hearty homemade fare is based on recipes from the late 1700s. The atmosphere is very Early America. What's more, costumed servers and Living History interpreters re-create the lively social interactions shared by past travelers seeking food, drink and lodging.

As you will discover, taverns have satisfied a very wide range of social needs. In addition to exploring the main-floor dining area, you will walk upstairs to a large, sunlit room that once served as a ballroom, makeshift school room, worship center and extra sleeping quarters. You will see the elaborately decorated Ladies' Parlor and other public rooms. You might even have the opportunity to taste an eighteenth-century punch, dance a tavern reel or write with a quill pen. Outside are the Tavern's dependencies (outbuildings) and the Virginia Wine Exhibit. Living History programs are offered from April through October.

Be sure to obtain a "Presidents' Pass" combination ticket if you plan to tour other historic attractions nearby, such as Jefferson's Monticello and James Monroe's Ash-Lawn Highland. It may be purchased onsite or ordered in advance (www.monticello.org/visit/pres_pass.html).

Located in Charlottesville, VA, less than a mile from Monticello. Take I-64 exit 121; drive 1/2 mile south on SR 20; then 1 mile east on SR 53/Thomas Jefferson Pkwy. Open daily except major holidays. Admission charged.

▲ Michie Tavern is an exceptional building on a beautiful hillside near Jefferson's Monticello. Immerse yourself in the eighteenth-century ambiance and include a stroll of the grounds.

◀ The Rising Sun Tavern may appear humble, but inside are all the amenities that an eighteenth-century traveler could want. It was especially pleasant for women, who were glad to have their own cozy parlor away from the noisy, "unseemly" behavior of men.

◀ Business signs in the 1700s were noticeable but not ostentatious. They didn't need to be read from a speeding vehicle or compete with a lot of other street advertising.

Old Bethpage Village Restoration

SEE MAP PAGE 11, LOCATION #57
Old Bethpage, New York
Phone: (516) 572-8400
http://www.oldbethpage.org

markedly. John Layton has stocked his shelves with general manufactured products ranging from kitchen appliances and pottery to children's toys and penny candy. John Luyster makes brooms and has filled his store with an odd assortment of goods: tobacco, molasses, hardware, whale oil, powdered paints, farm implements and bulk foods.

▲ John Noon operated this typical Long Island country hotel for 11 years. Its Georgian-style central hallway enables it to have a split personality – one pubic and one private. Downstairs are the public barroom as well as a private parlor and kitchen. Upstairs are the public ballroom and several bedrooms.

▶ Hat shops are rare in Living History villages. Even rarer is the opportunity to meet a hatter and observe his craft. Be sure to visit this shop at Old Bethpage.

▶ The concept behind Old Bethpage Village has its roots in the mid-1600s, when colonists founded town "spots" on Long Island. The spots served as commercial and social centers for outlying homes and farms.

▶ Farmhouse tools of the 1800s are often curiosities today. The object on the left is a common candle mold. But what is the large object in front? Ask when you visit.

In the 1960s, as progress swept through Long Island destroying irreplaceable landmarks, civic minded individuals took action. They purchased the Powell family farm in Old Bethpage and began moving buildings to the property. Today more than 50 historic buildings and seven reconstructions – representative examples of the early 1700s to mid-1800s – are spread throughout 209 beautiful acres. Costumed interpreters portray farmers, teachers, storekeepers, civic leaders, the blacksmith, the cooper, the hat maker, the tavern keeper, musicians and others who would have been attracted to a prosperous New York community.

Enjoy a self-guided walking tour. At the crossroads, stop at the Noon Inn, Layton General Store and Luyster Store. The inn is a two-story Georgian-style house with a very unusual feature: a barroom that was originally built as a barroom. (In the 1800s, taverns were typically renovated farmhouses.) The two nearby stores differ

Down the road, the hatter is molding stylish felt hats, and the blacksmith is working at his forge. The home of Peter Cooper, inventor of the "Tom Thumb" steam locomotive, is nearby. Cooper began his entrepreneurial career here. Furnishings include his fanciful baby cradle, which played music and shooed away bothersome flies.

Further down the road are several other homes and the Powell Farm, which became the basis for Old Bethpage. In other parts of the village are several additional farms and homes plus the one-room District No. 6 School and the Manetto Hill Church. In many cases, interpreters beckon visitors to enter. Old Bethpage also has many special activities – such as regular Old Time Baseball games; planting and sheep shearing in May; a Civil War Battle in July; and a County Fair in the fall. This is a fun place to spend a day and gain insight into domestic, agricultural and commercial activities central to village life in the 1800s.

Located ¹/₂ mile south of Long Island Expy. exit 48, on Round Swamp Road in Old Bethpage, NY. Follow brown signs. Open Wednesday-Sunday March-December; closed Thanksgiving and December 25. Admission charged.

Spring Mill Pioneer Village

SEE MAP PAGE 17, LOCATION #22
Mitchell, Indiana
Phone: (812) 849-4129
http://www.in.gov/dnr/parklake/properties/park_springmill.html

"Let's go to town." We say those words casually today, little realizing how important they were centuries ago. Towns were a lifeline to goods and services (both purchases and sales), friends and neighbors, mail and special orders. And although days away by horse and wagon, the entire family wanted to make the trip. Spring Mill – now a restored and reconstructed showplace in a lush Indiana park – was such a place.

This vital village came to life in the early 1800s. Following the establishment of a gristmill, workers were hired by the mill operators to provide a tavern, tannery, weaver, distillery, general store, apothecary/doctor office, post office, blacksmith, lumber mill and other businesses – all to serve a 50-mile radius of farmers and their families. The primary draw was, of course, the gristmill.

As you might imagine, fall was the busiest time of year at Spring Mill. Farm families made a special trip to town not only to grind their corn but also to enjoy the excitement and camaraderie they craved after a long season of hard work. Some stayed overnight in the tavern; others camped out nearby and slept under their wagons. Stagecoaches made extra trips, bringing more travelers to town. Farmers lined up their wagons at the mill, loaded with bags of husked corn, and the noise of grinding cornmeal was heard around the clock. Hogs, raised for sale, rooted in the yard near the mill. Children played. People gathered to catch up on news, to gossip and to say "hello" to friends and neighbors they had not seen for months.

By comparison, today's Pioneer Village is remarkably quiet; but it is not empty. All homes and businesses are fully outfitted, and a number of Living History interpreters in period attire go about their daily tasks and crafts. A highlight is the restored, water-powered gristmill which grinds cornmeal the way it did 175 years ago. When not driving the gristmill, the water wheel diverts its power to the saw mill, which also operates as it did long ago. A variety of special events and daily programming are offered, and handcrafts made by the re-enactors are sold in the mercantile.

For a change of pace, we recommend exploring some of the 1,319-acre public park's other offerings. Spring Mill has an artificial lake and virgin timberland. Here you will be able to enjoy a wide range of outdoor activities, including boating, camping, cave exploring, fishing, hiking, mountain biking, picnicking and swimming. Other attractions include the nature center, a memorial to astronaut Virgil I. "Gus" Grissom and guided boat tours through Twin Caves.

Located on SR 60 in Spring Mill State Park, about 3 1/4 miles east of Mitchell, IN, via SR 37. Open daily April-October. Park entry fee charged; Pioneer Village is free.

▲ Lovingly restored, the gristmill is the centerpiece of Spring Mill Pioneer Village. Here the miller makes cornmeal using a water-powered grinding stone. Next door, in the smaller building, the sawyer cuts lumber, also with equipment powered by water.

◀ Inside the gristmill, the maze of wooden gears and shafts rumble and roar to life when water is released from the raised aqueduct onto an immense water-powered wheel.

◀ Twenty historic buildings have been restored or reconstructed at Spring Mill Pioneer Village. Their idyllic environment belies the fact that the community was a noisy place in its heyday.

Hopewell Furnace National Historic Site

SEE MAP PAGE 11, LOCATION #48B

Birdsboro vicinity (south), Pennsylvania
Phone: (610) 582-8773
http://www.nps.gov/hofu

▲ The village around the foundry (red roof with steeple) is a peaceful place to stroll. During apple harvest season (early September through October), stop by the orchard and pick your own apples from the historic varieties.

▶ Iron was cast into a wide variety of products at Hopewell Furnace, but heating stoves were a mainstay. They often included intricate stove plates such as the ones shown here.

▶ Inside the foundry building, you will see the huge mouths that encircle the furnaces. Nearby rigging stands ready for use in lifting molten iron.

When colonists brought blast furnace technology to America in the mid-1600s, England paid attention. It did not want competition with its own ironmasters. For self-protection, officials of the English Crown tried to limit colonial production to only pig iron, a brittle material that needed further processing for many uses. Their goal was to send this pig iron to England, where it could be refined into wrought iron and profitable goods for shipment back to the colonies. Americans had a different plan: they wanted to reap the rewards of their hard work. So Parliament passed a law that actually prohibited the building of more ironworks. This effort also failed. By the time of the Revolution, one-seventh of the world's iron goods came from America.

Hopewell Furnace, which was founded in 1771, is a particularly well-preserved example of a rural American iron plantation. Its huge charcoal-fired and water-powered furnaces supplied a wide variety of iron products to cities along the American east coast until 1883, when more advanced production technologies made Hopewell obsolete. What remains today are 14 restored structures, most furnished and tourable, on 848 beautiful acres. A self-guided tour enables visitors to explore the ironmaster's mansion and several workers'

homes, as well as the general store, blacksmith shop and rebuilt iron furnace complex. This company town also has a working farm, which in past times would have provided much of the meat and produce needed to sustain furnace workers and their families. Late June through Labor Day, Living History programs and demonstrations represent life in the iron making industry during the 1820s to 1840s – the height of Hopewell's success.

Located about 50 miles northwest of Philadelphia, PA, and about 5 miles south of Birdsboro on SR 345. Open Wednesday-Sunday except certain holidays. Admission charged.

IRON PLANTATIONS

While northern states had the factory mentality needed to make high-grade iron, the South did not. In fact, establishing an iron industry in the South was counter to the well-ingrained agricultural way of life. Southern iron plantations were typically small and only produced low-grade pig iron, not wrought iron. (This was a weakness during the Civil War. Confederate-made guns and other military equipment apparently were not as durable as weaponry in the Union Army.) Northern iron plantations, like southern agricultural plantations, faced stiff foreign competition. The ironmaster had to pay low wages to keep prices down; so he had to find other ways to compensate employees, most of whom were married and had children. To attract workers, he built homes, provided farmland, set up a company store, and often established a school and a church. For this, he was well rewarded. The successful ironmaster in the North usually held a social position comparable to that of a cotton or tobacco planter in the South, with an impressive dwelling and gentrified lifestyle.

Cornwall Iron Furnace

SEE MAP PAGE 11, LOCATION #51
Cornwall, Pennsylvania
Phone: (717) 272-9711
http://www.cornwallironfurnace.org

Allaire Village

SEE MAP PAGE 11, LOCATION #54
Farmingdale, New Jersey
Phone: (732) 919-3500
http://www.allairevillage.org

Hundreds of iron furnaces dotted the American landscape, but Cornwall has the only charcoal-fueled blast furnace to survive fully intact. Primarily a producer of molded domestic products and pig iron, the Cornwall Iron Furnace operated for 140 years. It began in 1742 and continued until 1883, when newer furnace operations fueled by anthracite coal made it obsolete.

On a guided tour, you have the opportunity to walk through the entire facility, learning step-by-step what an iron furnace is all about. We found it fascinating.

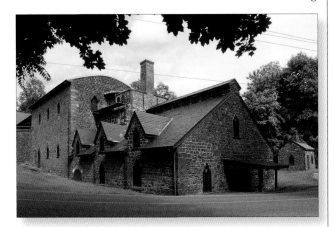

When the facility was operating, iron ore, limestone and charcoal were loaded into the hot stone furnace in the charging room. The blowing apparatus, including a 24-foot Great Wheel, pumped in air to raise the temperature. Nearby boilers harnessed exhausted heat from the smelting process and produced steam to drive a 20-horsepower, single-cylinder engine, which powered this huge equipment. It was blazing hot! Finally, in the casting house, the furnace was tapped for molten iron – twice each day – to make stove plates, pans, cannons, cannon balls and other items. The remaining molten iron was directed into channels on the floor to create bars of pig iron that were later processed into wrought iron. It's an interesting place – to both men and women.

After your tour, stroll through the community that grew up around the furnace. A short drive away are the former miner's villages (now private homes).

Located at Rexmont Road and Boyd Street in Cornwall, PA, northwest of Lancaster and Ephrata Cloister (Religious & Secular Groups, page 126). Take Pennsylvania Turnpike (I-76) exit 266 to Route 72 north and to Route 419 north, or take Route 322 east to Boyd Street. Open Tuesday-Sunday except certain holidays. Admission charged.

James P. Allaire built The Howell Iron Works in the 1820s to provide a source of bog iron for his thriving manufacturing business. Allaire Village grew up around it. Here blacksmiths, carpenters, leather workers, molders, tinsmiths and other craftsmen are working as they did back then. In addition, women are re-creating the old domestic life, including hearth cooking, spinning and quilting. Ironically, today we think of the handcrafts as art forms. Back then, they were life's necessities.

Special weekend programs re-create a nineteenth-century funeral, a wedding and other events that reflect the customs and mannerisms of the period. Guided tours are offered in the Allaire Home. The museum has lots to share, too, including examples of bog iron and the "holloware" products made here – cauldrons, pots, kettles, bakeware, stoves, pipes, sash weights, etc.

Located in Farmingdale, NJ. From I-195 West take exit 31B to Route 547 North; turn right onto Route 524 (Allaire Road). Open May-November – Wednesday-Sunday Memorial Day-Labor Day; weekends rest of season; closed major holidays. Admission charged.

▲ Allaire Village was a true company town, and the buildings reflected their owner's sense of practicality. The bakery, general store, carpenter's shop and other structures were built for durability. They showed little style but much fine craftsmanship.

◀ Pointed Gothic windows are not an architectural feature one would expect to find on an industrial building, especially a blast furnace. Then again, Cornwall Iron Furnace is not an ordinary facility. The Gothic Revival red sandstone buildings were erected in the mid-1800s to protect the equipment operating inside.

◀ Row houses with multiple apartments were America's first "tenements." In the 1800s, they were viewed as pleasant, economical alternatives to single-family dwellings. The ones pictured here provided egalitarian quarters for Allaire Village's many employees and their families.

Chesapeake & Ohio Canal Nat. Hist. Park

SEE MAP PAGE 15, LOCATION #33A & 31
Washington, DC, and Potomac, Maryland
Phone: (202) 653-5190 (Georgetown Visitor Center)
Phone: (301)299-3613 (Great Falls Tavern Visitor Center)
http://www.nps.gov/choh

△ A cross between a female horse and male donkey, mules were the preferred "engines" of canal boats. They had the endurance and cooperative disposition of their mothers plus the intelligence and sure-footedness of their fathers. Two sets of two or three mules could pull a 150-ton cargo boat for up to six hours before needing a break.

▶ Cover your ears. This stamp mill doesn't just sit here – it works! When the levers are pulled for demonstration purposes, ore pours into a hopper behind the railing and down to the stamps (large, heavy cylinders at the end of the chute). It is then crushed into a fine sand and combined with water to make a slurry for further processing.

This important part of history is remarkably well preserved. As so often is the case, credit goes to the Civilian Conservation Corps, which began the restoration in the 1930s. Since 1971, when the C & O Canal became an historical park, our National Park Service has been working to protect, stabilize and restore over 1,000 original structures along the canal.

While the park has several visitor centers, your first stop should be the one in Georgetown, Washington, DC. Georgetown was a tobacco port when the C & O Canal began construction here on July 4, 1828. Over the next 22 years, the canal extended 184.5 miles. It was six feet deep and 60 to 80 feet wide, with a 12-foot-wide towpath alongside where mules walked, canal boat in tow. There were 74 locks that raised or lowered boats to accommodate changing elevations, plus seven dams and a 3,118-foot-long tunnel. As many as 800 boats traversed this system, carrying coal, lumber, grains and other raw materials to major industrial centers.

Six visitor centers. Georgetown: 1057 Thomas Jefferson St., NW, Washington, DC. (Wednesday-Sunday, April-October; Saturday-Sunday in winter). Great Falls Tavern: 11710 MacArthur Blvd., Potomac, MD (daily). Also in Maryland: 40 West Potomac St., Brunswick (Friday-Sunday); 205 West Potomac St., Williamsport (Wednesday-Sunday); 326 East Main St., Hancock (Friday-Tuesday, summer only); 13 Canal St., Cumberland (daily). Admission charged only at Great Falls, which is a very scenic park with walking trails and picnicking.

Reed Gold Mine National Hist. Landmark

SEE MAP PAGE 15, LOCATION #26
Concord, North Carolina
Phone: (704) 721-4653
http://www.reedmine.com

The earliest documented gold find in America began with a boy playing in a creek on his family's farm. In 1799, he found a rock that was pretty enough to bring home. The 17-pound gold nugget became a doorstop. After three years, it was sold to a jeweler for the asking price of $3.50.

Imagine the shock of learning the rock was worth $3,600! With that news, the farmer and three local men formed a mining partnership. The team worked part-time, side-by-side with their slaves, using pans and rockers to wash gravel in search of more gold. Amazingly, one of the slaves found a 28-pound nugget. News traveled quickly, and gold fever struck our nation.

Placer (creek) mining led to underground mining when veins of gold were discovered in quartz. By the mid-1820s, North Carolina had about 300 gold mines – most of them dug in crop land by farmers and their slaves. More North Carolinians were engaged in gold mining than any other occupation except farming.

At the original farm, however, a family squabble led to a court injunction in 1835, which closed the mining operation. When re-opened a decade later, the mine was under new ownership. Today, the entire area is an historical landmark. Portions of the mine tunnels have been restored for guided tours; an ore-crushing stamp mill has been reconstructed; and exhibits provide insight into gold geology and mining technology. Seasonally, you can try their luck panning for gold.

Located 20 miles east of Charlotte, NC, and 12 miles southeast of Concord, via US 601, NC 200 or NC 24/27. Open Tuesday-Saturday except major holidays. Admission charged.

Historic Roscoe Village

SEE MAP PAGE 17, LOCATION #19
Coshocton, Ohio
Phone: (740) 622-9310 or toll-free (800) 877-1830
http://www.roscoevillage.com

Part shopping district and part Living History park, Historic Roscoe Village is a charming, restored nineteenth-century Ohio and Erie Canal town. The Village is open year-round. From April through December, many of the historic buildings are peopled with costumed interpreters who provide intriguing glimpses into daily life in the 1800s. Brick pathways wind through colorful gardens and lush courtyards. Shops and restaurants present a tempting array of old and modern pleasures.

Be sure to tour the doctor's distinctive home and office. Visit the teacher's one-room school. See the boat exhibit near the end of town, where you will learn about family life on the canal. Also stop along the way to hear what the artisans and craftspeople have to say about blacksmithing, broom and bucket making, pottery making, printing and weaving.

In the Visitor Center complex, miniature displays provide a bird's-eye view of nineteenth-century canal construction. The Hands-On facility offers children and adults the chance to try Canal Era crafts such as

tin punching, candle dipping, weaving, printing, rope making, top painting and quilting. At nearby Lake Park, you can take a ride down a restored portion of the Ohio and Erie Canal on the horse-drawn Monticello III. Annual festivals and special events add to the fun.

Located on SR 16 and SR 83 at junction of US 36 in Coshocton, OH, 70 miles east of Columbus. Open daily except Easter, Thanksgiving, Dec. 25 and Jan. 1. Building tours April-December. Admission charged for tours.

▲ You can glide down a section of the old Ohio and Erie Canal, hearing little more than the bird songs in the trees, the clip-clop of the horses and the commentary of your boat captain.

◄ At the Montgomery Print Shop, you can watch as old platen presses print cards and fliers using hand-set type. You can also examine wooden printing plates that were carved long ago with amazing precision and artfulness.

◄ Captains of canal boats usually took their families with them as they traveled. At the boat display in town, you can see an example of the single small cabin that housed them all. It had bunks for parents and children, plus a tiny kitchen area with a wood-burning stove.

CANAL BOAT TRAVEL

In the early days, passenger travel on a canal boat was anything but glamorous. It was simply a means of getting from point "A" to point "B" via the fastest, most direct route possible. On board, a single central cabin served as the small dining hall, game room and unventilated communal bedroom. At night, benches lining the cabin were unfolded into sleeping cots, and hammocks were slung from the ceiling. Most people slept fitfully, packed like sardines. Their only privacy was a curtain that separated the men from women and children. The rooftop served as a viewing platform. Sitting up there was understandably a relief on good-weather days, despite the heaps of luggage that also shared this small space. Passengers had plenty of time to enjoy the scenery – canal boats traveled at about four miles per hour.

Slater Mill Historic Site

SEE MAP PAGE 11, LOCATION #58
Pawtucket, Rhode Island
Phone: (401) 725-8638
http://www.slatermill.org

▲ Although located in the center of town, the mill complex feels like it is a world away. You can relax near the garden, enter a mill worker's home, explore the manufacturing operations, and sense what life was like when this was a bustling textile center.

▶ The power looms sit quietly now, but when just one is turned on for demonstration purposes, the racket is intense. The din created when all were running must have been deafening!

▶ Though it isn't impressive by modern standards, the carding machine seemed to be a miracle in its day. Using just a few rollers with brush-like wire bristles, it straightened cotton fibers after the seeds had been removed by the cotton gin. Previously, this process was done by hand – a slow and tedious task.

With its abundant supply of water and timber, Pawtucket was destined to play a central role in the production of American goods. As far back as the mid-1600s, the village attracted blacksmiths and other skilled craftsmen. Although nearly destroyed during King Philip's War, it thrived. Pawtucket's watershed event occurred in 1793, when Samuel Slater began operating the nation's first successful cotton manufacturing mill. That production facility, highly innovative for its time, marked the beginning of the American Industrial Revolution. Today Slater Mill Historic Site keeps the memory of that exciting time alive and meaningful to the modern visitor.

We were frankly startled by the completeness of this exceptional visitor attraction. In its operating days, Slater Mill and the surrounding support buildings were focused on what might seem simple enough in today's age: the production of thread to be woven elsewhere into cloth. But simple, this was not. In fact, it was a relatively novel concept that required the invention of new machinery, the careful training of employees and the practice of a new way of working –

in assembly lines. People of all ages participated. Children were especially adept at handling precise tasks amidst the cramped machinery. (Of course, this was often dangerous; so it was only a matter of time before concerns about child labor changed the working practices.)

Interpreters have a remarkable amount to show you. The water-power system has been restored, along with the leather belts and pulleys that operated machinery. David Wilkinson's machine shop has been replicated to show how machine replacement parts were made and how other needed items, including thousands of wooden spools, were produced. The manufacturing facility is filled with equipment. Here interpreters will take you from the harvested cotton, the cotton gin and automated carders, to the thread pullers and spinners, and finally to the finished goods. (Although cloth and end-products were not made here, representative sock

makers, ribbon makers and other weaving machines are included to complete your understanding.) You will hear how textile manufacturing progressed in complexity and capability, and you will see the equipment function. There's nothing else quite like this.

Located at 67 Roosevelt Avenue in Pawtucket, RI, less than an hour's drive from Mystic, Sturbridge, Boston, Plymouth, Cape Cod, Newport and other New England attractions. Open March-November – weekends March-April; daily May-November. Admission charged.

Hagley Museum & Library

SEE MAP PAGE 15, LOCATION #34
Wilmington, Delaware
Phone: (302) 658-2400
http://www.hagley.lib.de.us

This is the first du Pont family home in America, built in 1803. It is a place full of stories about one remarkable, very influential family and the people they knew – a place where you can see, hear and imagine how five generations lived during the 1800s and how their lives changed with the Industrial Revolution.

Eleuthère Irénée (E.I.) du Pont, the family patriarch, emigrated to America from France in 1799. While on a hunting trip, he realized the need for low-cost,

high-quality gunpowder and decided to erect a powder works near Wilmington, Delaware. Sales grew steadily from inception. Then came the War of 1812, and success was guaranteed. E. I. du Pont became known as the premier gunpowder and explosives manufacturer in America. From this beginning emerged the present-day multinational DuPont company, famous for numerous products contributing to people's lives around the world – in food and nutrition, healthcare, apparel, safety and security, construction, electronics and transportation.

At the Hagley Museum, exhibits and interpretive demonstrations bring history back to life, not only at the du Pont powder mills, estate and gardens but also in a restored portion of the workers' community. You can walk to most sites but must take the museum bus to tour the du Ponts' Georgian-style residence and hear about their private life. At the mansion, gracious room settings include furnishings from the Empire, Federal and Victorian periods. Outside the home, along the cascading waters of the Brandywine River, you can stroll through the lush landscaping and discover a nineteenth-century French-style garden. Centuries-old oaks and sycamores tower overhead.

In the workers' community, the Gibbons House provides a revealing look at the life of a foreman's family. Here you will learn about the foods workers ate, the furniture they used and the conveniences they acquired. Costumed guides provide insight into the benefits that ordinary folks gained when new

machinery and new production methods entered the workplace. Nearby is a schoolhouse where the children of mill workers learned reading, writing and arithmetic before Delaware provided public education.

Beside the river is the heart of the du Pont operations. Here, massive stone mills, storehouses and a wooden water wheel recall the time when waterpower was vital. The millstreams at Hagley still channel water to operate the machinery. Powdermen and machinists demonstrate a water turbine, a steam engine and a powder tester. A restored 1870s machine shop also is operated for the benefit of visitors.

Located on Route 141 in Wilmington, DE. Take I-95 exit 5B (from south) or exit 8B (from north). Follow sign near Tyler McConnell Bridge. Open year-round – daily mid-March through December; less often rest of year; closed Thanksgiving and December 25. Admission charged.

◢ Millraces, fed by the nearby river, powered dozens of mills and workshops throughout the facility. Steam engines were introduced later to provide supplemental power.

◢ Museum displays are housed in what was originally a cotton spinning mill. The building had been converted by du Pont into a factory for making metal gunpowder kegs.

◢ The du Pont mansion sat on a hill above the factory. It was not the safest place. One of several gunpowder explosions at the factory substantially damaged this elegant home and caused Mrs. du Pont to suffer a hearing loss.

Salem Maritime National Historic Site

SEE MAP PAGE 11, LOCATION #61A
Salem, Massachusetts
Phone: (978) 740-1660
http://www.nps.gov/sama

▶ *Friendship*, moored at the Derby Wharf, is a replica of a 171-foot East Indiaman built in 1797. She carries 17 sails on her three masts and 55 miles of rigging. The original made 15 voyages to China, Java, Sumatra, Madras, London, Hamburg, Archangel, St. Petersburg and other ports, trading for exotic spices, sugar and coffee. She was captured by the British during the War of 1812.

▶ The fine furniture, ceramics and glassware on display at the Derby House are representative of the high stature that America's first millionaire achieved as a merchant in Salem.

▼ A portion of Derby Street has been restored as closely as possible to its 1800s appearance, with a clear view of Derby Wharf and Salem Harbor.

Salem was once the seat of America's maritime prowess. As far back as the 1630s, local merchants were sending vessels laden with salted cod, lumber and other goods to the West Indies and Europe. Business rapidly grew to include most of the world's major ports and brought great wealth and prosperity. During the Revolutionary War, much of Salem's merchant fleet was adapted for wartime use and managed to capture or sink 455 British vessels. After the war, Salem resumed its growth, becoming the sixth largest city in the country and the richest per capita by 1790. Sea captains used this prosperity to build grand Federal-style buildings. They also founded the East India Marine Society to share the glories of their maritime adventures. Surprisingly, though, this great success came to an abrupt halt in 1807 when President Jefferson ordered an embargo on all foreign commerce to counter attacks on American vessels during the Napoleonic Wars. Then came the War of 1812. Salem never fully recovered.

Salem Maritime National Historic Site protects and shares this city's grand waterfront legacy. For many visitors, the best part is boarding *Friendship*, a tall sailing ship. Unlike other replicas of historic vessels, this one had a perfect model for its construction: a large, exceptionally skillful copy of the original ship made by early crew members, apparently for their captain's son. (See the model at the Peabody Essex Museum, Salem.)

Also enjoyable are the guided tours of three furnished buildings: the 1819 Custom House, 1762 Derby House and 1675 Narbonne House. The Custom House was the place where merchants interfaced with the Federal Government – obtaining permits to land cargo, getting seamen's protection certificates and paying customs taxes. Nathaniel Hawthorne, one of America's great authors, once worked here and is said to have used co-workers and townspeople as models for characters in his books. (His clerk's desk is on display.) The Derby House was built for America's first millionaire, Elias Hasket Derby. A leading shipowner, Derby was also a Revolutionary War privateer. The house he built next door supposedly served as a warehouse for privateer prizes. A short distance away is the eclectic Narbonne House, which served as a home and shop for tradesmen.

Located at 174 Derby Street in Salem, MA. Open daily except certain major holidays. Admission charged for daily guided tours of the buildings and Friendship.

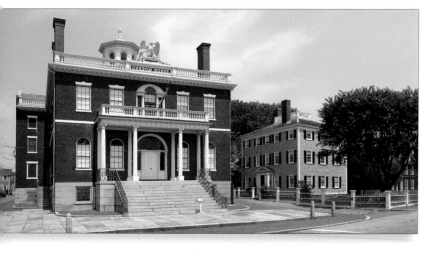

Lincoln's New Salem

SEE MAP PAGE 17, LOCATION #24
Petersburg, Illinois
Phone: (217) 632-4000
http://www.lincolnsnewsalem.com

There is a mystery to solve here. A young man came to this commercial village in 1831. He could read, write and do simple arithmetic but seemed to have no special skills and no idea what he wanted to do for a living. He landed his first job taking goods on a flatboat to New Orleans but settled into being a shop clerk, soldier in the Black Hawk War, general store owner, postmaster, land surveyor and rail splitter. Financially strapped, he also took on odd jobs and earned a bit of money as a wrestler. How was this restless young man able to "find himself"? How was he able to become one of America's greatest leaders: President Abraham Lincoln?

New Salem had only one reason for existing back then: to provide goods and services to the outlying community. It had four general stores, two doctors' offices, a grist mill, a tavern, a grocery store, a schoolhouse/church and several residences. Other buildings included shops for skilled craftspeople – the carpenter, blacksmith, cooper, hat maker, shoemaker and tanner. In all, 20-25 families lived and worked here.

For a few years, the village thrived. But in 1840, many buildings were moved and others abandoned, the victims of competition from nearby Petersburg. Little would anyone have guessed that New Salem would be remembered as the place where Abraham Lincoln lived for six years, began to satisfy his lifelong quest for knowledge and finally settled on a career path. (He had seriously considered blacksmithing but chose lawyering.) Years later, Lincoln became our sixteenth President.

The village we see today is a reconstruction on the original foundations. Built by the local community, a general contractor and the Civilian Conservation Corps during the Great Depression, it is an Illinois State Historic Site. You will find it to be complete, with period furnishings and costumed interpreters representing

the time of Lincoln's residency. One building, the Onstot Cooper Shop, is original. It had been moved to Petersburg but was returned in 1922.

The tales to be learned here are at once fascinating, enchanting, curious and startling. Seeing the village, walking into the buildings, talking with the people – it's all so much better than just reading a book about a great man at a pivotal point in his life! Still, if you know only a little about Lincoln, we recommend some reading in advance of your visit. It'll make your experience all the more satisfying.

Located on Route 97, just 2 miles south of downtown Petersburg, IL, and 20 miles northwest of Springfield. Open year-round – daily from mid-April through Labor Day; Wednesday-Sunday rest of the year; closed on certain major holidays. Free.

▲ Twelve log houses, the tavern, the school where church services were held, and ten workshops, stores and mills re-create New Salem, IL. Furnished as they might have been in the 1830s, they have interesting stories to tell through well-informed Living History guides.

◄ The cooper made and sold wooden-staved vessels such as casks, barrels, buckets, tubs, butter churns and hogsheads. Tools of his trade included a winch for cinching up the staves so that hoops could be fitted tightly, to hold them in place.

◄ The store which Lincoln co-owned with a partner was also the place where he slept (apparently on the counter). It is easy to visualize the lanky young Abe here, swapping stories with the local folks, reading by the fire and finally owning trousers that were not six inches too short for his unusually long legs.

WAR OF 1812

most of the issues which had sparked the war just faded away

While America was trying to build a new nation and expand its reach, relations with Great Britain deteriorated. There had been an uneasy peace ever since the Revolutionary War, partly because the British continued to support their former Native American allies who opposed white settlement of the fertile Ohio River Valley and other Indian territories. Matters worsened when the British took up arms against America's former ally, France. In the midst of an escalating battle with Napoleon, British ships blockaded American vessels laden with goods bound for France and other European countries. In addition, they drafted American sailors to help fight British battles. Many Americans were infuriated, and President Madison agreed with them. At the same time, however, anti-war sentiment was strong.

A dark cloud of dissent loomed over our country after Congress took a hard line against Great Britain on June 18, 1812. New Englanders were bitterly opposed to military action; in fact, the states of Massachusetts and Connecticut refused to fight. Furthermore, America was ill-prepared for a "second war of independence." But War Hawks from western and southern states dominated both the House of Representatives and Senate. So we declared war against Britain.

With fewer than 12,000 troops in the regular army and just over 20 seagoing naval vessels at the start of the war, our nation could have met disaster. (The British Navy had nearly 100 ships in American waters.) As it was, the 2 ½ year war caused serious collateral damage, took more than 2,200 American lives and

settled nothing. Americans struck first, temporarily disrupting British merchant shipping to and from Canada. The Royal Navy countered by strengthening its blockade of major American ports and further restricting our nation's trade. Americans attempted to invade (and annex) Canada on three fronts but ultimately failed, with decisive victories and painful losses on both sides. Along the way, we almost lost our major shipbuilding base at Sacket's Harbor on Lake Ontario – it became a target of British-Canadian warships while American forces were occupied across the lake at Fort George. Worst of all, British forces invaded Washington, DC, in 1814 and burned public buildings, including the Capitol and White House. The greatest battle of all – in New Orleans – was a resounding American victory but completely unnecessary. It occurred two weeks after the December 1814 peace treaty was signed, because news of the war's end had not yet reached General Andrew Jackson.

In the end, the Treaty of Ghent simply restored captured land to the original owners and established commissions to handle boundary disputes. Most of the issues which had sparked the war just faded away following Napoleon's ouster in Europe and the end of British support to Native Americans. Still, there was one positive outcome: America's survival against a world power increased patriotism countrywide and helped unite the states into one nation.

ERIE MARITIME MUSEUM

In the late 1700s, a coveted tract of land on Lake Erie was acquired by our Federal Government and then purchased by the state of Pennsylvania to gain shipping access to Lake Erie. Emerging from that event was a rich maritime history, skillfully presented at the Erie Maritime Museum. The reconstructed *US Brig Niagara* (at right) is berthed outside the museum and open for public boarding. As a Sailing School Vessel inspected by the U.S. Coast Guard, it offers one-day history-based educational sails as well as a traditional square-rig seamanship training course.

Inside the museum – a former steam-powered electricity generating station – the exhibits are equally unusual. They include a reconstruction of the mid-ship section of the *USS Lawrence* (sister ship of the *Niagara*); a "live fire" display of the *Lawrence* blasted with 53 rounds (re-creating the carnage inflicted upon both the *Niagara* and *Lawrence* at the Battle of Lake Erie during the War of 1812); and exhibits about the 1844 *USS Wolverine* (previously named the *USS Michigan*), our nation's first iron-hulled warship. Located at 150 East Front Street in Erie, PA. http://www.brigniagara.org

Fort McHenry National Monument

SEE MAP PAGE 15, LOCATION #23
Baltimore, Maryland
Phone: (410) 962-4290
http://www.nps.gov/fomc

It was the valiant defense of this star-shaped fort on September 13-14, 1814, that inspired lawyer Francis Scott Key to write a poem called "The Star-Spangled Banner." His stirring words, "O say can you see, by the dawn's early light..." later became our national anthem.

Key, who was in the process of seeking the release of a civilian prisoner on a British warship, saw the entire battle from sea, unable to do anything but pace and hope. It must have been a terrifying, desperately frus-

trating sight as night came and the sky was lit and relit by the flames of red Congreve rockets and the fiery explosions of mortar-fired bombs. Fort McHenry was strategically located on the Patapsco River, the one place where the Americans could stop the British advance on Baltimore and help preserve our nation's independence. It had 1,000 troops equipped with 57 guns and a furnace for heating

"THE STAR-SPANGLED BANNER"

Nearly 150 years would pass before America had an official national anthem. Ironically, what is now a patriotic melody began life as a British Colonial drinking song, an ode to Venus and Bacchus. In 1890, John Philip Sousa gave the popular tune a more stately arrangement, which was played by the Navy during the raising of the flag and later became official music for military occasions and other appropriate events. In 1918, the tune was heard for the first time at a baseball game during the seventh-inning stretch. Still, as a Ripley's "Believe it or Not!" cartoon pointed out in late 1929, we had no national anthem. This was a sore point – America would be hosting the next Olympic Games and needed official music. Finally on March 3, 1931, President Herbert Hoover signed a Congressional resolution naming "The Star-Spangled Banner" as our national anthem. The song was heard many times the following year at the Olympics. Interestingly, like the British "God Save the Queen," ours is one of the few national anthems that does not mention its home country.

cannon balls (to burn enemy ships). But the Americans were fighting a far larger British force that was attacking by both land and sea. Remarkably, at daybreak, the immense American flag – 30 feet by 42 feet – was still flying, and the British were in full retreat. It was a decisive victory and the only time the fort ever came under attack. Fort McHenry had served its purpose.

For the next 100 years, the fort remained an active military post. Then it fell into disrepair. Our National Park Service came to the rescue in 1933, making it the only park that is both a National Monument and Historic Shrine. Today, you will find a beautifully reconstructed fort. On weekends during the summer months, it is manned by interpretive soldiers, sailors and citizens dressed in replica early nineteenth-century clothing. For your enjoyment, they perform military drills, artillery and musket demonstrations, barracks duties and a variety of civilian activities. Ranger and children's programs are offered during the summer months. Special events include the Star-Spangled Banner Weekend in September, which is typically a three-day encampment and extravaganza with War of 1812 re-enactors, parades, military bands, fireworks, a symbolic ship-to-shore bombardment and much more.

Located on Fort Avenue in Baltimore, MD, 3 miles southeast of Baltimore Inner Harbor, just off I-95 exit 55. Open daily except Thanksgiving, December 25 and January 1. Admission charged.

▲ On days when the wind is not too strong, a replica of the original, huge flag is raised with the help of visitors. This symbol of our nation dwarfs all around it – the people and the buildings – and is visible from miles away.

◀ The officers' quarters weren't large but they were fairly comfortable. The bed was near the fireplace, and its tent-like cover could be closed for added warmth in winter. There was a mantel to keep everyday items handy. And a few elegant touches could be added to make off-duty time quite enjoyable.

PRESIDENTIAL HOMES

▲ Monroe's Ash Lawn-Highland home offers an important reminder: American Presidents come from all walks of life. In comparison with Monticello, a short distance away, it is a modest, working farm. From the yard, you can see how the house was modified to accommodate a growing family.

▶ Montpelier is in the final stages of a stunning restoration – returning it in size, form and furnishings to the home that the Madisons knew in the 1820s. Open for tours, it is thrilling to visit. The 2,700-acre estate includes a panoramic landscape as well as family and slave cemeteries.

▶ In Jackson's day, The Hermitage was an 1,100 acre plantation with 150 African slaves. The mansion has been beautifully restored and has its original furnishings. Nearby are the previous Jackson home (a log cabin) as well as three remaining slave cabins, a formal garden and the Jackson Tomb.

Every American should visit the homes of our nation's early Presidents. This is not because the homes are extraordinarily beautiful – some are; some are not. What is most significant is the insight each provides about the men who led America through its most defining years.

Our early Presidents were not all well educated. George Washington, for example, was born into an upper class family; but because of his father's untimely death, he received little formal education, a fact which sometimes made him self-conscious.

They were not all secure in their jobs, either. Thomas Jefferson, for instance, received a tie vote against Aaron Burr and thus was not elected by the Electoral College to his first term. The final choice fell to the House of Representatives, whose members argued among themselves before finally electing Jefferson as our third President and Burr as Vice President.

Our early Presidents weren't even necessarily well-to-do. In fact, some "kept up appearances" by amassing heavy debts that had to be paid after their deaths. Consequently, several Presidential homes passed out of family hands or were virtually abandoned by heirs who could not afford their upkeep. Among the earliest, Monticello fell into serious ruin, and Montpelier was so remodeled that its Presidential essence was completely hidden. We owe a great debt of gratitude to private philanthropists and civic-

minded organizations who preserved these treasures. Within the time period covered by this book are the following Presidents and their homes.

George Washington, President 1789-1797:
   Mount Vernon in Mount Vernon, VA
John Adams, President 1797-1801:
   Adams National Historical Park in Quincy, MA
Thomas Jefferson, President 1801-1809:
   Monticello near Charlottesville, VA
James Madison, President 1809-1817:
   Montpelier in Montpelier Station, VA
James Monroe, President 1817-1825:
   Ash Lawn-Highland near Charlottesville, VA
John Quincy Adams, President 1825-1829:
   Adams National Historical Park in Quincy, MA
Andrew Jackson, President 1829-1837:
   The Hermitage near Nashville, TN
Martin Van Buren, President 1837-1841:
   Martin Van Buren Nat. Hist. Site in Kinderhook, NY
John Tyler, President 1841-1845:
   Sherwood Forest Plantation in Charles City, VA

Courtesy The Montpelier Foundation, James Madison's Montpelier

Mount Vernon

SEE MAP PAGE 15, LOCATION #29A
Mount Vernon, Virginia
Phone: (703) 780-2000
http://www.mountvernon.org

George Washington inherited Mount Vernon in 1754 from the widow of his half-brother, Lawrence. Thinking of himself as a farmer – much more than as a President or military leader – he spent the rest of his life, when time permitted, transforming the property into a magnificent estate that extended over 8,000 acres. In his day, the plantation was divided into five farms, each operating as self-contained units. The Mansion House Farm, where George and Martha lived, is the portion that visitors see today. It stands in a park-like environment of rolling meadows, meandering walkways, groves of trees and panoramic views of the Potomac River.

Even if you have been here before, you may wish to return. Many new attractions have been added. Begin by seeing a dynamic film portraying pivotal

moments in Washington's life. Then tour his elegant home and explore the grounds, which include gardens, outbuildings, a demonstration farm with innovative 16-sided treading barn, and the tomb of George and Martha Washington. Steps from the historic area is the Donald W. Reynolds Museum and Education Center, which has 23 galleries and theater experiences, including interactive displays, films, life-size models of Washington and over 700 original artifacts.

You will discover that our first President's passion was his land. He especially enjoyed the challenge of cultivating crops and improving his farm's productivity. Consider, for instance, his gristmill – it was the only one in America using the advanced Oliver Evans system of water power. You can see an operating reproduction three miles from the main estate. Another example was Washington's whiskey distillery, which by size and volume ranked among the most important structures of

its kind in eighteenth-century America. A reproduction has been built next to the gristmill.

Located at 3200 Mount Vernon Memorial Highway in Mount Vernon, VA, 8 miles south of Alexandria. Open daily including government holidays and December 25. Admission charged. Combination ticket available with the gristmill and the distillery.

RELUCTANT PRESIDENT

When George Washington became President, America had less than 4 million people. Most were spread out on farmland, and many could not read or write. The best way to communicate was face-to-face; but traveling a distance of just 30 miles took all day. Politicians frequently battled over differing viewpoints, making consensus-building nearly impossible. And the very infrastructure of our capital was yet to be established. In this climate, Washington agreed to serve, not because he wanted the job but because he knew he was needed. He tried to retire after his first term, only to be persuaded to accept reelection. The nation was still in its formative years, he was reminded, and only he could hold it together. When he finally did retire, relations between America and France deteriorated, and President Adams asked for help. On July 4, 1798, Washington accepted the commission of "Lieutenant General and Commander in Chief of the armies raised or to be raised." All along, though, what he really wanted was to enjoy the life of a retired gentleman farmer at Mount Vernon.

▲ Washington's home is a true reflection of his sense of style and practicality. Among the many interesting features is the "rustication" of exterior walls, which involved using bevel-edged pine blocks coated with a mixture of paint and sand to create the appearance of stone but maintain the versatility of wood.

◄ Slave cooks Lucy and Nathan had their hands full in the kitchen at Mount Vernon. They prepared at least three generous meals a day when George and Martha were at home. They also had to accommodate many dinner guests.

Adams National Historical Park

SEE MAP PAGE 11, LOCATION #60A

Quincy, Massachusetts
Phone: (617) 770-1175
http://www.nps.gov/adam

At the huge library table, Charles compiled his father's Memoirs, and his son Henry wrote the *History of the United States: During the Administration of Jefferson.*

Located in Quincy, MA, 10 miles south of Boston. From I-93 or Route 128 south, take exit 7 (Route 3) south. Take exit 18 (Washington St. and Quincy Adams T). Follow signs to Quincy Center, turning right at seventh light onto Dimmock and right onto Hancock. National Park Service Visitor Center in President's Place, 1250 Hancock Street. Tours daily, April 19-November 10. Admission charged.

▲ Remodeled and enlarged under the supervision of Abigail Adams, the Old House served as the residence for many generations of the Adams family: John and Abigail, their son John Quincy Adams and his wife Louisa Catherine Adams, their son Charles Francis Adams (ambassador to the United Kingdom during the American Civil War), and historians Henry Adams and Brooks Adams.

▶ With so many highly educated, important people residing in the Old House, one can imagine the great words that must have been read and written in the handsome office.

▶ This was the birthplace of John Quincy Adams and the home where his parents, John and Abigail, began their life together. As became the pattern, Abigail tended to the house and farm while John focused on matters vital to the formation of our nation.

What a exceptional collection of buildings, gardens and family possessions! This national park provides vital insight into two great men – John Adams, our second President, and John Quincy Adams, our sixth President. Here is the saltbox house where John was born and raised. Here too is the pre-Revolution home where John and his wife Abigail lived and where John Quincy was born and raised. The centerpiece, however, is the "Old House," occupied from 1788-1927 by these illustrious Americans and their descendants. At one point, 17 members of what John Adams called "my complicated family" were living here. In the garden stands the impressive Stone Library, which was constructed by Charles Francis Adams (son of John Quincy Adams) to house his father's and grandfather's books and papers.

REMEMBERING JULY 4

In 1776, America's leaders were very passionate about their Declaration of Independence. For them, July 4 was a defining day – the beginning of a whole new life and a whole new way of governing a nation. Three of our first five Presidents seem to have felt so strongly about July 4 that, even on their deathbeds, they apparently willed themselves to stay alive just long enough to see that day one more time. In 1826, as America celebrated the fiftieth anniversary of Independence Day, 83-year-old Thomas Jefferson lay dying. "Is it the fourth?" he asked. Yes, he was assured. He passed away in the early morning hours. Fellow founding father 90-year-old John Adams died later that day, hoping and believing that his friend, Jefferson, was still alive. Exactly five years later, in 1831, James Monroe died at the age of 73. So the next time you celebrate with fireworks and a family picnic, take a moment to remember them, too. Celebrate their wisdom, their dedication, their courage.

Monticello

SEE MAP PAGE 15, LOCATION #25

Charlottesville, Virginia
Phone: (434) 984-9822
http://www.monticello.org

The contrasts between Washington and Jefferson are perhaps no more apparent than in their homes and plantations. While Washington was deliberate in his actions, Jefferson was a creative genius who could not be contained. His Monticello is a masterful statement about a man determined to surround himself with the ultimate in beauty and expressiveness. He designed and redesigned Monticello, built and partially demolished it, rebuilt it again, then expanded and improved it – for more than 40 years. The first design, begun in 1769, had 14 rooms. The last, completed by 1809, had 43 rooms, including 33 in the main house, four in the pavilions and six under the South Terrace. Thomas Jefferson really didn't have the financial resources for such a fine home, but there was no stopping him. He died more than $107,000 in debt (a sizable fortune in his day).

The house tour, which provides a comprehensive overview of the first floor, is marvelous. About 60 percent of the furnishings are believed to be items original to Jefferson; the rest are period pieces or reproductions. You will see the dramatic entrance hall, with its towering ceiling and balcony connecting two mezzanine-level wings. You will walk into the room that once held Jefferson's libraries, the largest of which

consisted of more than 6,000 books that ultimately formed the nucleus of what is now the Library of Congress. You will stop by Jefferson's bedroom and learn about its many creative features. The alcove bed, for example, is open on both sides to provide handy access to the adjoining office, presumably when late-night inspirations came into Jefferson's head. You will also visit the elegant dining room, the parlor (with its Jefferson-designed parquet floor of cherry and beech) and various other first-floor rooms where our third President lived, worked and entertained.

Outside is a re-creation of the working plantation that once served as a center of agriculture and industry. Living here during Jefferson's time was an extended

community of workers, including 130 African American slaves. These industrious people raised agricultural crops and tended livestock, made the tools needed for farm work, wove cloth and sewed clothing, built the house, crafted many of its furnishings, cultivated the gardens, and took care of numerous personal matters for Jefferson and his extended family.

Take a guided tour of the gardens and grounds or wander at your leisure. During Jefferson's time, Monticello was viewed as a botanic laboratory of plants obtained from all over the world. His orchards and vineyards had 170 varieties of fruit – apples, apricots, peaches, cherries, berries, figs, grapes. A 1,000-foot-long garden terrace had over 250 varieties of vegetables. Ornamental flower beds were strategically placed to add color and beauty.

If you have the time, take the guided tour of the plantation community. Its focus is on the African Americans at Monticello and the contributions they made to the economic operation of Jefferson's plantation. The tour will take you to Mulberry Row and other plantation-related sites near the mountaintop.

Located 70 miles from Richmond, VA, and about 2 miles southeast of Charlottesville. From I-64, take exit 121, turn onto Route 20 South and then left on Route 53 (Thomas Jefferson Parkway). Continue 1 3/4 miles, following the signs to Monticello. Open daily except December 25. Admission charged. Combination ticket available with Ash Lawn-Highland and Michie Tavern (pages 192 & 179).

▲ An exceptional treasure, Monticello has been designated a World Heritage Site by UNESCO. Many people believe that the west-facing portico shown here is the front entrance. It is, after all, pictured on the American nickel. However, Jefferson apparently didn't think in terms of one "front" to the house but rather an "east front" and a "west front."

◄ The garden pavilion was used by Jefferson as a quiet retreat overlooking an orchard, a vineyard and plots of figs, currants and berries. Today's pavilion is a reconstruction based on Jefferson's notes as well as archaeological excavations.

▲ The first white men in the West weren't looking for scenic beauty. Many were seeking abundance of another kind - beaver. (The dam and lodge shown here are in Grand Tetons National Park, WY.)

▶ In addition to farming, ranching and hunting, the Russians brought their Orthodox Christian religion to Fort Ross, CA.

▶ Although the continent was vast, it was widely populated when European fur traders arrived. Native Peoples had lived here for thousands of years. A replica of the birch bark lodge of the Ojibwe can be seen at the North West Company Fur Post, MN.

▶ As Euro-Americans spread across the West, they built high walls to protect themselves and their goods. Still, they wanted friendship and trade with the Indians. At Fort Union, ND, a mural over the gate was meant to encourage good relations.

OPENING THE WEST

It started innocently enough with the eagerness of pioneers, traders and fur trappers who wanted to see the frontier and tap into a wealth of natural resources. Then fiction writers and newspaper reporters, painters and photographers, businessmen, civic leaders and politicians became captivated by the allure of the West. They excited the general public. Gradually, what had been fear of the unknown became avid curiosity and ultimately an obsessive desire to own the land. The original inhabitants, America's Native Peoples, didn't have a chance against white encroachment and a government convinced that its destiny was to build a nation that stretched from coast to coast and beyond. So we could end our story where we began: with invading peoples taking from indigenous peoples, who had little choice but to accept a dangerous fate. Yet, the drama that unfolded wasn't so straightforward – not for Indians or for whites.

HISTORICAL PERSPECTIVE:
OPENING THE WEST

How easy it is to get caught up in the mystique surrounding the opening of the American West! As we travel through time, a wide-screen panorama unfolds before us, revealing a panoply of characters...

▨ Daniel Boone with 30 woodsmen, carving a route through the Cumberland Gap in the mid-1770s. Their Wilderness Road enabled an estimated 200,000-300,000 hopeful settlers to cross the Appalachian Mountains into Kentucky and the Midwest from 1775 to 1810.

▨ The colorful crew of the Corps of Discovery, heading out in 1804 on the Lewis & Clark Expedition. Among them was a moody former secretary of President Jefferson, a long-time friend and former army captain, a one-eyed fiddle player, an Irish carpenter, an African American slave, a French Canadian guide, his Shoshone wife and their newborn child, and the requisite crew of military men. Not only did they map an unknown wilderness, they also established cordial relations with nearly 50 Indian tribes and brought back a wealth of data about natural resources.

▨ The mountain man Zebulon M. Pike crossing the center of our continent in 1806 with 23 men. He split up his team in what is now central Kansas, to explore both the Red River region and Rocky Mountains. While he increased our knowledge about this vast territory, he also shaped early misconceptions about the Great Plains as a sandy desert not suitable for farming.

▨ The American fur traders who, when beaver hats became fashionable in the 1820s, sought to challenge long-established British trading companies by funding a number of trapping/trading ventures of their own. Their efforts resulted in a line of fur posts stretching from the Great Lakes to the Pacific Northwest.

▨ The men who built the National Road, financed by our government but delayed by the War of 1812 and disinterested politicians. They constructed bridges and created a road of solid stone topped by gravel all the way from Cumberland, Maryland, in 1811; to Wheeling, West Virginia, in 1818; to Vandalia, Illinois, in 1850.

With the stories of such legendary people comes a realization: the opening of the American West was not so much a period in history as a state of mind. It came from curiosity, wanderlust, independence, dreams for a better life, ambitions for wealth and power, and great determination to gain a foothold in new territories.

> ▶ Fort Union in North Dakota was a center of peaceful economic and social exchange between Euro-Americans and the plains Indians. As such, it was the most important fur trading post on the upper Missouri River from 1828-1867. Here Indians traded buffalo robes for a variety of goods, including beads, guns, blankets, knives, kettles and cloth.

the real opening of the American west began with the courageous pathfinders

Holding Back

In the early years of European colonization, such westward expansion was inconceivable. Few people ventured out alone into Indian territory. For one thing, it was unsafe. For another, the people had come to the New World to live together in communities; not many were pathfinders. Growth came by establishing new colonies nearby. Since disease had decimated Native Peoples, there was plenty of land. What's more, when colonists wanted to capitalize on additional natural resources, they had only to venture a short distance.

There was no incentive – in fact, there was a great disincentive – toward westward expansion. Pioneers risked igniting wars with the Native Peoples, who were prepared to defend their long-held territories. In addition, the British Proclamation of 1763 forbade Euro-American settlement west of the Appalachian Mountains. A few years later, new Indian treaties shifted the Proclamation line westward and opened the way for white settlement in what are now West Virginia and southwestern Pennsylvania. But that was all.

Gaining Independence

The Revolutionary War seems to have changed American attitudes about expansion. The land was no longer under British control, it was OURS. (Forget the fact that France and Spain still had sizable holdings.) Although formal laws and treaties recognized and guaranteed Indian rights to certain lands, Americans were determined to see what was in "our own backyard." Government efforts to maintain control proved futile. Even our Presidents could not resist the lure of

virgin country, extensive natural resources and new discoveries that awaited the nation further west.

Some whites conducted armed invasions into Indian territories, intent on gaining fertile land and other advantages for themselves. Some Native Peoples raided pioneer settlements to protect their interests and discourage white incursions. Although the majority of settlers were never attacked, they lived in constant fear of hostile Indians; so they built forts to defend their claims on the frontier. Progressively more and more Indian tribes, unable to stop the white advance, were forced to sign treaties giving up territory to land-hungry pioneers. Many others stood their ground and paid the price with heavy fighting against government troops. The battles became legendary and were most often tragic for the Indians. There was no stopping the flood of people heading west.

Shifting Boundaries

From a big-picture perspective, two westward movements occurred in America. The first was from about 1760 to about 1840; the second, much larger movement began in the mid-1840s. Because of them, "The West" was in an almost perpetual state of redefinition. At first, it was any western land within the English colonies and, later, within the United States. By the late-1700s, the West included settled lands over the Appalachian Mountains. Then it was beyond the Tennessee River; across the Mississippi River in the newly obtained Louisiana Purchase lands; the Texas Republic; over the Rocky Mountains. Somewhere along the way, it included the

unknown "wilderness" beyond settled territories and became known under new names: the Southwest, the Far West, the Northwest.

Our focus in this chapter is on the early forces behind these movements – before we won the Mexican territories, before we acquired Britain's Oregon Country, and before we annexed Texas. What followed was the 1840s view of Manifest Destiny as America's right (by Divine Providence) to expand across the continent.

Building America

The shape of our nation would not be fully established until the acquisition of Alaska in 1867 and Hawaii in 1898. At that point, the vision of Manifest Destiny was more than fulfilled. America stretched across the entire continent, from the Atlantic to the Pacific and beyond. Yet this vast area would not be settled in a few generations. Small, incremental steps were necessary: cabins in the woods, forts on the plains, trails through the wilderness, frontier farms, small businesses, communities with law and order, churches and schools. Who could have known where it would lead, this remarkable effort to build our nation?

▲ By 1837, America was comprised of 26 states and three organized territories that would soon gain statehood (Florida in 1845, Iowa in 1846 and Wisconsin in 1848). The land included in the Louisiana Purchase was still largely unsettled. Its development awaited further territorial gains to the West, which would then spark the second major migration and draw Americans all the way to the Pacific.

◀ Tall palisades appeared like giant footprints across the landscape as traders and settlers put down roots. They were made from hand-hewn tree trunks, set vertically in the ground. Often they were secured by cross beams, held together with wooden pegs. Clear indications that the newcomers planned to stay!

Frontier Culture Museum

SEE MAP PAGE 15, LOCATION #36

Staunton, Virginia
Phone: (540) 332-7850
http://www.frontier.virginia.gov

▲ The Scotch-Irish and their descendants were among the earliest settlers of the American "backcountry" (in and beyond the Appalachians). This farmhouse from Ulster is representative of their former life.

▶ Many Pennsylvania and Virginia immigrants came from Germany. In their homeland, kitchens often had a raised hearth that kept cooking fires at waist height. Without this innovation, most American women used a large fireplace and risked setting their clothes on fire. (The cast-iron cookstove was not common until the mid-1800s in cities and later in rural areas.)

▶ Most slept on mattresses stuffed with down or straw, supported by ropes strung across the bed frame. This mode of sleeping continued until the availability of bedsprings developed in 1865.

traditions. Walk inside the farm houses. Visit with the costumed interpreters. See their heritage farm animals and heirloom gardens. Watch the blacksmith at work. You'll learn much about the vastly different cultures and lifeways of early immigrants. More importantly, you will come to understand the character of people who could leave the safety and comfort of friends and family to travel across the intimidating Atlantic Ocean and settle in unfamiliar territory.

Located in Staunton, VA. Take I-81 exit 222; drive ¹/₃ mile west on US 250. Open daily. Admission charged.

To truly understand the westward movement, we must look back to the European immigrants and what they experienced before and after venturing across the Atlantic. One fascinating source of information is the Frontier Culture Museum. It has transported three historic farm houses from their countries of origin, reconstructed them on museum property and peopled them with Living History interpreters. These "snapshots" of the Old World represent the lives left behind in Germany, Northern Ireland and England. They stand in contrast to two relocated American farmsteads and their Living History occupants.

What a marvelous opportunity you have here! Witness the rich European influence on our cultural

LAND OWNERSHIP

At first, settlers simply took possession of the land they wanted or paid a small price to local Indians for usage rights. But many land companies and wealthy individuals saw America as a business venture, and they quickly staked out areas that looked promising. These enterprising speculators divided their claims into smaller home sites and sold them for a profit. Shortly after the American Revolution, our government decided to stake its own claims and reap the financial gain. The first area of interest was the land north of the Ohio River between the Appalachian Mountains and the Mississippi River. Thomas Jefferson proposed the Land Ordinance of 1785. Passed by Congress, it provided for the division and sale of this land after it was surveyed. Anyone who had settled on public land before it was surveyed was a "squatter." Many were evicted before Congress finally passed a law in 1841 enabling them to buy the rights to their homesteads.

Historic Mansker's Station Frontier Life Center

SEE MAP PAGE 17, LOCATION #27
Goodlettsville, Tennessee
Phone: (615) 859-3678
http://www.cityofgoodlettsville.org/historic

Middle Tennessee was far from the civilized eastern seaboard of America. Travelers had to make their way over the Cumberland Gap in the Appalachians and through a forested region of Indian territories. It was a difficult and potentially dangerous journey. When they finally reached the Middle Ground, Mansker's Station awaited them with a hot meal, a sound sleep and the protection of a Euro-American settlement. Recalling those days from the late 1700s, Historic Mansker's Station encompasses two staffed Living History sites.

Mansker's Fort

This reconstructed fortified frontier station was built with hand-hewn timbers and sits very near the site of the station raised by Kasper Mansker in 1779. The original rest-stop and resupply center was three times its current size, due to a larger number of cabins, but the spirit of the place is still very much in evidence. Living History encampments bring the fort to life throughout the year. Call for dates and times.

Bowen House

Among the oldest standing brick structures in Middle Tennessee, this large home provides an opportunity to understand the transition that frontier settlers were able to make from rustic fort life to elegant estate living. The Bowen House was completed in 1787 by William Bowen, a Virginia Militia captain, for his wife, nine children and future generations. (His grandson William Bowen Campbell, a governor of Tennessee, was born here.) Truly a home-grown house, it was constructed of local bricks, and except for the glass windows and hardware, all other materials were produced or harvested locally. About 70 percent of the woodwork and almost all of the floorboards are original. One exterior door still retains its mid-1700s lock.

Located off I-65 exit 97, half a mile east on Caldwell Road in Moss-Wright Park, Goodlettsville, TN. Open Tuesday-Saturday in season. Admission charged.

⬥ Great care was taken to create an authentic reconstruction of Mansker's Fort, and enthusiastic guides have much to share. During Living History encampments, which are open to the public, costumed interpreters live in the log cabins or in their own canvas shelters, re-creating life on the frontier in 1780.

◀ The fully furnished Bowen House is terrific to see any time, but you might want to chose the December Yulefest celebration of eighteenth-century Christmas customs. In the evening, both the fort and house are lit with candle lanterns; horse-drawn wagons carry visitors between the house and the fort; and the festivities include period music and dancing.

GROWING POPULATION

A major reason for America's westward expansion was population growth. Our nation more than quadrupled between 1790 and 1840 – increasing from 3,929,214 people to 17,069,453 according to official census reports. The bulk of this growth seems to have been due to better living conditions and longer survival rates rather than a significant increase in births or immigration. New arrivals from foreign countries seem to have accounted for less than ten percent of the growth during this 50-year period. In fact, immigration had slowed when our government sought to stabilize America's cultural identity by discouraging foreigners and instituting rules that delayed citizenship. Waves of immigrants still came, of course – Germans, French, Irish, British, Norwegians and others. (About 151,000 new immigrants arrived in 1820 alone.) After 1840, the percentage of newcomers rose substantially as people from all over the world came seeking freedom, opportunities and refuge from both natural and political disasters.

Old Fort Harrod State Park

SEE MAP PAGE 17, LOCATION #28

Harrodsburg, Kentucky
Phone: (859) 734-3314
http://parks.ky.gov/stateparks/fh

▲ In March of 1774, Captain James Harrod and 32 of his men left Pennsylvania to claim land for settlement in Kentucky. Old Fort Harrod is a replica of their resulting fortified town – a group of log buildings linked by tall fence posts.

▶ A natural spring, originally just outside the fort walls, was a major asset. In times of strife, it would enable settlers to withstand a long siege by Indians intent on forcing a surrender when food and water ran out.

▶ If you are interested in log cabin architecture, here is your opportunity to see an interesting assortment. Some are small cabins. Others started out as cabins but became the core of much bigger homes. One is a Quaker meeting house.

▶ The 1849 Friends Meeting House is a typical Quaker design. It has two doors, one for men and one for women/children, and no religious symbols.

This was the first English settlement west of the Alleghenies. It was also the place where military hero George Rogers Clark (William Clark's older brother) planned his great northwest campaign to secure the territory during the Revolutionary War. Today's Fort Harrod is an impressive reconstruction, with heavy timber stockade walls surrounding fully outfitted

settlers' cabins and blockhouses. Costumed interpreters engage in period tasks such as woodworking, weaving, basketry, blacksmithing and tin smithing. Delightful!

Nearby is the original log cabin where Abraham Lincoln's parents were married in 1806 and the Mansion Museum, which displays Civil War artifacts, a rare McIntosh Gun collection, Native American artifacts and Lincoln memorabilia.

Located 32 miles southwest of Lexington, KY. Take US 68 to 100 South College Street in downtown Harrodsburg. Open year-round – daily March-Nov.; weekdays Dec.-Feb.; closed major holidays. Admission charged.

Caesar's Creek Pioneer Village

SEE MAP PAGE 17, LOCATION #30

Waynesville, Ohio
Phone: (513) 897-1120
http://www.caesarscreekvillage.org

When the first white settlers came into this area, they were killed in a Shawnee attack. However, their African slave Caesar was captured, adopted into the tribe and given hunting rights along the creek that now bears his name. Years later, a community grew up in the valley.

Destined to be destroyed with the flooding of Caesar Creek Lake, 19 of the early-1800s buildings were saved by the Army Corps of Engineers and brought to this history-inspired setting. You can wander around the grounds any time, but the best time to be here is during special Living History days, when the buildings are open. Possibilities include an eighteenth-century Trade Fair and Spring Gathering in May, Ole' Time Music Festival in June, Civil War Encampment in September and 1800 Harvest Festival in October.

Located in Caesar Creek State Park east of Waynesville, OH. From I-71 exit 45, drive west on SR 73 about 3 miles; turn left on Oregonia Road and drive about 2 miles; then right onto Pioneer Village Road. Grounds open daily except major holidays. Free except during special events.

Pricketts Fort State Park

SEE MAP PAGE 15, LOCATION #35
Fairmont, West Virginia
Phone: (304) 363-3030 or toll-free (800) 225-5982
http://www.prickettsfort.org

Native Peoples did not take kindly to the continuing stream of white settlers moving into their territory, taking the land, depleting the resources, pushing Indians out of their long-established hunting grounds. It comes as no surprise that the settlers needed to build civilian forts for refuge when hostilities reached the breaking point. In 1774, Pricketts Fort was built by a civilian militia on private land for this very purpose.

While the original fort is long gone, extensive research by historians and archaeologists enabled a fine representation to be built at the site. History-oriented carpenters, blacksmiths and other specialists were involved, and authentic materials, such as old logs, were collected from around the state. The result feels eerily real, especially with the many costumed interpreters who people the buildings and talk about life on the West Virginia frontier.

Pricketts Fort is not a very big place – just 110 feet square with 12-foot-high outer walls – and it feels even smaller, crowded with 14 log cabins, blockhouses at each corner, a meetinghouse and a storehouse. There isn't much room in the common area where settlers would cook, children would play and life would go

on as best it could. The original fort was never meant to be comfortable, just safe enough for up to 80 nearby families to "fort up" if the need arose. (As it was, they seem to have camped just outside the walls instead, on several occasions.) Today's Living History museum provides an evocative reminder that too much independence was dangerous – settlers needed to stick together.

Located just north of Fairmont, WV. From I-79 exit 139, drive about 2 miles; follow signs. Open mid-April through October – daily Memorial Day to Labor Day; Wednesday-Sunday rest of season. Admission charged.

▲ "Fort" was a broad term on the frontier. It may not have served military purposes; it may not have been used frequently; and it may not have had stockade walls. While Pricketts Fort was fenced, many civilian forts were just a single, sturdy building with gun ports. Here family members and perhaps neighbors could take temporary refuge against an Indian attack.

◀ During our visit, leaves of lemon balm, a member of the mint family, were being dried on the kitchen table. We learned that this herb had many uses in early America: a garnish for salads, a refreshing tea, a mild sedative and an antibiotic extract.

◀ As we walked from cabin to cabin, we took note: rustic as they were, their presence would have been very comforting. Everyone knew the value of community on the untamed frontier. When confronted by angry Indians, there was safety in numbers.

FINDING A HOME

Land troubles were all-too-common as our nation grew. Even Daniel Boone, one of the most famous American pioneers, was embroiled in controversy. He claimed nearly 100,000 acres of land in Kentucky but was sued over defective titles. By the age of 65, Boone had lost nearly everything through legal battles and was heavily in debt. So he headed west into what was then Spanish Louisiana and settled in Missouri under a land grant from the Spanish governor. But when the territory became part of America under the Louisiana Purchase, Boone again lost his property. Although Congress reissued the original 850 acres to Boone 11 years later, he had to sell the land in order to pay off his debts. He did manage to live out his life in a comfortable four-story home, which you can visit just 30 minutes from downtown St. Louis. (See *Road to Independence*, page 150.) Along with an adjoining historic village, it offers an interesting look into our Old West.

LEWIS&CLARK EXPEDITION

Jefferson National Expansion Memorial

SEE MAP PAGE 19, LOCATION #30
St. Louis, Missouri
Phone: (314) 655-1700
http://www.nps.gov/jeff

▶ Reports from Lewis and Clark opened up a world of exciting possibilities. Ordinary Americans headed west to a new life, carrying their possessions in prairie schooners.

Perhaps no other story about the American West is as spell-binding or as awe-inspiring as this one. Meriwether Lewis was the 29-year-old former private secretary and aide-de-camp to President Thomas Jefferson. Captain William Clark was Lewis' long-time 33-year-old friend. Together they would lead an odd collection of very courageous and hard-working people into the unknown American wilderness during scorching summers and freezing winters; through rough waters, insect-infested terrains and hostile Indian territories; up the some-times treacherous Missouri River; across the rugged Rocky Mountains; and down the rushing Snake and Columbia rivers to the Pacific Ocean. Their directive from President Jefferson was to find the most practical westward route across this continent for the purposes of American commerce.

8,000 miles in 28 months, by boat and canoe, on foot and on horseback

The expedition began near St. Louis, Missouri, in May 1804 and returned to that city in September 1806. Remarkably, only two men deserted along the way, and only one died (probably from a ruptured appendix). The Corps of Discovery, as Jefferson called the group, numbered 45-50 at the start. Most were unmarried soldiers. Others included Clark's African American slave, York, and a scout/hunter named George Drouillard. Hired boatmen and six of the soldiers traveled only on the initial leg of the trip. During the first winter, a French Canadian trader named Toussaint Charbonneau and his wife Sacagawea, a Shoshone Indian, joined them as guides and interpreters. All told, the Corps covered approximately 8,000 miles in 28 months, by boat and canoe, on foot and on horseback. They returned to a heroes' welcome with invaluable maps, detailed journals and a wealth of material about the plants, animals, natural resources and Native Peoples. Most important, their success prompted America to claim Oregon, Washington and Idaho – despite prior British claims – and ultimately set in motion the great westward movement of the mid-1800s.

▲ Bull boats such as this one at the Museum of Westward Expansion were used by many Native Peoples instead of canoes. Clark wrote about them in his journal, noting that a bison hide stretched over the frame created a "perfect basin."

To fully grasp the monumental impact of the Lewis and Clark Expedition and subsequent westward movement, begin your own exploration here. The Jefferson National Expansion Memorial is comprised of the 630-foot-high Gateway Arch, the Museum of Westward Expansion beneath the Arch, and the nearby Old Courthouse where a slave named Dred Scott and his wife sued for their freedom in the mid-1840s. The museum, especially, is a must-see. Here an interactive timeline, presented in concentric circles, charts the history of our nineteenth-century American West from the Louisiana Purchase to the closing of the frontier in 1890. Be sure to see the peace medals – the single largest collection of their kind in the world. Other exhibits provide valuable insight into major mass migrations, bitter conflicts, epic explorations and technological advances. You will learn about fascinating people from all walks of life – government officials, explorers, mountain men and trappers, soldiers, Native Peoples, farmers, buffalo hunters, miners, settlers and others. And you will come away amazed by all you have learned. Check the website for special events and activities, including ranger programs with Living History.

Located in downtown St. Louis, MO. For garage parking, drive past the Arch and onto Washington Avenue. Traveling east, the garage is on the right. All 3 sites are open daily except major holidays. Free. Admission charged for tram ride inside Arch to a spectacular view.

Lewis & Clark Interpretive Center & Fort Mandan

SEE MAP PAGE 19, LOCATION #33
Washburn, North Dakota
Phone: (701) 462-8535 or toll-free (877) 462-8535
http://www.fortmandan.com

November 3, 1804, six months into the Lewis & Clark Expedition, William Clark wrote in his journal: "We commence building our cabins." He was referring to the crude log structures christened "Fort Mandan." The Corps of Discovery remained in these winter quarters, just across the Missouri River from several Native villages, for about five months – until the spring thaw enabled them to resume their difficult trip upriver. During that period, Lewis and Clark established diplomatic and trade relations with the Mandan-Hidatsa Indians. They interviewed those who had been west, learned about obstacles which lay ahead of them and sketched maps to guide their journey.

They also hired Toussaint Charbonneau and his Shoshone wife, Sacagawea (pronounced sah-cah-gah-we-ah, based on the Clark and Lewis journals). This proved to be particularly fortuitous months later, when the Corps met a band of Shoshone led by Sacagawea's brother. (Abducted as a child, she had not seen him or her tribe in years.) The unexpected reunion enabled the group to secure much-needed pack horses along with valuable information about the terrain yet to be crossed.

As is typical of early log structures, nothing remains of the original Fort Mandan, but it has been reconstructed as authentically as possible and is well worth the visit. You will see the re-created quarters of Captains Lewis and Clark, their men and the Charbonneau family, as well as the storage rooms that contained their supplies. All are furnished as they would have been during the winter of 1804-1805. On-site interpreters provide highly informative tours. Also interesting is the nearby Interpretive Center, where exhibits include a buffalo robe (which you can try on), a cottonwood keelboat, a "cradle-board" much like the one Sacagawea probably used to carry her baby, and period watercolors by famous artist Karl Bodmer.

Lewis & Clark Interpretive Center is located at the intersection of US 83 and ND 200A on McLean County Highway 17 in Washburn, ND, 38 miles north of Bismarck. Just 2 miles west of the Interpretive Center is Fort Mandan, also on McLean County Highway 17. Both are open daily. Admission charged.

▲ The construction of Fort Mandan greatly interested local Indians. From its beginning, the Mandans crossed the river daily just to watch the men work and to trade with them.

◀ Fort Mandan was rebuilt using drawings from the journal of Meriwether Lewis. Intended only as a temporary winter shelter, the compact fort barely had enough room for the men and supplies. The addition of the Charbonneau family only made the living conditions tighter.

◀ As many as nine men slept in each room, with some in the loft above. A fireplace provided warmth as well as a place to cook meals.

◀ Captain Lewis' office was just a narrow alcove in one corner of the room he shared with Captain Clark.

Lewis & Clark National Historic Trail Interpretive Center

SEE MAP PAGE 19, LOCATION #26
Great Falls, Montana
Phone: (406) 727-8733
http://www.fs.fed.us/r1/lewisclark/lcic

▲ A life-size exhibit at the Interpretive Center shows how the Corps of Discovery hauled supply-laden boats up the steep river bank to get around a series of waterfalls, including the Great Falls, on the Missouri River.

▶ On July 16, 1805, Lewis wrote in his journal: "After breakfast I determined to leave Capt. C. and party, and go on to the point where the river enters the Rocky Mountains and make the necessary observations..." Three days later, he and his men maneuvered their canoes through a dramatic river canyon where limestone cliffs towered all around them.

April 7, 1805, the Corps of Discovery headed west from Fort Mandan. They made relatively good time by water until mid-June. But then: the Great Falls and four other cascades stood in their path. The crew had no choice but to begin a grueling 18-mile detour around the falls.

Beaching their boats and concealing the pirogue, they hauled their dugout canoes and supplies up the steep river bank. In rain, hail and intense heat, they proceeded over land carpeted with cactus, using crudely made wagons. It was tough going, and getting back to the water brought new troubles: Lewis' experimental iron-frame boat failed. Before continuing, they had to construct two new dugouts.

The Interpretive Center at Great Falls provides exceptional insight into this arduous journey and the Expedition as a whole. Besides unusual displays, it offers a 30-minute introductory movie by filmmaker Ken Burns; informative talks; Living History demonstrations; and outdoor trails overlooking the Missouri River. To experience more, sign up for field trips, workshops and other activities offered each year. Opportunities include exploring history, geography and Native cultures; learning expedition-era skills; and visiting sites associated with exploration in the American West.

Although hydroelectric plants now harness the power of the Missouri, the waterfalls are still breathtaking much of the year. At the Interpretive Center, ask for a road map to the cascades, including the "Great Falls" at Ryan Dam. You can see the Black Eagle Falls and Dam at an overlook on your way to the Center; the others are just a short distance away by car.

Located in Giant Springs Heritage State Park, at 4201 Giant Springs Road on the northeast edge of Great Falls, MT; reached via River Drive. Open year-round – daily Memorial Day-September 30; Tuesday-Sunday rest of year; closed major holidays. Admission charged.

Gates of the Mountains

SEE MAP PAGE 19, LOCATION #27
Helena vicinity (north), Montana
Phone: (406) 458-5241
http://www.gatesofthemountains.com

On the evening of July 19, 1805, members of the Lewis & Clark Expedition entered a deep-water channel on the Missouri River. They were in the foothills of the Rocky Mountains not far from present-day Helena, Montana. Rugged limestone cliffs came to the water's edge on both sides and rose 1,200 feet overhead. At each bend in the waterway, the great stone walls seemed about to converge and block their passage, only to spread wide like giant gates as the boats approached. In his journal, Meriwether Lewis wrote: "the river appears to have forced it's way through this immense body of solid rock for the distance of 5 ¾ miles and where it makes its exit

below has thrown on either side vast columns of rocks mountains high...from the singular appearance of this place I called it the *gates of the rocky mountains*."

This is a thrilling natural wonder, to be enjoyed from your own boat or on a commercial cruise. In addition to the canyon scenery, you will see Indian pictographs painted on the rock walls. At the Meriwether Picnic Area, you can go ashore where Lewis and his advance party are believed to have camped for the night. You also have the potential for wildlife sightings – the canyon is home to Bighorn Sheep, Mountain Goats, otters, deer, ermine, beaver, mountain lions, black bears and large birds (including golden and bald eagles, peregrine and prairie falcons, ospreys and vultures).

Located 20 miles north of Helena, MT, just 3 miles off I-15 exit 209. Reasonably priced cruises offered late May to late September, weather permitting, from the boat marina. Call or check website for schedule and rates.

Fort Clatsop, Lewis & Clark National Historical Park

SEE MAP PAGE 23, LOCATION #31

Astoria, Oregon
Phone: (503) 861-2471
http://www.nps.gov/lewi

Soon after the Corps of Discovery reached the Three Forks of the Missouri River in Montana, water travel was no longer possible. What lay before the men was a hard struggle by land. Yet they continued on, succeeding in part because friendly Indians fed them when they ran out of food, provided pack horses to ease their travel, and traded Indian apparel when their European-style garments wore out or became unsuitable. In mid-October 1805, almost without warning, the Corps came upon the broad waters of the Columbia River. In mid-November, they paddled their canoes into the Columbia's estuary. There, finally, the Pacific Ocean stretched before them.

Their excitement was short-lived, however. Winter rains were intense, and they had to focus on survival needs. After hurriedly building Fort Clatsop, the men fell into a routine – making salt from seawater, hunting for food, tanning hides, and crafting footwear and cloth-

ing. Captains Lewis and Clark compiled scientific observations about the local flora and fauna. They also met and traded with the nearby Clatsop and Chinook Indians.

On March 23, 1806, at the first sign of spring, the explorers set out for home. They had achieved their goals. They had discovered a route to the western edge of the continent, amassed valuable data on the land and its inhabitants, and positioned our nation to claim the Pacific Northwest. Five years later, the first American settlement – a Pacific Fur Company post – would be established at the mouth of the Columbia.

Today, a replica of the expedition's 50-foot by 50-foot Fort Clatsop camp stands on the original site amidst the coastal forest and wetland. The rooms are outfitted with animal skins, blankets, clothing and personal items; dried plants and cooking utensils; weapons and bullet-making equipment. All of the furnishings are handcrafted. Here is your chance for a realistic hands-on interaction with a remarkable time in America's past. Engaging Living History videos are shown in the Visitor Center. Costumed rangers staff the Fort and conduct interpretive programs mid-June through Labor Day.

Fort Clatsop is just one of 12 sites protected by the Lewis and Clark National and State Historical Parks on the Oregon and Washington coast.

Located 5 miles south of Astoria, OR. Take business US 101 to Fort Clatsop Road. Summer shuttles to other park sites. Open daily except Dec. 25. Admission charged.

EXPEDITION CLOTHING

The men started their trip wearing civilian or Army-style clothes made primarily of wool or linen. Gradually they acquired Indian apparel – leather shirts, leggings and moccasins as well as buffalo robes. By the time they reached the Pacific Ocean, they were clad almost entirely in leather or fur. At Fort Clatsop, Sgt. Gass noted in his journal that men who were not hunting for meat or working at the salt works were employed "in dressing elk skins for mokasins, which is a laborious business, but we have no alternative..." Capt. Lewis wrote: "Had a large coat completed out of the skins of the Tiger Cat and...a small animal about the size of a squirrel...these skins I procured from the Indians who had previously dressed them and formed them into robes." Sgt. Ordway and Pvt. Whitehouse repeatedly recorded that they and others spent their days "making Cloathing, moccasins & dressing Elk Skins." Footwear and clothes were a constant concern.

▲ Even though the current Fort Clatsop is a 2006 reconstruction, seeing it is an eye-opening experience. The men of the Corps of Discovery did the best they could with what was available. All things considered, they built a fine home to get them through the wet and miserable winter of 1805-1806. (It rained all but 12 days during the four months they camped here.)

◀ Walking into the living quarters and listening to what the interpreters have to say, one can only marvel at the fortitude of people so determined to map the pathway west. It seems amazing, indeed, that none of the Corps of Discovery died from starvation, injury, animal attacks or exposure. (One man – Charles Floyd – died during the first summer, but apparently this was due to a ruptured appendix.)

FUR TRADING

▲ The heart of every fur trading post, including this room at Fort Vancouver, was the place where furs were collected, evaluated, weighed and packed in 275-pound bundles for shipment to the East and to Europe.

Well before the Lewis & Clark Expedition, fur traders had opened trails westward, moving in advance of civilization and contributing to the development of British, French and Russian empires in America. Known as "mountain men," many were free spirits, working their own traps and exchanging their pelts for supplies at trading posts. Others were employees of trading companies that dominated the North American frontier from the late 1600s to early 1800s – most notably the Hudson's Bay Company, North West Company (which merged with Hudson's Bay), Russian-American Company, American Fur Company (with Pacific Fur Company and South West Company subsidiaries), Rocky Mountain Fur Company, and Missouri Fur Company.

Overall, fur trade promoted friendly relations between the traders and Native Peoples. But it also brought disease and "demon whiskey," sparked rivalries between competing tribes, and prompted attacks against white settlers who cleared away vital animal habitat. In addition, intense commercial competition led to conflicts between the French and British, and between the Russians and Indians. Fur trade rights even played a part in establishing the border between the United States and Canada.

Fur-bearing animals were plentiful in America, and demand for their pelts remained high for a very long time. After all, fur was soft and warm; leather was supple and elegant; and beaver-felt hats were high style. Predictably, though, a glut of furs and leather over-saturated the marketplace. The most popular animals began to disappear due to over-trapping and the encroachment of civilization on their habitat. Clothing styles changed. And the financial rewards diminished. By 1850, most fur trading activity had ended.

With no other choice, fur traders and trappers changed careers. Some served as trail blazers and guides for settlers emigrating west. Others settled down to raise livestock, to farm or to operate trading posts. Among the more renowned, Christopher (Kit) Carson, William Sublette and Jedediah Smith played major roles in exploring and settling the West. Jim Bridger established Fort Bridger, a crudely built but important trading post that supplied travelers on the Oregon Trail. William Wolfskill explored a route that would become the Sante Fe Trail and then established himself as an extraordinarily successful California farmer. (Wolfskill had the largest orange grove in America and, later, the largest vineyard, with some 85,000 grapevines. He has been credited as being the father of California's wine industry.) Thriving settlements grew from the fur trade business to become major cities as diverse as New Orleans, Chicago, St. Louis, Albany and Detroit.

EXPLORER TURNED TRAPPER

John Colter, one of the more famous fur trappers, started his mountain man career as a member of the Lewis and Clark Expedition. When the Corps of Discovery neared the Mandan villages on their way home in 1806, he asked to be discharged early, eager to see more of the American West. In 1807, Colter joined the Missouri Fur Company and became the first white person to see what is now Yellowstone National Park. He also had a fur trapping experience that became legendary. The year was 1809. The place: near the headwaters of the Missouri River, in forbidden Blackfoot Indian territory. He and his partner were on the river, trapping beaver, when they were discovered by angry Indians. The Blackfeet killed his partner, stripped Colter naked and told him to run for his life. Apparently it was a game of sport, with the Indians in pursuit. After a few miles, Colter managed to kill the nearest Indian, steal his blanket and thus evade other pursuers. Colter reached safety 11 days later, naked and emaciated. Undaunted, he continued to trap for a few more years before using his fur-trade profits to buy a plot of land in Missouri, build a cabin, marry and have a son.

Museum of the Fur Trade

SEE MAP PAGE 19, LOCATION #22

Chadron, Nebraska
Phone: (308) 432-3843
http://www.furtrade.org

Although comprised mostly of indoor exhibits, this specialized museum is well worth going out of your way to visit. It has rare and unusual things that will peak your interest and increase your understanding of both the fur trade and the people who gave their lives to it – the voyageurs, mountain men, professional hunters and Native Peoples. What's more, you will gain intriguing insight into the business enterprises of British, French, American and Spanish traders. A major museum expansion and renovation project was completed in 2006.

Three galleries focus entirely on fur trading from early colonial days to the present. On display is the entire range of trade items used during centuries of interface between diverse cultures. Here are the cutlery, axes, firearms, munitions, textiles, costumes, paints and beads exchanged by traders with Native Peoples from Canada to Alaska and from Hudson's Bay to the Gulf of Mexico. What the Europeans and Americans received in return were primarily beaver pelts and bison hides, especially the dense, even coats of female bison.

A short path from the museum leads to the Bordeaux Trading Post, originally built by the American Fur Company and operated from 1837 to 1876. The museum grounds also include a garden of Native American crops farmed for centuries in the Missouri Valley. Among the historic varieties grown during the summer, you can see the midget tobacco smoked in peace pipes by the Mandan Indians; the Assiniboine flint corn used at the distillery in Fort Union; and the blue-kerneled little corn grown by the Blackfoot tribe on the Montana plains.

Located 3 miles east of Chadron, NE, on US 20. Open daily April-October. Admission charged.

North West Company Fur Post

SEE MAP PAGE 19, LOCATION #29

Pine City, Minnesota
Phone: (320) 629-6356
http://www.mnhs.org/places/sites/nwcfp

The Montreal-based North West Company moved a lot of beaver fur from the hands of Native American hunters to the heads of fashion-conscious men and women. It had over 100 wintering posts in a vast network extending from the St. Lawrence River Valley to beyond the foothills of the Rocky Mountains. In the fall of 1804, wintering partner John Sayer and his crew established one of these posts two miles up the Snake River from Cross Lake. The site was intentionally near the local Ojibwe hunting and trapping camp that would become the post's main source of beaver pelts.

Today's Living History interpretation of Sayer's business venture is exceptional. Based on extensive archaeological findings and historic documents, the reconstructed post includes a fully outfitted six-room row house, surrounded by a 100-foot by 61-foot palisade with defensive bastions in the north and south corners. It is manned by well-informed costumed interpreters, including a "fur trade clerk" and others representing the time period. A nearby Ojibwe encampment and a trapper's cabin add to the authenticity of the place.

We recommend the guided tour – you will have plenty of time afterwards to take a closer look at the fur post and ask further questions. In addition, the Visitor Center has a very informative museum.

▲ Many fur trading forts were temporary structures that were abandoned as the local fur resources were depleted. Indoor kitchens were considered an unnecessary luxury; so cooking was done outside, weather permitting.

◄ To better withstand the intense weather common on the open plains, this trading post was built mostly below ground. The re-creation contains a fully outfitted trade room plus modest accommodations for the trader.

Located in Pine City, MN, about 1 1/2 miles west of I-35 at exit 169 (Pine County Highway 7). Open daily from May-Labor Day; Fridays-Sundays from Labor Day-October. Admission charged.

Forts Folle Avoine Historical Park

SEE MAP PAGE 17, LOCATION #26
Danbury vicinity (south), Wisconsin
Phone: (715) 866-8890
http://theforts.org

▲ As the territory was depleted of fur-bearing animals and Native Peoples migrated, the fur traders moved on to new sites as well. Their well-crafted palisade and cabins fell to ruin and were hidden in the forest for 165 years. In 1969, the trading site was discovered.

▶ Birch bark was a versatile resource for Native Peoples. It was used for everything from houses and canoes to storage containers and cooking utensils. On a winter lodge, the waterproof orange inner bark was turned up to repel water. On a summer wigwam, the light outer bark faced outward to reflect the sun's rays.

▶ Thanks to iron pots received from the Europeans in trade, the Ojibwe could make large amounts of maple sugar for use not only as a sweetener but also as a preservative.

local Native Peoples – the Ojibwe, Odawa, Cree, Dakota, Fox and Sauk – not only for furs but also for food, family life and winter survival. At the Ojibwe village, interpretive demonstrations cover all aspects of Native life and reveal in very interesting detail how Indians used their limited resources. Our guide showed us a winter camp, a workcamp for making maple sugar and a

One cannot help but wonder: two competing companies, less then 100 feet apart, trading with the local woodland Indians? But then, we all know what happens when people identify the same business opportunity at the same time. No one backs down. The North West Company arrived in the spring of 1802 and built a trading post, cabin and stockade. The XY Company arrived that winter and built a single structure, combining its trading post and living quarters. The two were friendly enough. In fact, the XY traders moved inside the North West stockade at one point, fearing attack by hostile Indians. Such was life in the Folle Avoine (fohl av-WAHN), or the "crazy oats" (wild rice) region of northwestern Wisconsin 200 years ago.

The four traders' cabins have been reconstructed on their original sites, alongside a remarkably complete woodland Indian village. In both areas, traditionally dressed interpreters interact with visitors. As you will learn, the traders relied heavily on the cooperation of

hunting area with various kinds of traps for fishing, catching small animals and killing a bear.

Tours and demonstrations are offered throughout the tourist season. Special programs include a fur trade rendezvous. The Visitor Center has archaeology displays, maps and artifacts.

Located between Danbury and Webster, WI. Take SR 35 to County Road U; drive 2 1/2 miles west. Open Wednesday-Sunday, Memorial Day-Labor Day. Admission charged.

THE AMERICAN PLAINS

As the first settlers moved westward, they had little regard for the Great Plains. Headed for the rich land and flowing rivers of the Pacific Northwest, they saw only difficulties in a dry region carpeted by treeless fields of deep-rooted grass. The tallgrass prairies they passed through were altogether different from our modern experience. The big bluestem, switchgrass and Indiangrass could reach a height of six to eight feet by late summer. Cordgrass (sloughgrass) could reach ten feet – taller than a boy standing on his dad's shoulders and taller than a man on horseback! What's more, farmers needed to use heavy plows pulled by as many as 20 animals just to break up the root system. Still, there was one great advantage to dense prairie sod: it was strong enough to be cut into large bricks which could be stacked to form the walls of a house. Some historians estimate that more than a million sod houses were built in America and Canada.

Colonial Michilimackinac

SEE MAP PAGE 17, LOCATION #29
Mackinaw City, Michigan
Phone: (231) 436-4100
http://www.mackinacparks.com/parks/colonial-michilimackinac_7

This marvelous reconstruction of a fur trading village and military outpost recounts a lively history. Back in 1715, French traders and soldiers built a fort here, overlooking the Straits of Mackinac (MAK-in-naw), which connects Lake Huron and Lake Michigan. The location proved ideal, and Michilimackinac (MIH-shil-uh-MAK-in-naw) became the center of a fur trading industry which extended north into Canada, west across the Mississippi River, south into the Illinois Country, and along the shores of Lake Michigan.

It was a busy place! The French used the post until 1761, when the British took control during the French and Indian War. But the British almost lost Michilimackinac because the Ottawa and Chippewa Indians resented their policies. The Indians attacked and killed most of the fort's occupants in 1763. Through the sheer force of will, Michilimackinac managed to remain in British hands and was active until 1780. It was then dismantled and moved to nearby Mackinac Island.

Too important to forget, Michilimackinac has been reconstructed on its original site as a Living History museum, complete with costumed eighteenth-century interpreters. Behind the fortified 18-foot walls are a priest's house, guardhouse, storehouse, blacksmith shop, French church and British trader's house, as well as blockhouses and barracks. All are furnished.

In addition to its visitor attractions, Colonial Michilimackinac is the site of the longest ongoing archaeological excavation in America. An underground exhibit entitled "Treasures from the Sand" displays more than 350 of the artifacts found at Michilimackinac since 1959. Mid-June through mid-August, you can even watch an archaeological dig in progress and talk to the archaeologists about their work.

Located on the southwest side of the Mackinac Bridge in Mackinaw City, MI. Open daily from early May to early October. Admission charged.

▲ With dozens of people to be fed in this large and busy place on the frontier, productive gardens were vital. The exotic foodstuffs available locally were combined with fruits and vegetables familiar to settlers from the East or across the Atlantic.

◀ The post commander was generally well educated and lived a very different lifestyle from the rest of the fort. His status afforded luxuries and privileges available only to the very well-to-do. However, advancement also brought loneliness. The leaders missed the camaraderie of their former peers.

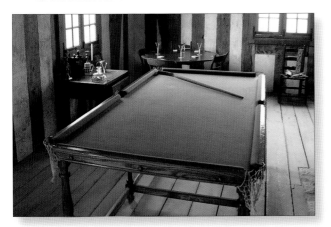

Walk inside. Colorful colonial times will come to life for you through vivid re-enactments of the French and British occupations. You can meet village residents; witness a traditional French Colonial wedding; see the boisterous Arrival of the Voyageurs; visit the Native American camp; watch demonstrations of colonial cooking and blacksmithing; and enjoy the drama of cannon and musket demonstrations.

BLACKSMITHS

Village "smithies" were the most numerous craftsmen in America and as essential to every community as the general store. They were often the primary source for tools, knives, utensils, agricultural implements and construction hardware. Many were locksmiths, gunsmiths, shipsmiths, heavy-tool makers and nailers. They repaired wagons and carriages, and they fixed worn and broken tools. They manufactured shoes for horses and oxen; some even fit them to the animals; others, having gained a working knowledge of the animals they shoed, served as veterinarians as well. So the blacksmith shop was a very busy place at Michilimackinac. Men and women gathered to talk and share gossip while waiting for service. Children hung around, watching the smithy and his apprentice at work – heating iron to a bright orange glow, steadily moving from forge to anvil and back again, pounding the hot metal and shaping it into its final form.

Grand Portage National Monument

SEE MAP PAGE 19, LOCATION #25
Grand Portage, Minnesota
Phone: (218) 475-2202 (summer) or (218) 387-2788 (winter)
http://www.nps.gov/grpo

▲ Company outposts such as Grand Portage hosted the summer rendezvous. Note the separate kitchen on the left. Had it been connected to the main building, the warmth and odors would have been unbearable in the summer heat. Besides, the French-trained chefs undoubtedly wanted some distance from the rowdy goings-on next door.

▶ Even though this facility was remote, company officers visited every year to ensure that their financial interests were well-managed. While here, they dined as well as they did at home, having brought livestock, personal chefs, fine china and silverware with them.

▶ Canoes were the primary means of transportation for the fur industry. They were light weight, built of wood slats, covered with birch bark and sealed with pine pitch. The largest were 40 feet long and capable of carrying eight men plus their belongings and three tons of supplies.

It was an opportunity fur traders could not resist: low-cost items such as mirrors, axes, iron kettles, beads and guns could be exchanged for tens of thousands of valuable beaver pelts from Canadian and American Indians. The potential for big profits was enough to spur hundreds of men to risk the perils of northern winters to trade with the Indians and then take an arduous journey in summer, laden with furs, to receive their pay. One of the worst parts of the trek was Le Grand Portage, a rugged 8 1/2 mile trail developed by American Indians to bypass waterfalls and rapids that blocked canoe access to the western end of Lake Superior.

Capitalizing on this strategic location, the North West Company built an outpost at the foot of the portage. Everyone associated with its fur trade business came together here for the big midsummer rendezvous – the French voyageurs, Indian families, Scottish clerks, guides and interpreters, wintering partners from outlying posts, and senior company officials from Montreal and London. They exchanged goods, divided profits and had a grand old time (accompanied by substantial drinking and frequent fighting). That was in 1778. By 1802, company partners had decided to leave.

They were tired of the pressure from an emerging United States; beaver pelts were becoming scarce; and the market was diminishing. So they dismantled or destroyed the 18 buildings constructed from spruce, pine and birch. They took down the more than 2,000 cedar pickets surrounding them. And they transported the valuable materials in company schooners far into Canada for use in constructing Fort William. The new location enabled the Nor'Westers to continue their lucrative business and capture 78 percent of all fur sales. In our modern times, journal research and archaeological excavations uncovered the facts needed to rebuilt much of the original post in an intriguing 710-acre park.

Don't be put off by the long drive to nearly the Canadian border. You will find much here to make the trip worthwhile. The palisade, main gatehouse, great hall, kitchen complex, warehouse, Ojibwe village, voyageur encampment, historic gardens, fur press area and canoe dock have all been rebuilt. In addition, Living History interpreters offer a wealth of information. They even invite visitors to feel the furs and handle the European trade items.

Located entirely within the boundaries of the Grand Portage Ojibwe Indian Reservation, this reconstructed supply and transfer depot celebrates not only fur trade but also Ojibwe lifeways. Annual events include the Grand Portage Rendezvous Days and Pow-Wow held the second full weekend of August – it has an historic encampment, demonstrations and competitive events. Also popular is the "Winter Frolic" weekend in January – it showcases winter life at the North West Company depot with snowshoeing, an historic sled-dog race, sleigh rides and a snow snake toss (an Indian game).

Located on the north shore of Lake Superior, just off of SR 61 about 1/2 mile from the village of Grand Portage, MN. Open daily from late May through mid-October. Admission charged.

Old Fort Madison

SEE MAP PAGE 19, LOCATION #24
Fort Madison, Iowa
Phone: (319) 372-6318 in season
http://www.oldfortmadison.com

In 1808, Fort Madison became the first American military post on the upper Mississippi River. In part, its job was to protect the government "factory," or trading post, which was located just outside the fort walls so that local Native Peoples could exchange furs for manufactured goods. The post was also commissioned to secure the frontier in what is now southeast Iowa. But the times were difficult. Bands of marauding Indians would kill soldiers outside the stockade, slaughter garrison cattle, burn nearby settler's cabins and even attack the fort itself with burning arrows. Faced with this all-too-frequent harassment, the post commander finally decided to leave. In September 1813, under cover

of darkness, he and his men set fire to the buildings and stockade and then slipped away downstream in boats. It seemed that Fort Madison was lost to history.

But then, in 1965, part of the cellar of the burned middle blockhouse was uncovered by chance on the grounds of the W.A. Sheaffer Pen Company. This discovery led to excavations which revealed the fort site. Replicas of several major buildings were later hand-hewn by inmates at the Iowa State Penitentiary, and these authentically made log structures were assembled just blocks from where Fort Madison once stood. A number of Living History interpreters people the fort, providing perspective on the challenges that soldiers and settlers faced in the rugged Louisiana Territory.

Located on Highway 61 at Riverview Park in Fort Madison, IA. Open Wednesdays-Sundays, June-August; weekends only, May and September. Admission charged.

Fort Osage

SEE MAP PAGE 19, LOCATION #32
Sibley, Missouri
Phone: (816) 650-5737
http://www.historicfortosage.com

When the Lewis & Clark Expedition passed through this area in June 1804, Clark noted its "high command-ing position, more than 70 feet above high-water mark, and overlooking the river." It was a good place to establish a fort. In 1808, he returned and, under his direction, built Fort Osage – one of the first military outposts in the Louisiana Purchase. Just outside its walls was a United States Factory Trade House.

The four-story high trade house (half underground) was specifically set up to promote relations with Native Peoples and protect them from exploitation by unscrupulous traders. Osage Indians and other local tribes which signed treaties with our Federal Government were able to obtain trade goods here at low, uniform prices. Ultimately, however, private traders formed such a powerful lobby in Congress that they put the government factory system out of business. A few years later, with settlers pushing the frontier farther west, Fort Osage closed. It soon fell into ruin.

Today you can see the reconstructed Factory trade house as well as the fort blockhouses, officers' quarters, soldiers' barracks and surrounding log stockade, all on their original sites (and on their original foundations where possible). The buildings are outfitted to reflect 1812 and are staffed by costumed interpreters. You will feel the past as a tangible presence.

Located in Sibley, MO, on the Missouri River, 14 miles northeast of Independence. Open year-round – Tuesday-Sunday, March-November 15; weekends, November 16-February; closed major holidays. Admission charged.

▲ Situated high above the Missouri River, Fort Osage supported one of the most successful of the 28 government "factories" operating from 1795 to 1822. (Factory is an old term for a store which sells goods entrusted to it by others.)

◀ Based on archaeo-logical findings and the trader's drawing, Old Fort Madison is an exceptional full-scale replica of the main structures. The original fort was mistakenly built below a ridge that was hidden at the time by trees. Although a long protective passage and tail blockhouse (not reconstructed) were added, fort occupants could be shot from the ridge as they walked around inside the fort.

Fort Union Trading Post National Historical Site

SEE MAP PAGE 19, LOCATION #34

Williston vicinity (southwest), North Dakota
Phone: (701) 572-9083
http://www.nps.gov/fous

Fort Uncompahgre

SEE MAP PAGE 19, LOCATION #23

Delta, Colorado
Phone: (970) 874-8349
http://www.delta-fort.org

▲ Fort Union was unique among trading posts. Its headquarters was the elaborate Bourgeois House shown here. Just as noteworthy: the entire fort, including stockade walls, was painted gleaming white and accented in bright colors. No one was going to confuse it with a competing trading post situated nearby.

▶ Fort Uncompahgre was not a glamorous place, but it was very well stocked. The goods traded with the Ute Indians came from all over the world – pigments and tea from China, sugar from Mexico, tobacco from Virginia, rifles smuggled from the East Coast, knives and wool blankets from England.

Originally built in 1828, Fort Union became the fur trading center for the upper Missouri River region. It was 1,800 miles by water from its supply base, St. Louis, but ideally situated to attract Indian traders. North of the Missouri were the Assiniboine. Up the Yellowstone were the Crow. Also within range were the Mandan, Hidatsa, Plains Cree, Plains Chippewa, Blackfoot, Sioux and métis (mixed white-Indian heritage). All were eager to trade beaver pelts for European goods. When silk hats replaced beaver, the Indians brought bison hides, valued both for their fur and their leather (which was more sturdy than cowhide for wagon straps, mechanical pulleys and such).

Many prominent men spent time at Fort Union. Among them were artists George Catlin, Karl Bodmer and John James Audubon; mountain men Jim Bridger and Jim Beckwourth; and the Jesuit priest Pierre DeSmet. When no longer needed after the Civil War, Fort Union met a sad but honorable end: it was dismantled for use as construction materials to expand nearby Fort Buford.

The fortified post came back to life with its 1985-1991 reconstruction, thanks to the National Park Service. The walls and bastions were rebuilt. The trade house was replicated and furnished to its 1851 appearance. Indian encampments were set up around the fort. Costumed interpreters came to share their knowledge about the coexistence of white and Indian cultures. And special events were added, including a Rendezvous, Indian Arts Showcase and Living History Weekend.

Located 25 miles southwest of Williston, ND, via US 2 and SR 1804, and 24 miles northeast of Sidney, MT. (In 2 time zones, it uses Central time.) Open daily. Free.

A number of fur trading posts have been restored or reconstructed as Living History attractions throughout America. On the surface, one may wonder why. Look deeper. Fort Uncompahgre (un-com-PAW-gray) is a prime example: the former inhabitants and their lives inspired gossip in their day and became legendary.

Antoine Robidoux, the post's original owner and operator, was a remarkable individual. Some call him an accomplished explorer, robust mountain

man and astute politician. Others say that he was a ruthless businessman who became wealthy by taking advantage of others and by selling illegal guns and high-profit whiskey when the fur trade began to decline. He certainly seems to have been a paradox – a power-seeking Frenchman who took Mexican citizenship to gain trading rights and married the Sante Fe governor's daughter; a charmer equally comfortable socializing in high society, leading a fur trapping party or playing hand games with local Indians; and the owner of the only commercial posts in fur trade history to be burned to the ground by angry Indians.

Fort Uncompahgre, established in 1828, was one of the burned posts. Most of its inhabitants were killed. Today's costumed interpreters share fascinating stories and bring the fur business back to life during hands-on tours of the fully outfitted, reconstructed trading center.

Located in Confluence Park north of Delta, CO. Take Gunnison River Drive west from US 50 for two blocks. Self-guided tours Monday-Friday from April-October. Guided tours by appointment. Closed November-March. Admission charged.

Historic Fort Snelling

SEE MAP PAGE 19, LOCATION #31
St. Paul, Minnesota
Phone: (612) 726-1171
http://www.mnhs.org/places/sites/hfs

Strategically positioned at the junction of the Mississippi and Minnesota rivers, Fort Snelling was built in the 1820s in a time and place demanding great courage. The river iced over in winter. Supplies were hundreds of miles away. And the land was a wild place populated by Indians, criminals and fur traders. But the fort was vital here. It protected law-abiding citizens. It denied non-Americans commercial use of the rivers. It also prevented white encroachment on Indian lands ahead of government treaties.

Colonel Josiah Snelling's officers and soldiers did more than enforce American laws and policies. They also changed the landscape – establishing roads, building a gristmill and sawmill, planting crops, raising livestock, and gathering wood and stone for their buildings. For almost 30 years, the post was the hub of the Upper Mississippi. When the Civil War erupted, it became a training center for the Union Army. After the war, the regulars returned to serve in Indian campaigns and the Spanish-American War of

1898. Only after World War II was the fort finally closed. Destined to be saved from the threat of a freeway, it became Minnesota's first National Historic Landmark and was restored to its 1820s appearance.

Today within the walls of Historic Fort Snelling, Living History travelers can see a vivid picture of the lifestyle of soldiers, officers, domestics, tradesmen, fur traders and Indians who lived in the region long ago.

All of the personnel – from the Commander, to the soldiers, to the laundress – are in character, portraying people and events of the period. On the day we visited, the fort was dealing with the "death" of a soldier (apparently of a stroke). Each person had his or

her own way of coping with the loss. The doctor was puzzled and concerned by the mysterious death, having tried everything he knew, including drilling a hole into the soldier's skull to relieve the pressure on his brain. The laundress, who was paid for her services by individual soldiers, had lost one-sixth of her business. And two of the poor unfortunate's comrades were discussing how the dead man's personal effects would be divided up among various people.

Located in St. Paul, MN, at junction of Minnesota Highways 5 and 55, a mile east of Twin Cities International Airport. Open daily May-October. Admission charged.

◀ Filling the hours, days, months and years was a challenge on the frontier. For soldiers, much of the time was spent, as it still is, perfecting their marching drills on the parade ground. The soldiers shown here are dressed in their finest uniforms. In the 1800s, they would have had one other set of clothing, a uniform for everyday use.

◀ Life in the ranks was not glamorous, and it was rarely exciting. Endless hours were spent not only marching and training but also cleaning weapons and keeping a shared bunk in order.

◀ Soldiers in the upper ranks enjoyed an important perk: they were allowed to have their families live with them. However, the women were required to work to pay for their keep. This small but comfortable room (right-hand photo) was the home of a sergeant, his laundress wife and their children.

Fort Vancouver National Historic Site

SEE MAP PAGE 23, LOCATION #35
Vancouver, Washington
Phone: (360) 816-6230
http://www.nps.gov/fova

▲ The Chief Factor's House was the officers' home. The cannons seen here recall the Factor's power and symbolically protect the entrance, just as they did historically. To the right are the bakery and the well with its long sweep used to help lift heavy buckets of water.

▶ Unlike most fur trading posts, Fort Vancouver was fortunate to have a doctor and an infirmary as well as regular supplies of medicine to combat epidemics and treat accident-related injuries.

▶ Even in the officers' quarters, living space was at a premium. The three beds in this room were ingeniously designed to fold up and out of the way so that children had room to play.

many businesses here. Over time, Fort Vancouver became the center of not only commerce but also political and cultural activities in the Pacific Northwest.

Today at Fort Vancouver National Historic Site, the stockade and several buildings have been reconstructed on their original sites and furnished appropriately. Living History activities are presented in the kitchen, blacksmith shop, carpenter shop, bakehouse and garden. It all feels remarkably authentic.

Fort Vancouver was established at a time when the British, Spanish, Russians and Americans were still vying for control over lands west of the Rocky Mountains. Representing Great Britain's territorial interests from 1825 to 1860, it served as the administrative headquarters and main supply depot for the Hudson's Bay Company. As such, it was the hub of a fur trade network utilizing two dozen posts, six ships and about 600 workers (in peak seasons). And yet, Englishmen were in the minority, and spoken languages were primarily a Chinook jargon and Canadian French. In addition, fur trading was only one of

Demonstrations and guided tours are offered daily. In addition, a variety of cultural and evening programs are available to visitors. Among the special annual events is a September weekend Candlelight Tour featuring the unique lifestyle of Fort Vancouver.

Located on East Evergreen Boulevard in Vancouver, WA, reached via Mill Plain Boulevard off I-5 exit 1C, just across the Columbia River from Portland, OR. It is part of the Vancouver National Historic Reserve, which also includes several other historic sites. Open daily except major holidays. Admission charged.

BEAVER HATS

For more than 200 years, North American furs were among the most highly valued resources on the continent. When European hatters realized that the soft underhair of beaver fur made some of the finest felt, beaver hats became a status symbol, prized as family heirlooms. Traffic in beaver pelts escalated, and trading companies had to continually expand their territories to meet the demand. From eastern Canada and America, they advanced westward around Hudson's Bay in the Canadian Shield, through the Athabasca drainage, across the Rocky Mountains and finally all the way to the Pacific Coast. By the time the demand for beaver hats had run its course, the beaver had disappeared from much of North America. However, with the advent of protective laws and habitat restoration, it is back. In fact, the beaver has become a pest in many areas now populated by humans.

Fort Nisqually Historic Site

SEE MAP PAGE 23, LOCATION #34
Tacoma, Washington
Phone: (253) 591-5339
http://www.fortnisqually.org

This Hudson's Bay Company outpost, established in 1833, was the first European settlement on Puget Sound. Although called a fort, it never had a military purpose. Instead, it grew into a major fur trading center with a multi-cultural workforce and a large-scale agricultural enterprise exporting crops and livestock to Russian America, Hawaii, Spanish California, Europe and Asia. America's Native Peoples played key roles here – as friends, customers and fur traders, as farm and livestock employees, and even as spouses.

When Fort Nisqually was closed in 1869, the United States government paid the Hudson's Bay Company $650,000 for the fort and agricultural lands. In the mid-1930s, the original Factor's House and Granary – all that survived the passage of time – were relocated to Tacoma from their original site in the Nisqually River delta. In addition, portions of the fort were reconstructed, including the blacksmith shop and laborer's dwelling house. Today America's northwestern

history comes alive at this very interesting, well-outfitted re-creation. Costumed interpreters regularly re-enact the fur-trading era. A variety of special programs also are held throughout the year.

Located inside Point Defiance Park in Tacoma, WA, along with a replica of an early twentieth-century logging camp, a children's park, a zoo and an aquarium. Open year-round – daily May 30-Labor Day; Wednesday-Sunday rest of year; closed major holidays. Admission charged.

MARRIAGES TO NATIVE WOMEN
Most trading post employees, whether officers, clerks or voyageurs, chose to marry au façon du pays, or "in the fashion of the country," with varying degrees of commitment. Some men viewed their marriage as a temporary affair; others took multiple Indian wives; but many formed faithful, lifelong unions. Native women seemed to adapt easily to the fur trade lifestyle, and they contributed irreplaceable skills, tribal alliances and knowledge essential to their husband's survival. In fact, they were as important as voyageurs to the success of trapping brigades – cleaning and tanning skins, harvesting and cooking food, repairing clothing and moccasins, and protecting the camp from robbers and wild animals. Ultimately, fur trade marriages created a mixed-heritage culture known as métis (may-tees), with a sizable colony in Canada and several communities on the American border. The métis people could function well in either the Native American or white man's world, becoming French-speaking Roman Catholics or English-speaking Protestants while also speaking the Cree Indian language or a French-Cree dialect.

▲ A security zone was required around the commercial enterprise that was central to a Hudson's Bay Company trading post. So Fort Nisqually had bastions, or lookout towers, on two corners of its surrounding palisade. However, since the fort was never under attack, these bastions were used, more often than not, for extra housing or storage.

◄ Most of the Fort's buildings were constructed using a mortise and tenon framework with squared, standardized logs as infill. This "post and sill" technique enabled buildings to be easily added or recycled into other structures. Today at Fort Nisqually, you can visit the Trade Store, Granary and Blacksmith Shop.

◄ This original Factor's House (c. 1855) was home to the fort manager. Its four furnished rooms reflect the Chief Factor's prosperity as well as his active young family, which included a wife, sister-in-law and four little boys.

Bent's Old Fort National Historic Site

SEE MAP PAGE 19, LOCATION #28
La Junta vicinity (east), Colorado
Phone: (719) 383-5010
http://www.nps.gov/beol

⚠ This adobe trading post was built to obtain furs from the Cheyenne, Comanche, Arapaho, Kiowa and occasionally Ute Indians. One of its owners was Charles Bent, who became governor of New Mexico. Another was his brother William, who married Owl Woman, daughter of a Cheyenne medicine man, and raised four children with her.

▶ Bent's Old Fort is fully outfitted, not only in the trading room shown here, but also in the reception room for visiting dignitaries, dining room, kitchen and other quarters. The second floor social room has a replica of the large pocket billiard table that had been shipped in pieces over land in the 1840s and assembled before the room was completed.

This is a very engrossing place to visit. The reconstruction is based on original sketches, paintings and diaries from the period as well as archaeological excavations. All of the animals are historically accurate, including the Spanish Barb horses, oxen, peacocks, Dominique chickens and mule. In addition, Living History demonstrations are presented on weekends and during special events. They include blacksmithing, adobe construction and maintenance, frontier medicine, fur trading and general trading post life.

Although you can tour the fort on your own, we highly recommend the guided tour, available year-round. The interpreters welcome questions and have extensive information to share about the fort's colorful past and its powerful owners. Among the special events are an annual Santa Fe Trail Encampment, which includes the "Army of the West" as well as Santa Fe Trail merchants and plains Indians.

Located about 6 miles east of La Junta, CO, on SR 194E. Open daily except Thanksgiving, December 25 and January 1. Admission charged.

The Santa Fe Trail was a vital link to the Southwest. From 1821-1846, it was primarily a commercial highway between Missouri and Santa Fe, New Mexico. After the Mexican War (1846-1848), it was a national road connecting America to its newest territories and the route many settlers took west. The trail remained in widespread use until rail travel was available in 1880.

For 16 years, Bent's Old Fort was the only sizable, permanent, white settlement on the Santa Fe Trail. Playing a key role supporting travelers from 1833-1849, it was the one dependable place where soldiers, explorers, adventurers and early settlers could find what they needed – supplies, water and livestock; wagon repairs; a good meal and companionship; rest and medical care; and refuge during conflicts with Indians. So the fort's success stemmed from the abilities of its owners to serve as good hosts while also bartering, transporting and selling thousands of bison robes and beaver pelts.

FREIGHT WAGONS

Although you may doubt this: the brightly colored wagons at many historic trading posts are authentic. The bigger ones – Conestogas – were built by German farmers in Pennsylvania's Conestoga Valley; their red wheels and running gear were the tradition, as were their contrasting body colors (usually shades of blue, but not always). These commonly used wagons of American history were adaptations of the freight-and-passenger wagons of Europe. Built to withstand our more rugged terrain, they had high wheels to clear stumps and a deeply curved body to ensure that loads would settle toward the middle and stay put on steep hills. Conestogas carried most of the freight and people moving westward over the Allegheny Mountains from the 1770s until about 1850. During the time of Bent's Old Fort, smaller, lighter trade wagons were loaded with goods, and the wagoners walked or rode a horse beside them, driving their oxen or mules from there. The driver's position on the left of the team led him to steer the wagon to the right-hand side of the road and forced smaller wagons to do the same, thus establishing the national custom of traveling on the right.

Sitka National Historical Park

SEE MAP PAGE 23, LOCATION #33

Sitka, Baranof Island, Inside Passage, Alaska
Phone: (907) 747-0110
http://www.nps.gov/sitk

Russia pursued strong commercial interests in Alaska. However, early fur traders made serious mistakes. Rather than hunt for sea otters and other marine life themselves, they enslaved the capable Aleuts.

Even worse, they brought deadly diseases. Within two generations, 80 percent of the southwestern Natives had died. Later, when facing competition from other traders, the Russians lay claim to all of Alaska and made Sitka their capital. In response, the Tlingit people (KLINK-it) took up arms in 1804. Ultimately, local Russian Orthodox priests provided the vital stabilizing influence.

Sitka National Historical Park commemorates this difficult but interesting time in Alaska. It also offers you the opportunity to stroll through a temperate rain forest studded with beautifully carved totem poles and to see demonstrations of Native arts. Park rangers and volunteers offer interpretive programs at the Russian Bishop's House and other interesting sites.

Located on Lincoln Street in Sitka, AK. Open daily. Russian Bishop's House open for tours daily mid-May through September and at other times by request. Admission charged, except during winter.

Fort Ross State Historic Park

SEE MAP PAGE 23, LOCATION #32

Jenner vicinity (north), California
Phone: (707) 847-3286
http://www.fortrossstatepark.org

This was the southernmost outpost of the Russian-American Fur Company, established in 1812 to provide an expanded source of agricultural goods and furs. Although built in Spanish California and Indian territory, Fort Ross prospered. It also achieved harmony amidst great cultural diversity. (About half the population was Russian, and half was Alaska Native, California Indian and mixed Russian/Alaskan or Alaskan/Indian.)

The Russians left Fort Ross and California after less than 30 years. Their reasons were practical. Russian-American operations in Alaska and the Pacific Northwest were aimed at supporting the fur trade. As that business declined, due in large part to the depletion of fur-bearing animals, Russian settlements became military and economic liabilities. Fort Ross was sold in 1841 to John Sutter (of Forty-Niner Gold Rush fame). The entire Alaska territory was sold to America in 1867.

Visiting the restored and reconstructed fort is a delightful adventure. Fort Ross was originally modeled after traditional stockades, blockhouses and log buildings found in Siberia and Sitka, and today's resurrection is as authentic as possible. What's more, the coastal setting is stunningly beautiful; so plan some extra driving, north and south, to enjoy the vistas.

Try to time your visit to coincide with Fort Ross Cultural Heritage Day, held annually on the last Saturday of July. The many costumed interpreters and wide variety of re-enactments, including an old-style Russian Orthodox mass in the chapel, are marvelous. Also tour the Visitor Center Museum, which provides an overview of the fort's history, and stop by the bookstore.

Located on Coast Highway One, 12 miles north of Jenner, CA. Open daily; closed Thanksgiving and December 25. A parking fee is charged.

▲ Fort Ross was the southern-most Russian settlement in America. It is now a state historic park and includes this reconstruction of the first Russian Orthodox church south of Alaska.

◀ The authentically furnished Russian Bishop's House in Sitka represents the premier cultural icon of Russian influence in America. The second floor has been restored to its 1853 appearance, with original furnishings and artifacts.

◀ Totem poles record the legends and histories of Alaska Natives. Each builds its story from the bottom up, with stylized figures representing human ancestors, the Creator, the eagle of peace and friendship, and other animal and bird spirits.

INDEX

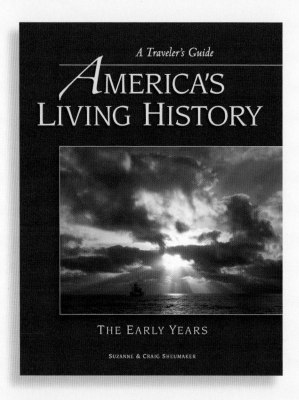

Give a gift to friends & family.

America's Living History-The Early Years is available at numerous retail outlets, including online stores and tourist sites.

To order direct from the publisher or receive an autographed book, please go to the Red Corral Publishing website:

www.AmericasLivingHistory.com

Or call toll-free: **1-888-733-7370**

Red Corral Publishing
505-1 South Highway 49, #240
Jackson, California 95642